井上雄彦

**Takehiko Inoue**

WHEN PEOPLE ASK ME WHAT I DO FOR FUN, I
NEVER KNOW WHAT TO TELL THEM.

I HAVEN'T HAD TIME TO PLAY BASKETBALL FOR
A WHILE. MY ROAD RACER'S SO UNUSED THAT
IT'S BECOME A PART OF MY INTERIOR DÉCOR,
AND THE ONLY MOVIES I EVER SEE ARE THE BIG
BLOCKBUSTERS. I DO WATCH VIDEOS, BUT THAT
SOUNDS LIKE SUCH A LAME ANSWER... "I'M TOO
BUSY FOR FUN!" IS PRETTY LAME TOO, THOUGH,
SO I GUESS I NEED TO FIGURE SOMETHING OUT.

Takehiko Inoue's *Slam Dunk* is one of the most
popular manga of all time, having sold over 100
million copies worldwide. He followed that series
up with two titles lauded by critics and fans
alike—*Vagabond*, a fictional account of the life
of Miyamoto Musashi, and *Real*, a manga about
wheelchair basketball.

D1293285

# SLAM DUNK
## Vol. 6: Nothing to Lose
### The SHONEN JUMP Manga Edition

STORY AND ART BY TAKEHIKO INOUE

English Adaptation/Kelly Sue DeConnick
Translation/Joe Yamazaki
Touch-up Art & Lettering/James Gaubatz
Cover & Graphic Design/Sean Lee
Editor/Kit Fox

VP, Production/Alvin Lu
VP, Publishing Licensing/Rika Inouye
VP, Sales & Product Marketing/Gonzalo Ferreyra
VP, Creative/Linda Espinosa
Publisher/Hyoe Narita

Printed in the U.S.A.

Published by VIZ Media, LLC
P.O. Box 77010
San Francisco, CA 94107

SHONEN JUMP Manga Edition
10 9 8 7 6 5 4 3 2 1
First printing, October 2009

www.viz.com

THE WORLD'S
MOST POPULAR MANGA

www.shonenjump.com

# SLAM DUNK

## Vol. 6: Nothing to Lose

STORY AND ART BY
TAKEHIKO INOUE

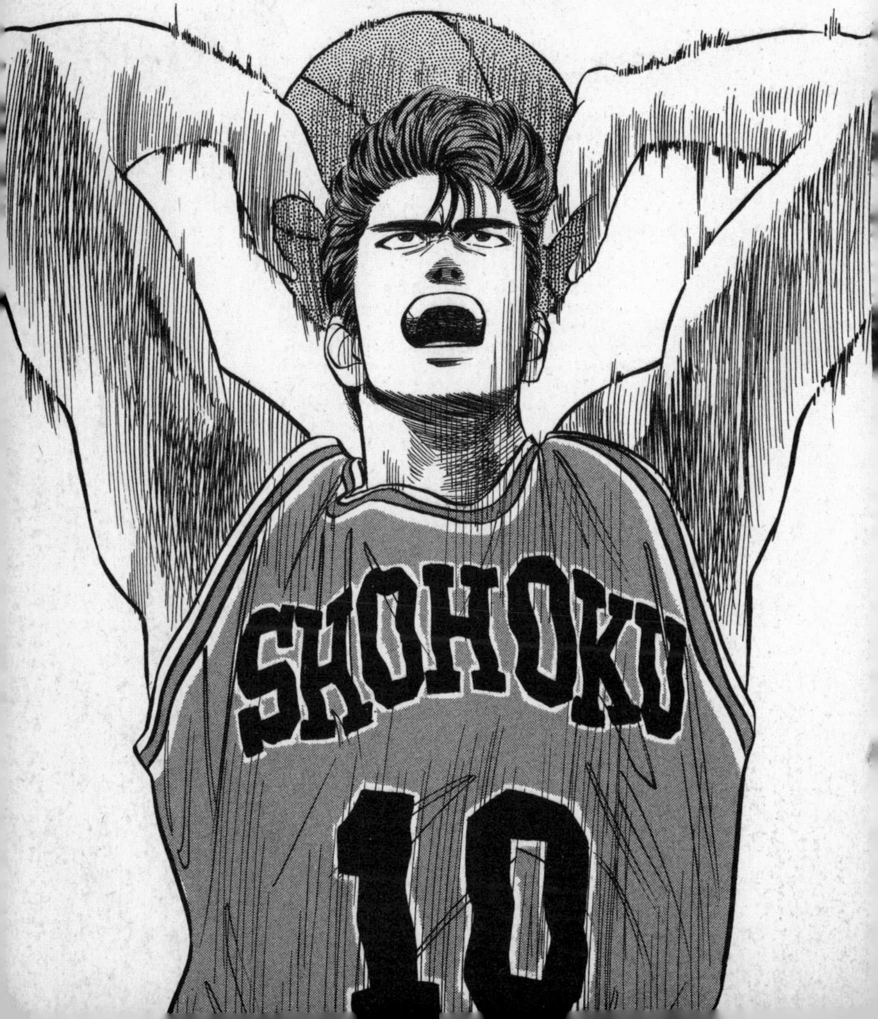
SHOHOKU
10

# Character Introduction

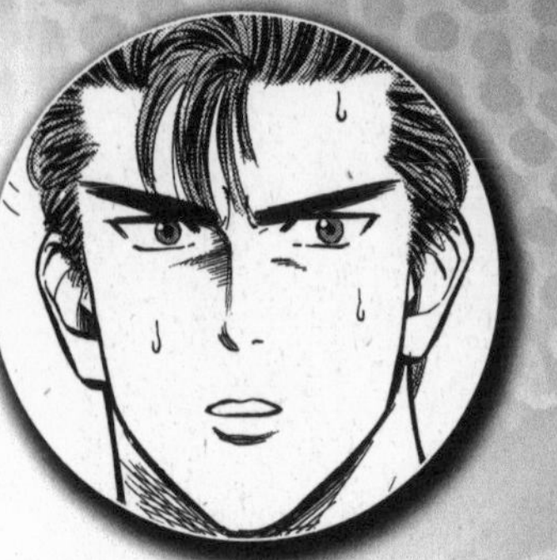

**Hanamichi Sakuragi**
A first-year at Shohoku High School, Sakuragi is in love with Haruko Akagi.

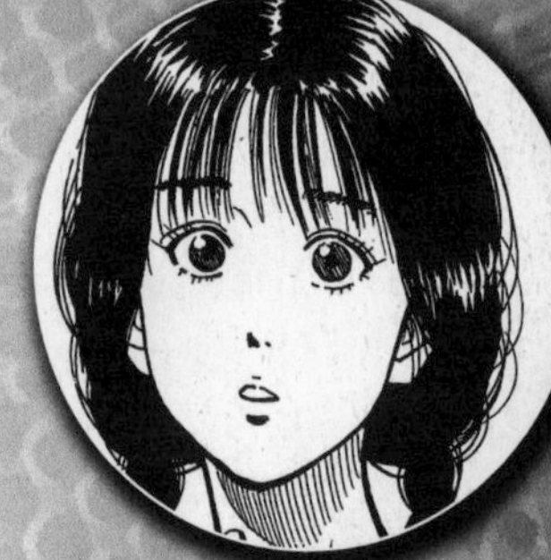

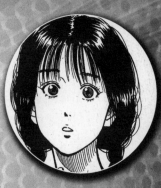

**Haruko Akagi**
Also a first-year at Shohoku, Takenori Akagi's little sister has a crush on Kaede Rukawa.

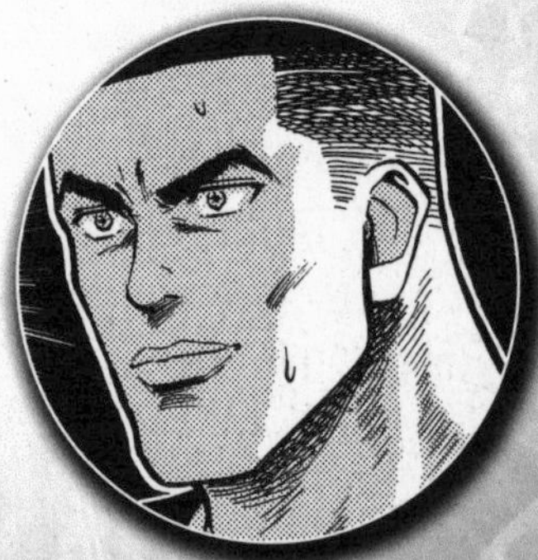

**Takenori Akagi**
A third-year and the basketball team's captain, Akagi has an intense passion for his sport.

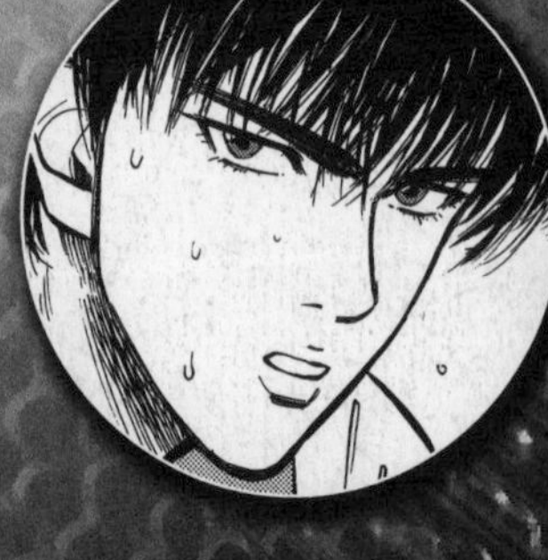

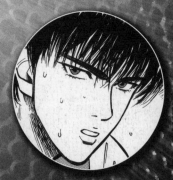

**Kaede Rukawa**
The object of Haruko's affection (and that of many of Shohoku's female students!), this first-year has been a star player since junior high.

Sakuragi's Friends

Ohkusu Mito Takamiya Noma

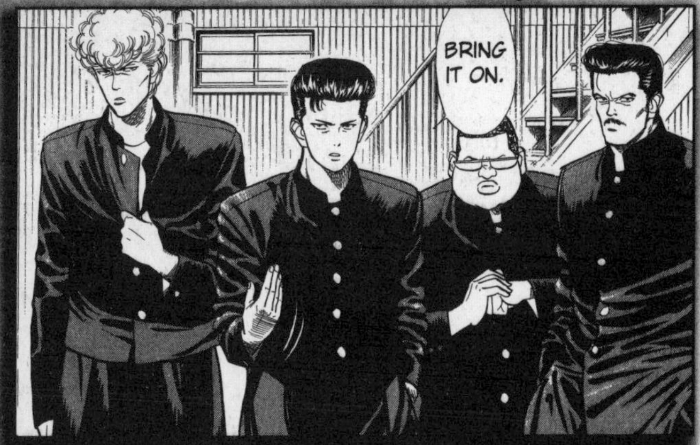
BRING IT ON.

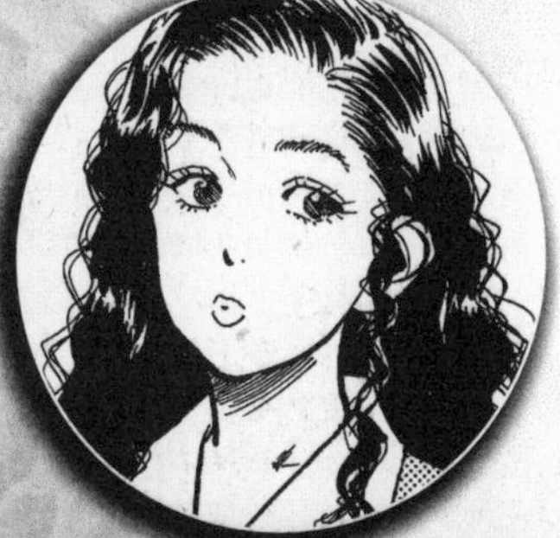

**Ayako**
**Basketball Team Manager**

# Our Story Thus Far

Hanamichi Sakuragi is rejected by close to 50 girls during his three years in junior high. In high school, he joins the basketball team in order to get closer to his beloved Haruko, whose brother is the team captain. However, the endless fundamental drills do not suit his personality, and he and Captain Akagi frequently butt heads.

During an exhibition game, Shohoku struggles against their opponents' powerful captain, Uozumi, and their star player, Sendoh. Sakuragi is put in to replace an injured Akagi, but first-game jitters get the best of him. A kick in the butt (literally!) from Rukawa snaps him out of it, and he finally starts to show what he can do. Akagi returns to the game and they close the gap to four points—with only a minute remaining!

# Vol. 6:
# Nothing to Lose

## Table of Contents

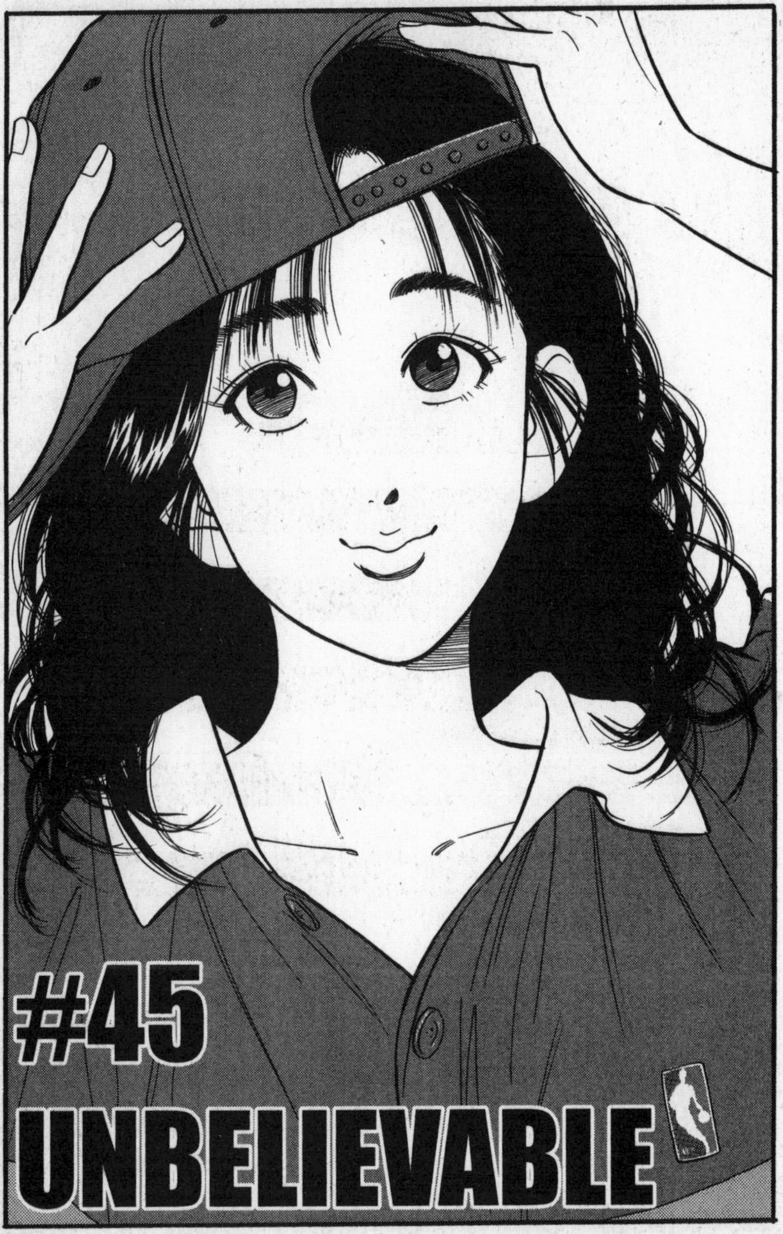
#45
UNBELIEVABLE

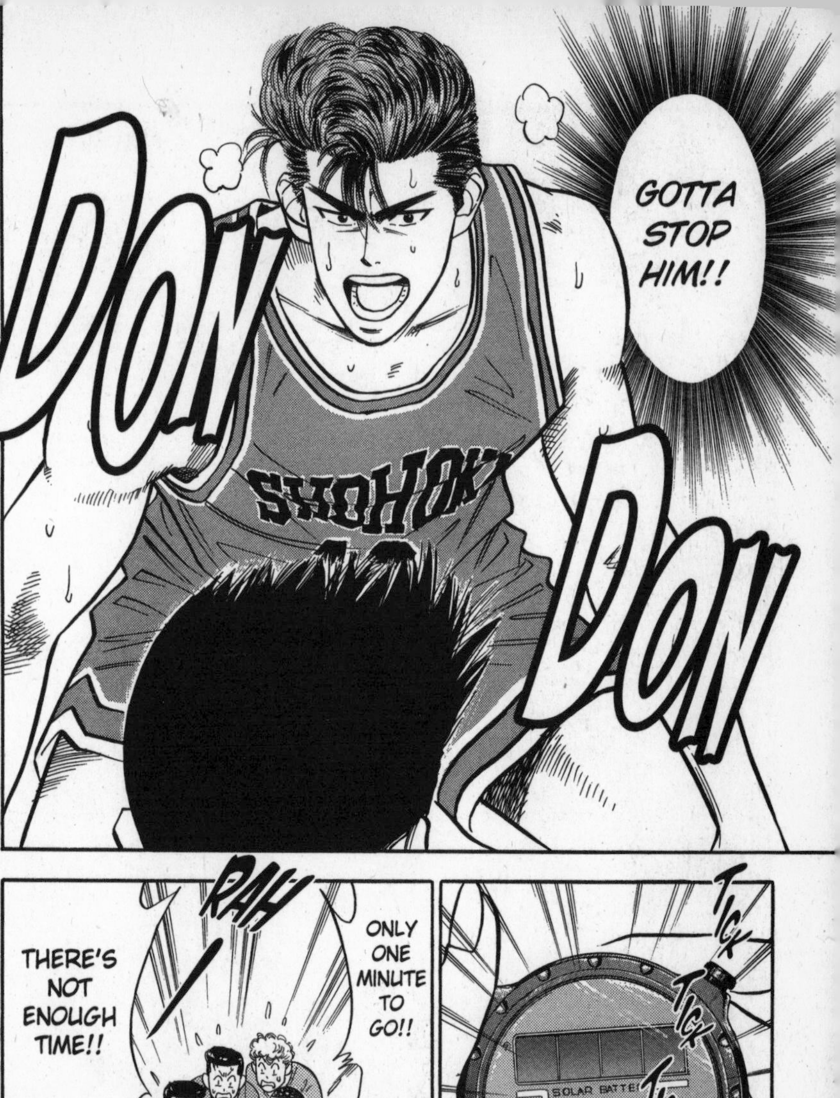
DON
GOTTA STOP HIM!!
DON
TICK
TICK
TICK
TICK
RAH
ONLY ONE MINUTE TO GO!!
THERE'S NOT ENOUGH TIME!!
CHILL!

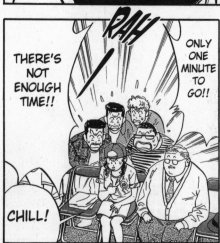

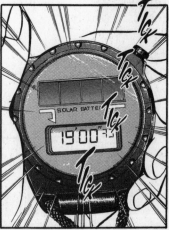

READ THIS WAY

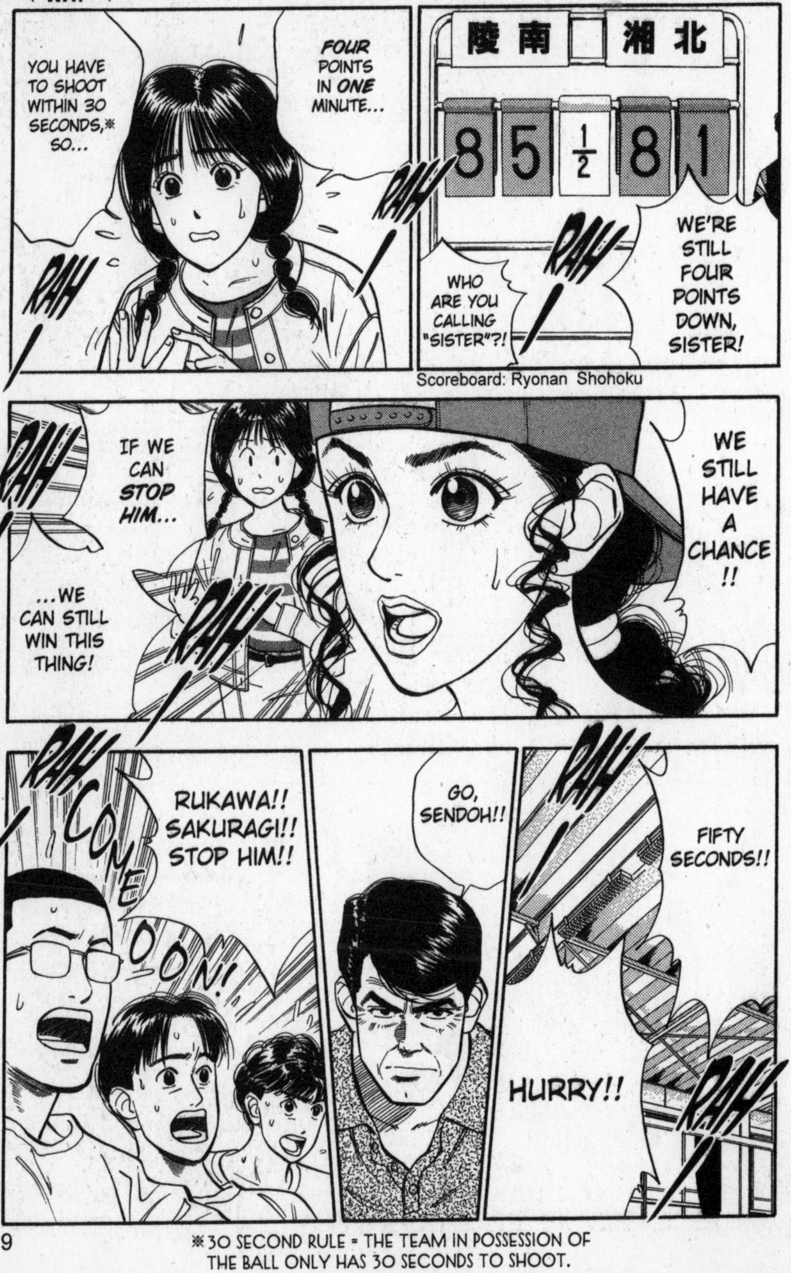
陵南 湘北
85 1/2 81
RAH
WE'RE STILL FOUR POINTS DOWN, SISTER!
WHO ARE YOU CALLING "SISTER"?!
RAH
FOUR POINTS IN ONE MINUTE...
YOU HAVE TO SHOOT WITHIN 30 SECONDS,※ SO...
RAH
Scoreboard: Ryonan Shohoku
WE STILL HAVE A CHANCE!!
IF WE CAN STOP HIM...
...WE CAN STILL WIN THIS THING!
RAH
RAH
RAH
FIFTY SECONDS!!
HURRY!!
RAH
GO, SENDOH!!
RAH
COME OON!
RUKAWA!! SAKURAGI!! STOP HIM!!

※30 SECOND RULE = THE TEAM IN POSSESSION OF THE BALL ONLY HAS 30 SECONDS TO SHOOT.

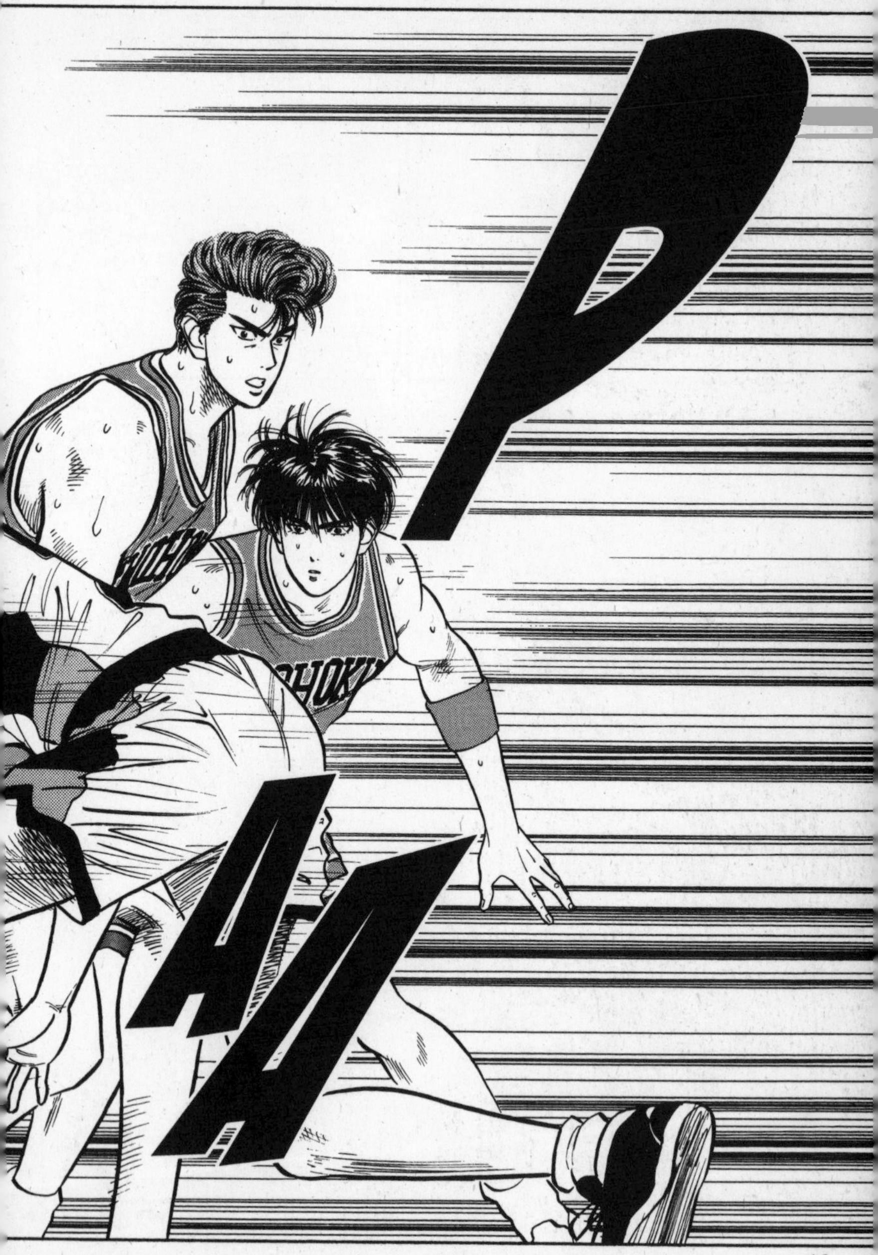
PAH

READ THIS WAY

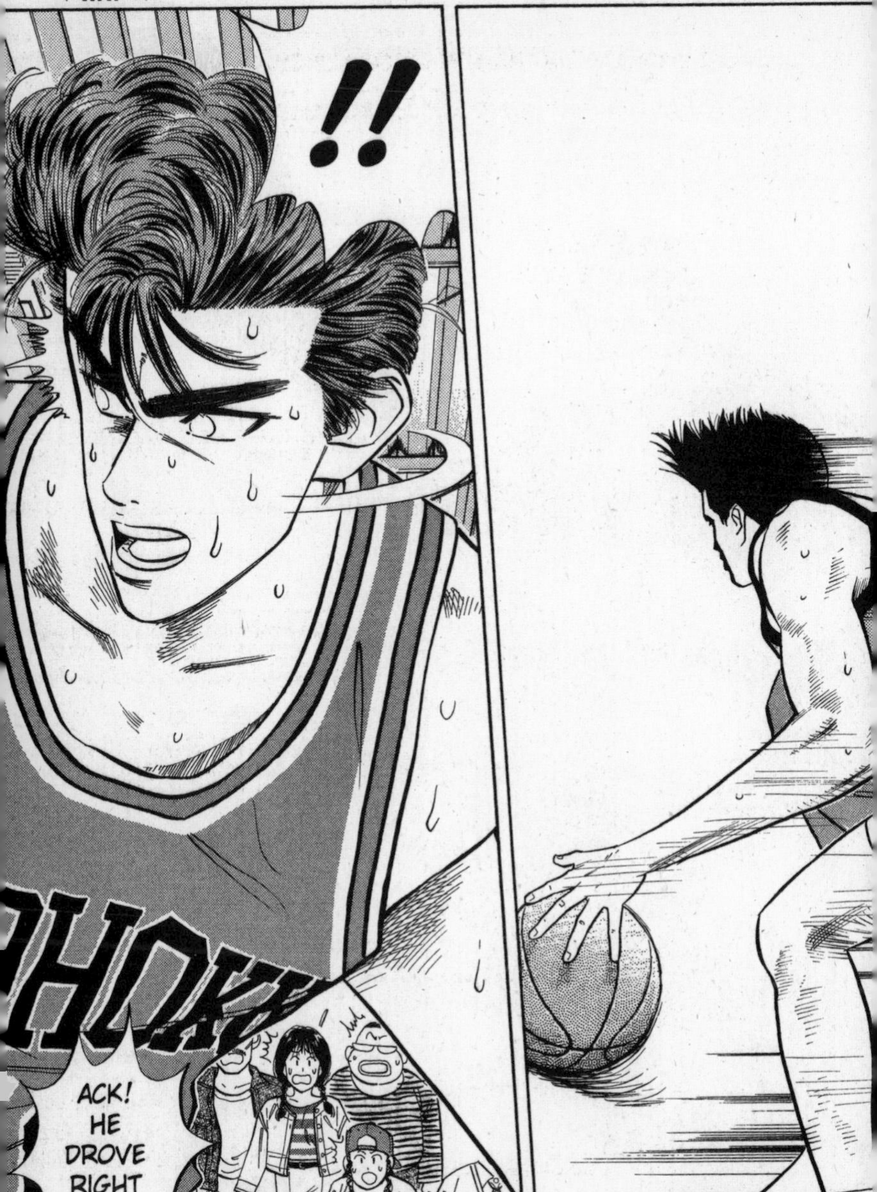
!!
ACK! HE DROVE RIGHT BY!!

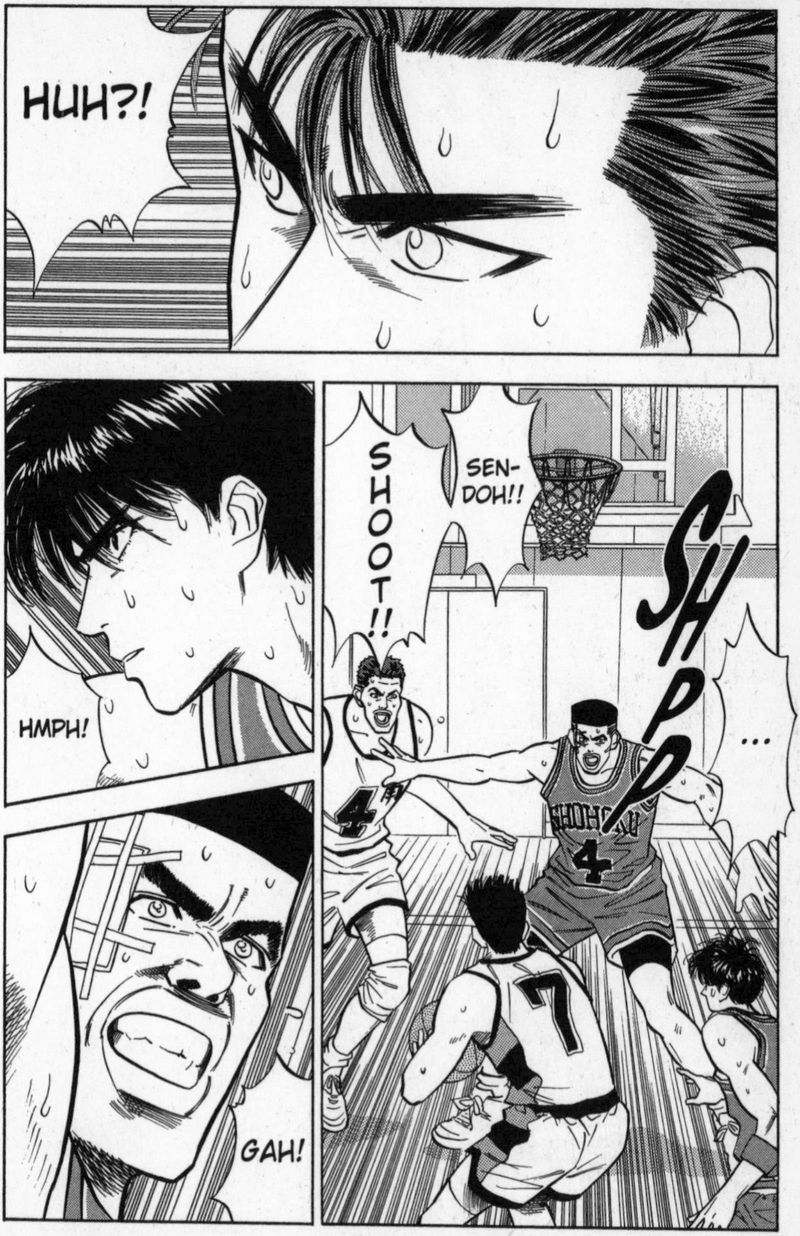
HUH?!
SHPP
SEN-DOH!!
SHOOT!!
...
HMPH!
GAH!

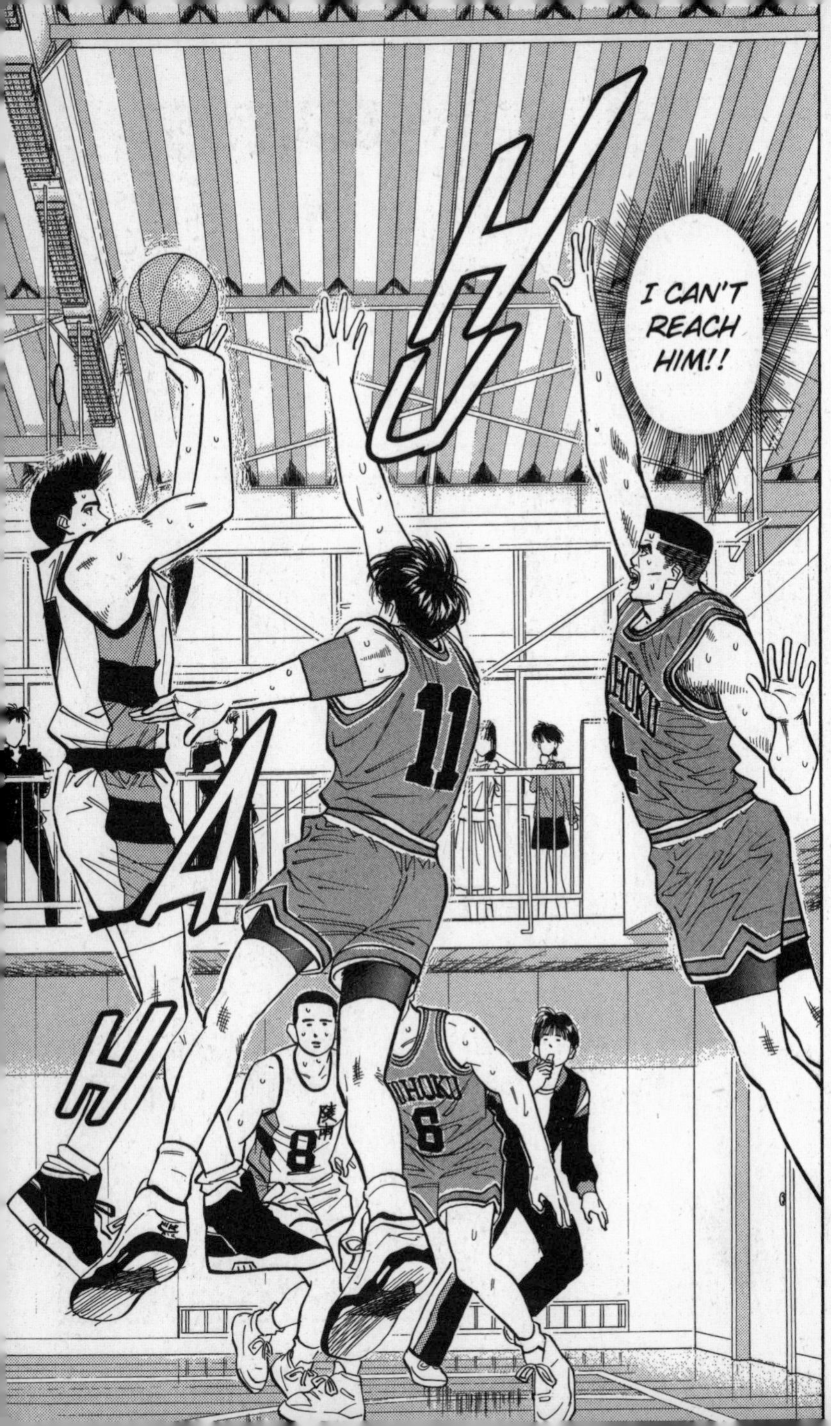

I CAN'T REACH HIM!!
HUH

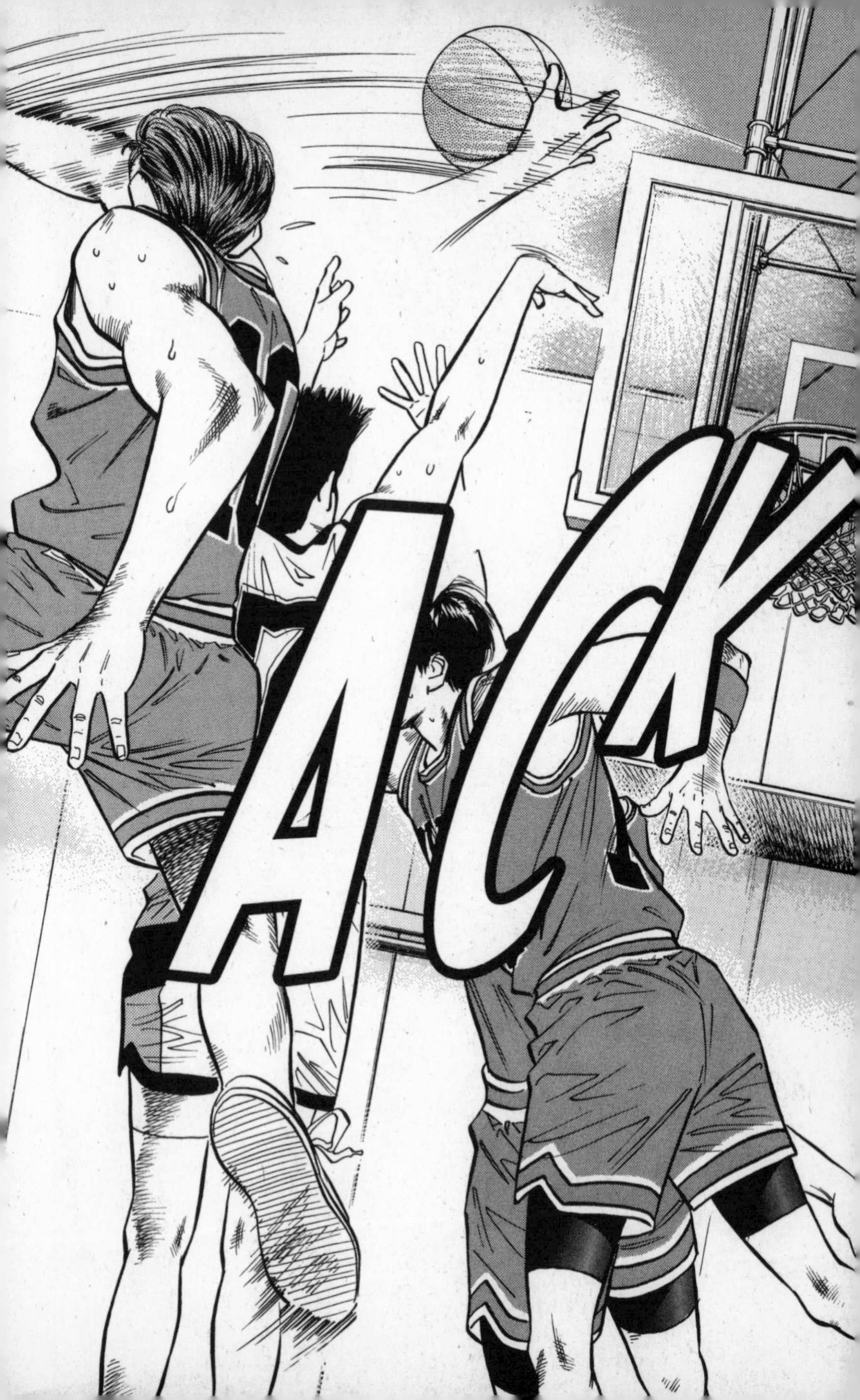
ACK

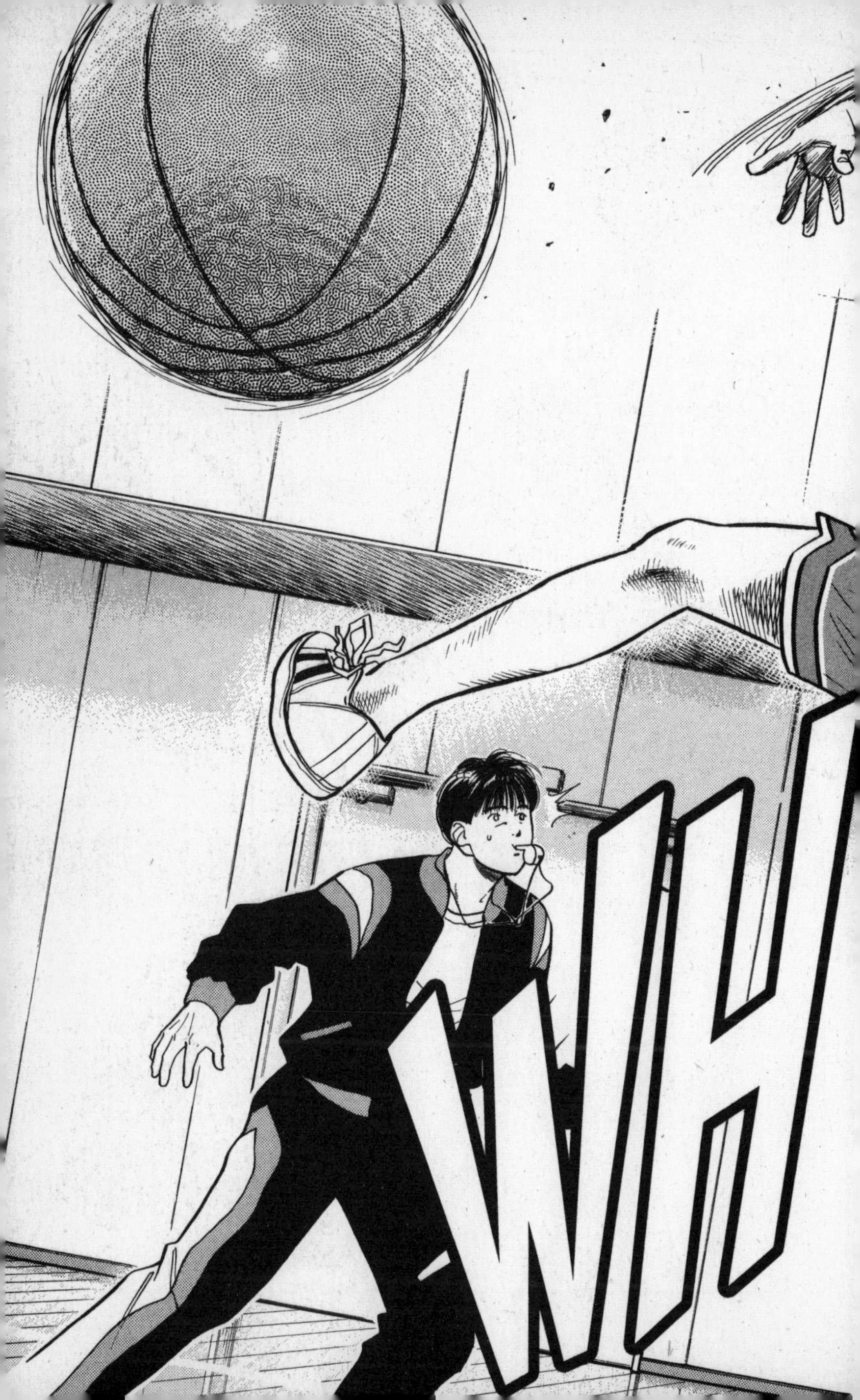
WH

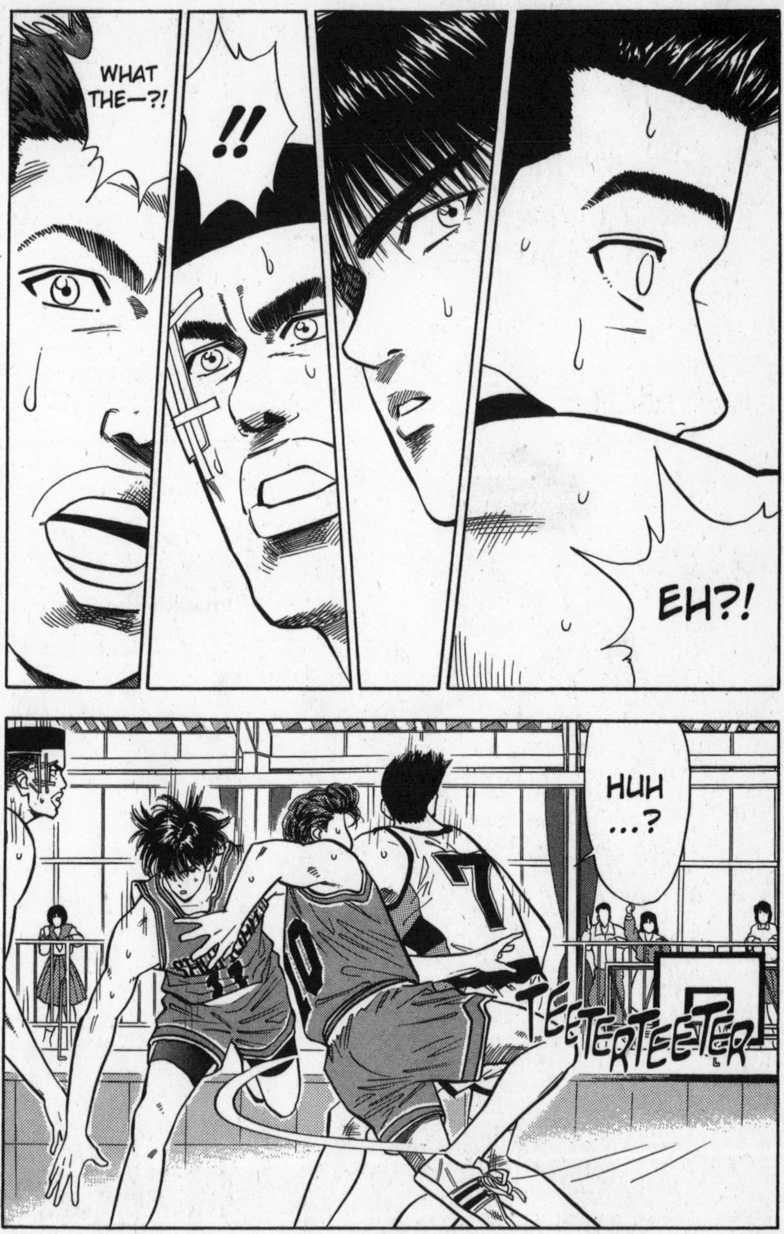
EH?!
!!
WHAT THE—?!
HUH ...?
TEETERTEETER

READ THIS WAY

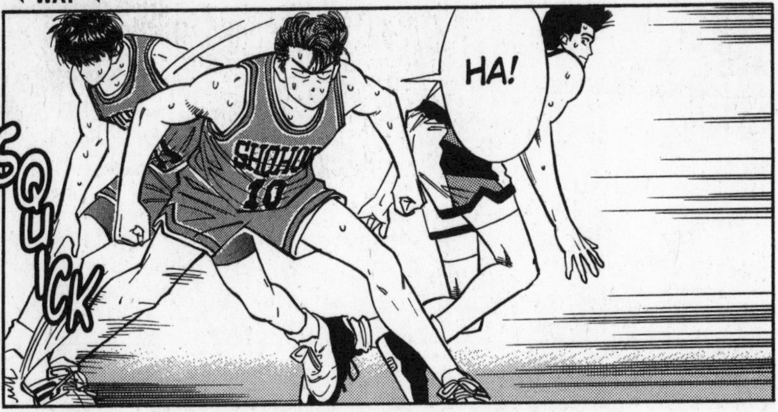
HA!
SQUICK

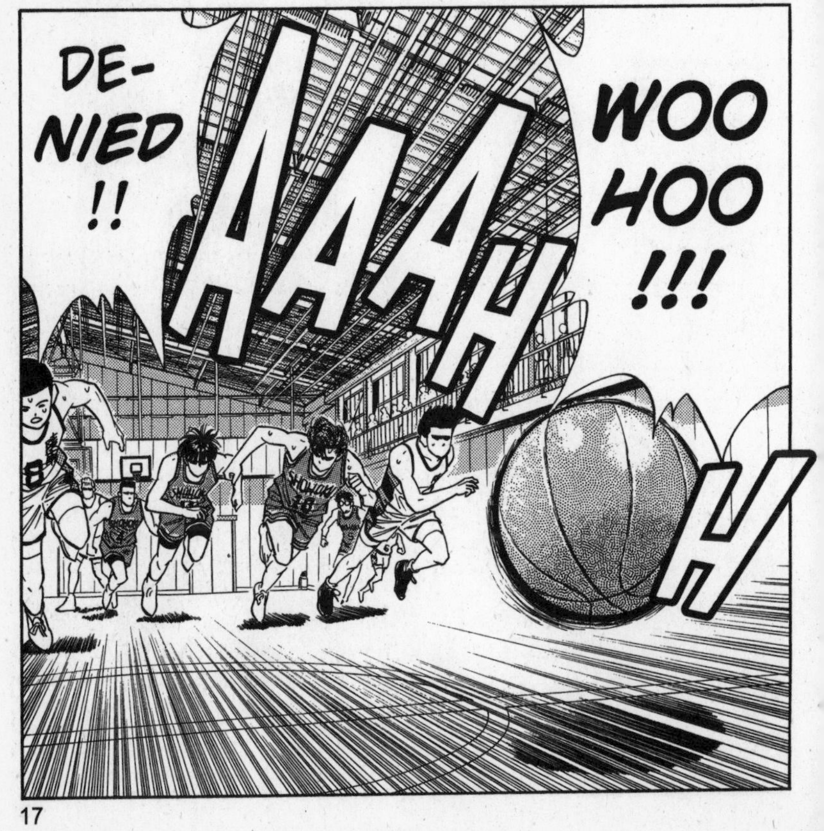
WOO HOO !!!
AAAHH
DE-NIED !!

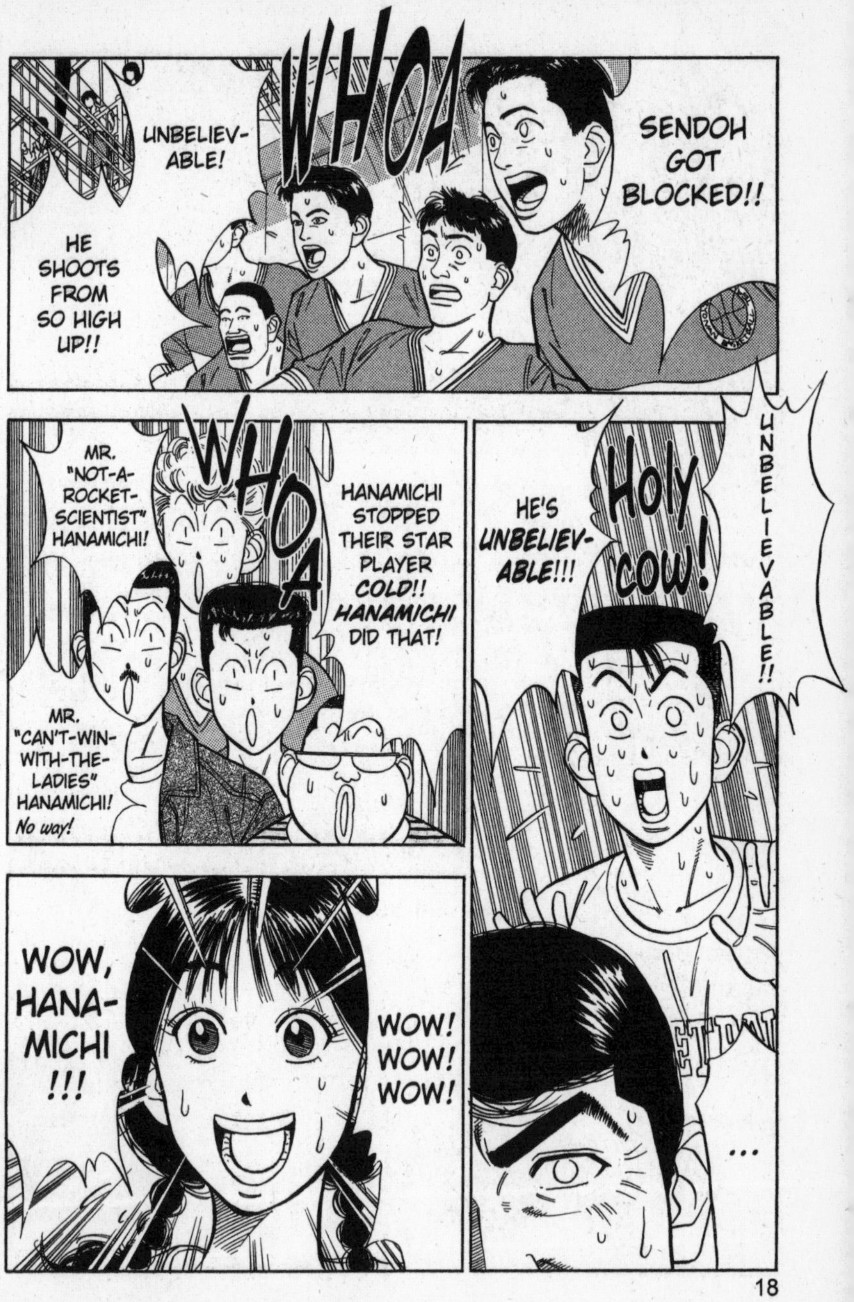
SENDOH GOT BLOCKED!!
WHOA
UNBELIEV-ABLE!
HE SHOOTS FROM SO HIGH UP!!
UNBELIEVABLE!!
Holy cow!
HE'S *UNBELIEV-ABLE*!!!
...
HANAMICHI STOPPED THEIR STAR PLAYER *COLD*!! *HANAMICHI* DID THAT!
WHOA
MR. "NOT-A-ROCKET-SCIENTIST" HANAMICHI!
MR. "CAN'T-WIN-WITH-THE-LADIES" HANAMICHI! *No way!*
WOW! WOW! WOW!
WOW, HANA-MICHI!!!

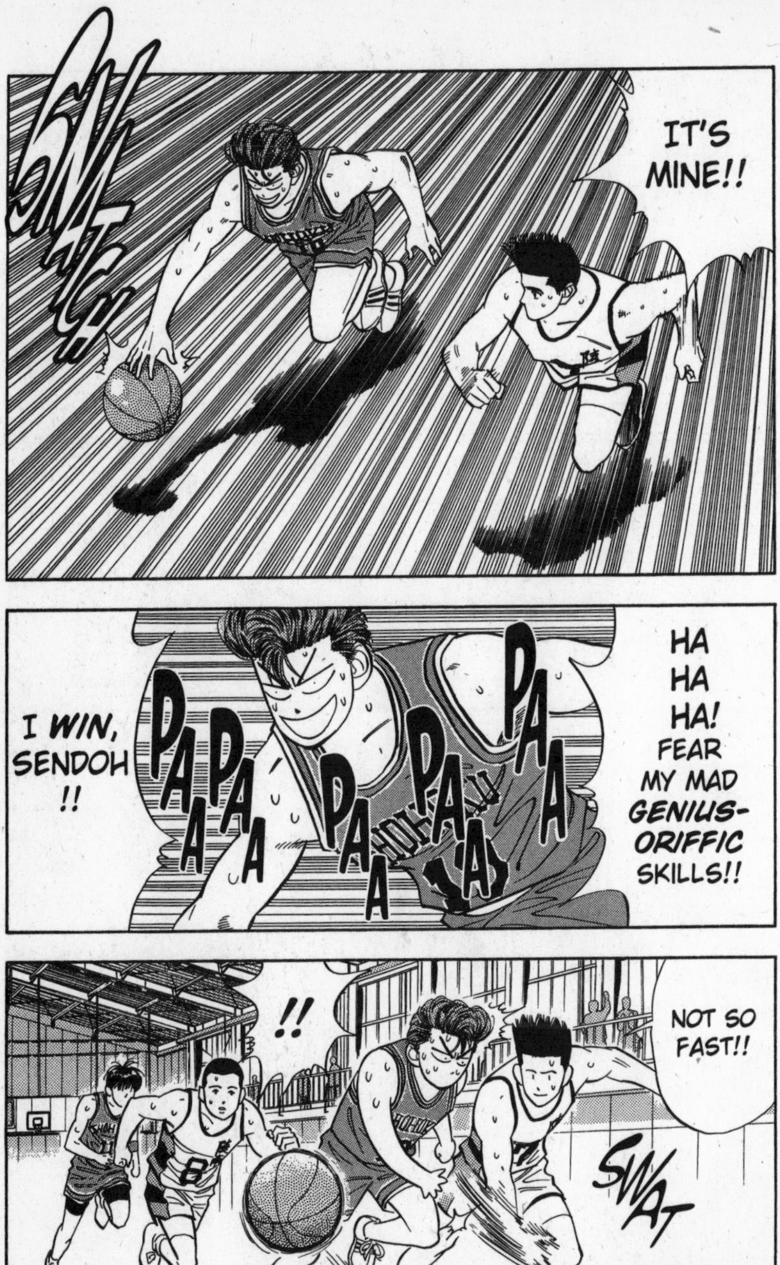
IT'S MINE!!
SNATCH
HA HA HA! FEAR MY MAD GENIUS-ORIFFIC SKILLS!!
PAA PAA PAA PAA PAA PAA
I WIN, SENDOH!!
NOT SO FAST!!
SWAT
!!

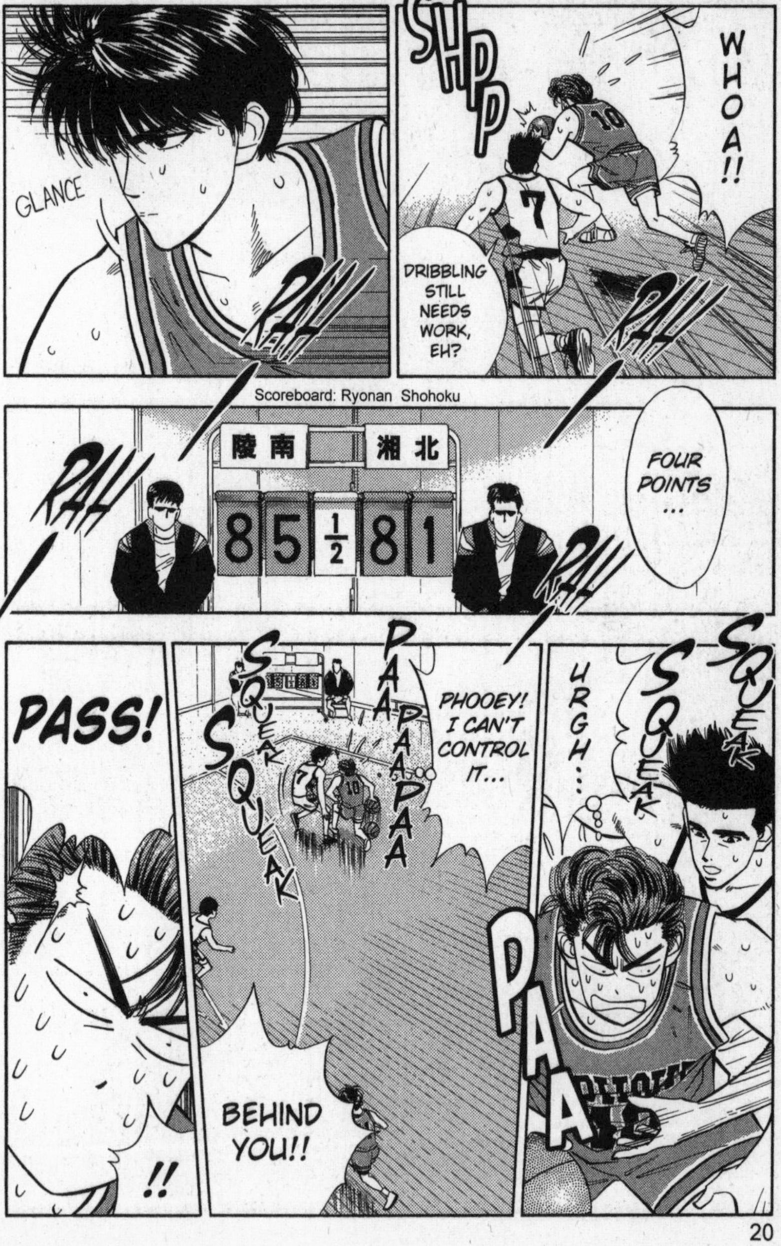
SHPP
WHOA!!
DRIBBLING STILL NEEDS WORK, EH?
RAH
GLANCE
RAH
Scoreboard: Ryonan Shohoku
FOUR POINTS...
RAH
陵南 湘北
85 1/2 81
RAH
SQUEAK
SQUEAK
URGH...
PAAA
PHOOEY! I CAN'T CONTROL IT...
PAA
PAAPAA
SQUEAK
SQUEAK
BEHIND YOU!!
PASS!
!!

READ THIS WAY

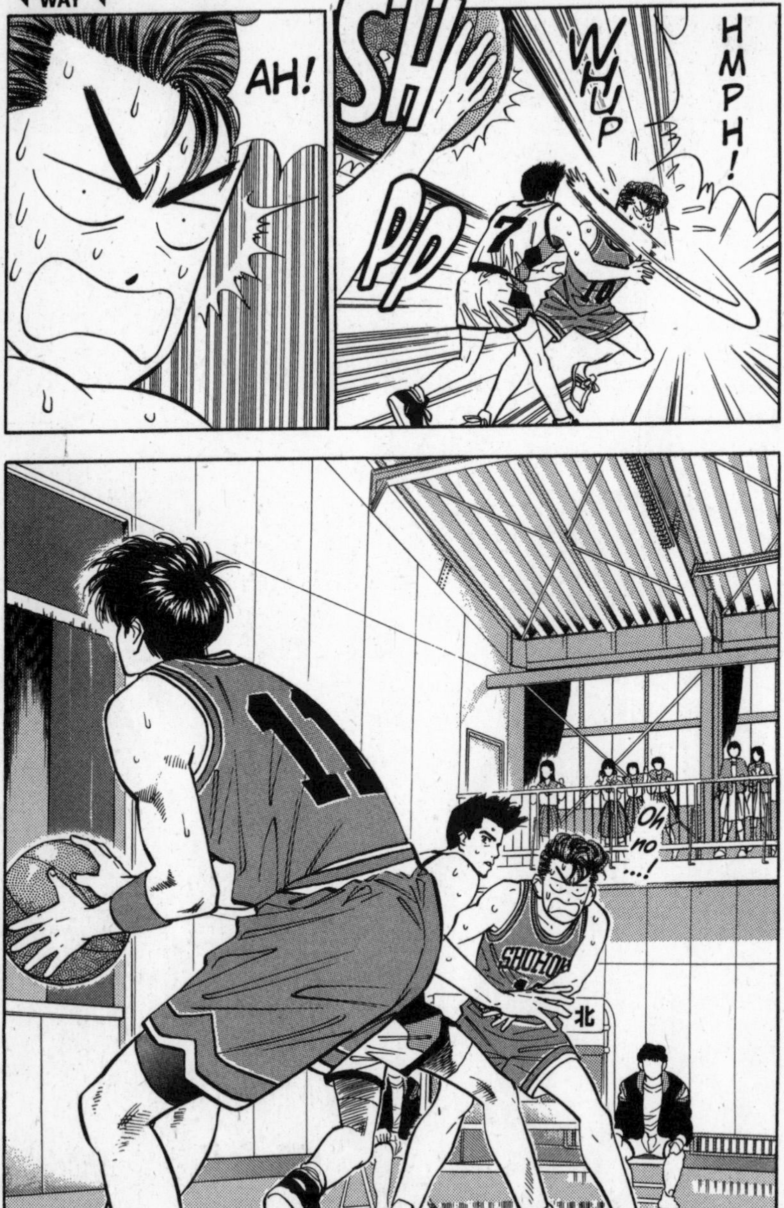
HMPH!
WHUP
SHPP
AH!
Oh no...!
北

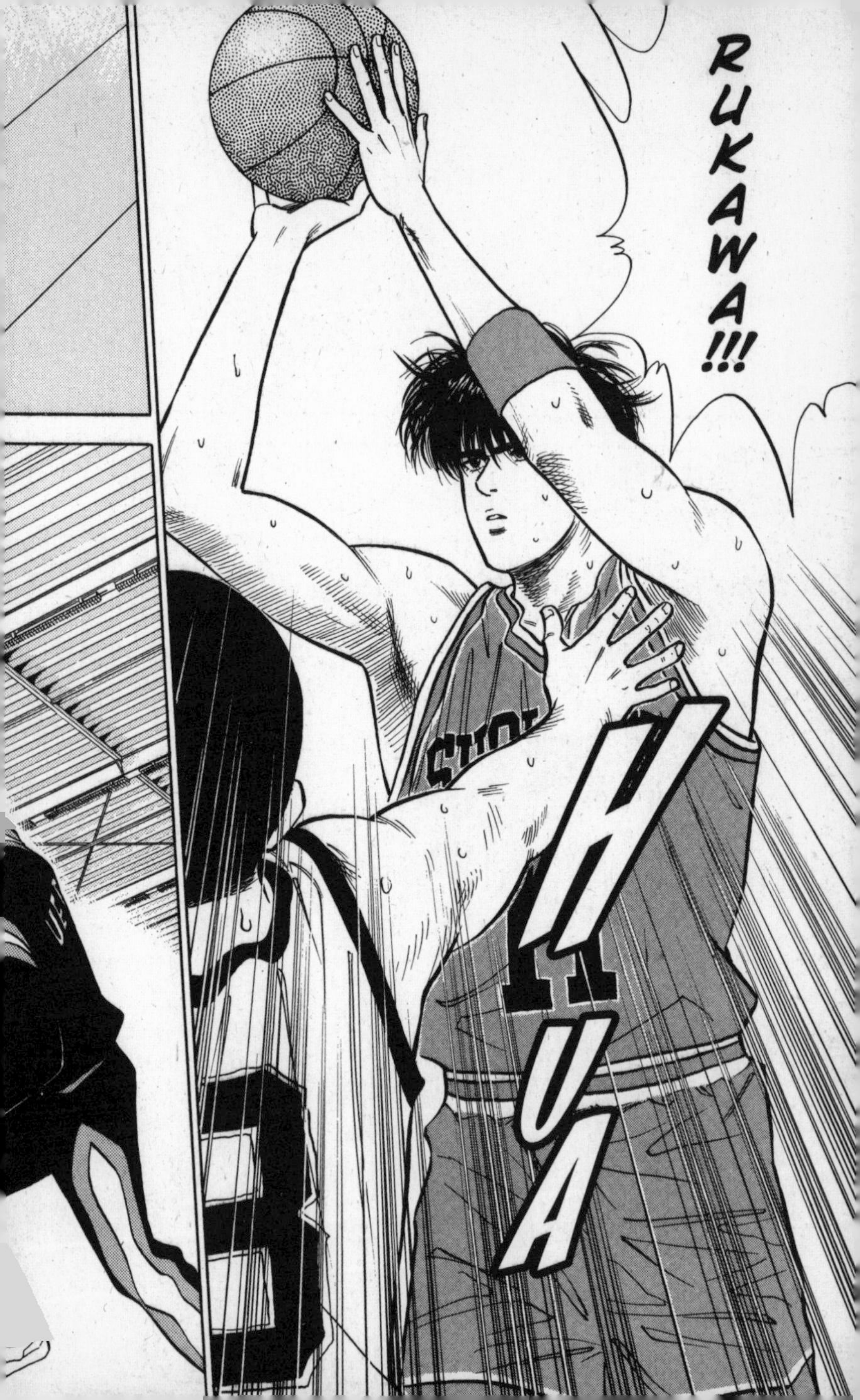
RUKAWA!!!
HUA

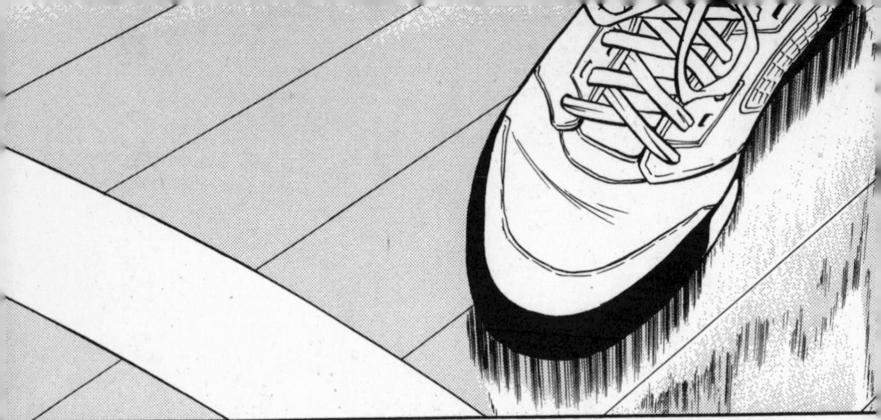
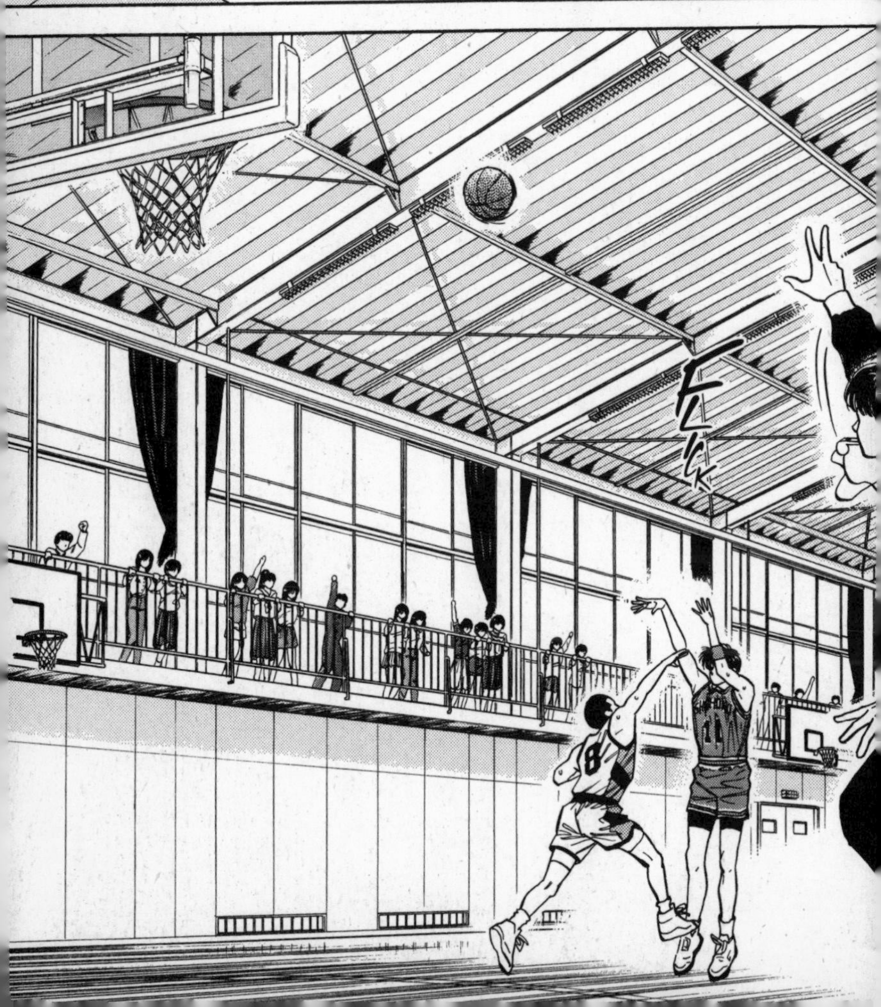
FLICK

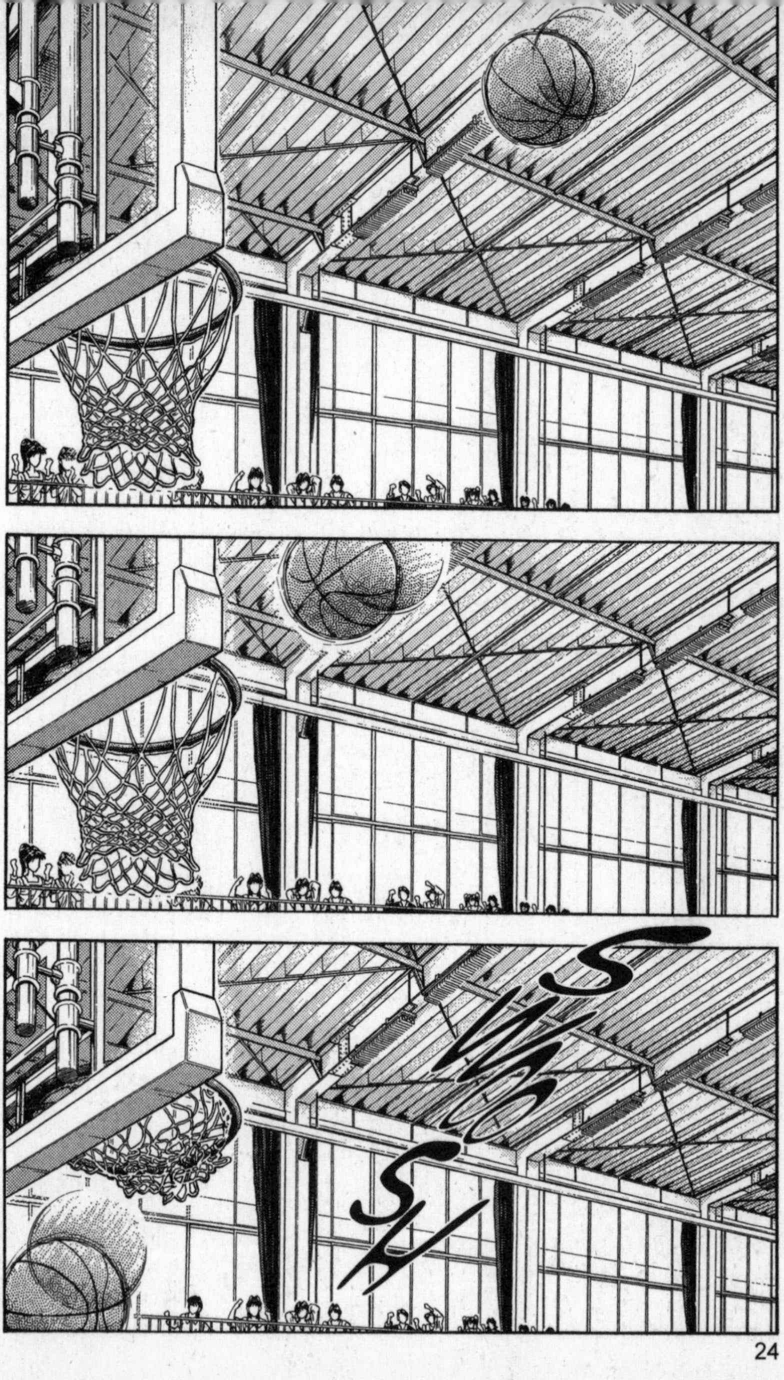
SWOOSH

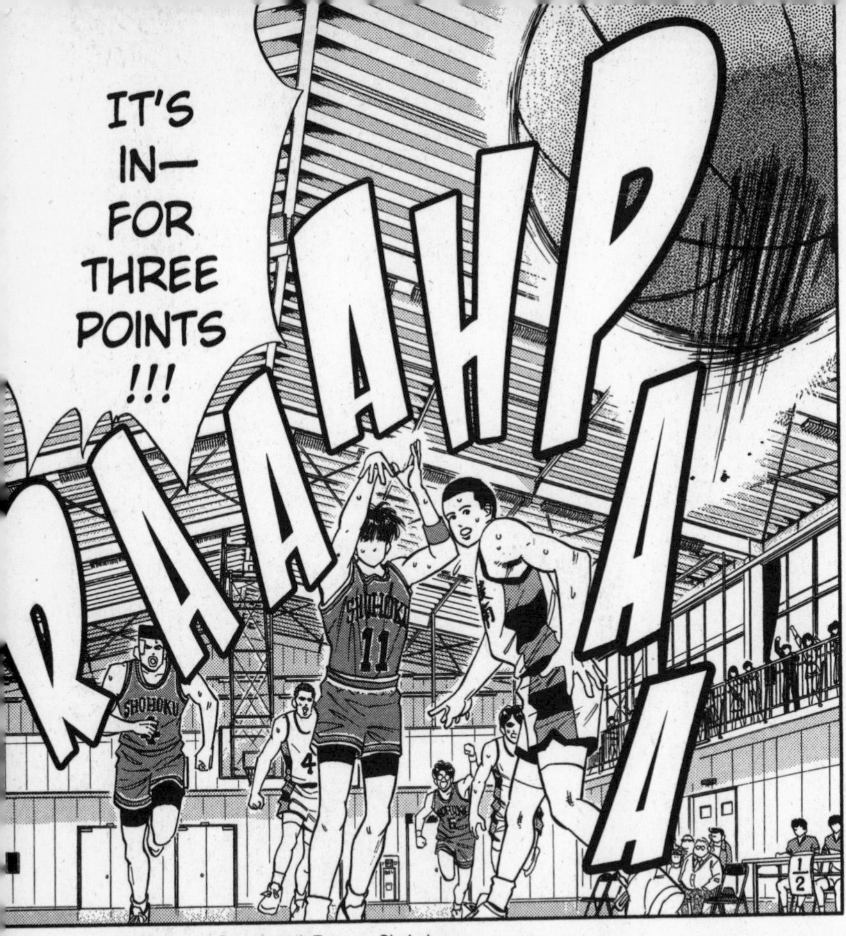
IT'S IN— FOR THREE POINTS!!!
RAAAHPAAA

Scoreboard: Ryonan Shohoku

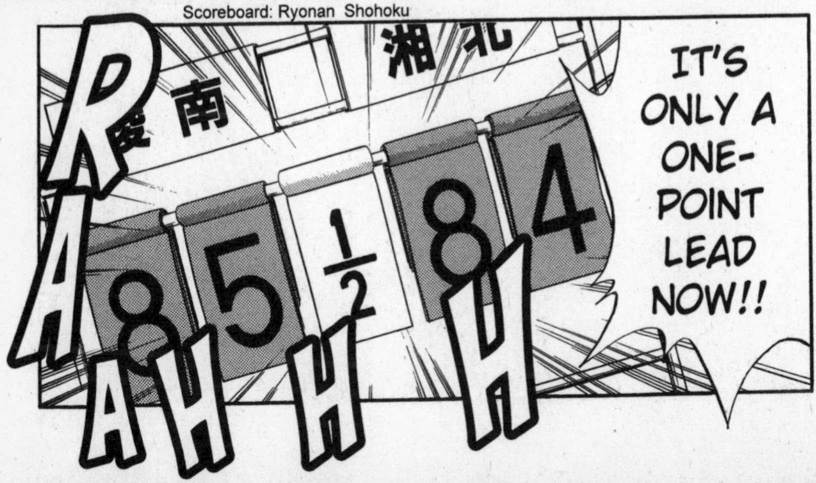
IT'S ONLY A ONE-POINT LEAD NOW!!
RAAAHHHH
85
84

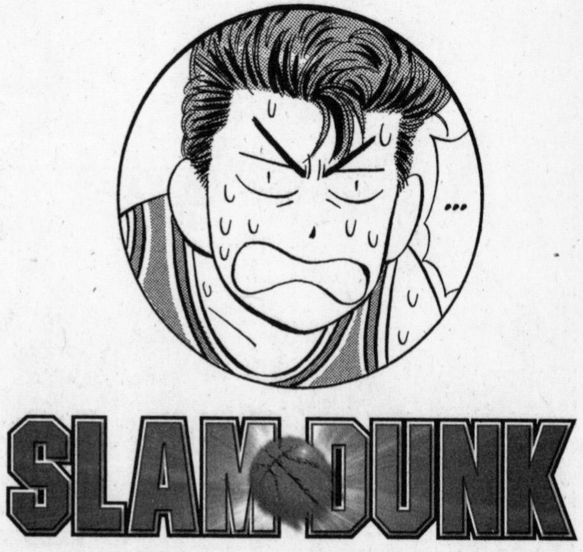
...

SLAM DUNK

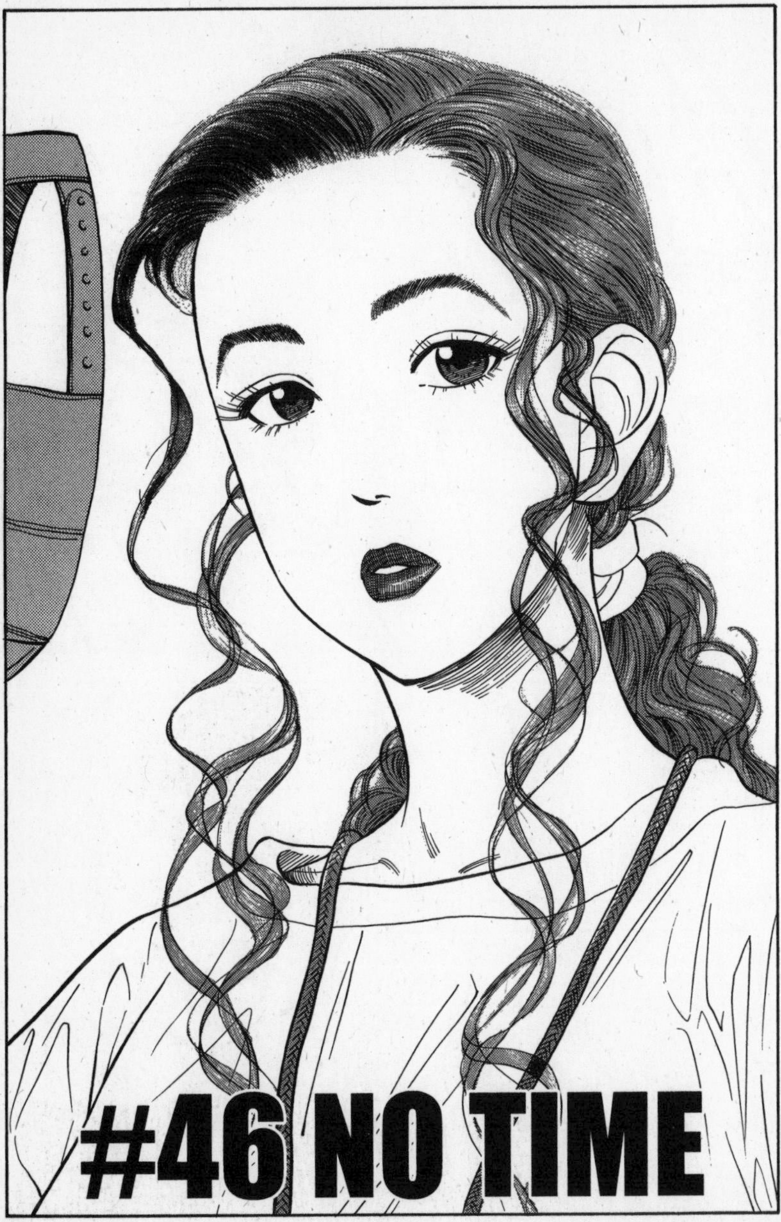

# #46 NO TIME

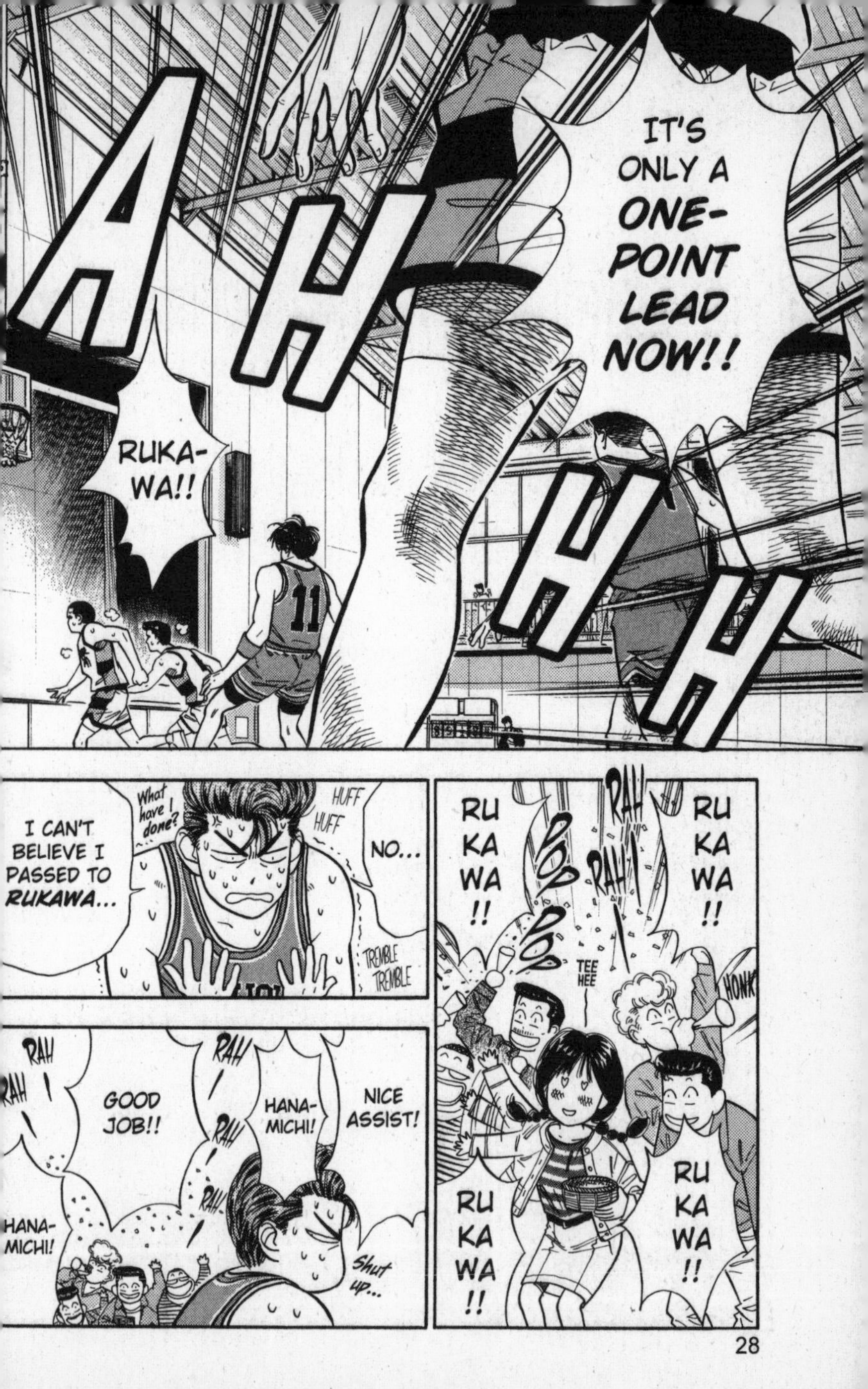
IT'S ONLY A ONE-POINT LEAD NOW!!
AHHHH
RUKA-WA!!
RU KA WA!!
RAH! RAH!
BOOO
RU KA WA!!
TEE HEE
HONK
RU KA WA!!
RU KA WA!!
NO...
HUFF HUFF
What have I done?
I CAN'T BELIEVE I PASSED TO RUKAWA...
TREMBLE TREMBLE
NICE ASSIST!
HANA-MICHI!
RAH! RAH! RAH!
GOOD JOB!!
RAH! RAH!
HANA-MICHI!
Shut up...

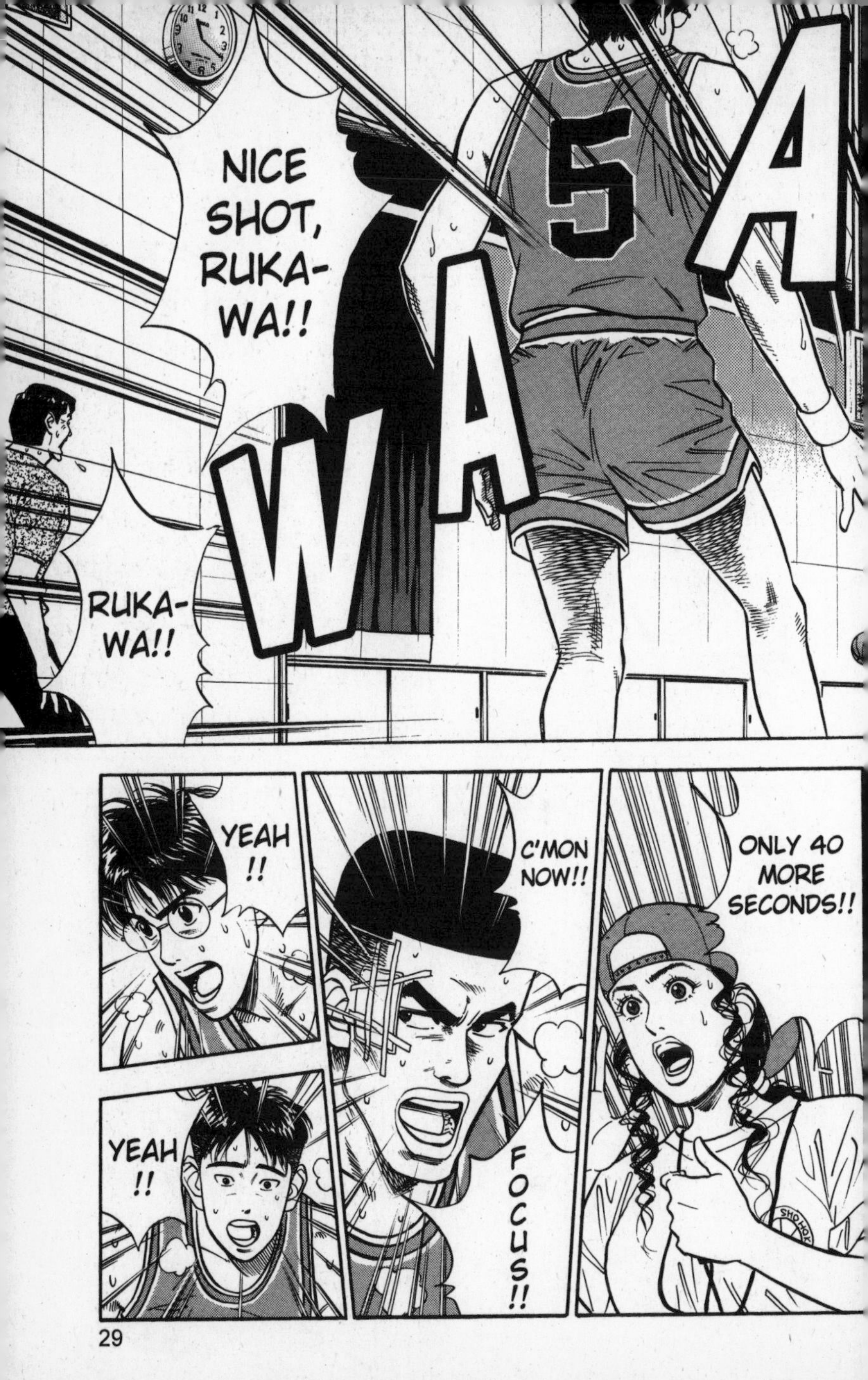

WAA
NICE SHOT, RUKAWA!!
RUKAWA!!
ONLY 40 MORE SECONDS!!
C'MON NOW!!
FOCUS!!
YEAH!!
YEAH!!

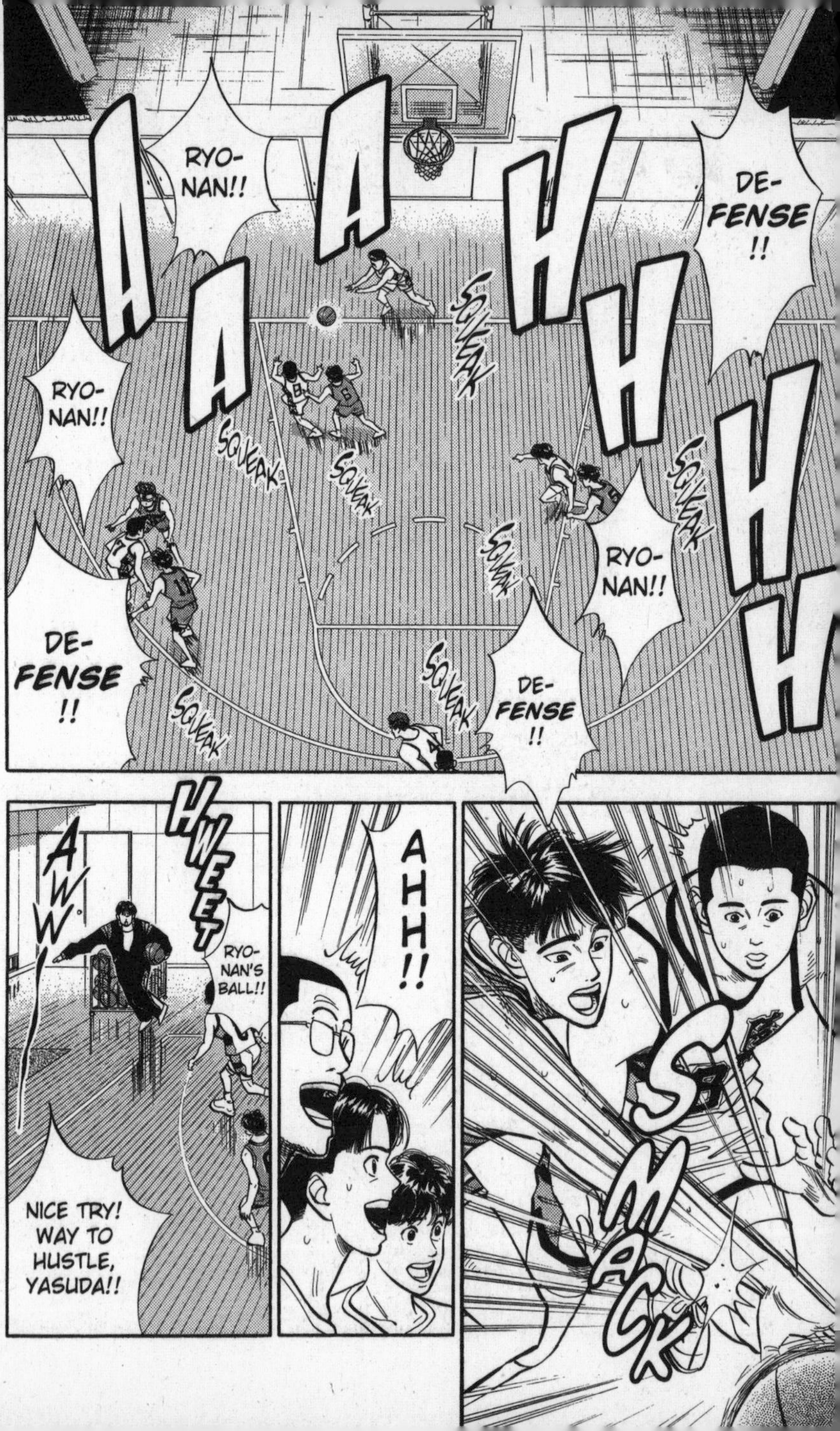

AAAHHHHH
DE-FENSE!!
RYO-NAN!!
SQUEAK
RYO-NAN!!
SQUEAK
SQUEAK
SQUEAK
SQUEAK
RYO-NAN!!
SQUEAK
DE-FENSE!!
DE-FENSE!!
SQUEAK
SMACK
AHH!!
HWEET
RYO-NAN'S BALL!!
AWW!
NICE TRY! WAY TO HUSTLE, YASUDA!!

READ THIS WAY

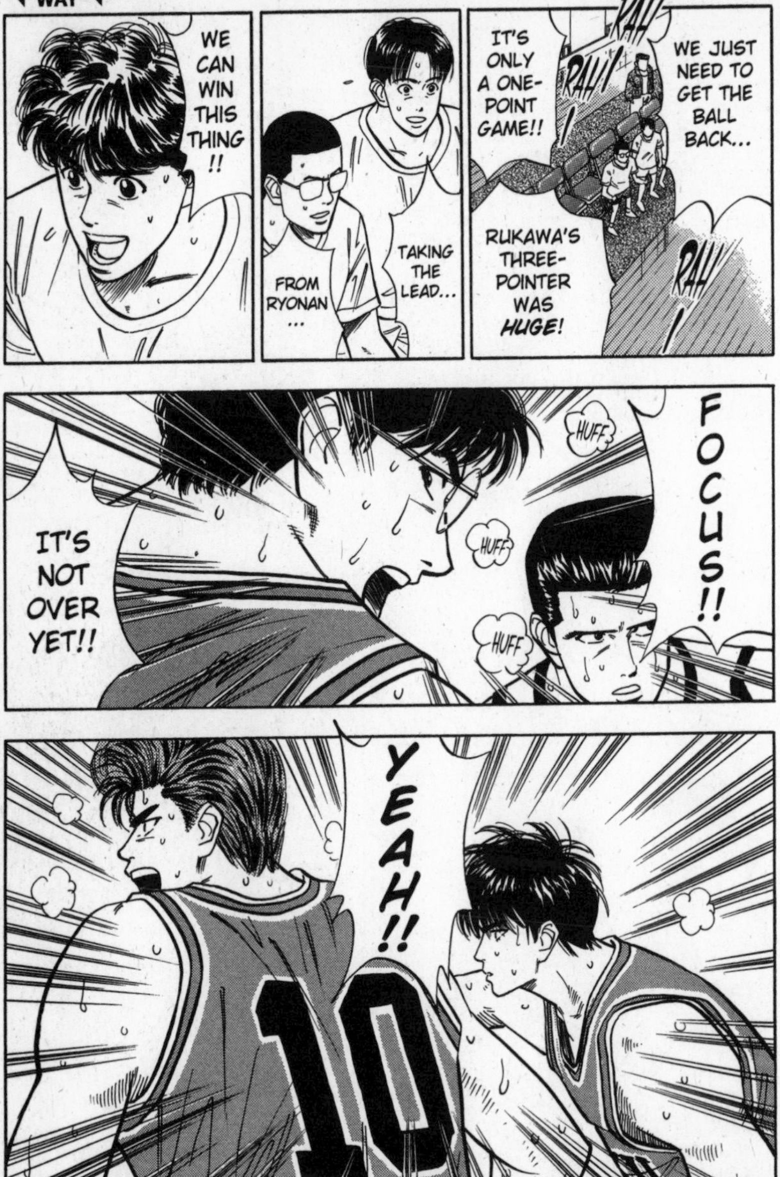
RAH
RAH
WE JUST NEED TO GET THE BALL BACK...
IT'S ONLY A ONE-POINT GAME!!
RAH
RUKAWA'S THREE-POINTER WAS HUGE!
TAKING THE LEAD...
FROM RYONAN...
WE CAN WIN THIS THING!!
FOCUS!!
HUFF
HUFF
HUFF
IT'S NOT OVER YET!!
YEAH!!

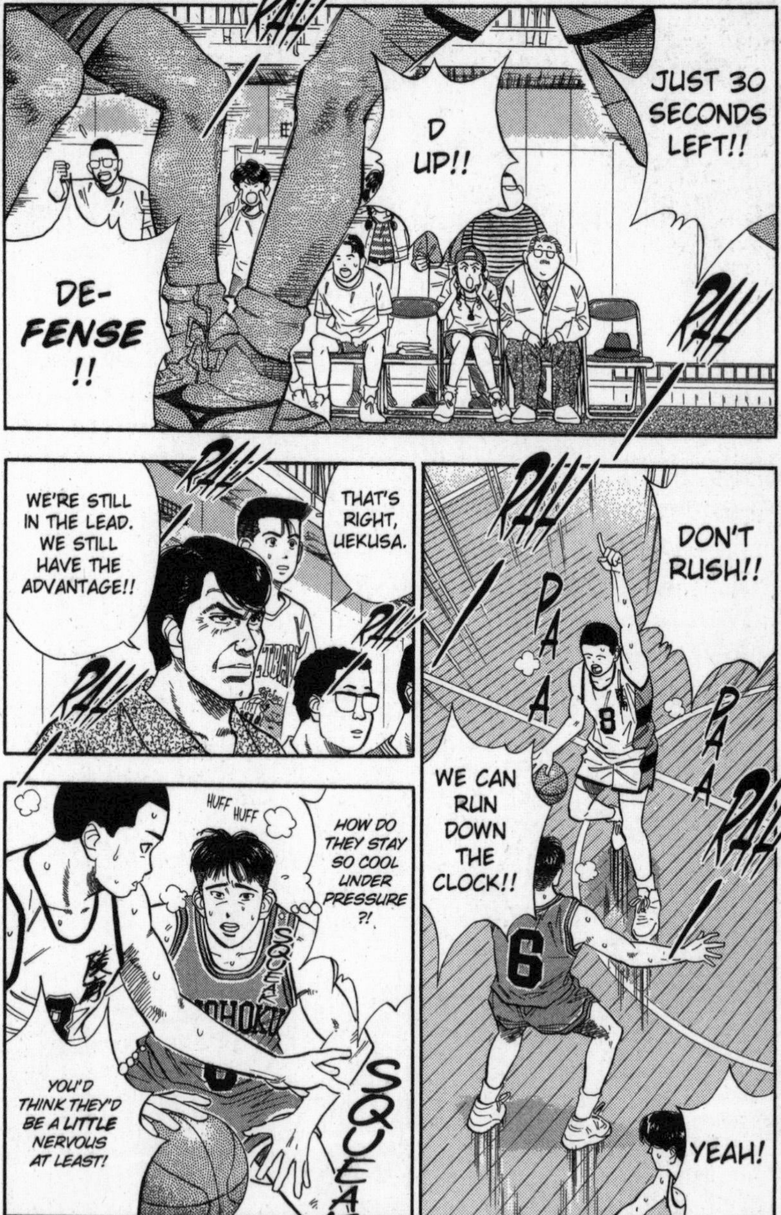
RAH
JUST 30 SECONDS LEFT!!
D UP!!
RAH
DE-FENSE!!
RAH
DON'T RUSH!!
PAA
PAA
RAH
WE CAN RUN DOWN THE CLOCK!!
YEAH!
RAH
THAT'S RIGHT, UEKUSA.
WE'RE STILL IN THE LEAD. WE STILL HAVE THE ADVANTAGE!!
RAH
RAH
HUFF HUFF
HOW DO THEY STAY SO COOL UNDER PRESSURE?!
SQUEAK
YOU'D THINK THEY'D BE A LITTLE NERVOUS AT LEAST!
SQUEAK

READ THIS WAY

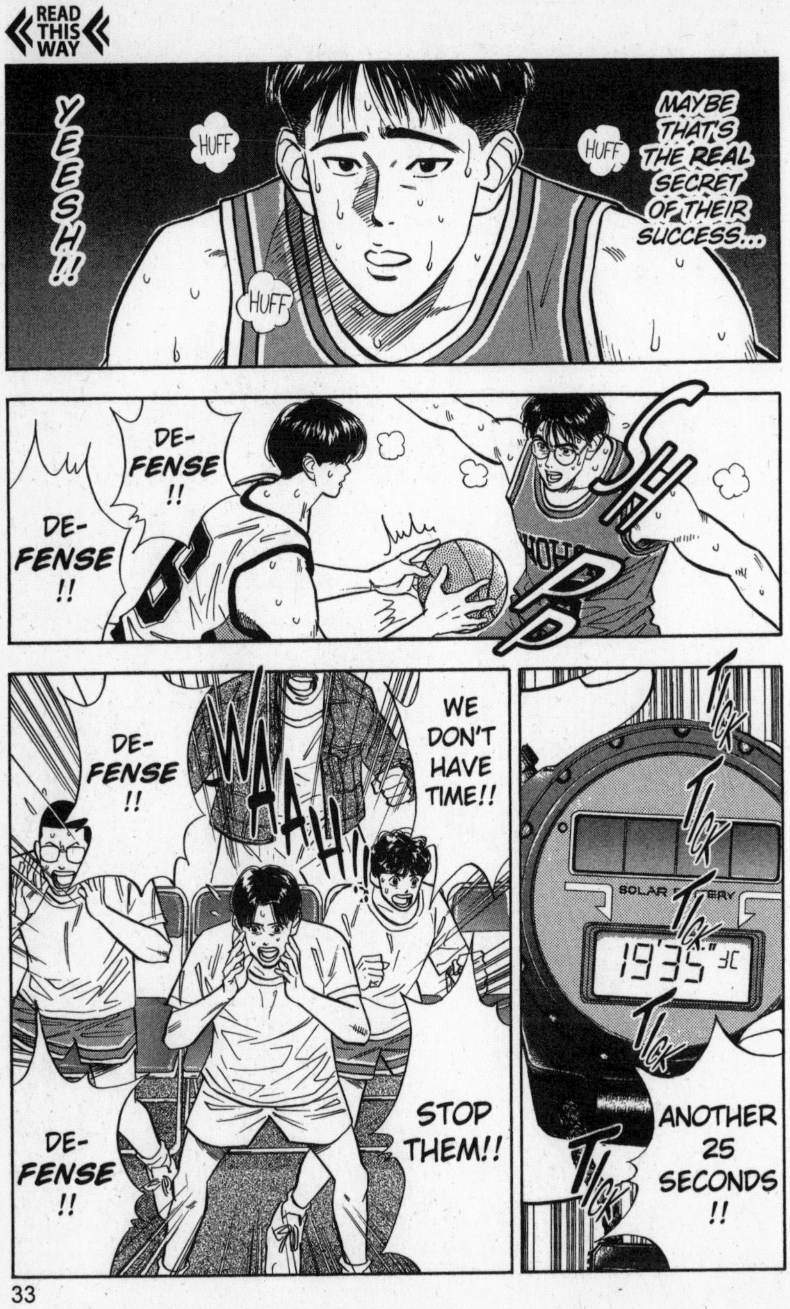

MAYBE THAT'S THE REAL SECRET OF THEIR SUCCESS...
HUFF
HUFF
HUFF
YEESH!!
SHAPP
DE-FENSE!!
DE-FENSE!!
TICK
TICK
TICK
TICK
TICK
19'35"
ANOTHER 25 SECONDS!!
WE DON'T HAVE TIME!!
WAAAH!!
DE-FENSE!!
STOP THEM!!
DE-FENSE!!

Scoreboard: Ryonan Shohoku

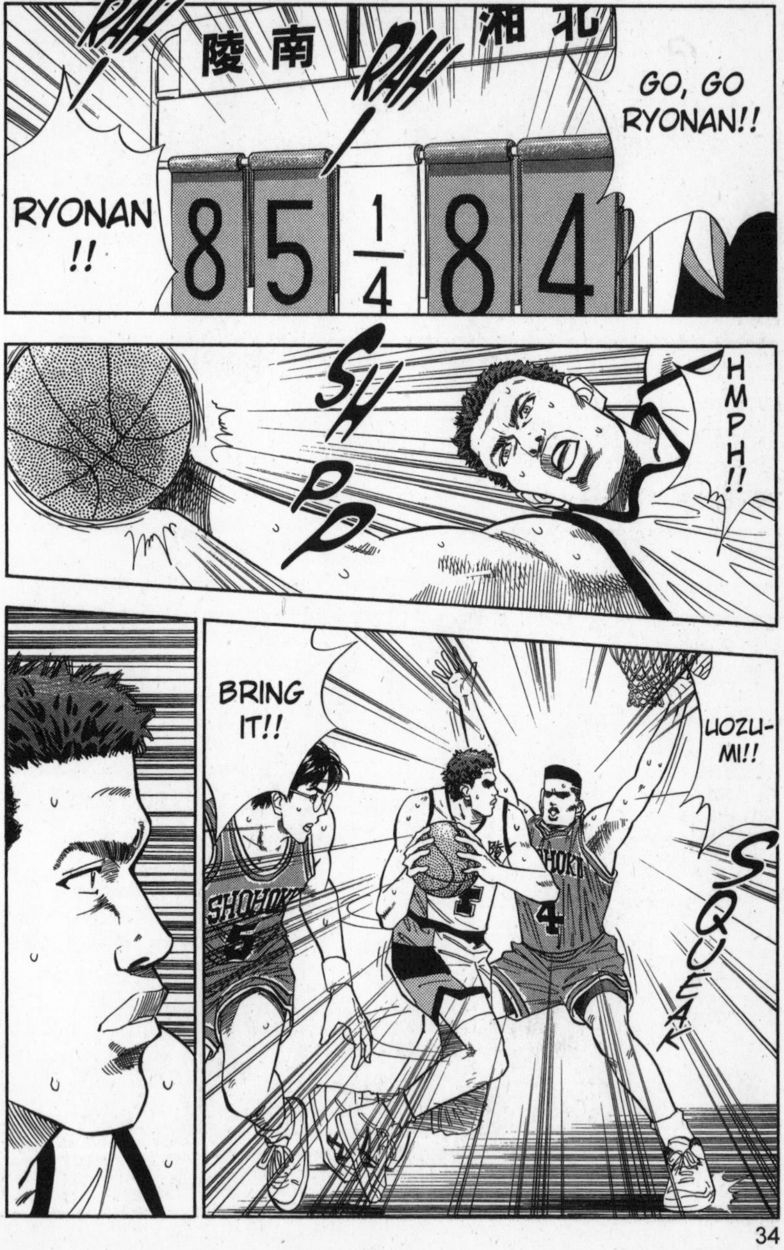
GO, GO RYONAN!!
湘北
陵南
RAH!
RAH!
RYONAN!!
85 1/4 84
HMPH!!
SHPP
UOZUMI!!
SQUEAK
BRING IT!!

READ THIS WAY

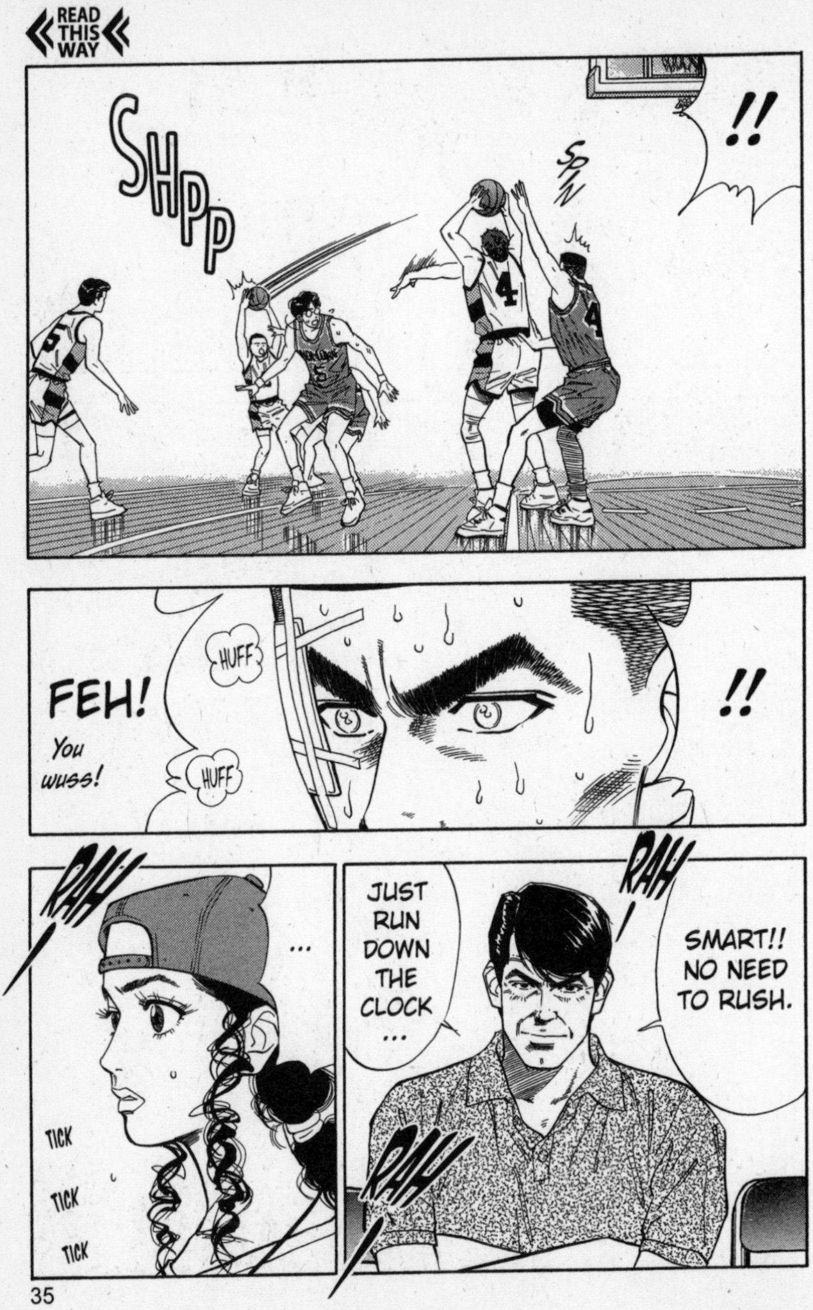

!!
SPIN
SHPP
!!
HUFF
HUFF
FEH! You wuss!
RAH
SMART!! NO NEED TO RUSH.
JUST RUN DOWN THE CLOCK...
RAH
RAH
...
TICK
TICK
TICK

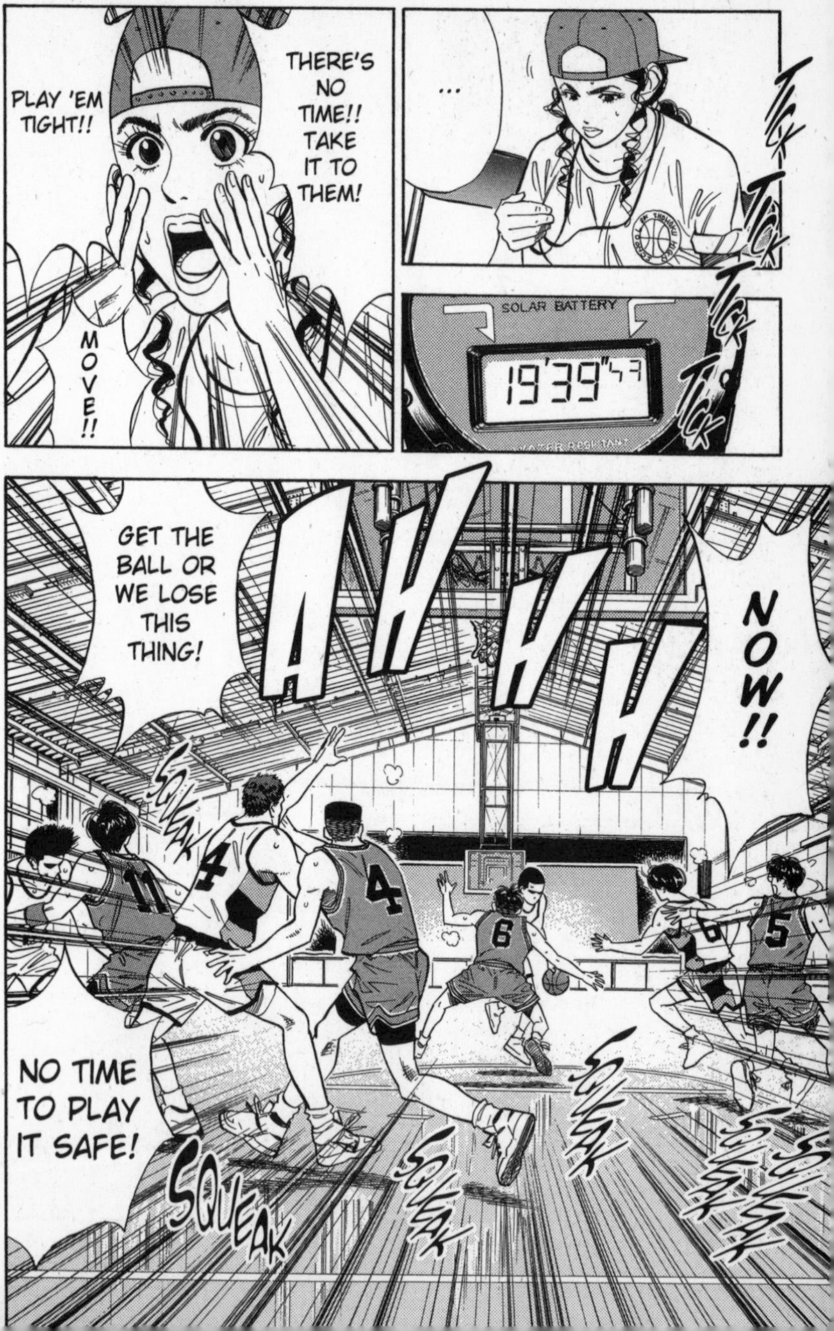
...
TICK TICK TICK TICK
SOLAR BATTERY
19'39"
THERE'S NO TIME!! TAKE IT TO THEM!
PLAY 'EM TIGHT!!
MOVE!!
NOW!!
AHHHH
GET THE BALL OR WE LOSE THIS THING!
SQUEAK
SQUEAK
SQUEAK
SQUEAK SQUEAK SQUEAK
NO TIME TO PLAY IT SAFE!
SQUEAK

READ THIS WAY

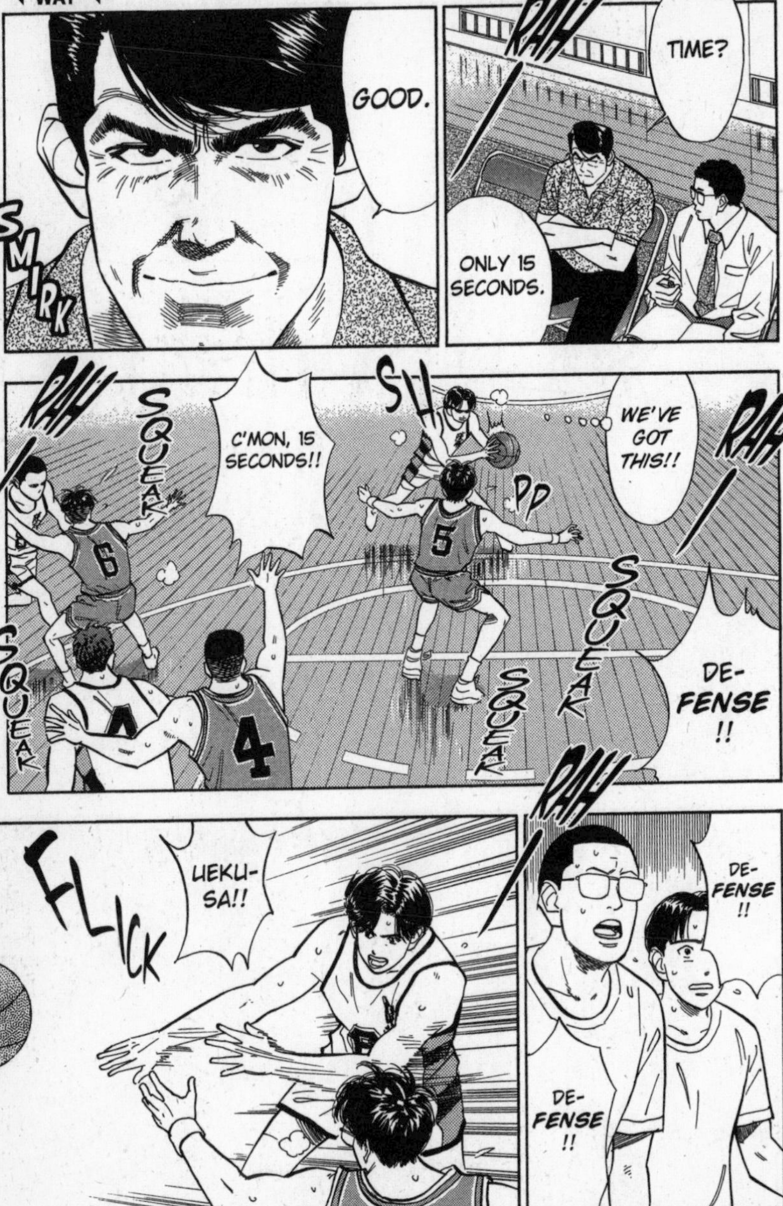
RAH
TIME?
ONLY 15 SECONDS.
GOOD.
SMIRK
RAH
WE'VE GOT THIS!!
DE-FENSE!!
SQUEAK
SQUEAK
SH
PP
C'MON, 15 SECONDS!!
SQUEAK
RAH
SQUEAK
RAH
DE-FENSE!!
DE-FENSE!!
UEKU-SA!!
FLICK

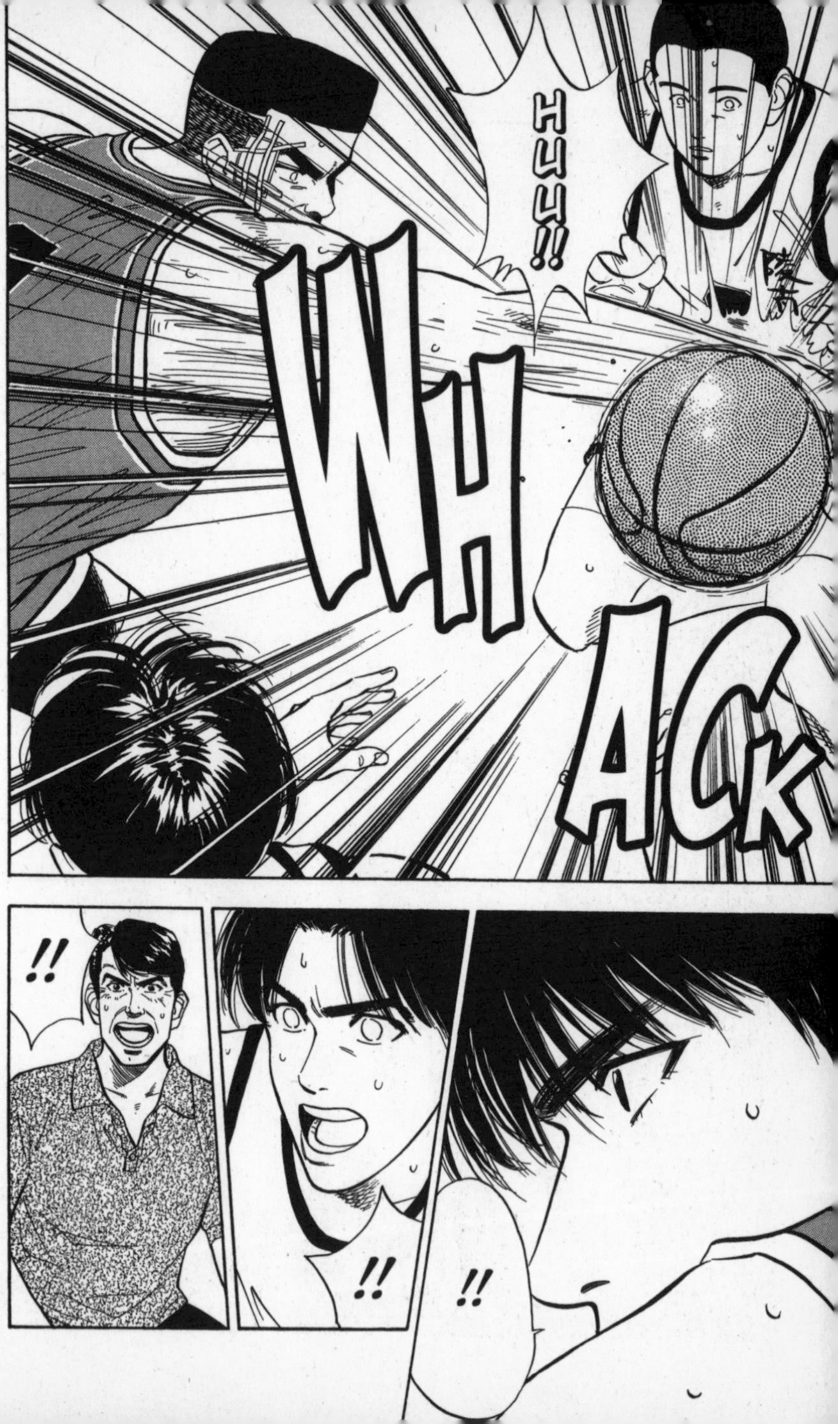
HUUU!!
WHACK
!!
!!
!!

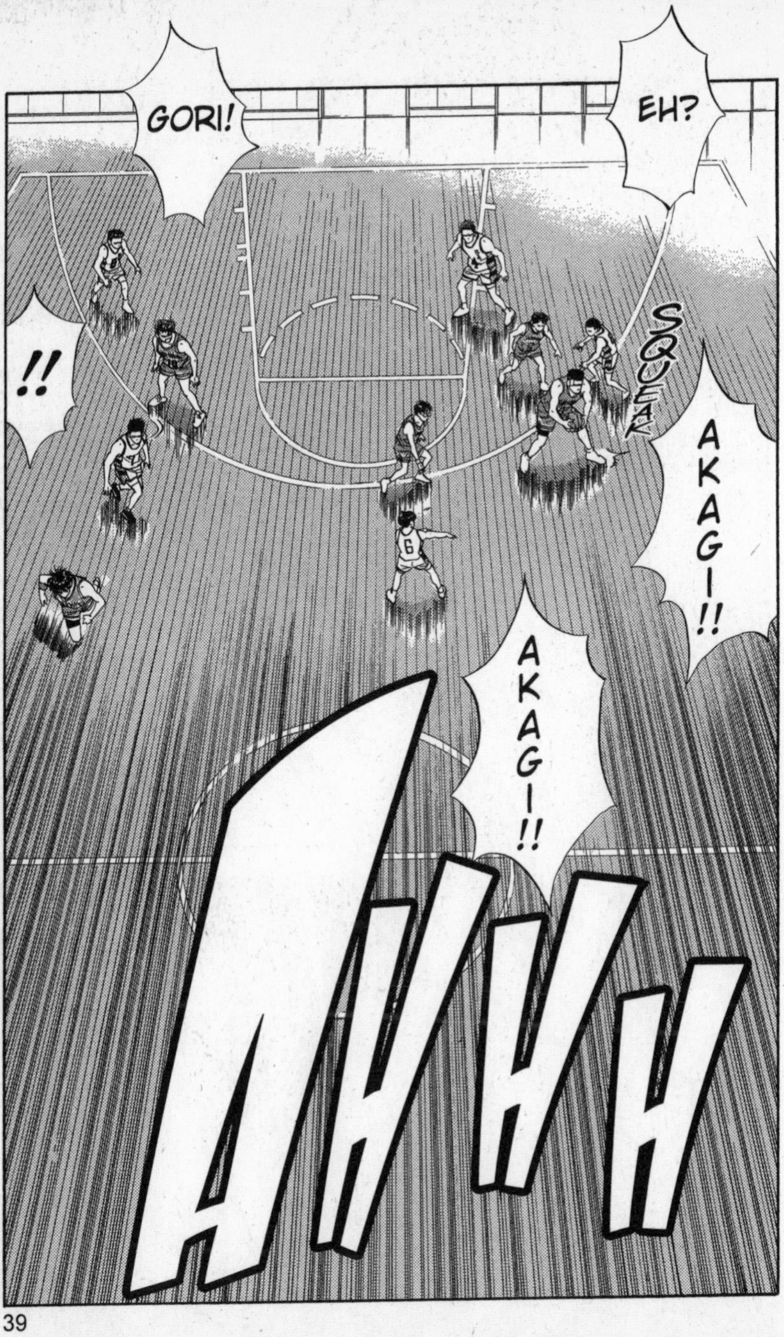
EH?
GORI!
SQUEAK
AKAGI!!
AKAGI!!
!!
AHHH

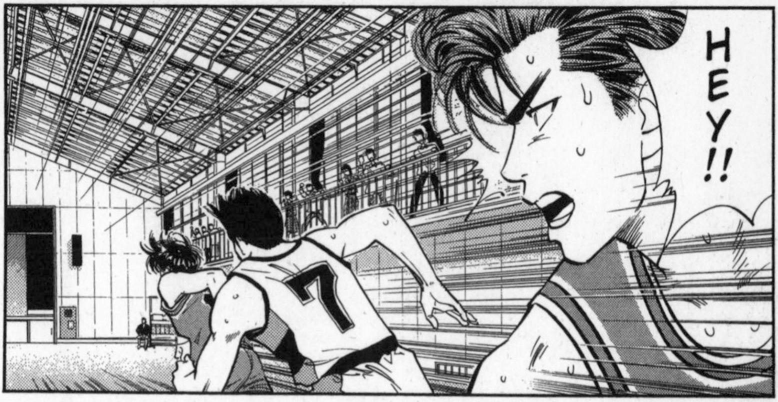
HEY!!

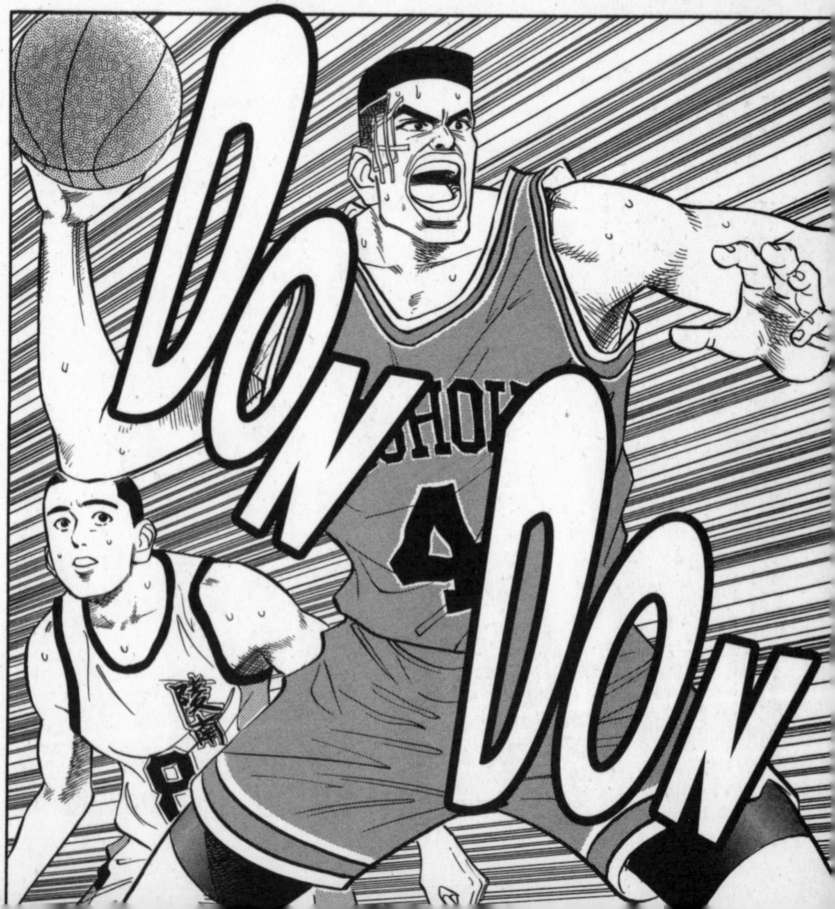
DON DON

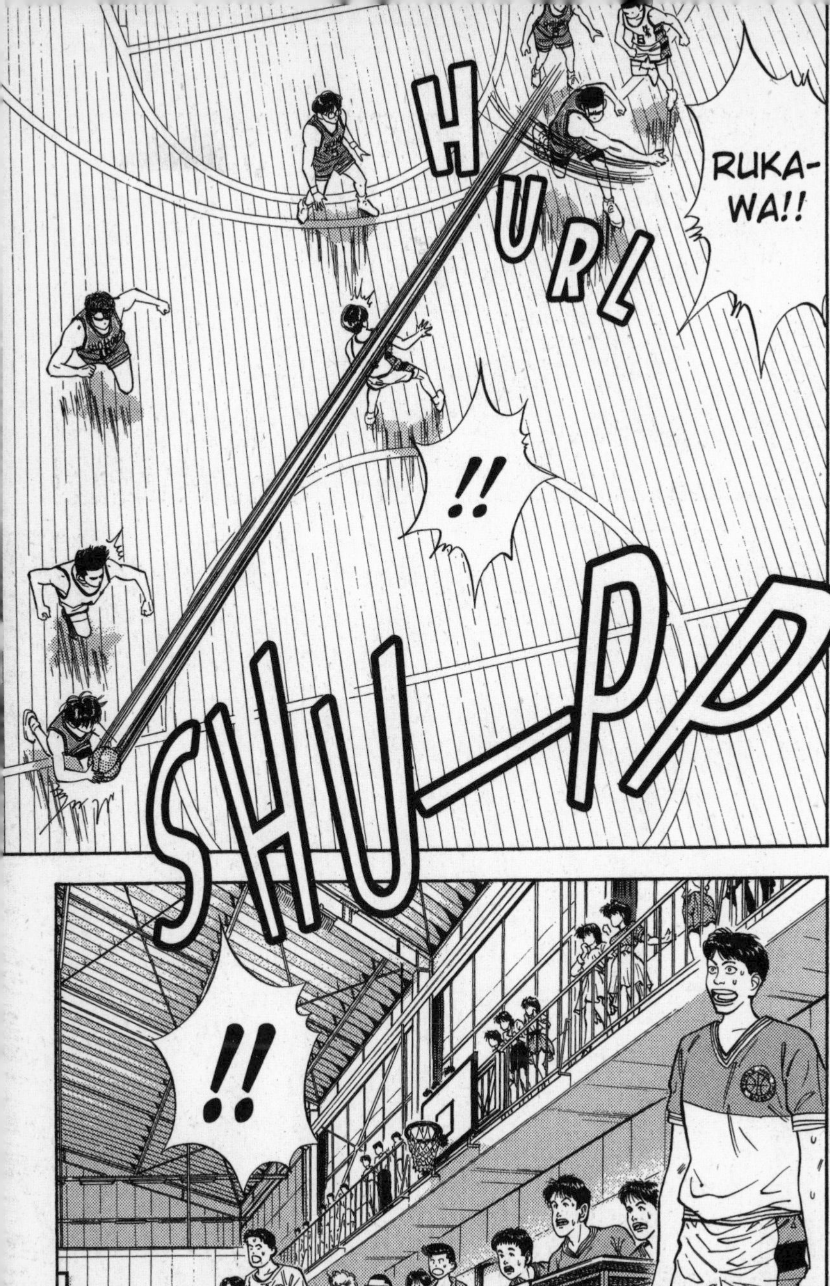
RUKA-WA!!
HURL
!!
SHUPP
!!

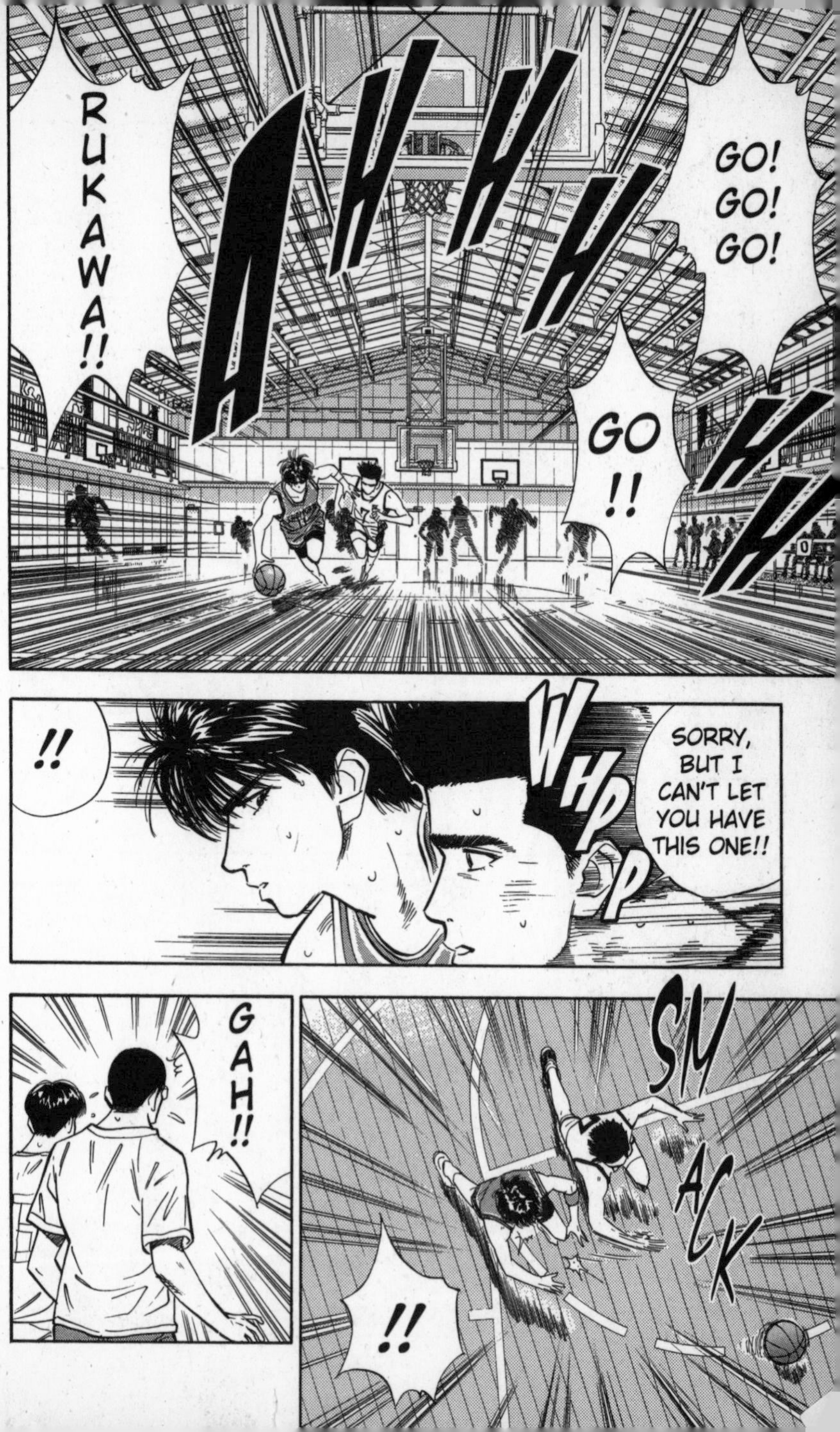
GO! GO! GO!
GO !!
AHHHH
RUKAWA!!
SORRY, BUT I CAN'T LET YOU HAVE THIS ONE!!
WHIP
!!
SMACK
!!
GAH!!

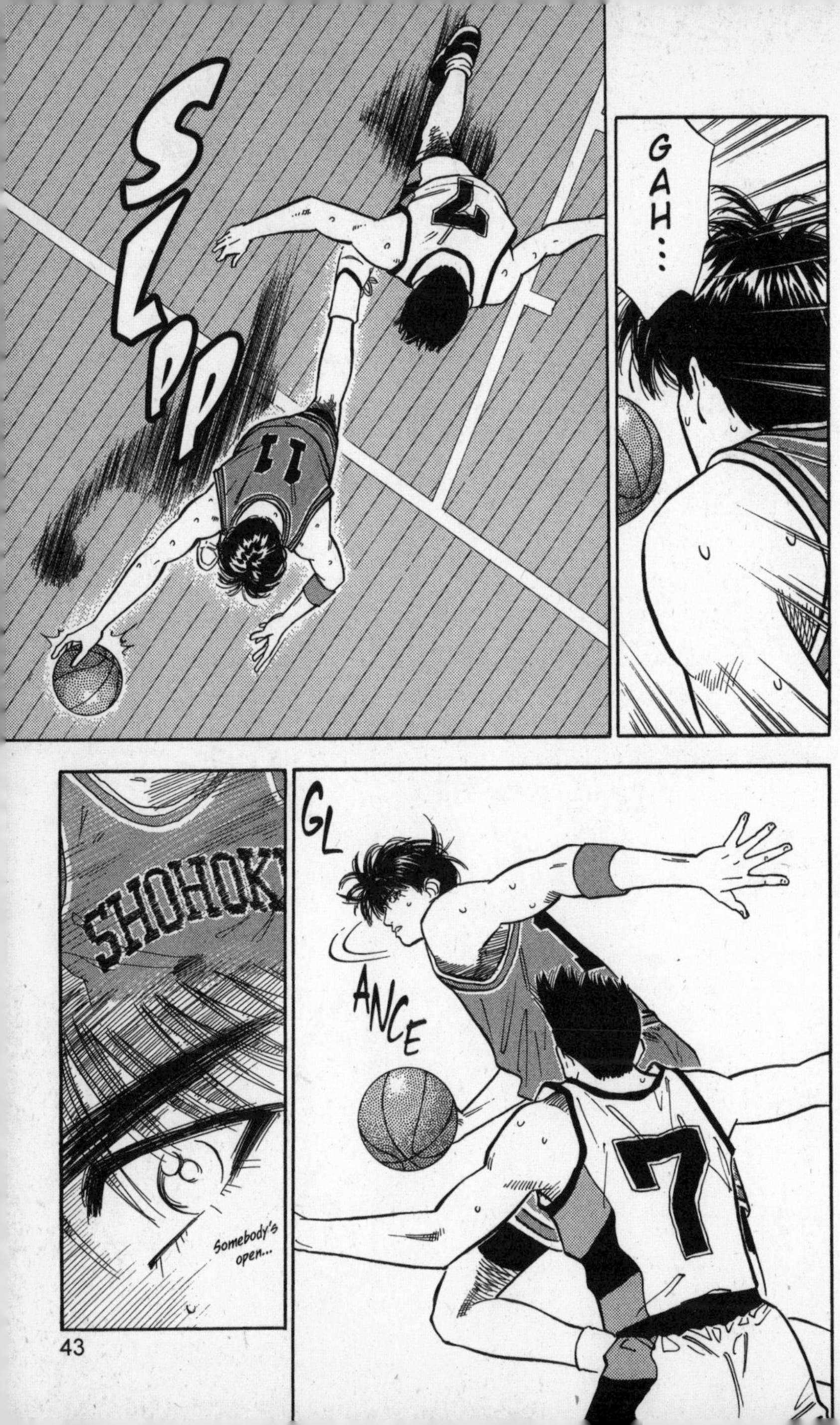
GAH...
SLPP
GLANCE
SHOHOK
Somebody's open...

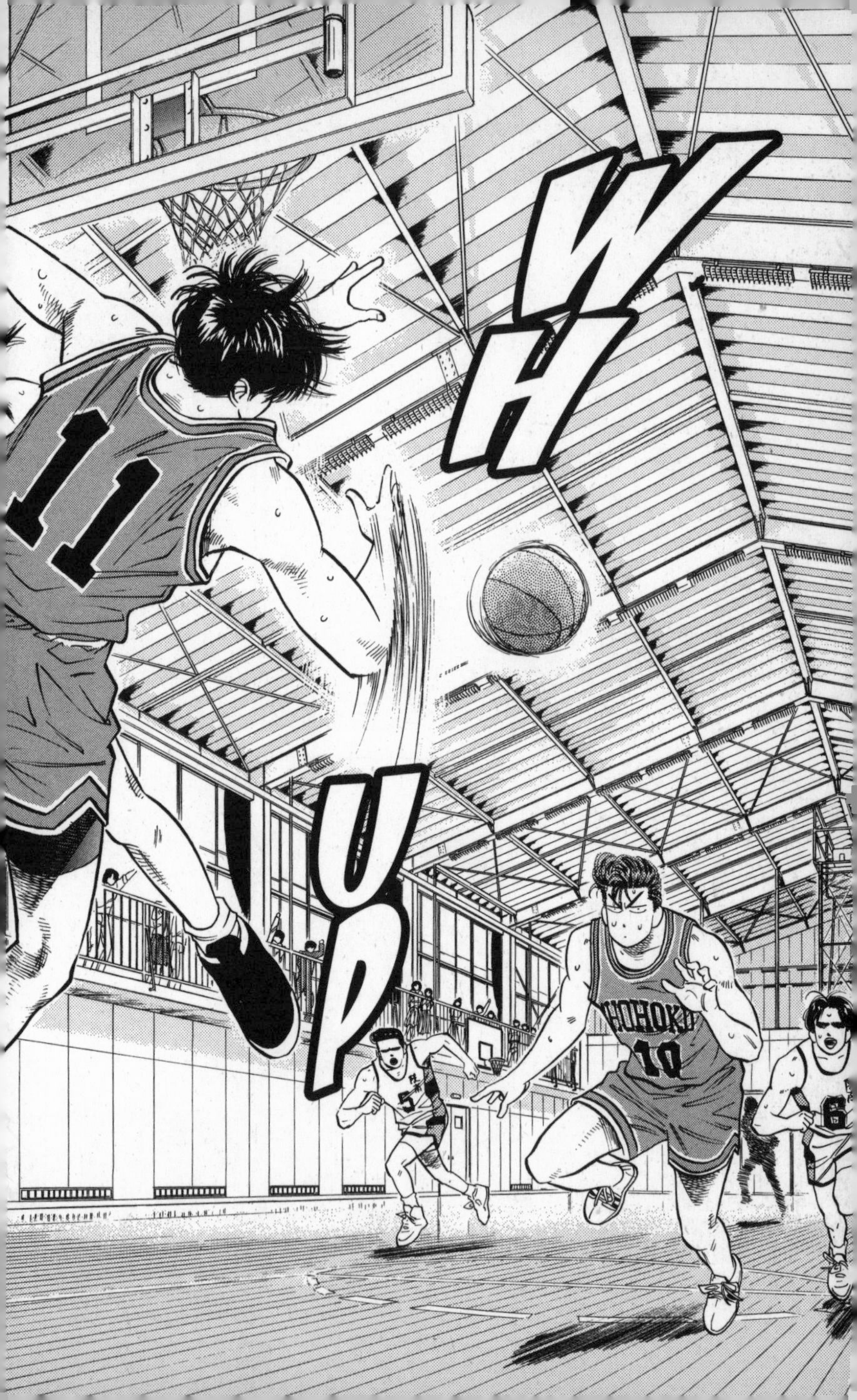
WHUP
SHOHOKU
10

READ THIS WAY

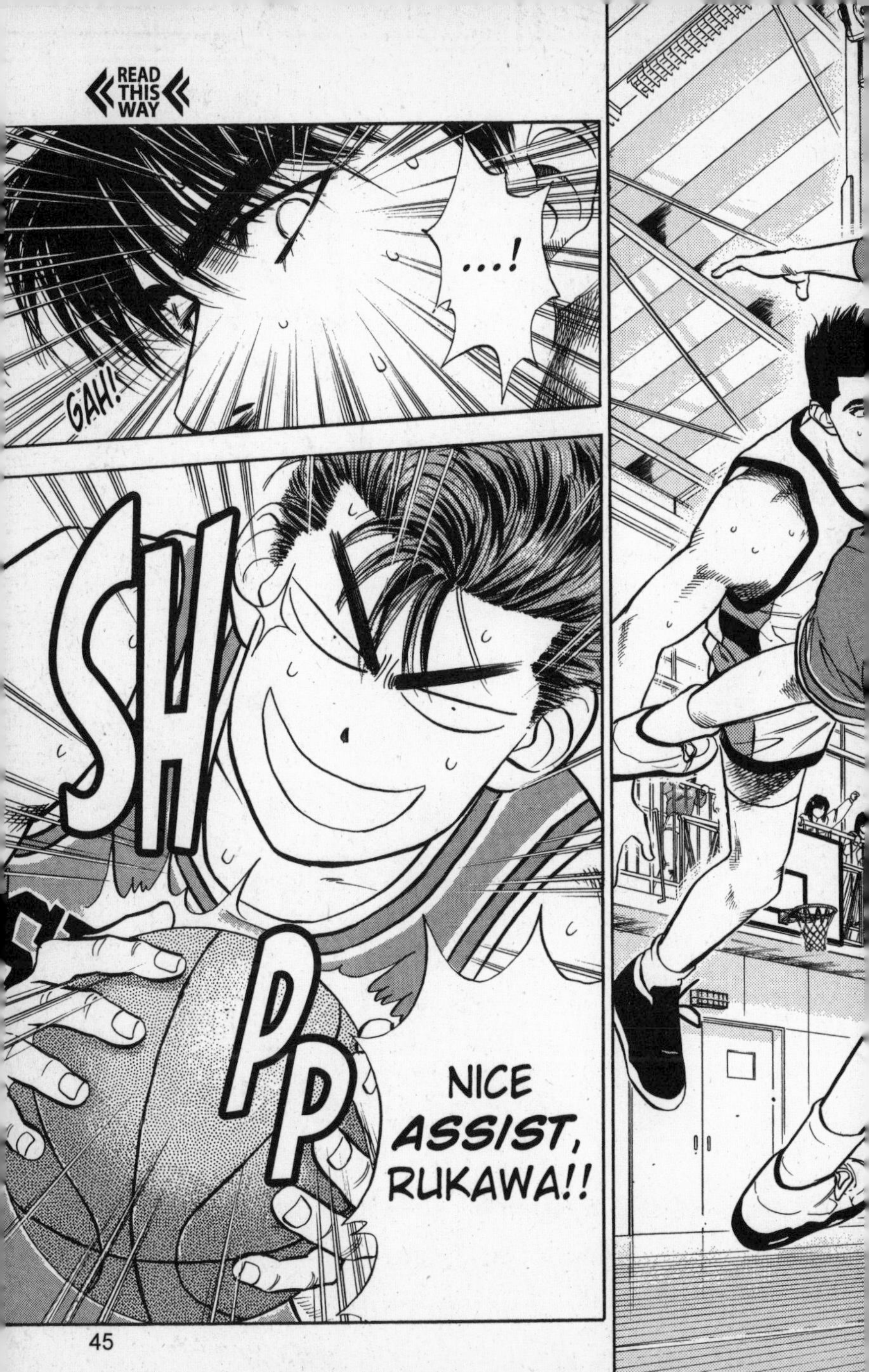

...!
GAH!
SHPP
NICE ASSIST, RUKAWA!!

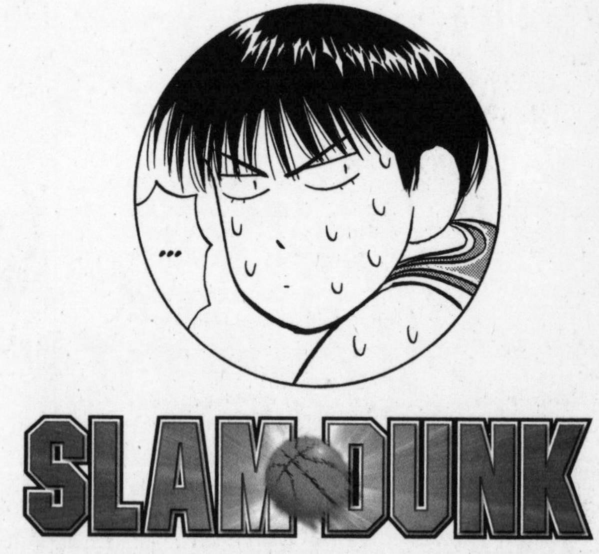
...

SLAM DUNK

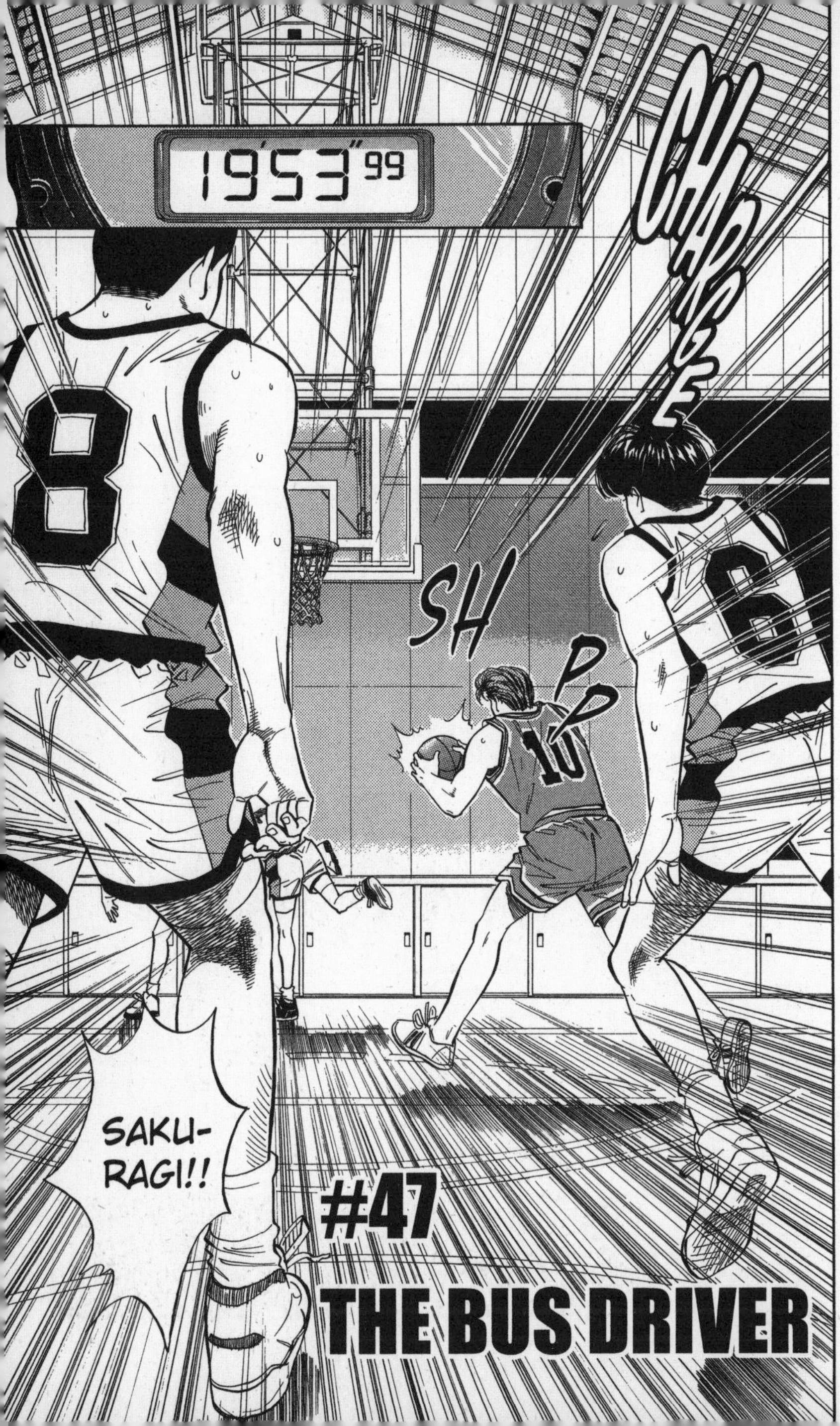

19'53"99
CHARGE
SH
PP
SAKU-
RAGI!!


# #47 THE BUS DRIVER

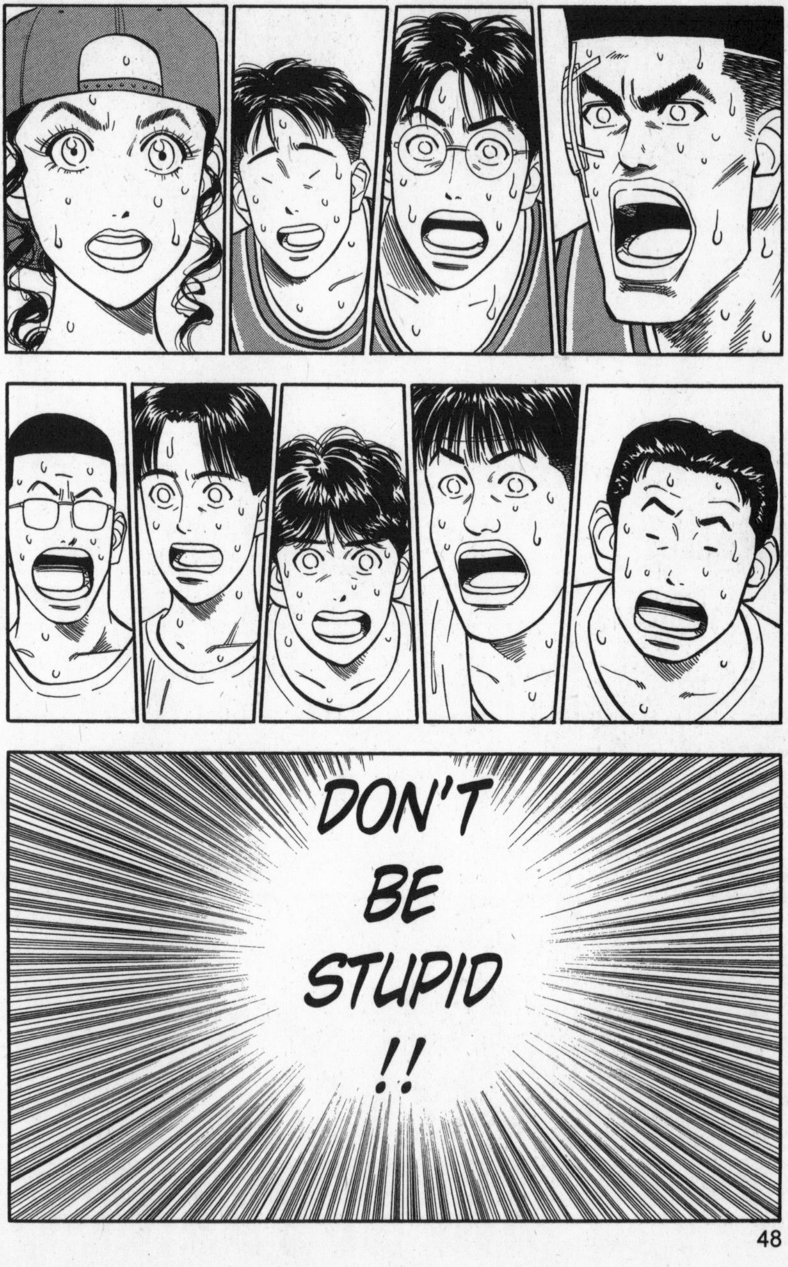
DON'T BE STUPID!!

READ THIS WAY

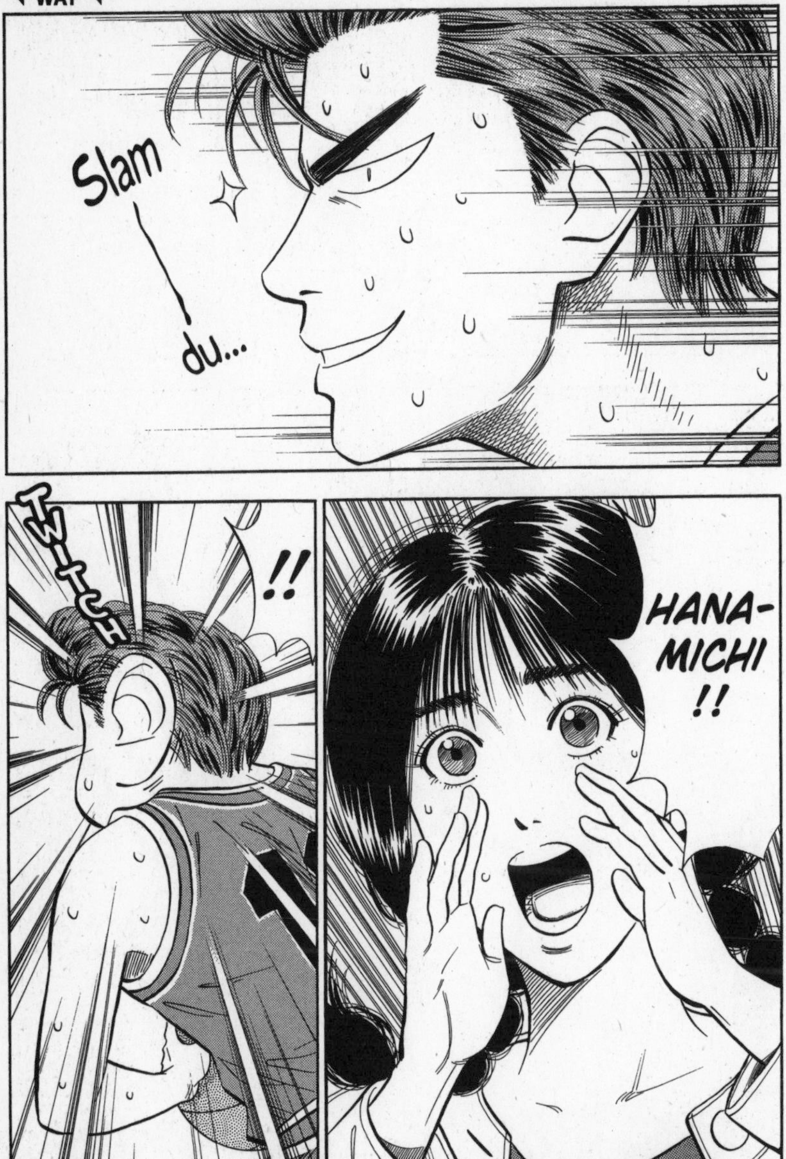
Slam du...
HANA-MICHI !!
TWITCH
!!

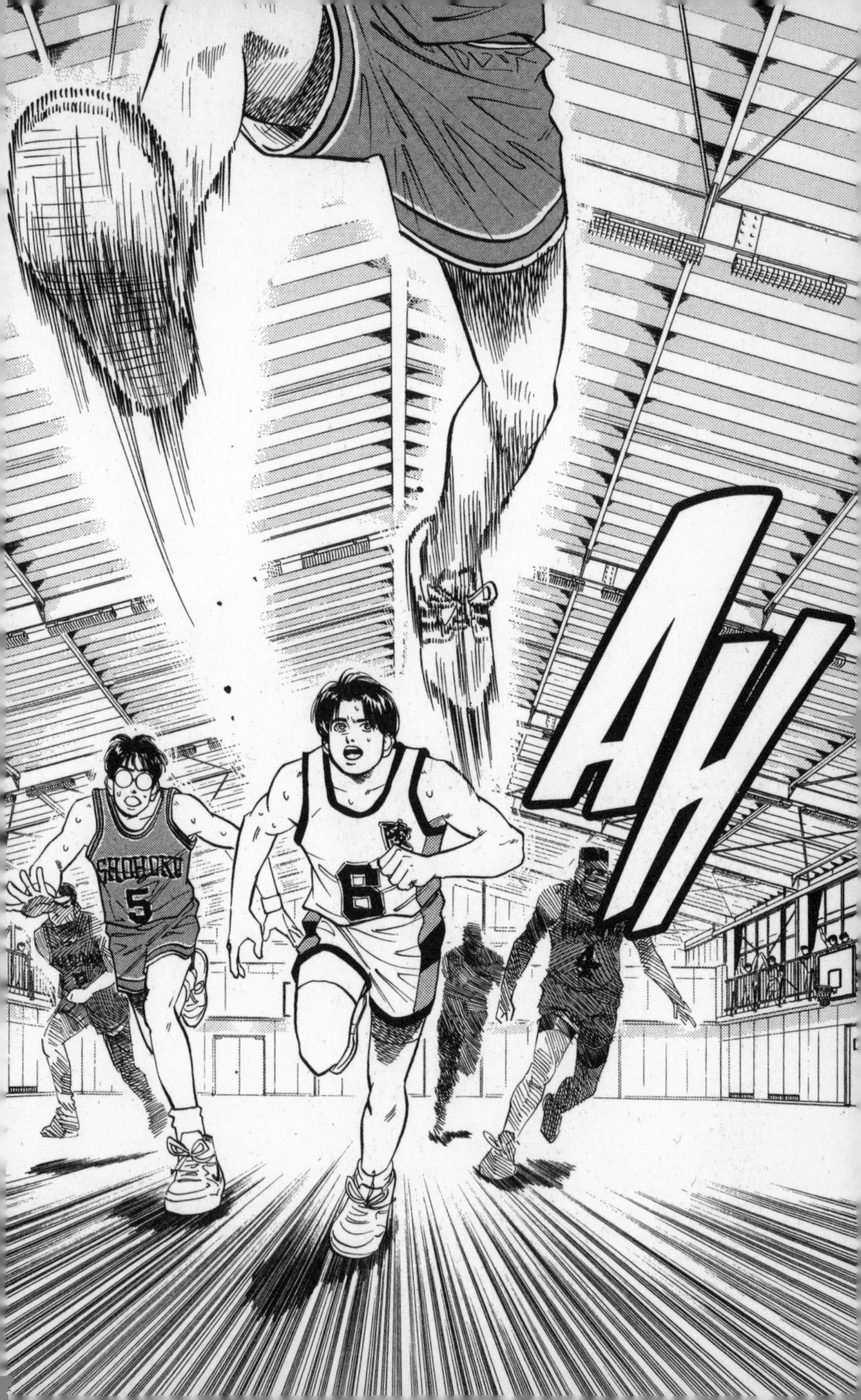
AH
SHOHOKU
5
6

READ THIS WAY

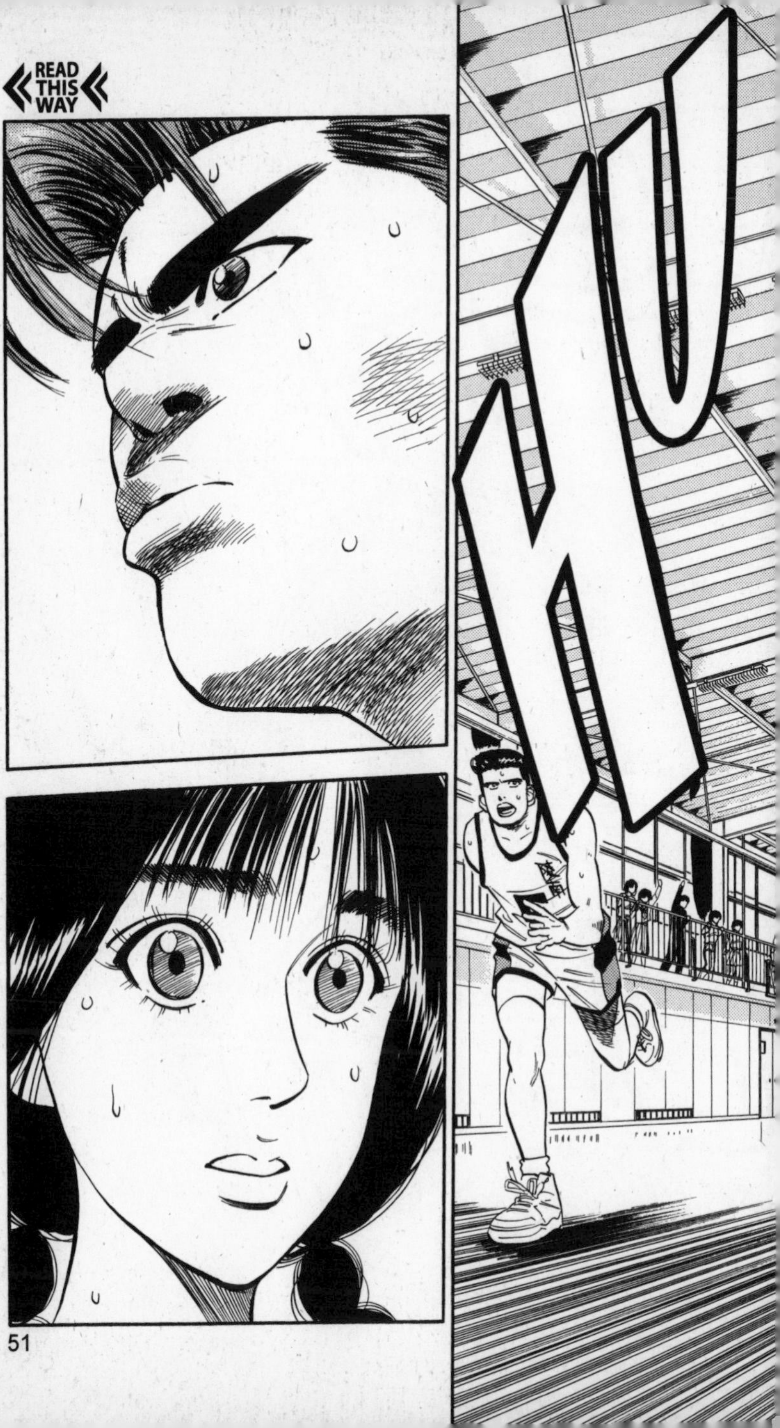
HU

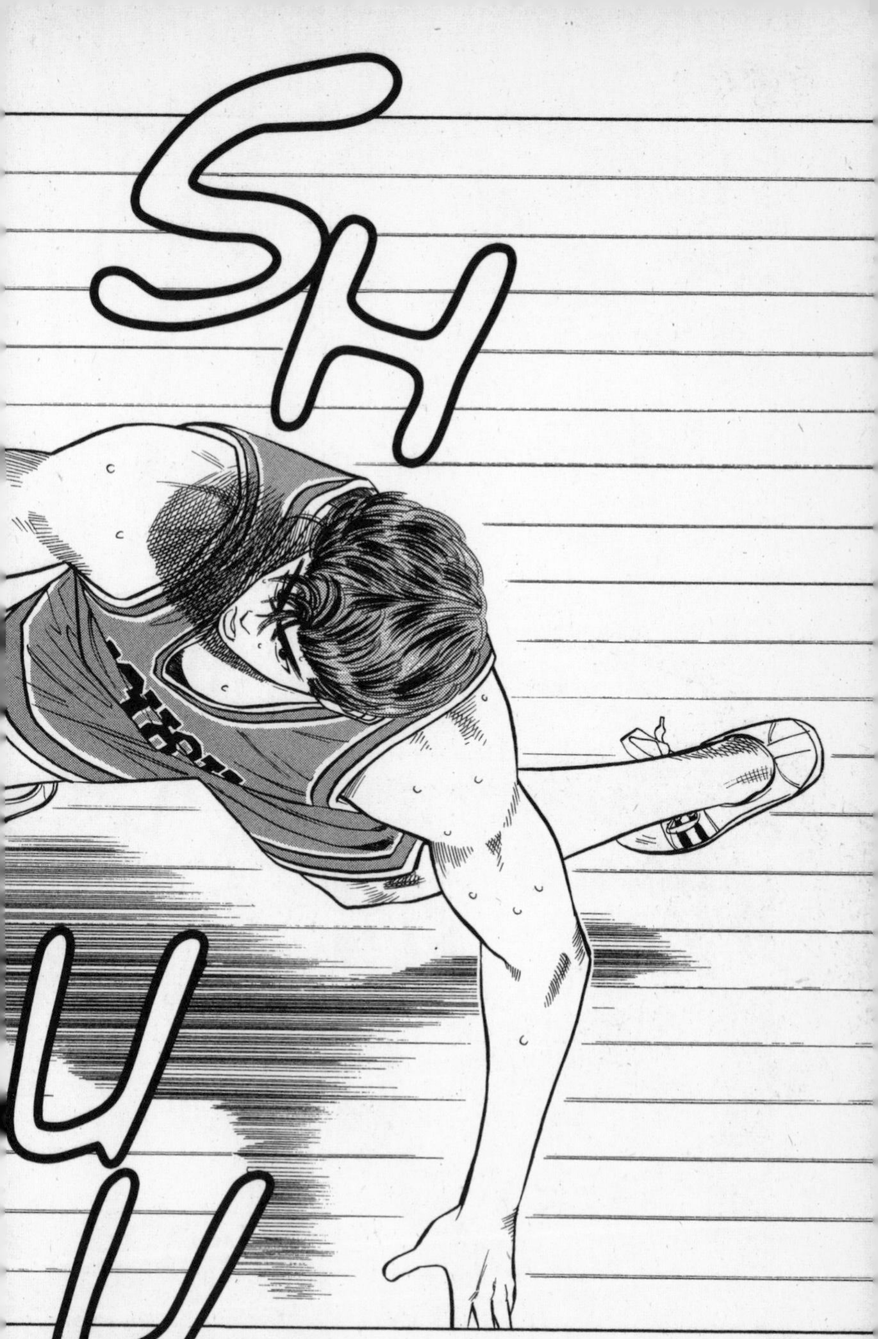
SHUU

READ THIS WAY

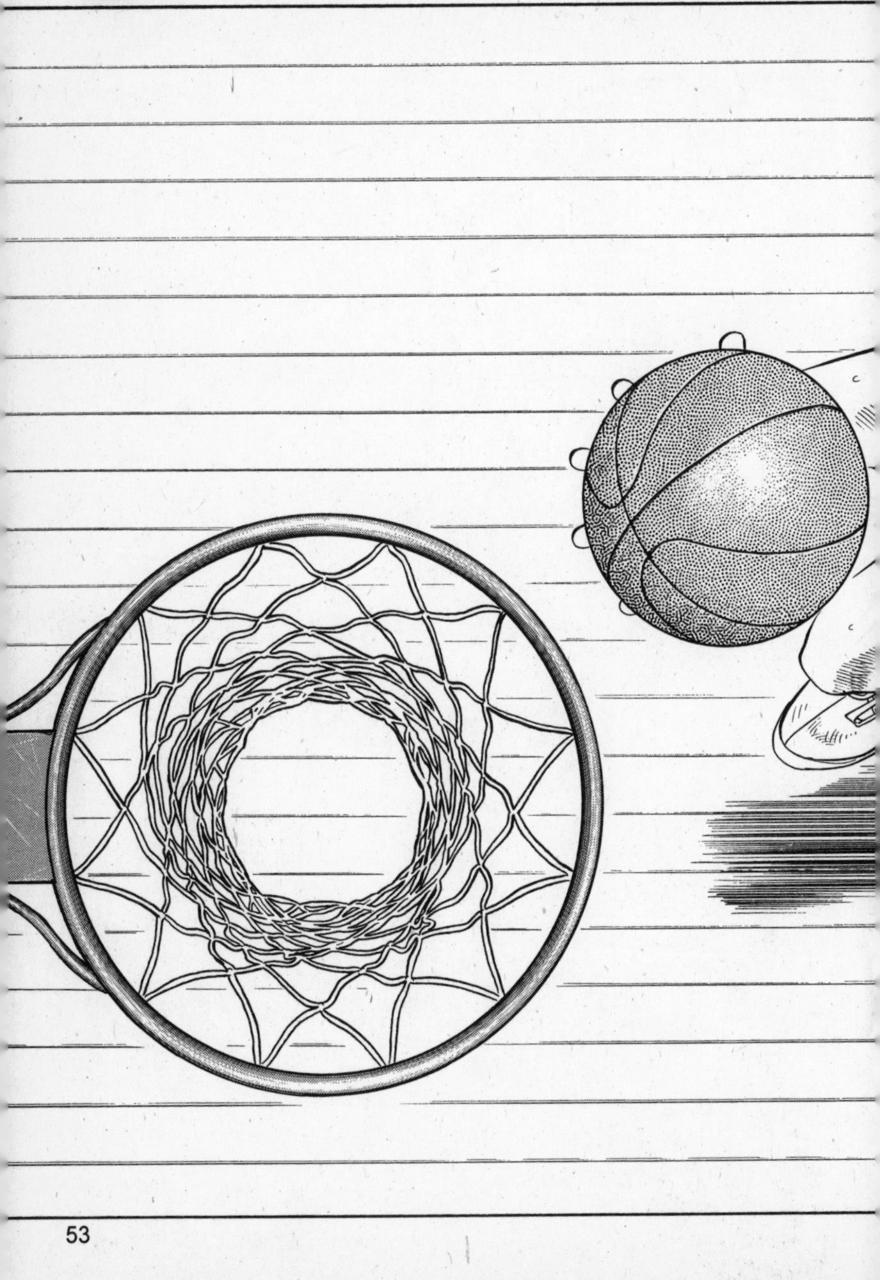

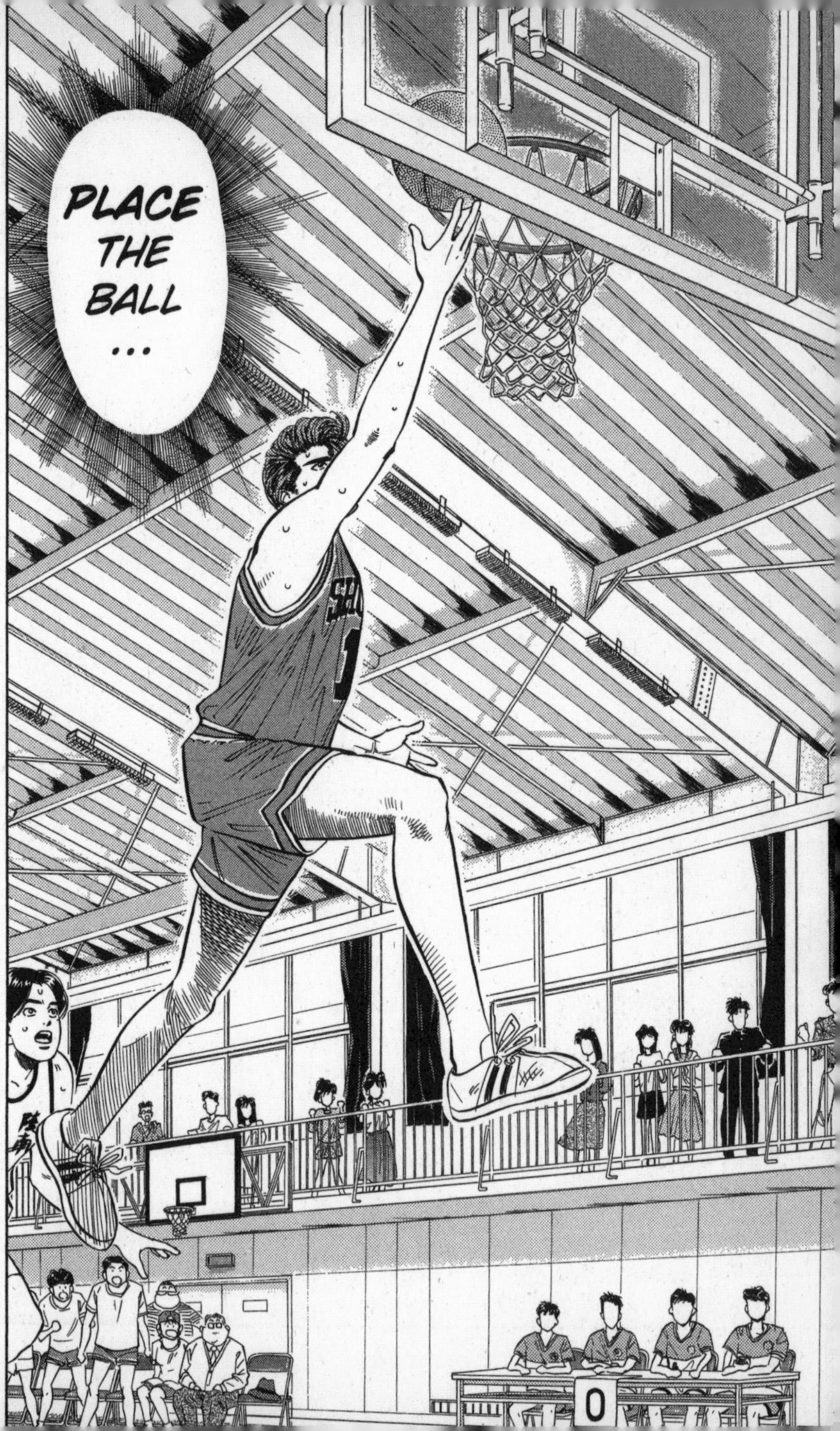
PLACE THE BALL ...

READ THIS WAY

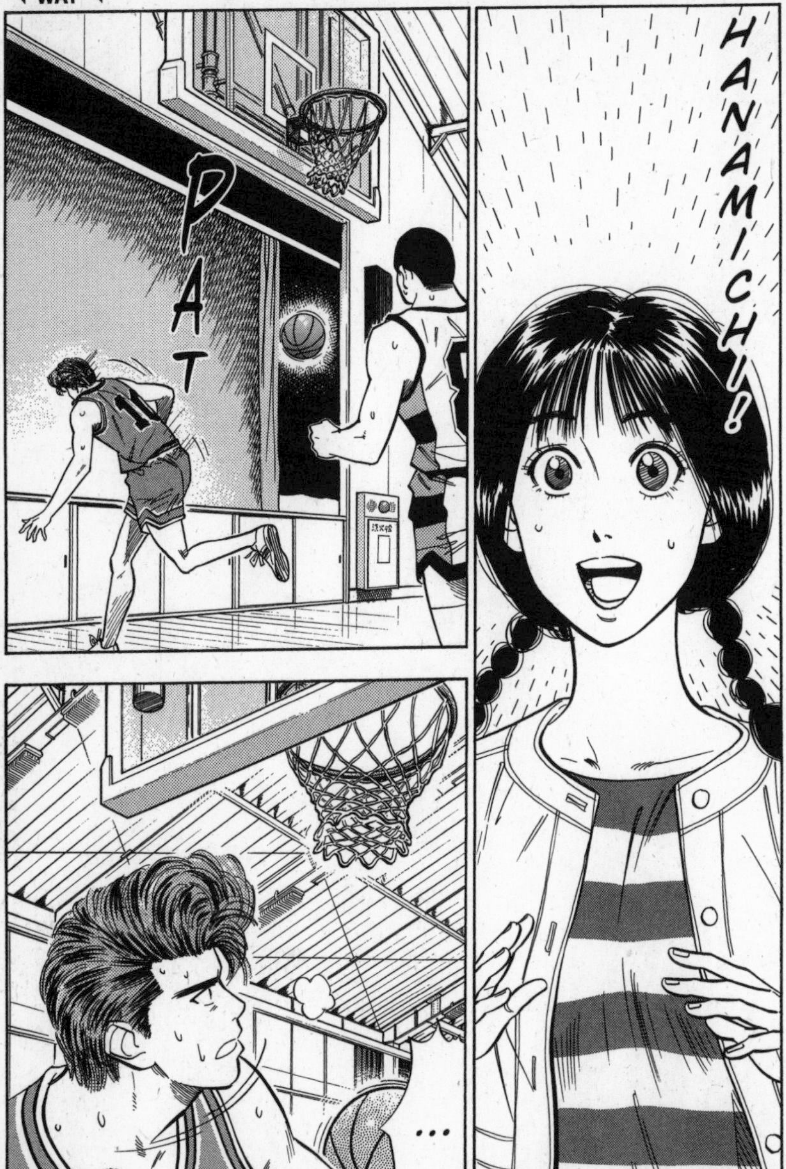
HANAMICHI!
PAT
...

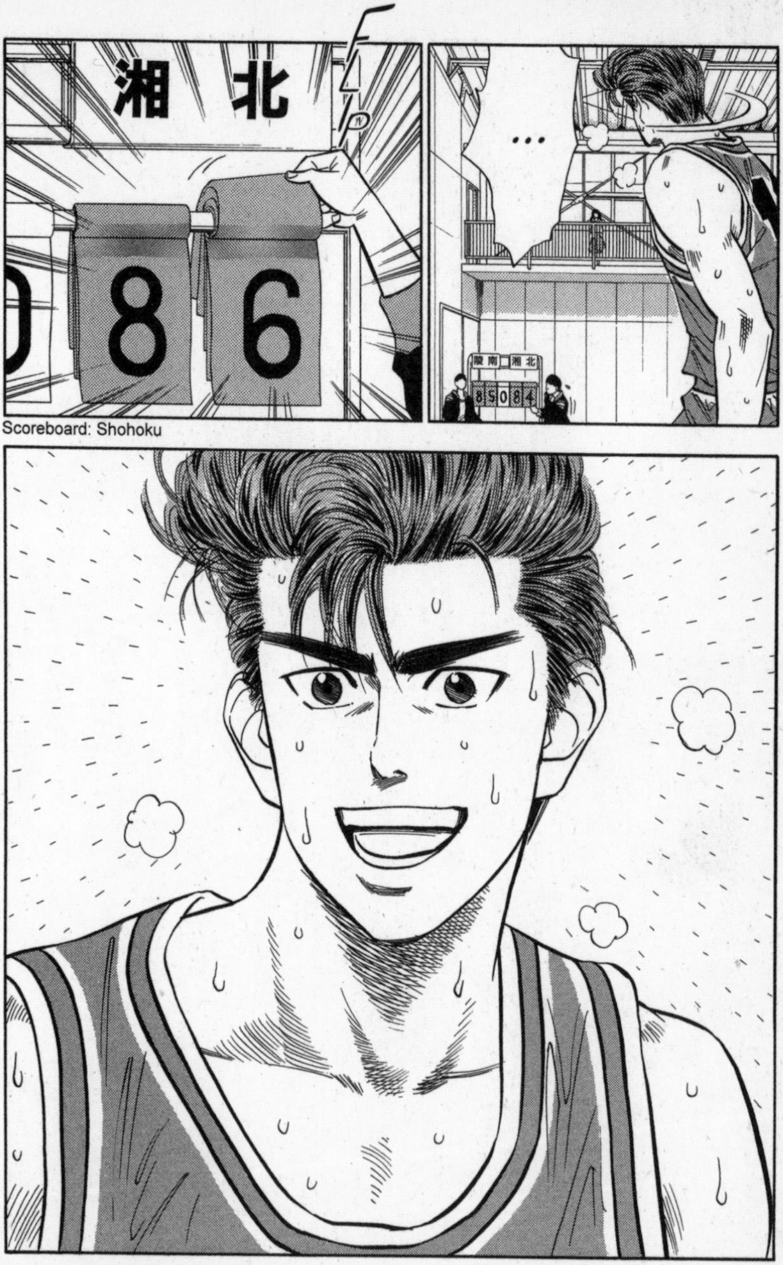
...
湘北
086
Scoreboard: Shohoku

READ THIS WAY

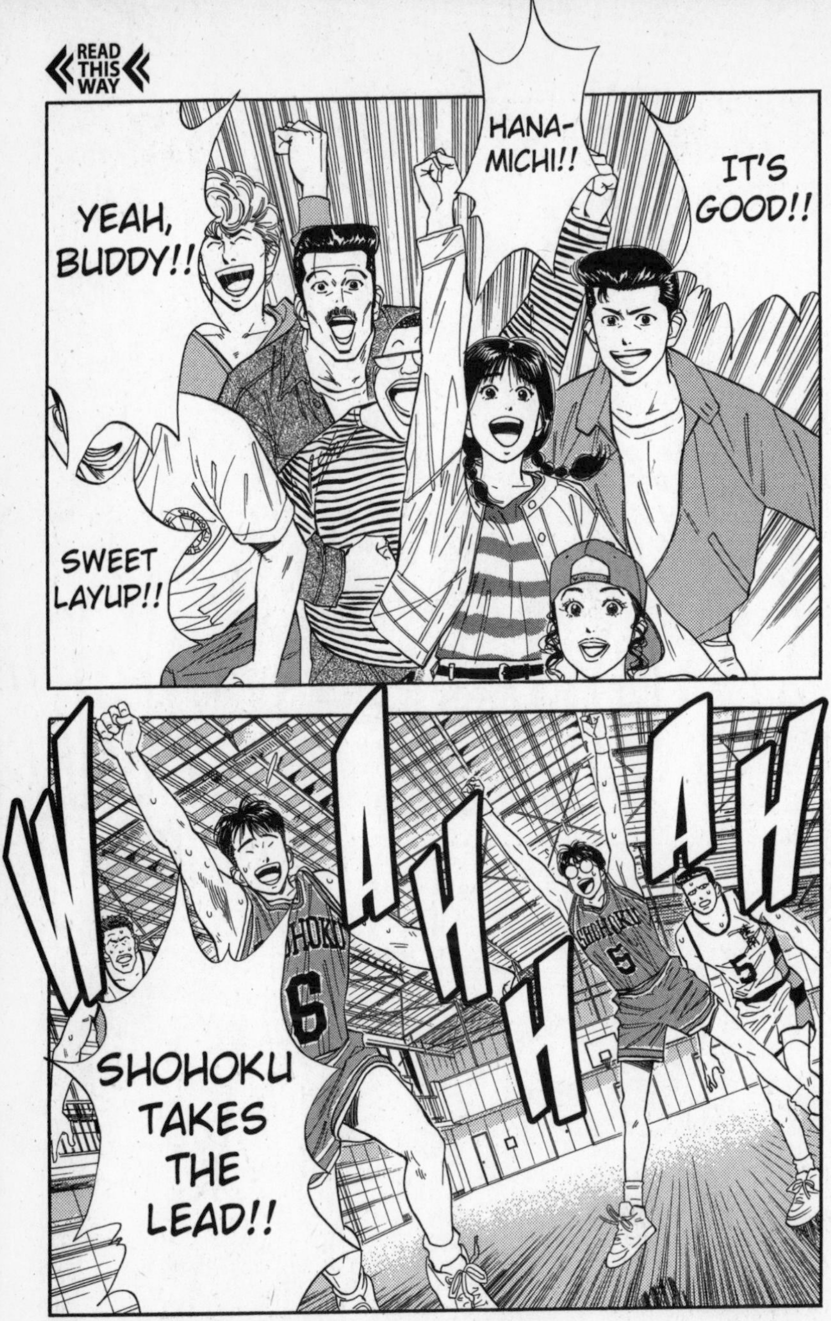
IT'S GOOD!!
HANA-MICHI!!
YEAH, BUDDY!!
SWEET LAYUP!!
WAHHHAH
SHOHOKU TAKES THE LEAD!!

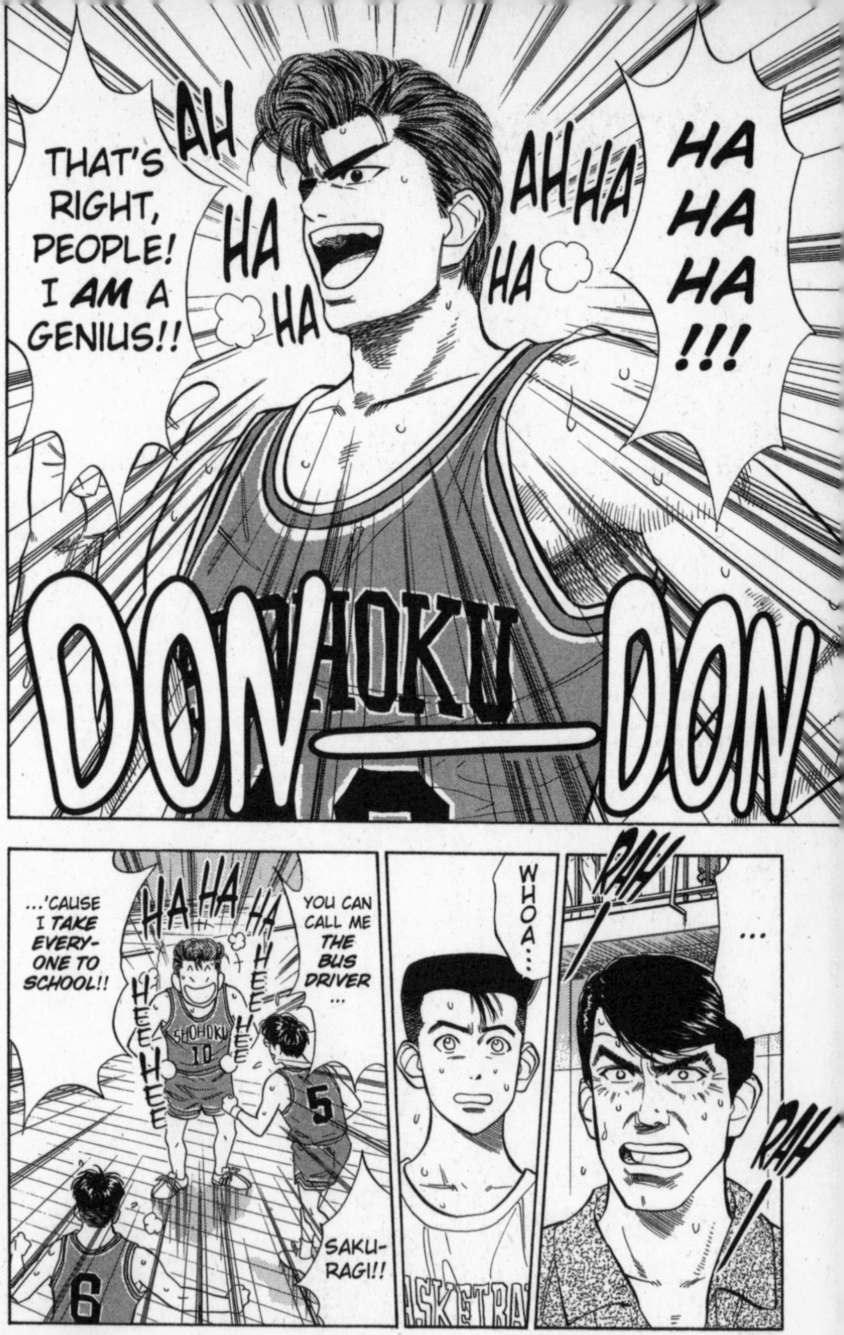
HA HA HA HA !!!
AH HA HA HA
THAT'S RIGHT, PEOPLE! I AM A GENIUS!!
AH HA HA HA
DON—DON
RAH
...
RAH
WHOA...
YOU CAN CALL ME THE BUS DRIVER ...
HA HA HA
...'CAUSE I TAKE EVERY-ONE TO SCHOOL!!
HEE HEE
HEE HEE HEE
SAKU-RAGI!!

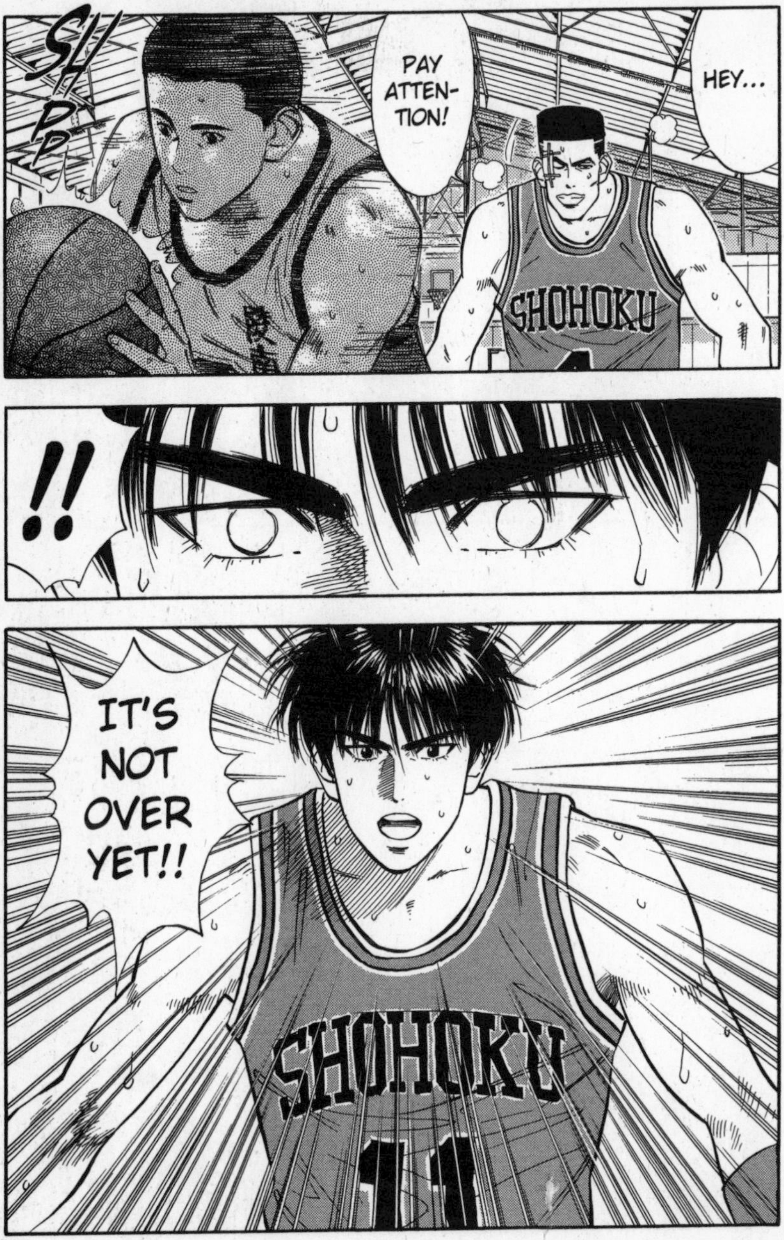
HEY...
PAY ATTEN-TION!
SHPP
SHOHOKU
!!
IT'S NOT OVER YET!!
SHOHOKU

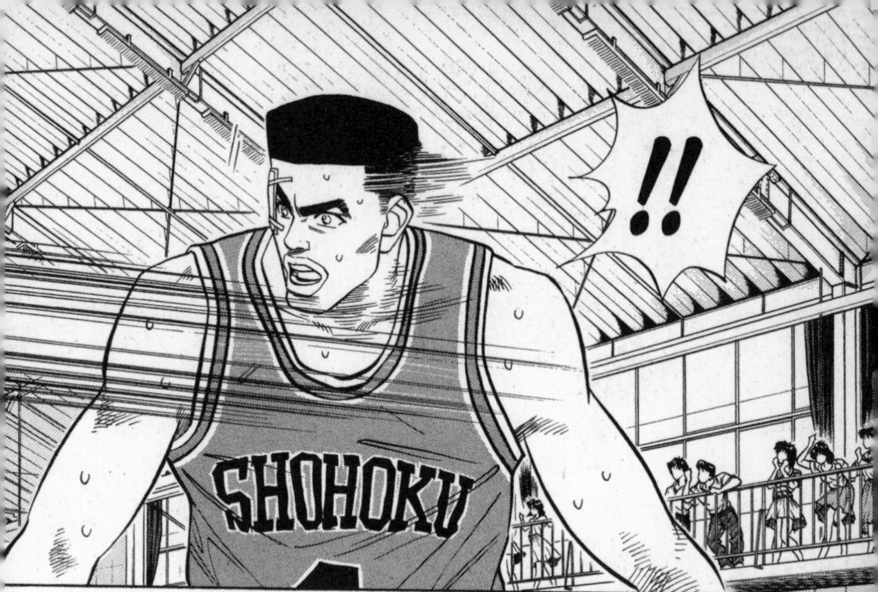
!!
SHOHOKU

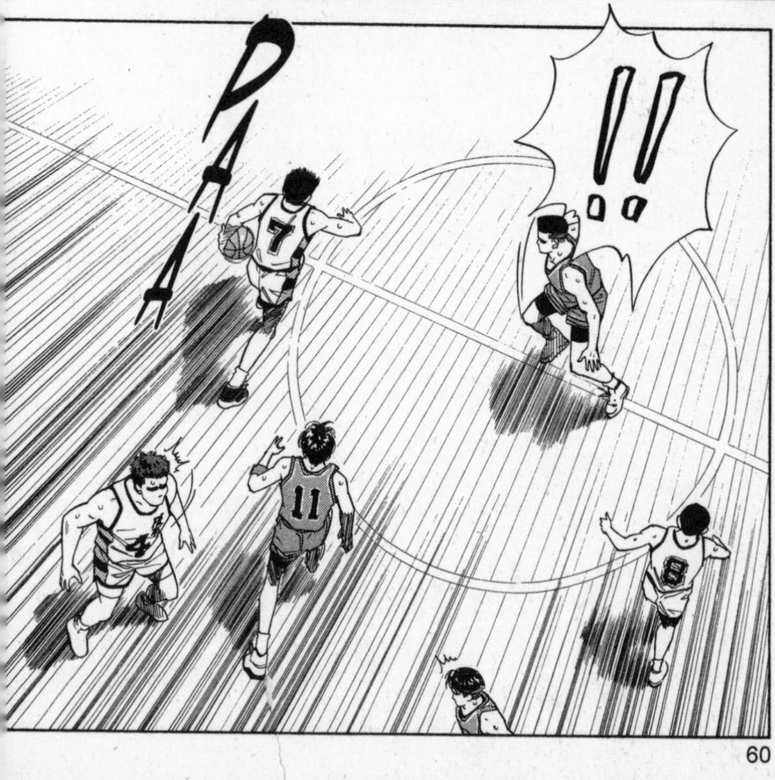
!!
PAAA

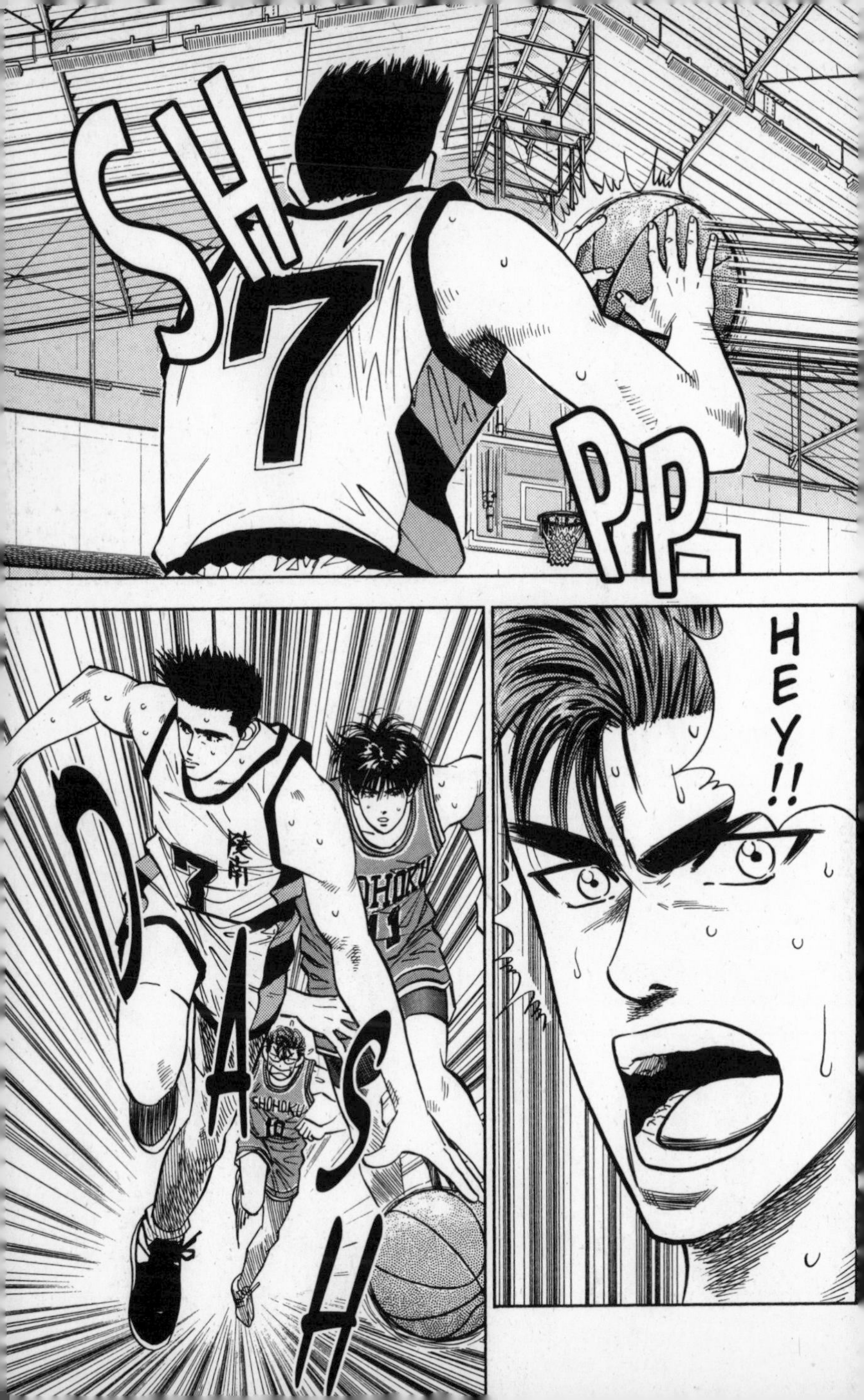
SHPP
HEY!!
DASH

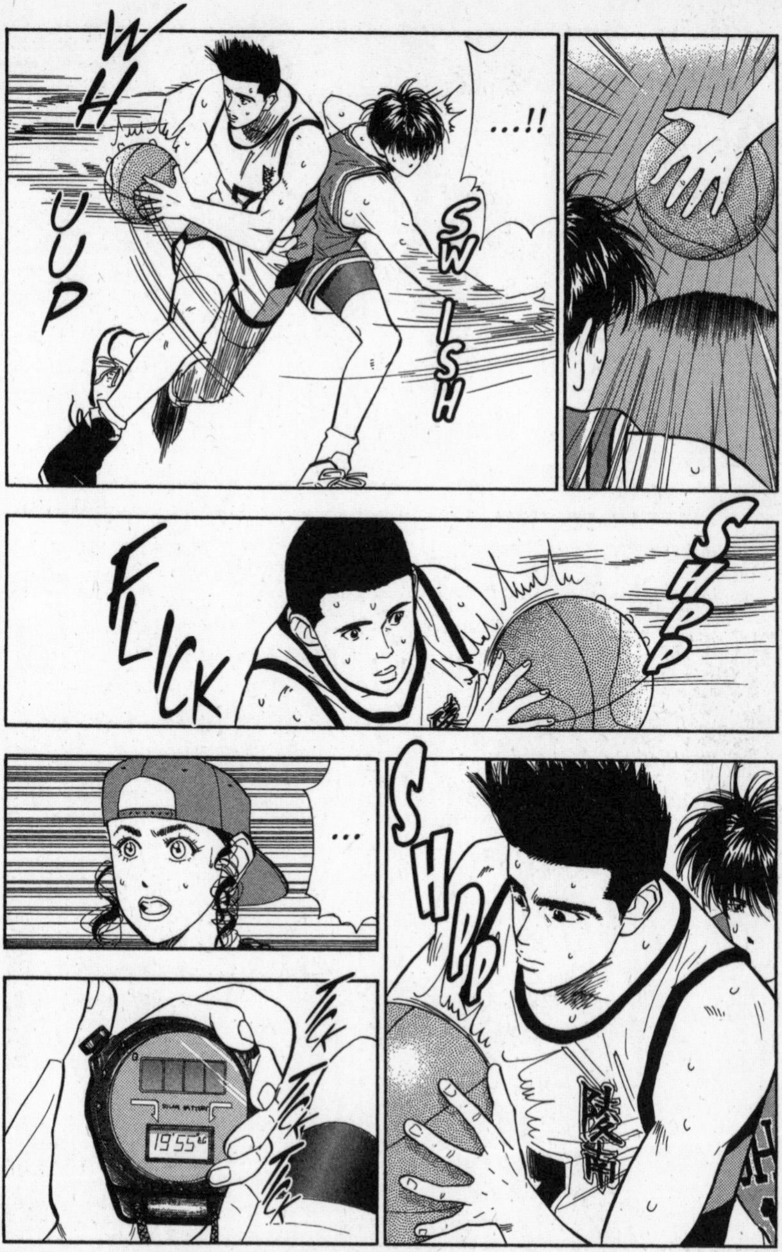
...!!
SWISH
WHUUUP
SHPP
FLICK
SHPP
...
TICK TICK TICK

READ THIS WAY

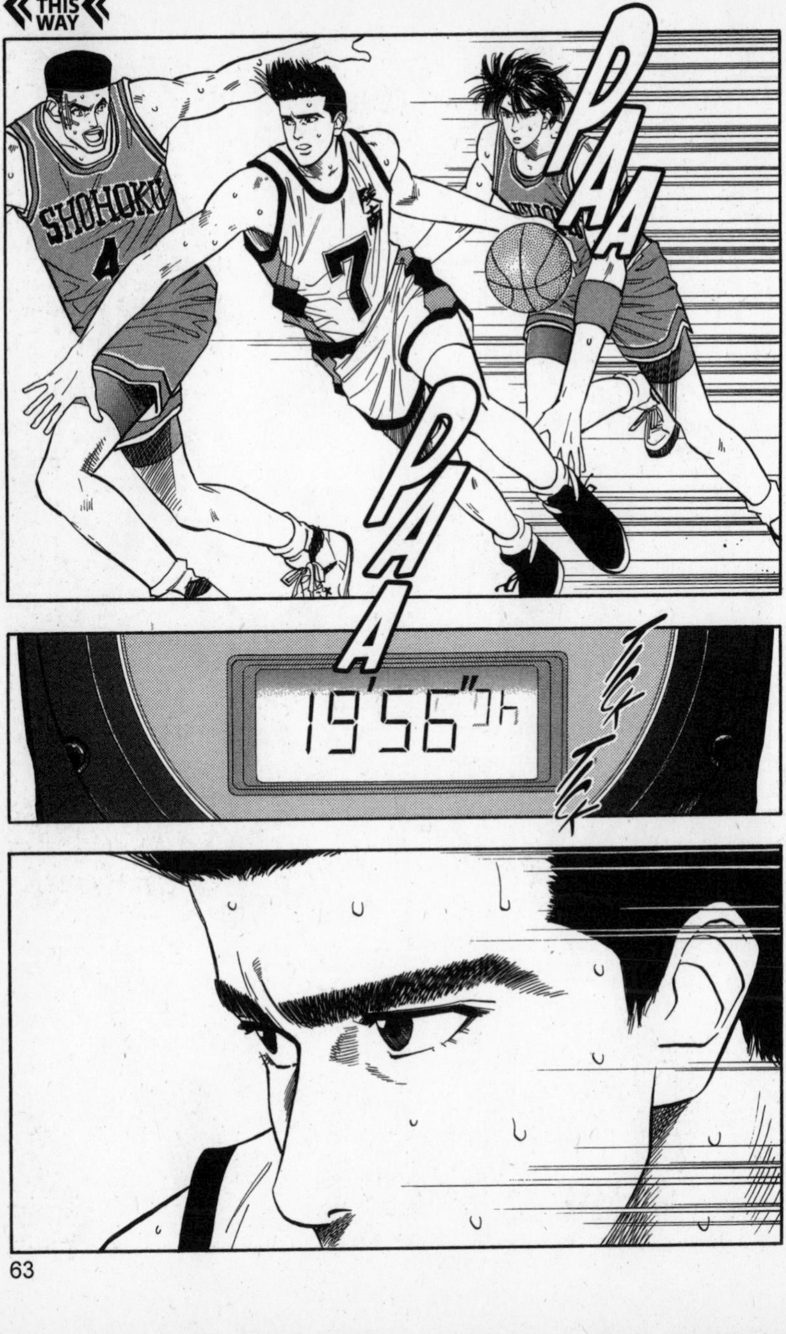
PAA
PAAA
SHOHOKU
4
7
19'56"
TICK TICK

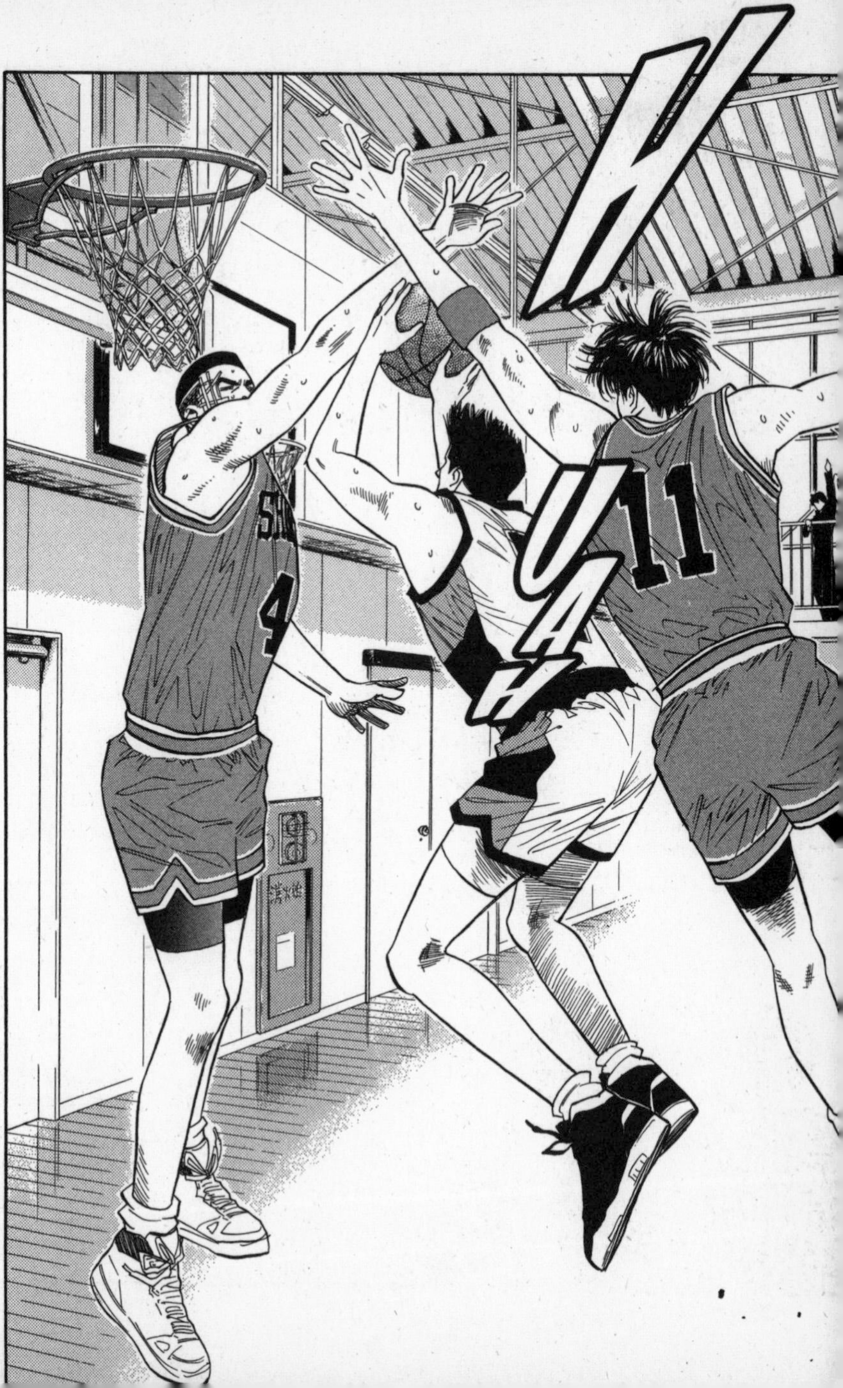

READ THIS WAY

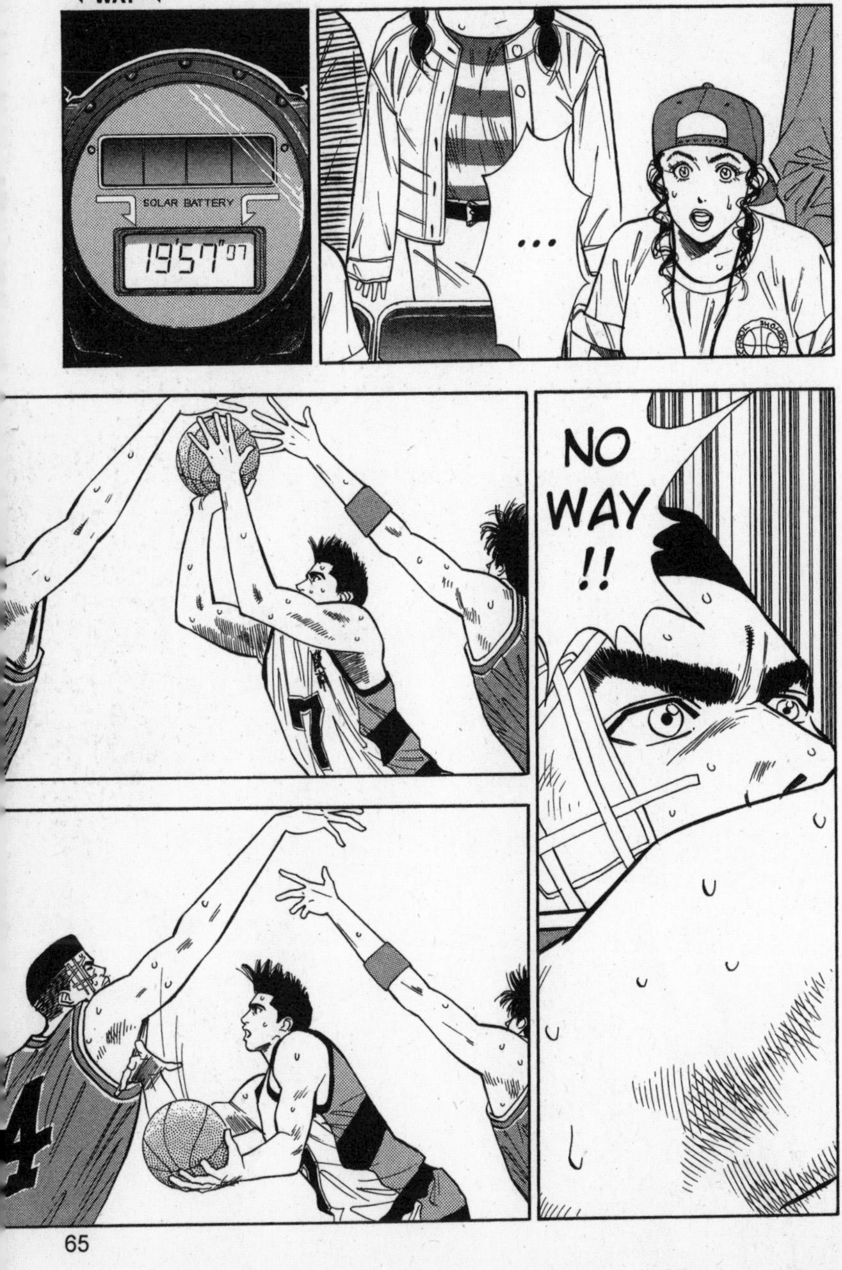
...
SOLAR BATTERY
19'57"07
NO WAY !!

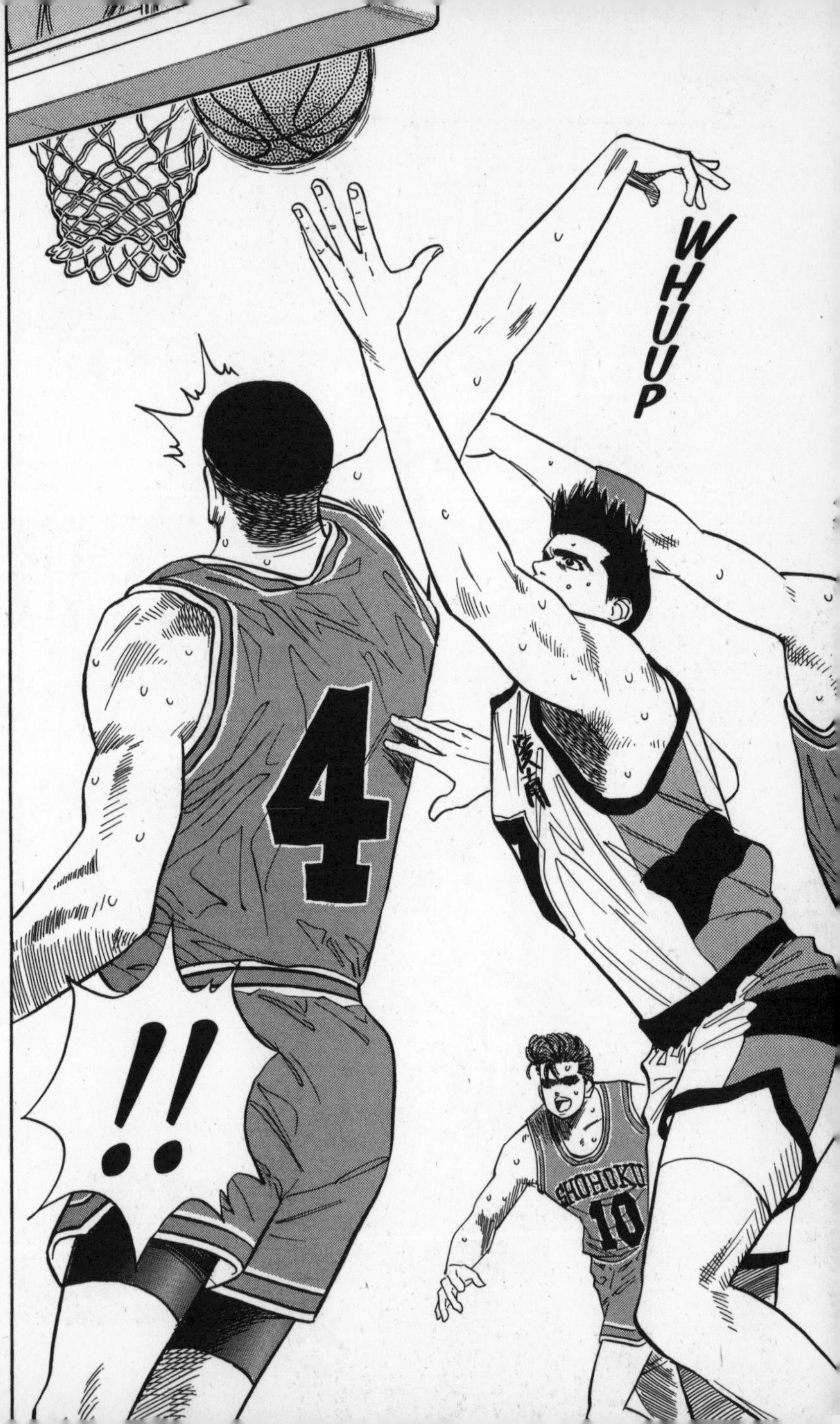
WHUUUP
!!

READ THIS WAY

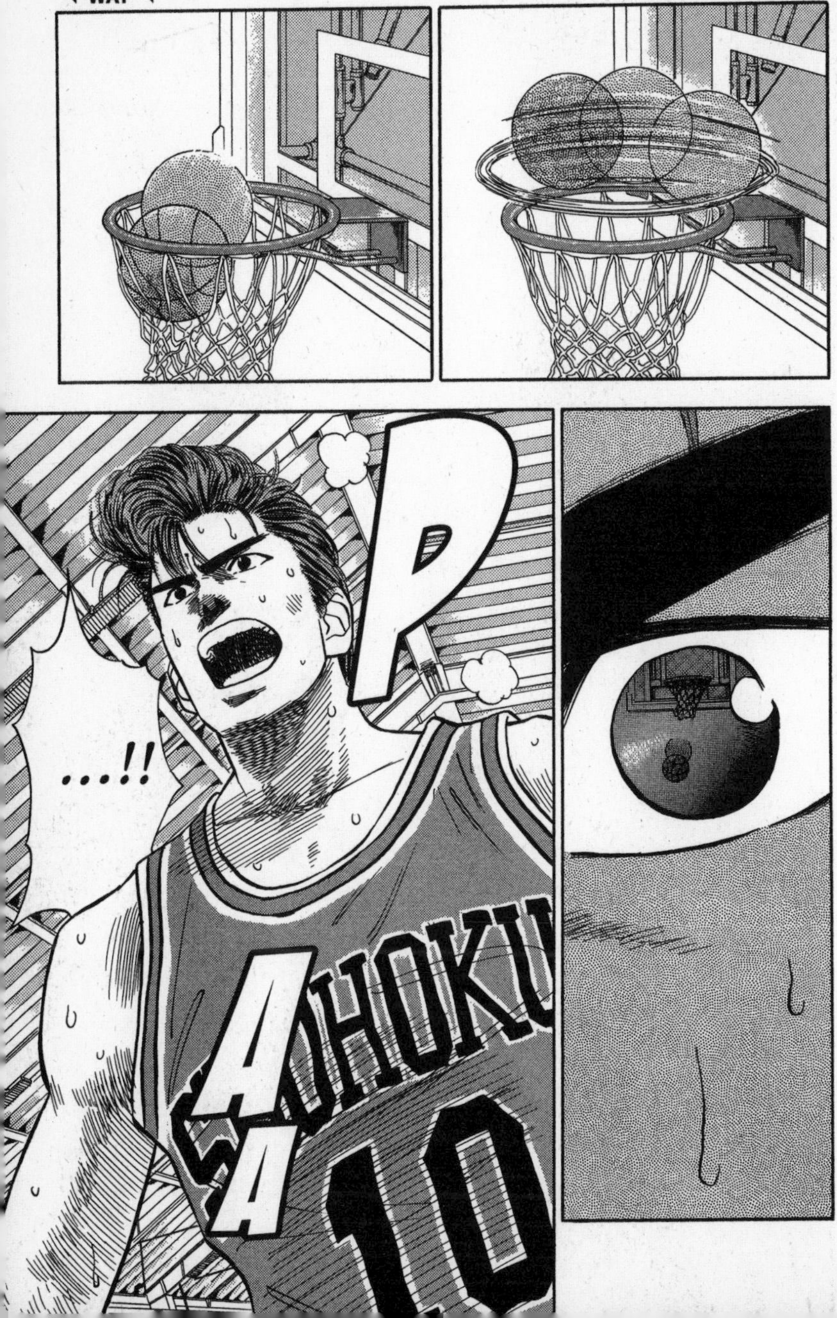
P
...!!

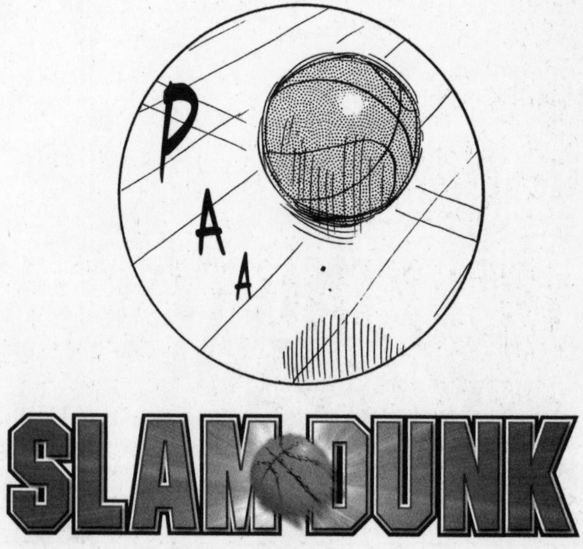
DAA

SLAM DUNK

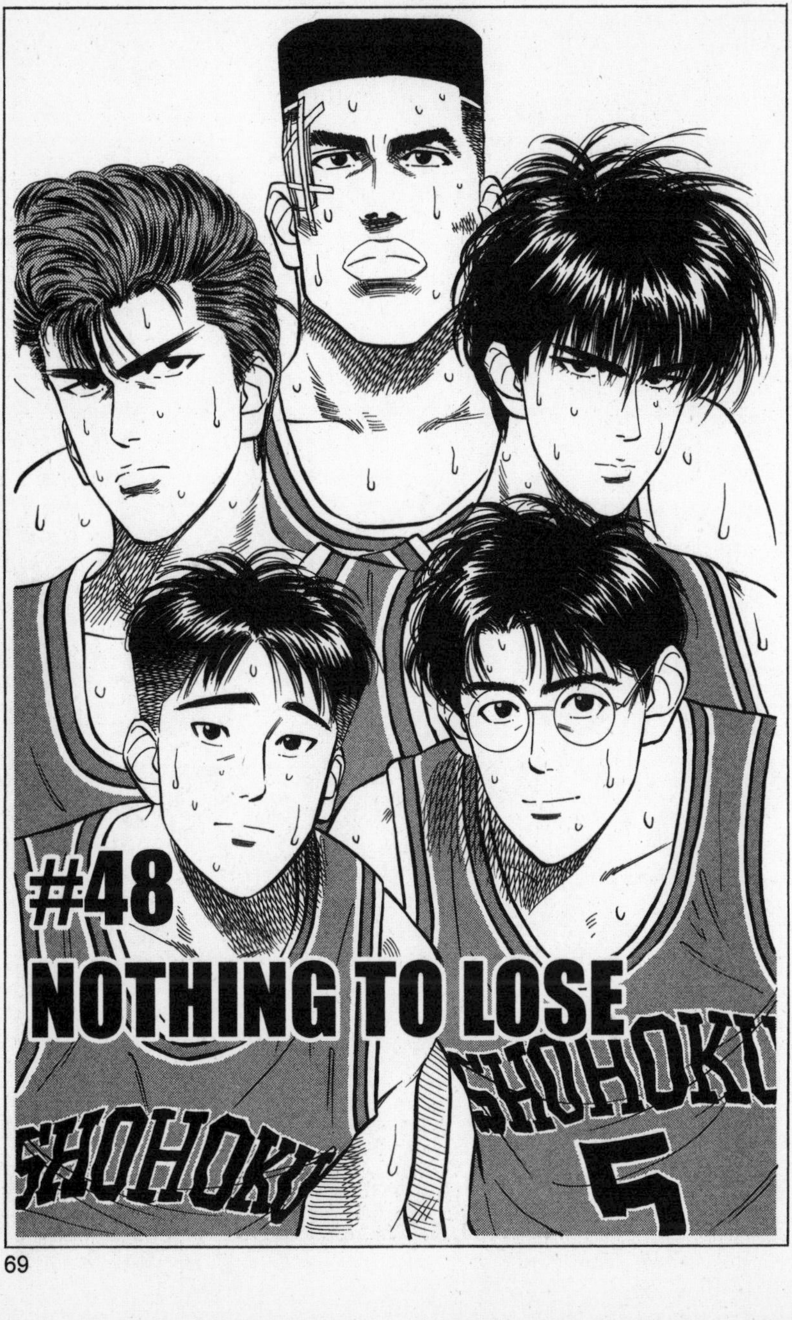
#48
NOTHING TO LOSE
SHOHOKU
SHOHOKU
5

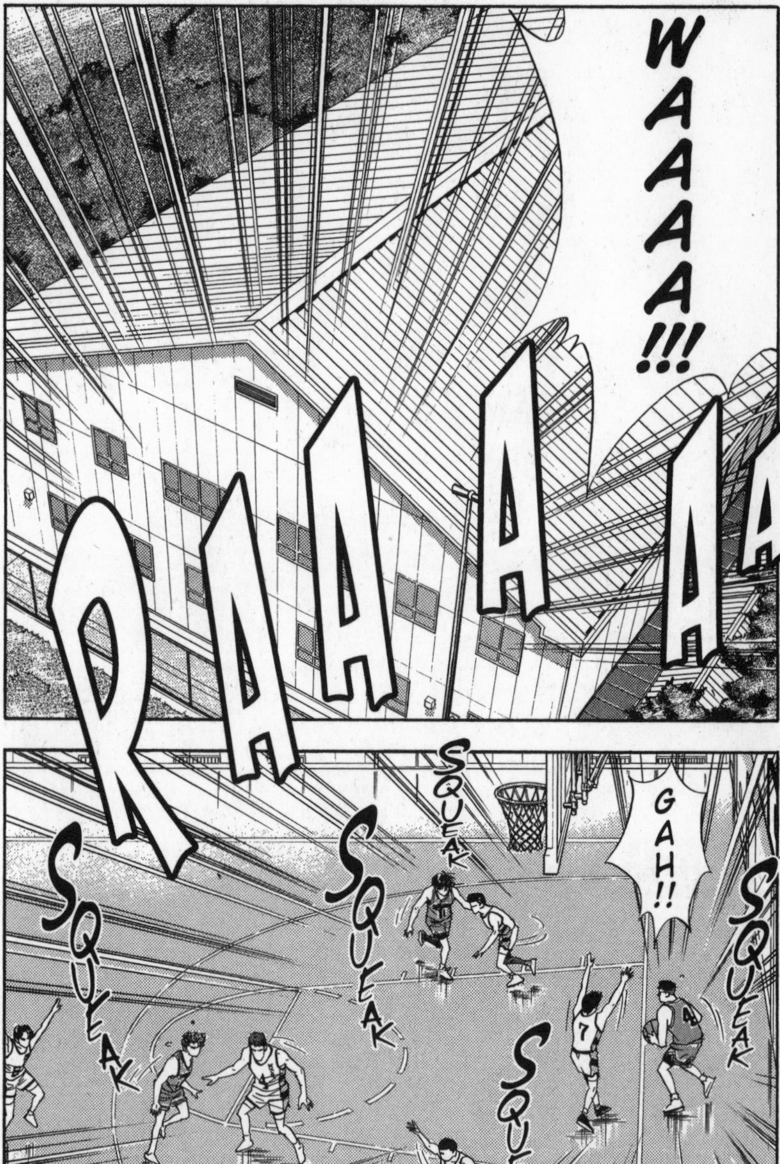
WAAAAA!!!
RAAAAA
GAH!!
SQUEAK
SQUEAK
SQUEAK
SQUEAK
SQUEAK

READ THIS WAY

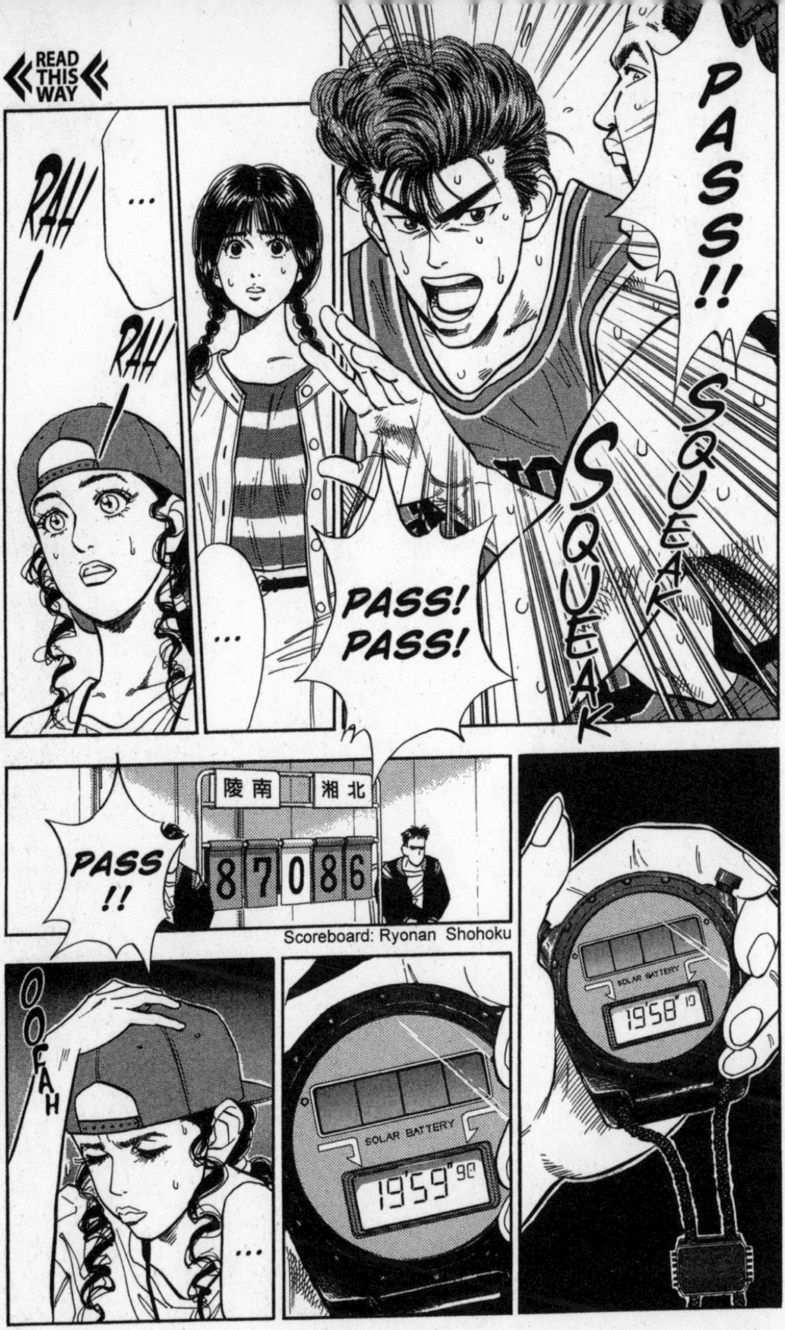
PASS!!
SQUEAK
SQUEAK
PASS! PASS!
...
...
RAH!
RAH!
SOLAR BATTERY
19'58"10
陵南 湘北
87086
PASS!!
Scoreboard: Ryonan Shohoku
SOLAR BATTERY
19'59"90
OOFAH
...

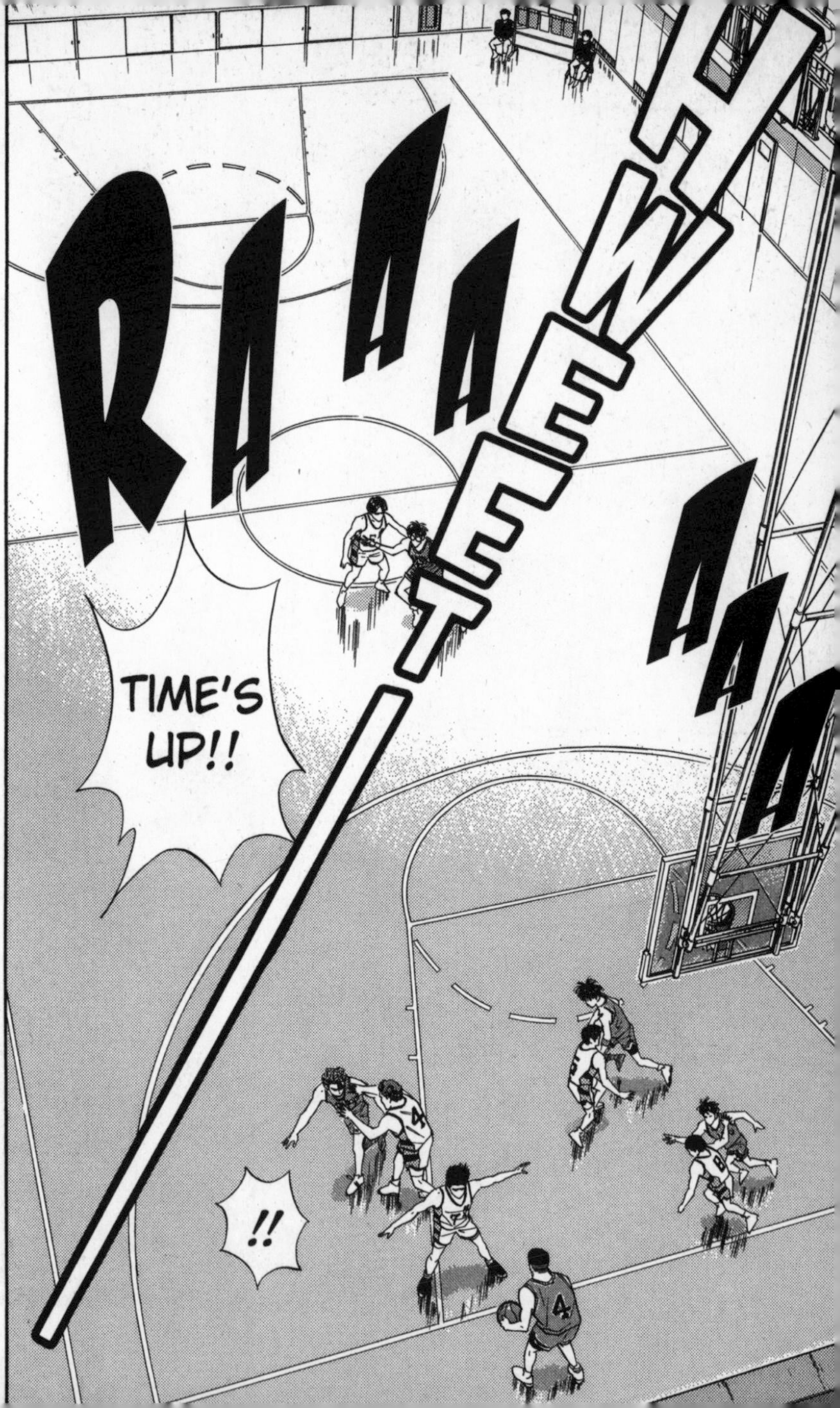

PHWEEEET
RAAAAAAAA
TIME'S UP!!
!!

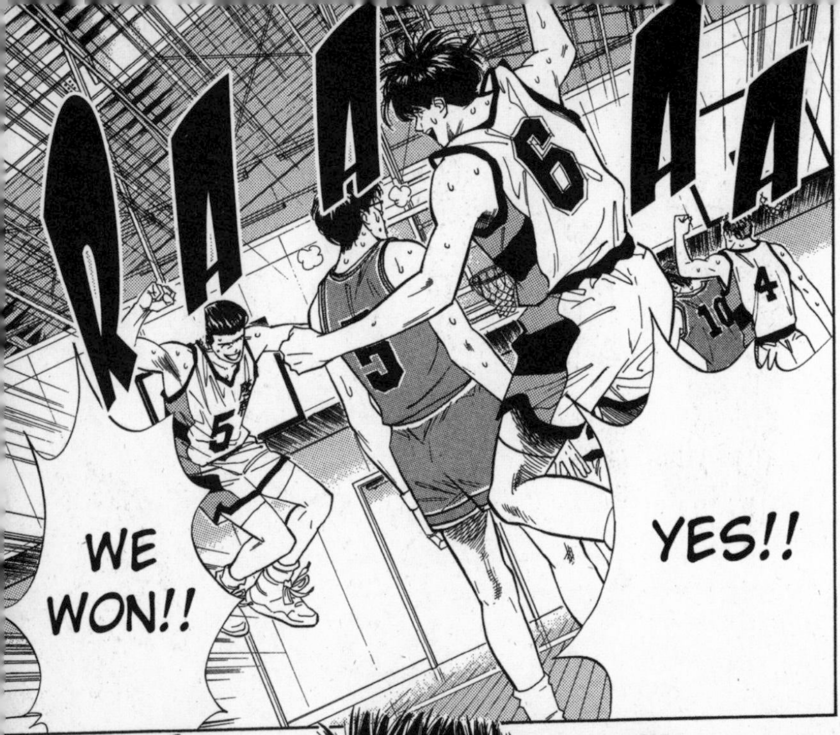
RAAAAA
YES!!
WE WON!!

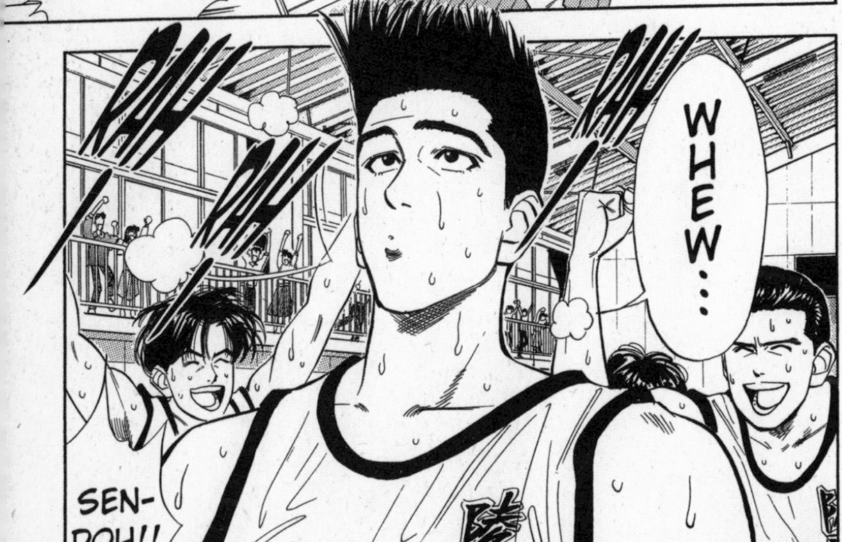
RAH
WHEW...
RAH
RAH
SEN-DOH!!

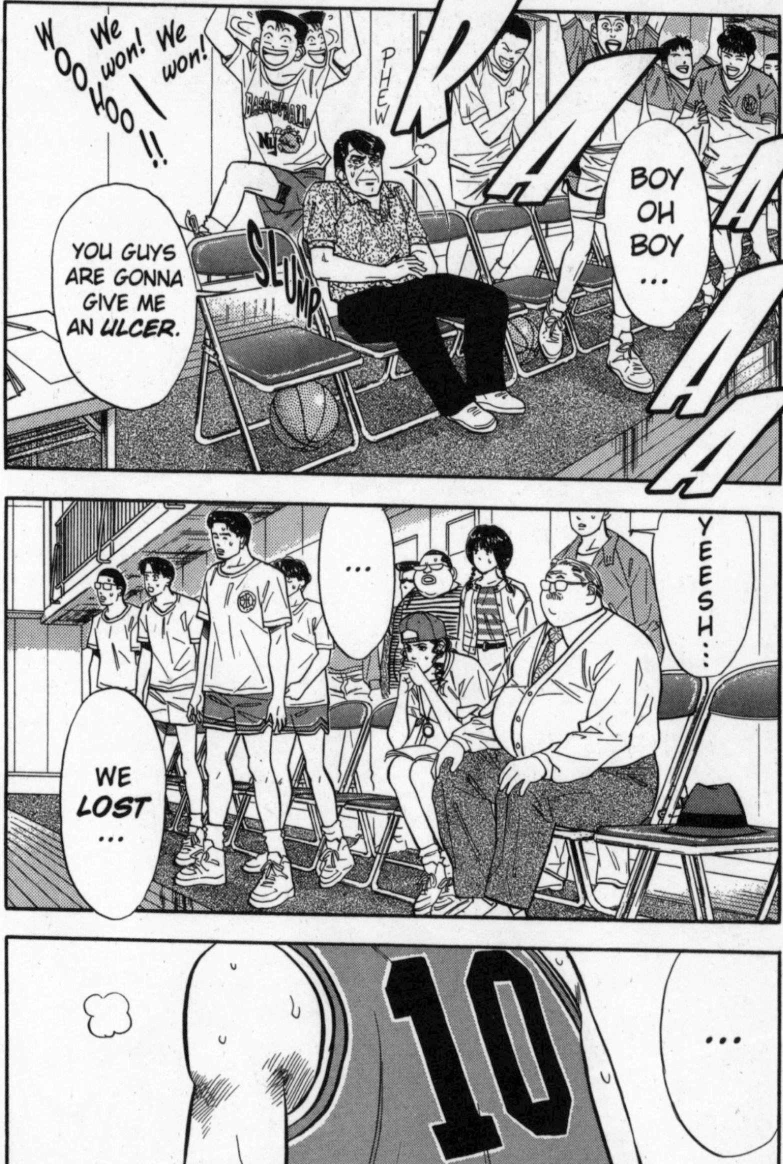
RAAAAA
BOY OH BOY ...
PHEW
We won! We won!
WOOHOO!!
SLUMP
YOU GUYS ARE GONNA GIVE ME AN ULCER.
YEESH...
...
WE LOST ...
...

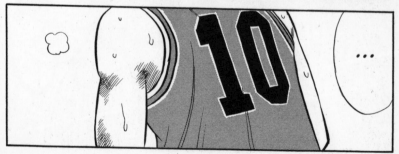

READ THIS WAY

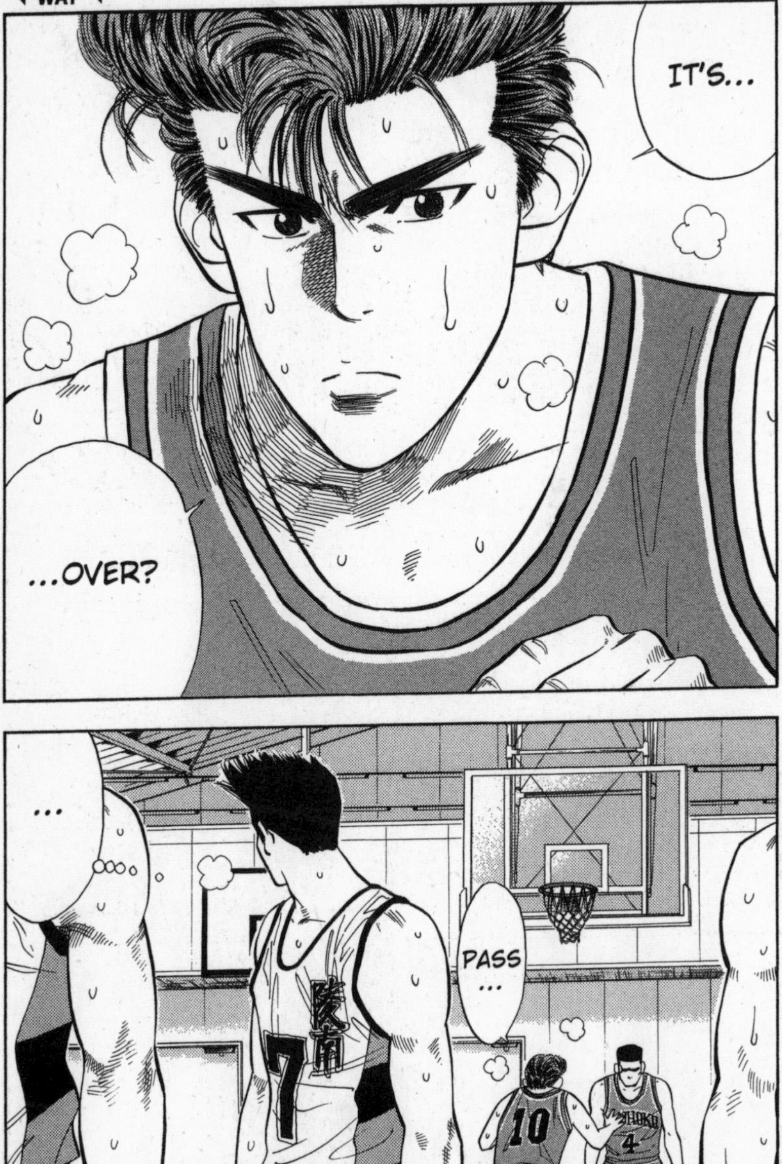
IT'S...
...OVER?
PASS ...
...

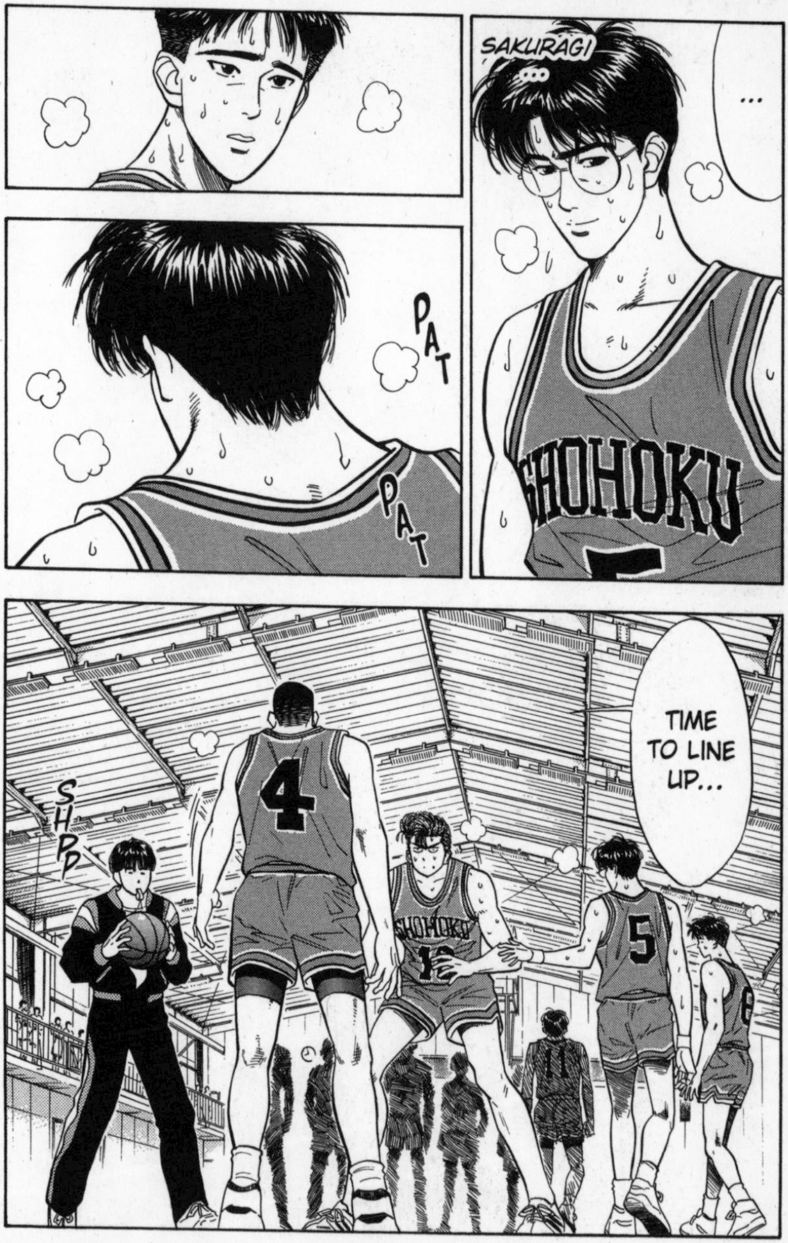
...
SAKURAGI ...
PAT PAT
TIME TO LINE UP...
SHPP

READ THIS WAY

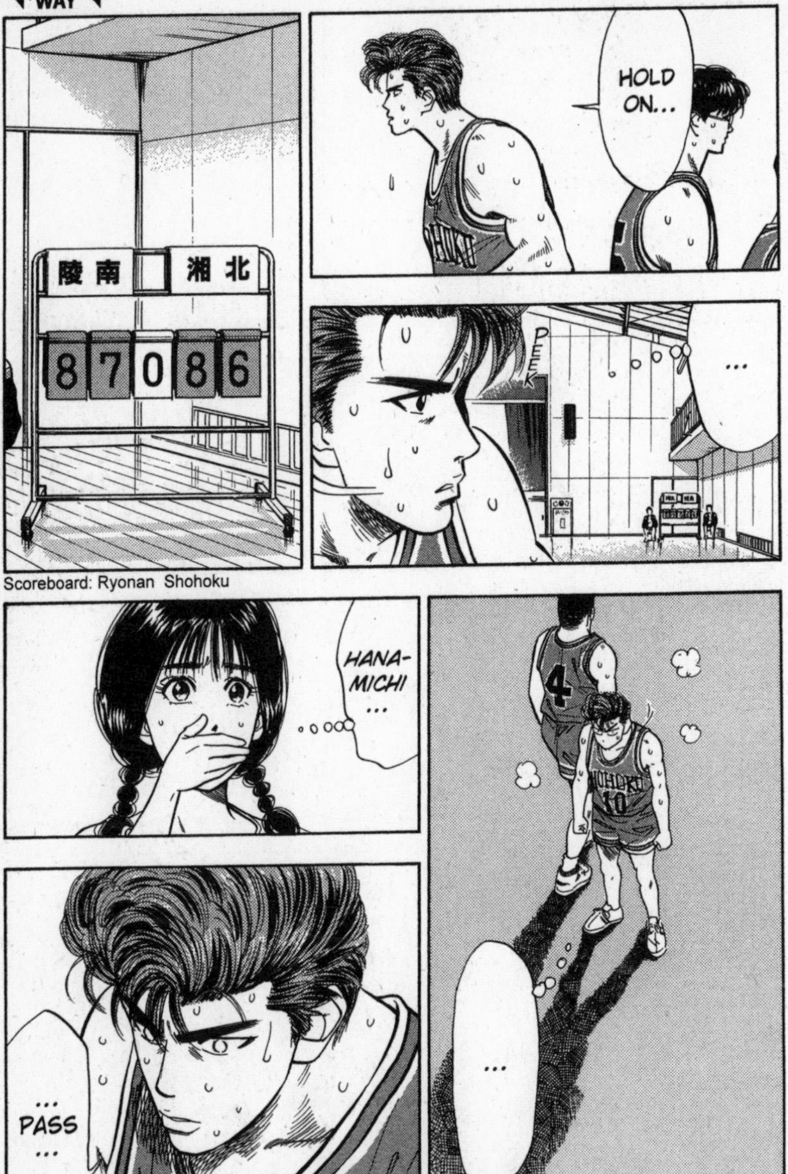
HOLD ON...
PEEK
...
陵南 湘北
87 0 86
...
HANA-MICHI ...
... PASS ...

Scoreboard: Ryonan Shohoku

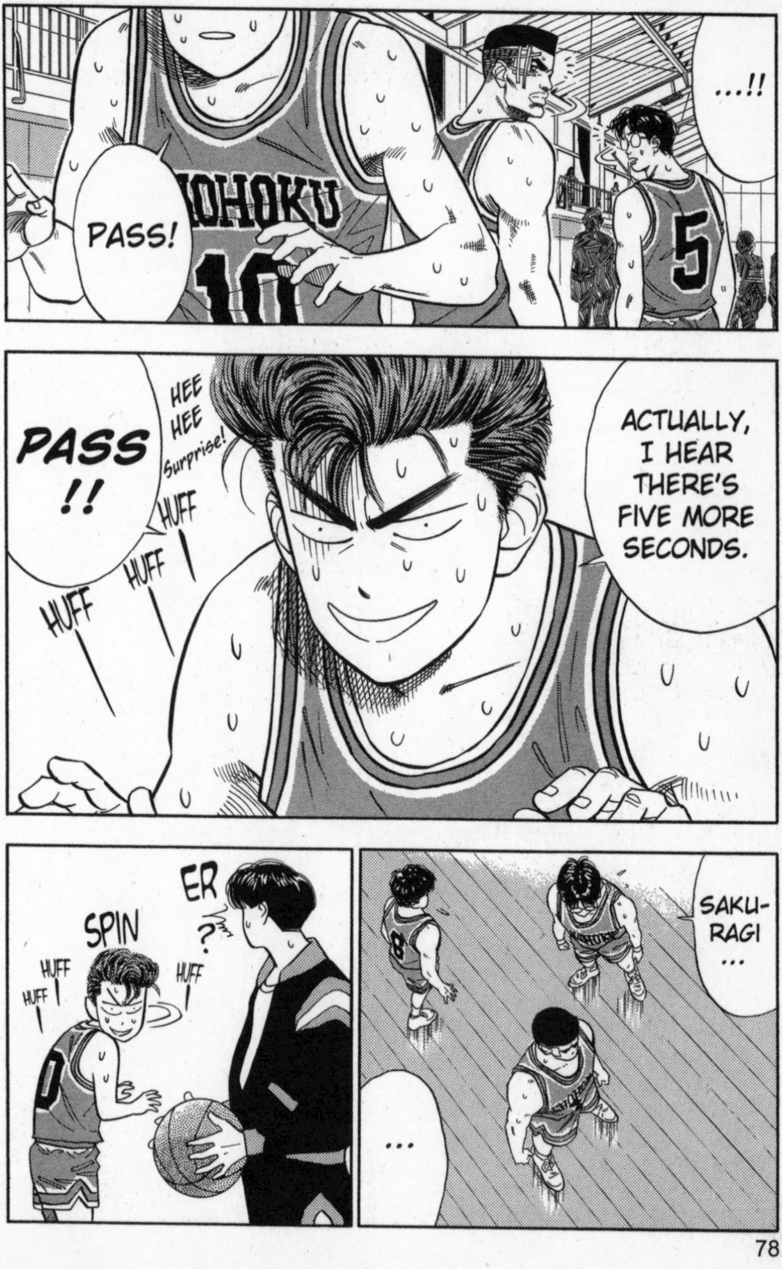
...!!
PASS!
ACTUALLY, I HEAR THERE'S FIVE MORE SECONDS.
HEE HEE
Surprise!
HUFF
HUFF
HUFF
PASS !!
SAKU-RAGI ...
...
ER
?
SPIN
HUFF
HUFF
HUFF

READ THIS WAY

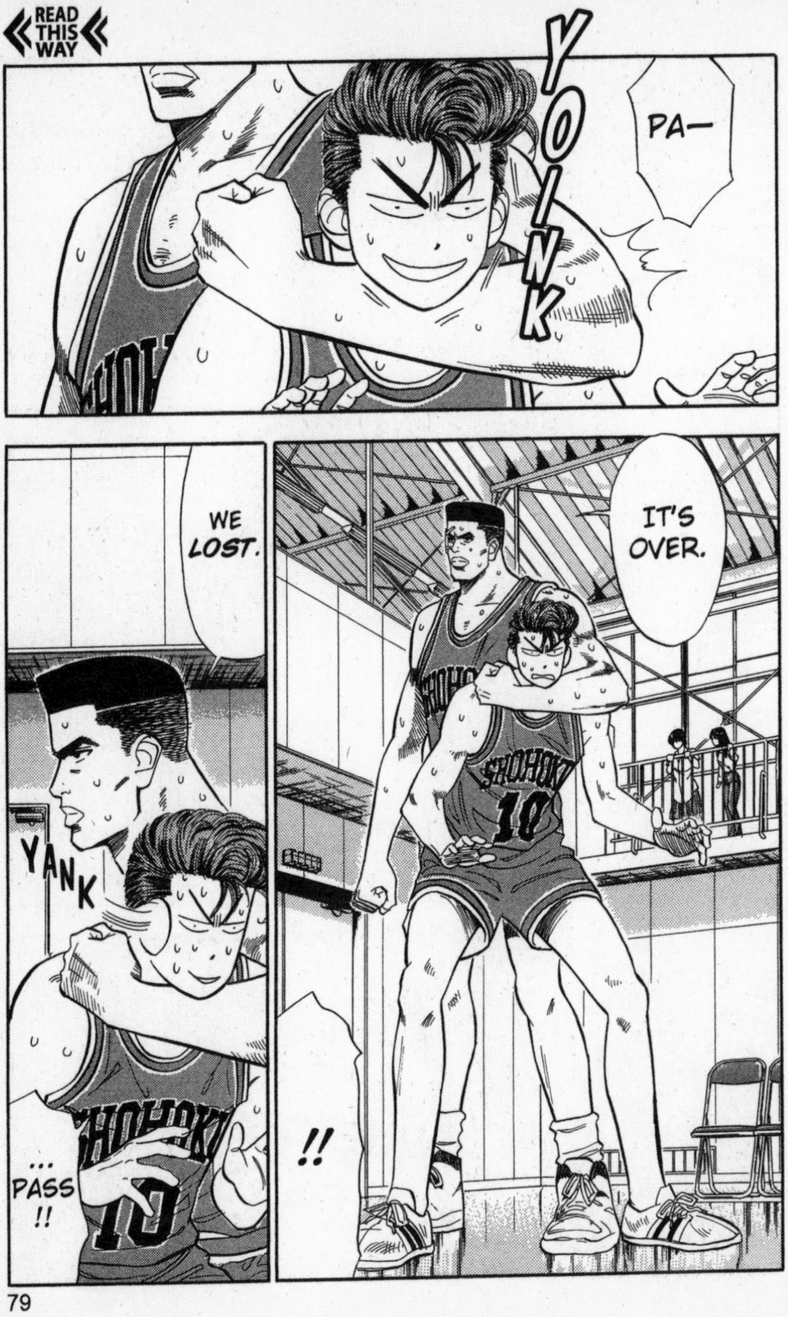
YOINK
PA—
IT'S OVER.
!!
WE LOST.
YANK
... PASS !!

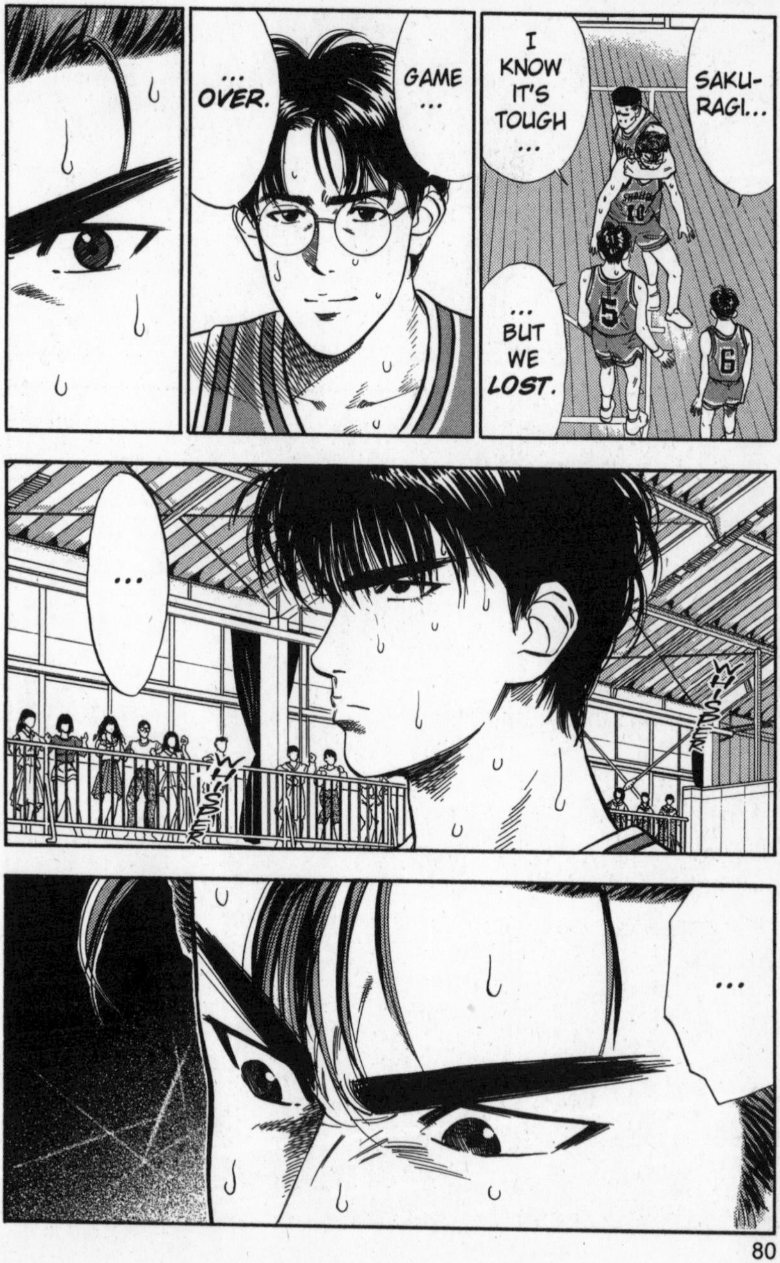
SAKU-RAGI...
I KNOW IT'S TOUGH...
...BUT WE LOST.
GAME...
...OVER.
...
WHISPER
WHISPER
...

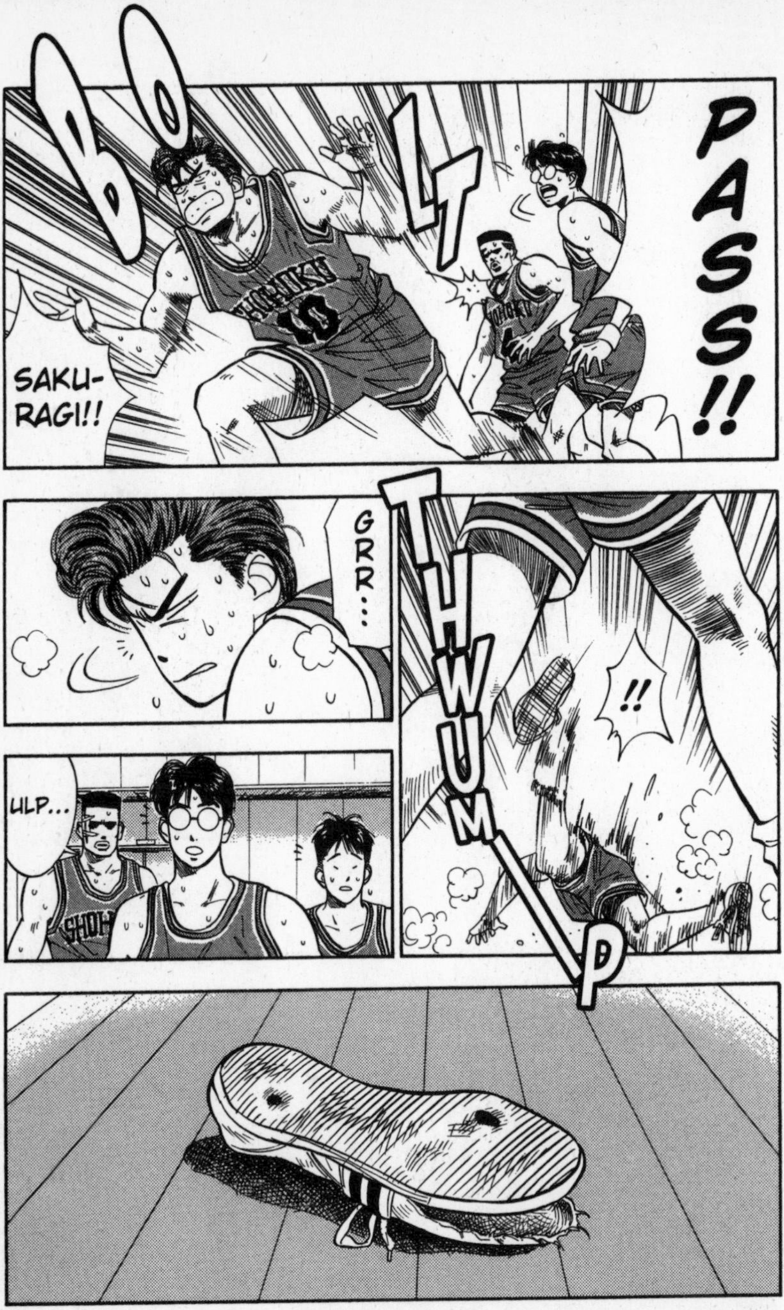
PASS!!
BOLT
SAKU-
RAGI!!
THWUMP
!!
GRR...
ULP...

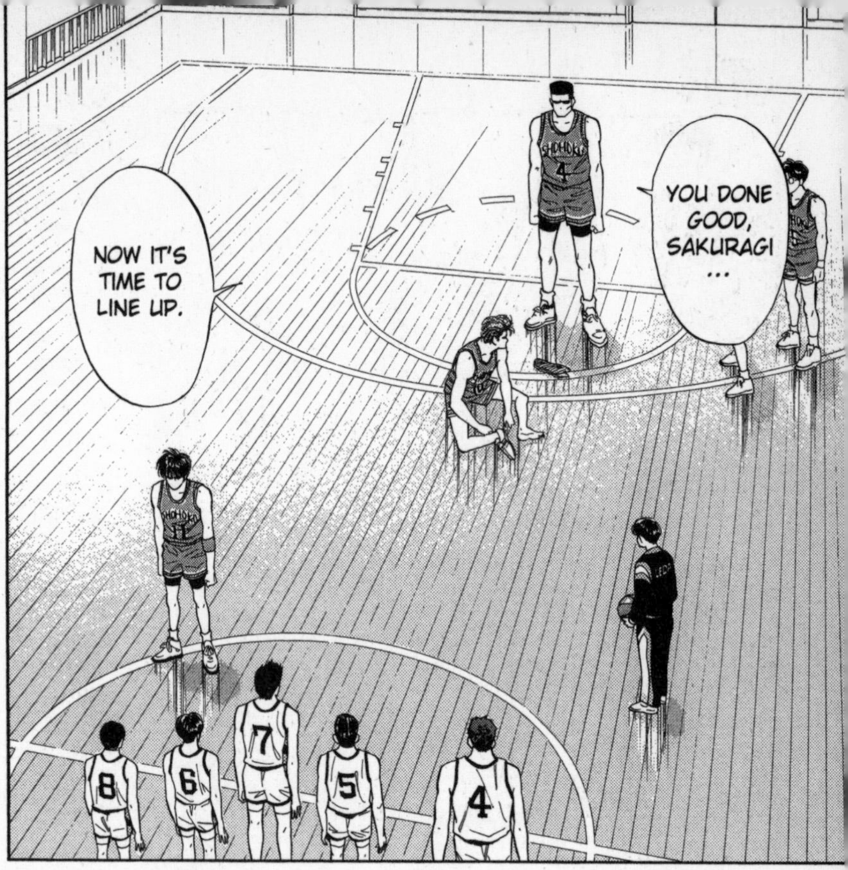
YOU DONE GOOD, SAKURAGI ...
NOW IT'S TIME TO LINE UP.

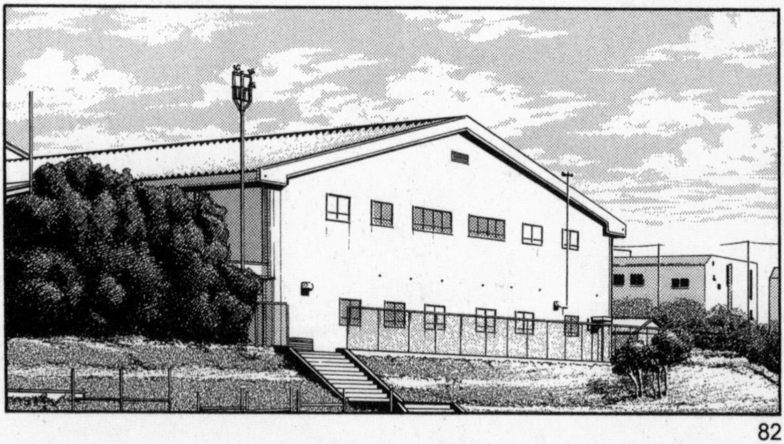

READ THIS WAY

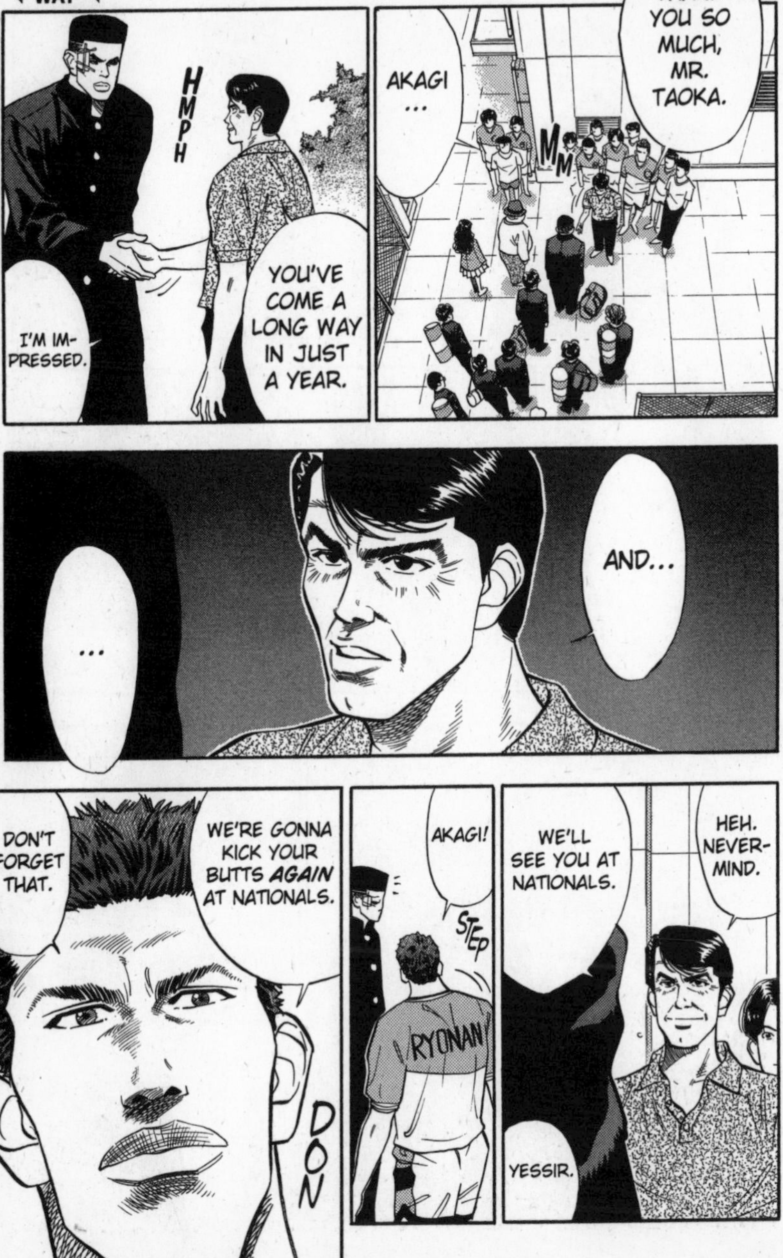

THANK YOU SO MUCH, MR. TAOKA.
AKAGI ...
MM
HMPH
YOU'VE COME A LONG WAY IN JUST A YEAR.
I'M IMPRESSED.
AND...
...
HEH. NEVERMIND.
WE'LL SEE YOU AT NATIONALS.
YESSIR.
AKAGI!
STEP
RYONAN
WE'RE GONNA KICK YOUR BUTTS AGAIN AT NATIONALS.
DON'T FORGET THAT.
DON

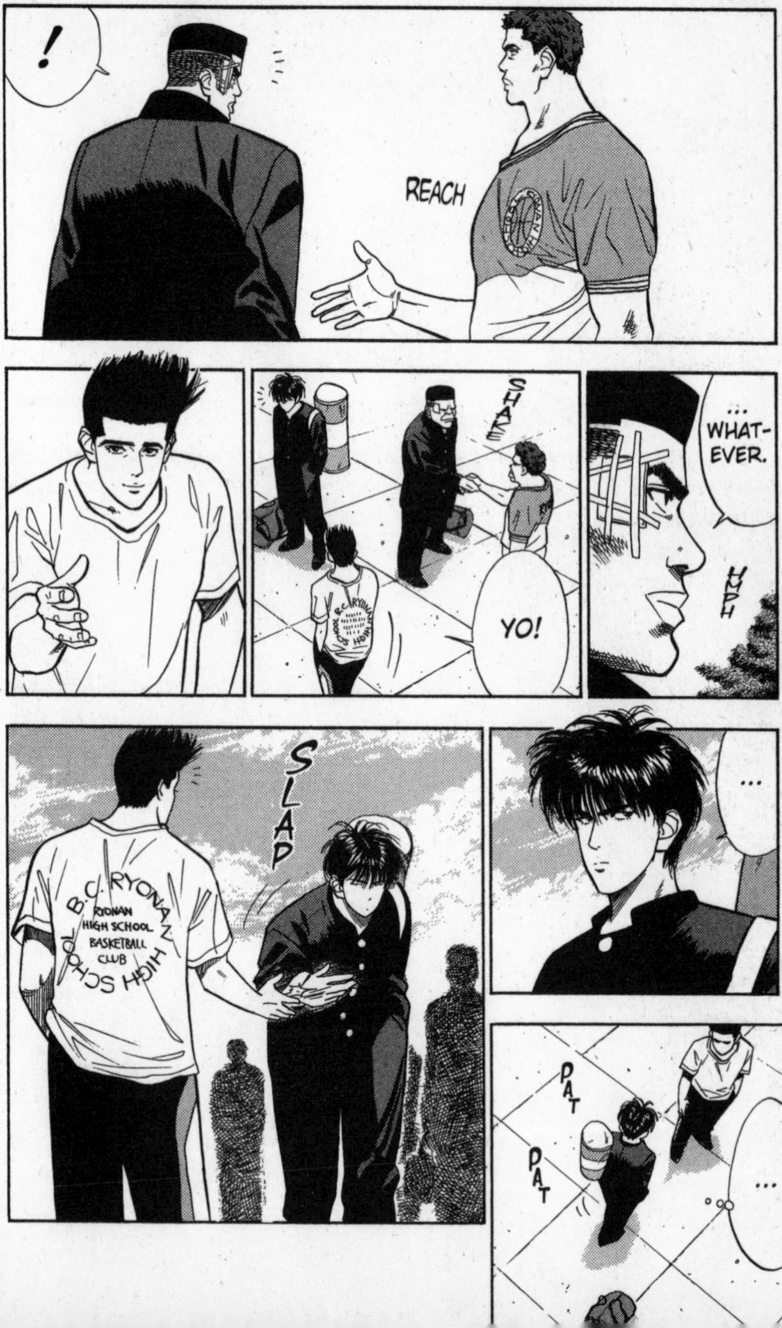
!
REACH
... WHAT-EVER.
HUMPH
SHAKE
YO!
...
PAT
PAT
...
SLAP
B.C. RYONAN HIGH SCHOOL
RYONAN HIGH SCHOOL BASKETBALL CLUB

READ THIS WAY

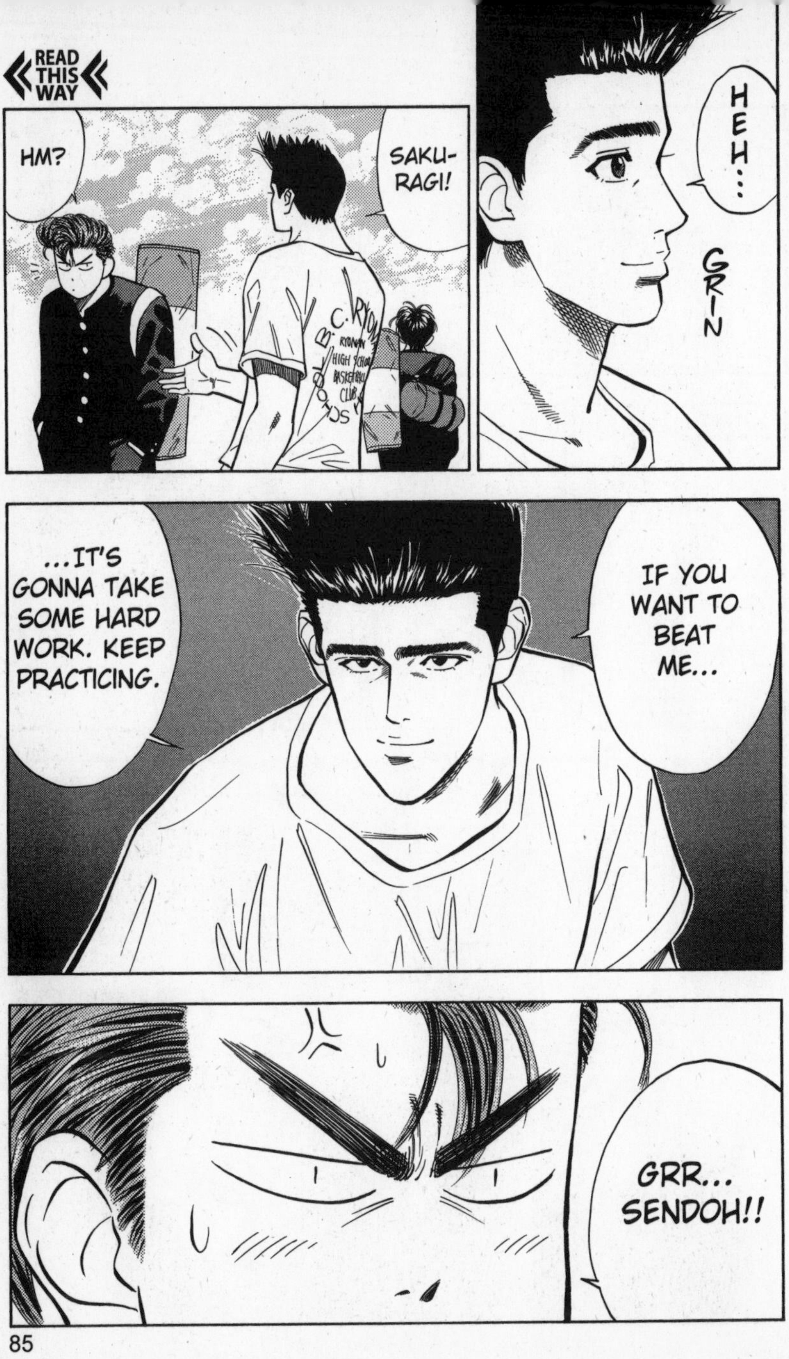
HEH...
GRIN
SAKU-RAGI!
HM?
IF YOU WANT TO BEAT ME...
...IT'S GONNA TAKE SOME HARD WORK. KEEP PRACTICING.
GRR... SENDOH!!

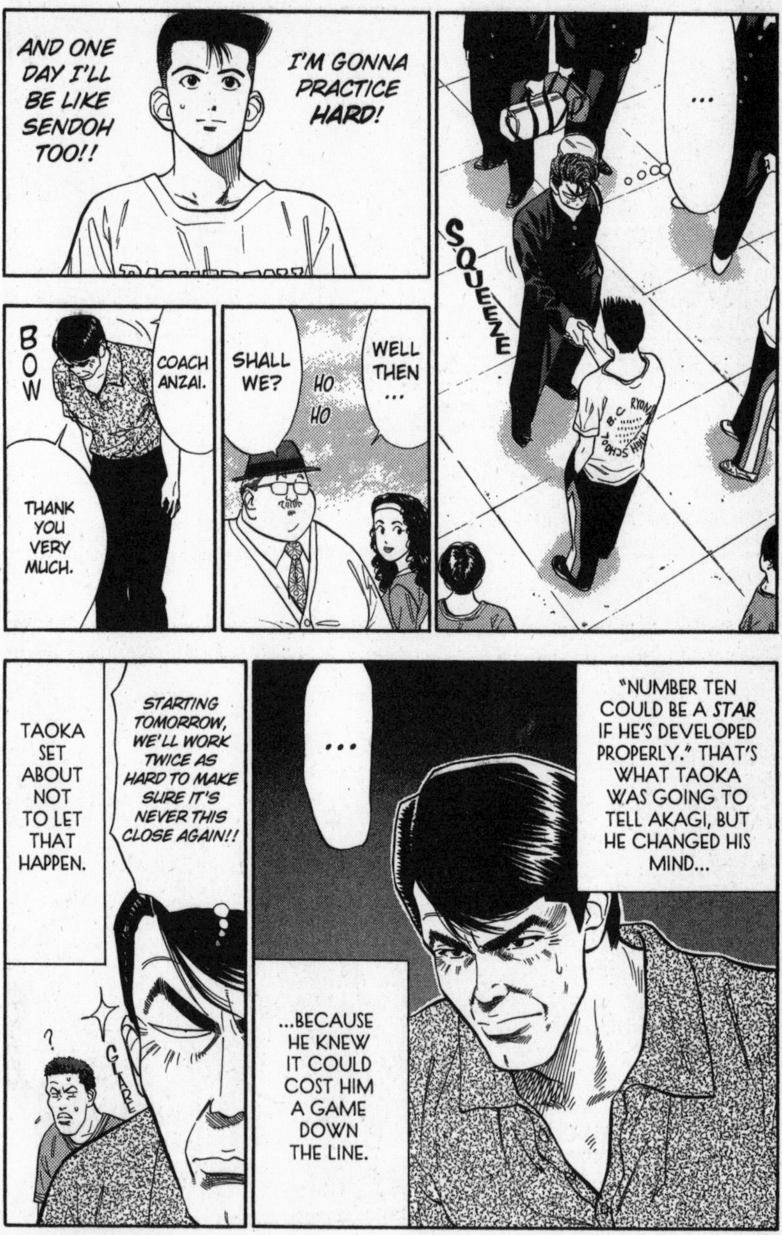
...
SQUEEZE
I'M GONNA PRACTICE HARD!
AND ONE DAY I'LL BE LIKE SENDOH TOO!!
WELL THEN ...
HO HO
SHALL WE?
COACH ANZAI.
BOW
THANK YOU VERY MUCH.
"NUMBER TEN COULD BE A *STAR* IF HE'S DEVELOPED PROPERLY." THAT'S WHAT TAOKA WAS GOING TO TELL AKAGI, BUT HE CHANGED HIS MIND...
...
...BECAUSE HE KNEW IT COULD COST HIM A GAME DOWN THE LINE.
TAOKA SET ABOUT NOT TO LET THAT HAPPEN.
STARTING TOMORROW, WE'LL WORK TWICE AS HARD TO MAKE SURE IT'S NEVER THIS CLOSE AGAIN!!
GLARE
?

READ THIS WAY

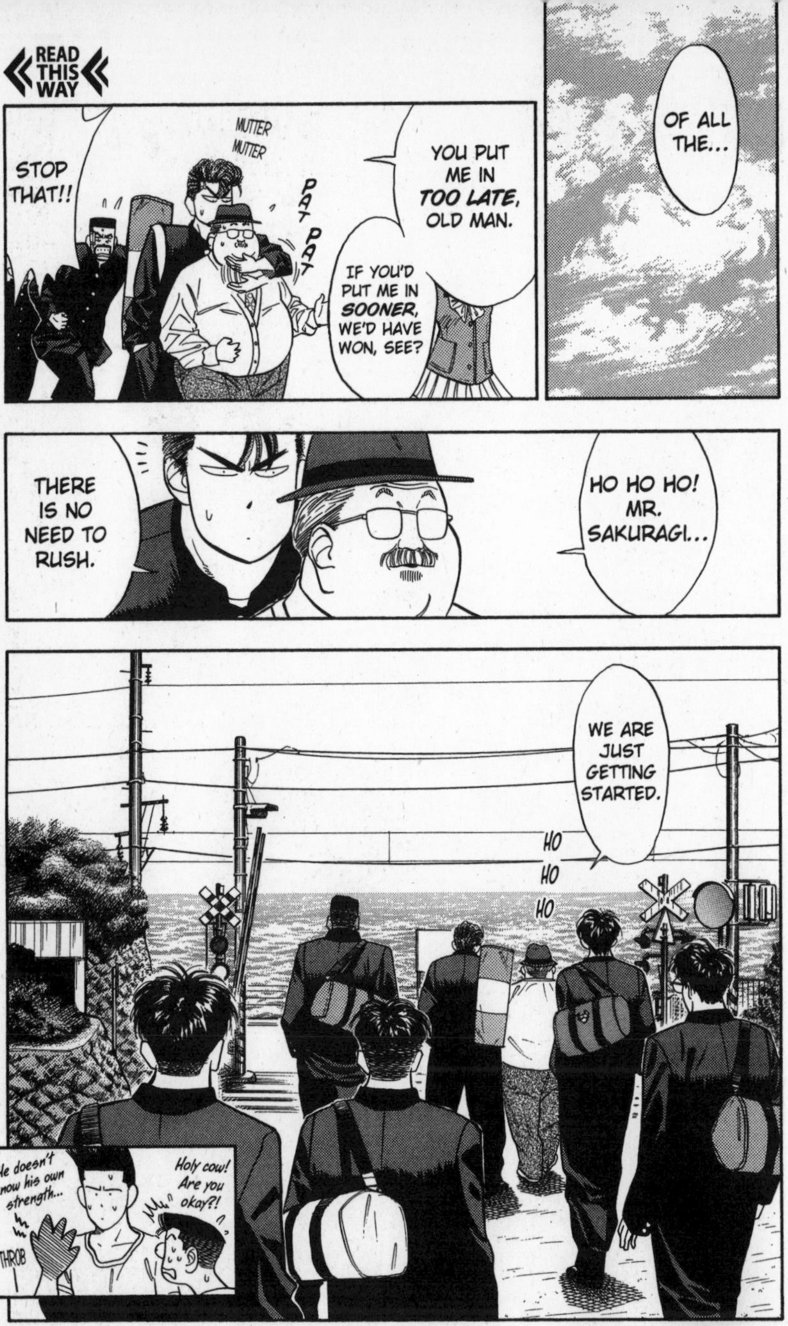
OF ALL THE...
YOU PUT ME IN TOO LATE, OLD MAN.
IF YOU'D PUT ME IN SOONER, WE'D HAVE WON, SEE?
PAT PAT
MUTTER MUTTER
STOP THAT!!
HO HO HO! MR. SAKURAGI...
THERE IS NO NEED TO RUSH.
WE ARE JUST GETTING STARTED.
HO HO HO
Holy cow! Are you okay?!
He doesn't know his own strength...
THROB

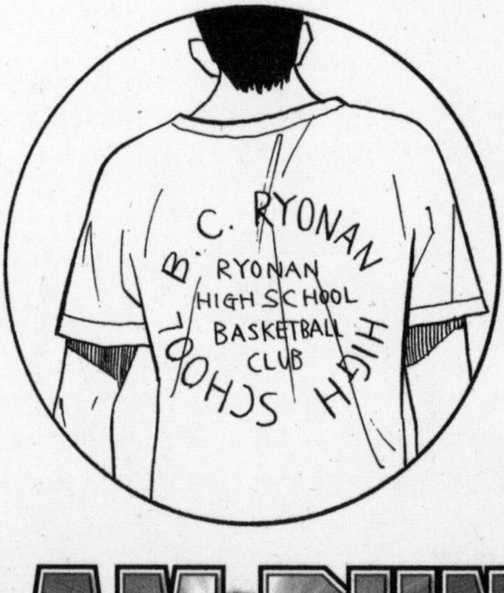
B.C. RYONAN
RYONAN
HIGH SCHOOL
BASKETBALL
CLUB
HIGH SCHOOL

SLAM DUNK

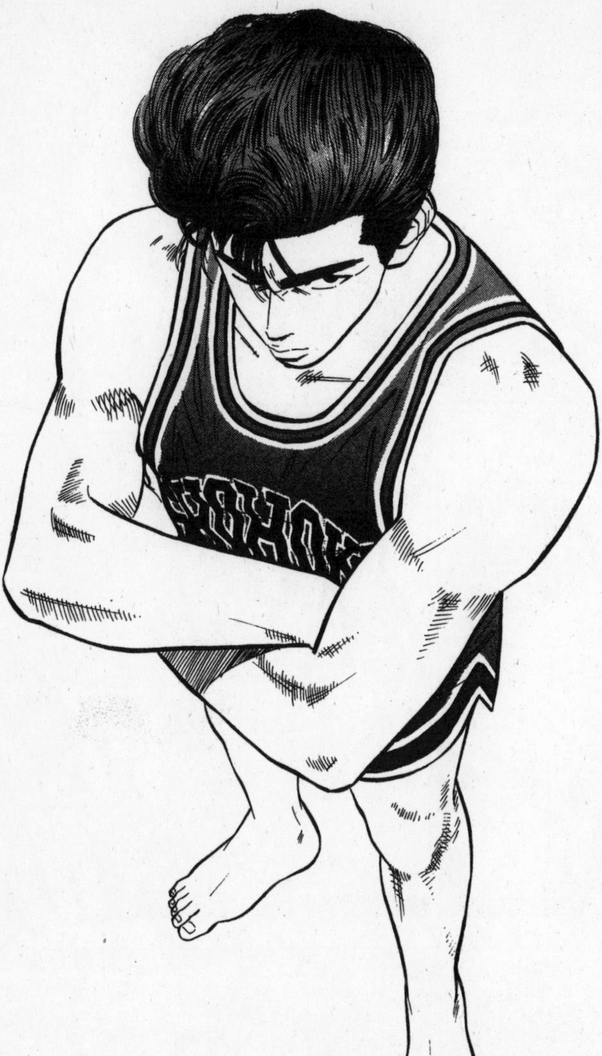

# #49 BASKETBALL SHOES

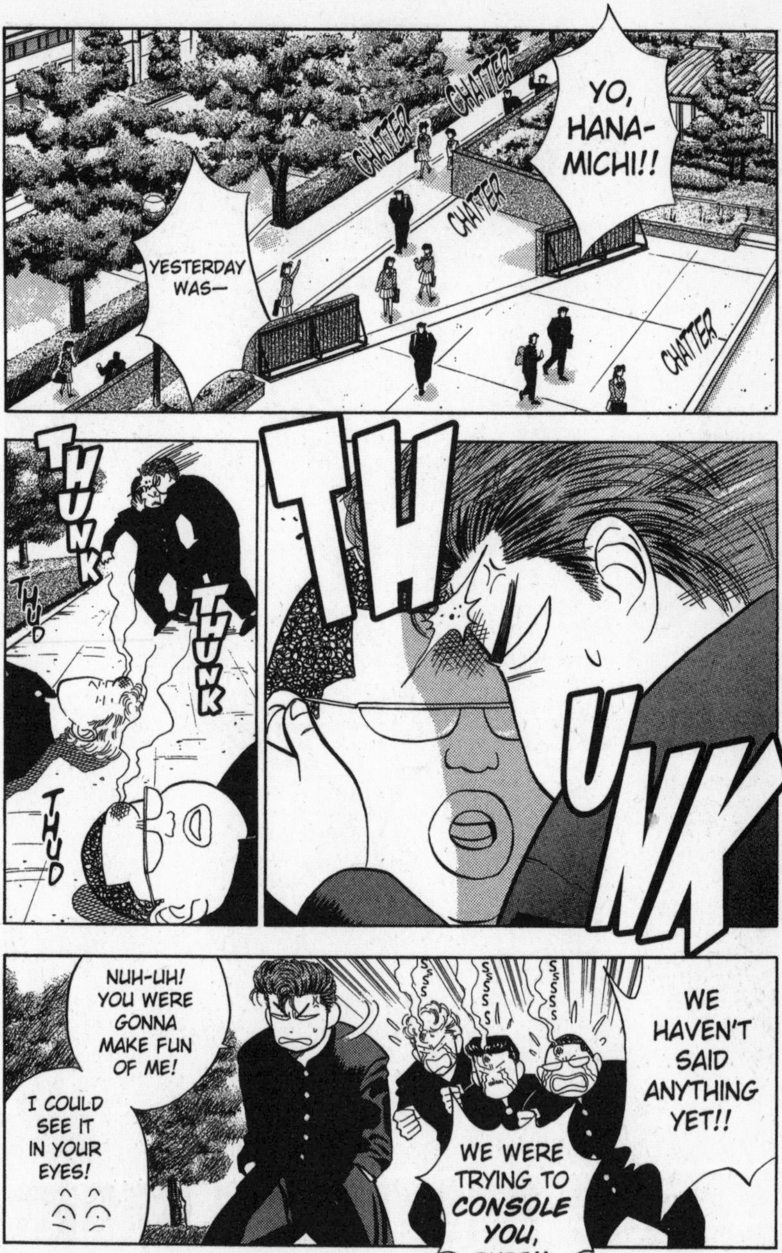
YO, HANA-MICHI!!
CHATTER
CHATTER
CHATTER
CHATTER
YESTERDAY WAS—
THUNK
THUNK
THUNK
THUD
THUD
WE HAVEN'T SAID ANYTHING YET!!
WE WERE TRYING TO CONSOLE YOU, DUDE!!
NUH-UH! YOU WERE GONNA MAKE FUN OF ME!
I COULD SEE IT IN YOUR EYES!

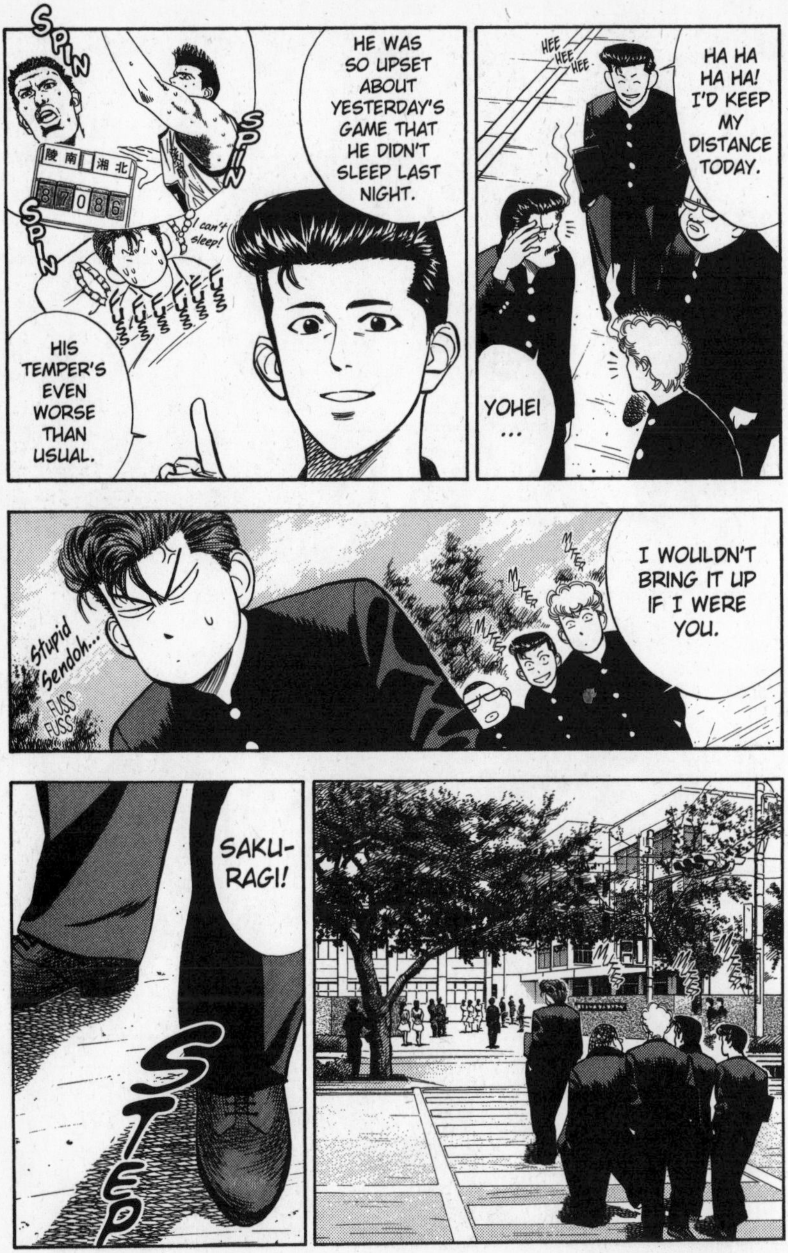
HEE HEE HEE
HA HA HA HA! I'D KEEP MY DISTANCE TODAY.
YOHEI ...
HE WAS SO UPSET ABOUT YESTERDAY'S GAME THAT HE DIDN'T SLEEP LAST NIGHT.
SPIN SPIN SPIN
陵南 湘北
I can't sleep!
FUSS FUSS FUSS FUSS FUSS
HIS TEMPER'S EVEN WORSE THAN USUAL.
I WOULDN'T BRING IT UP IF I WERE YOU.
MUTTER MUTTER MUTTER
Stupid Sendoh...
FUSS FUSS
MUTTER MUTTER
SAKU-RAGI!
STEP

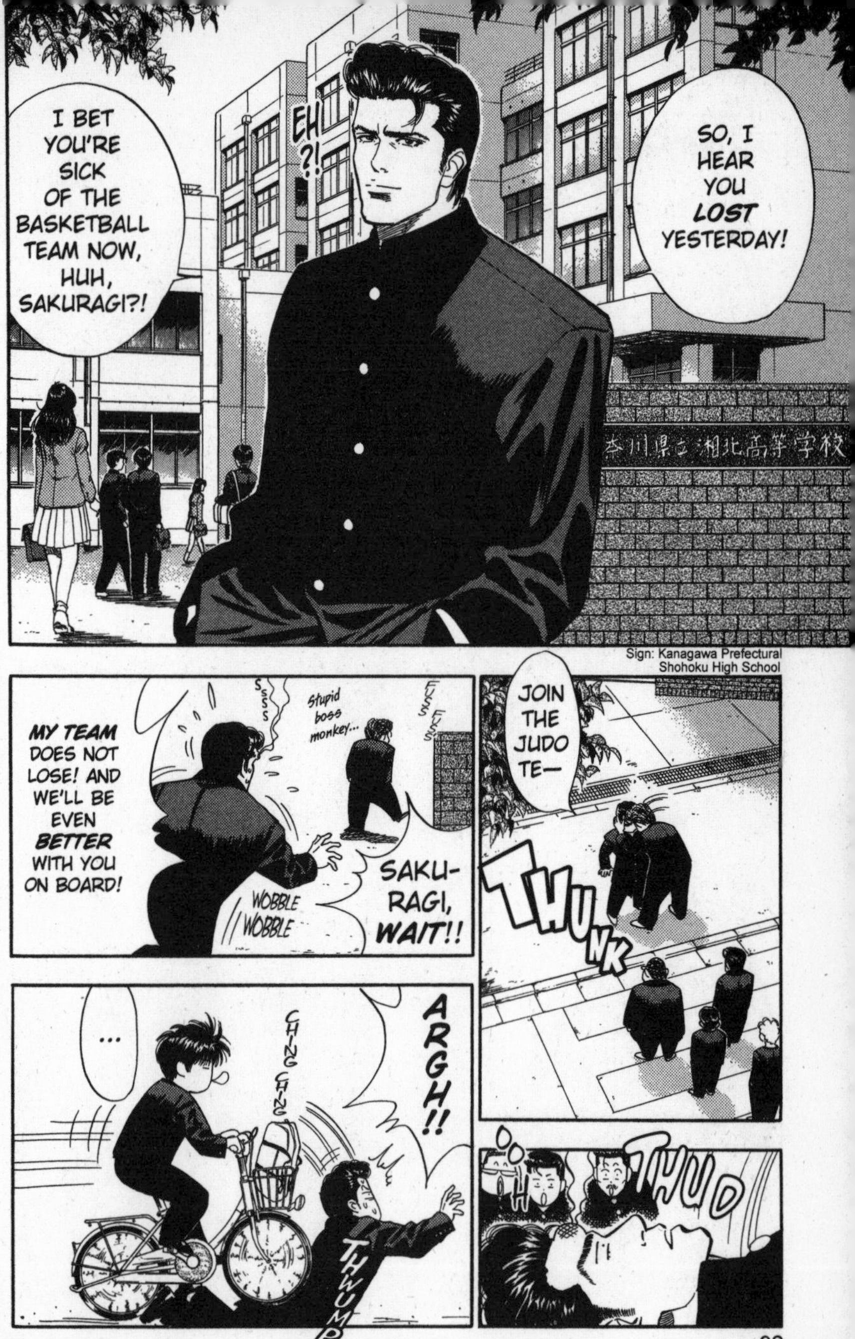
SO, I HEAR YOU LOST YESTERDAY!
EH?!
I BET YOU'RE SICK OF THE BASKETBALL TEAM NOW, HUH, SAKURAGI?!
JOIN THE JUDO TE—
THUNK
SAKU-RAGI, WAIT!!
FUSS FUSS
Stupid boss monkey...
SSSS
MY TEAM DOES NOT LOSE! AND WE'LL BE EVEN BETTER WITH YOU ON BOARD!
WOBBLE WOBBLE
OH
THUD
ARGH!!
CHING CHING
...
THWUMP
Sign: Kanagawa Prefectural Shohoku High School

READ THIS WAY

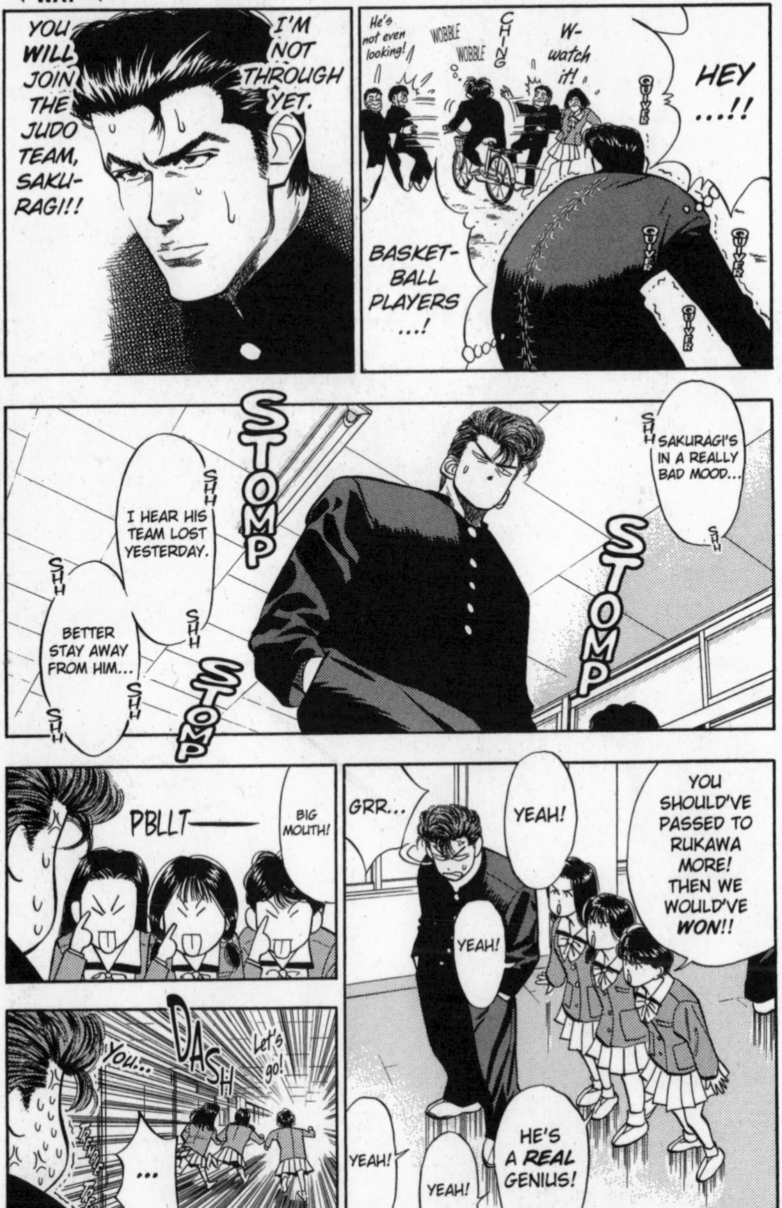
HEY ...!!
QUIVER
W-watch it!
CHING
WOBBLE WOBBLE
He's not even looking!
BASKETBALL PLAYERS ...!
QUIVER QUIVER QUIVER
I'M NOT THROUGH YET.
YOU WILL JOIN THE JUDO TEAM, SAKURAGI!!
SHH SAKURAGI'S IN A REALLY BAD MOOD... SHH
STOMP
STOMP
SHH I HEAR HIS TEAM LOST YESTERDAY. SHH
STOMP
SHH BETTER STAY AWAY FROM HIM... SHH SHH
YOU SHOULD'VE PASSED TO RUKAWA MORE! THEN WE WOULD'VE WON!!
YEAH!
GRR...
YEAH!
HE'S A REAL GENIUS!
YEAH!
YEAH!
BIG MOUTH!
PBLLT——
Let's go!
DASH
You...
TREMBLE TREMBLE
...

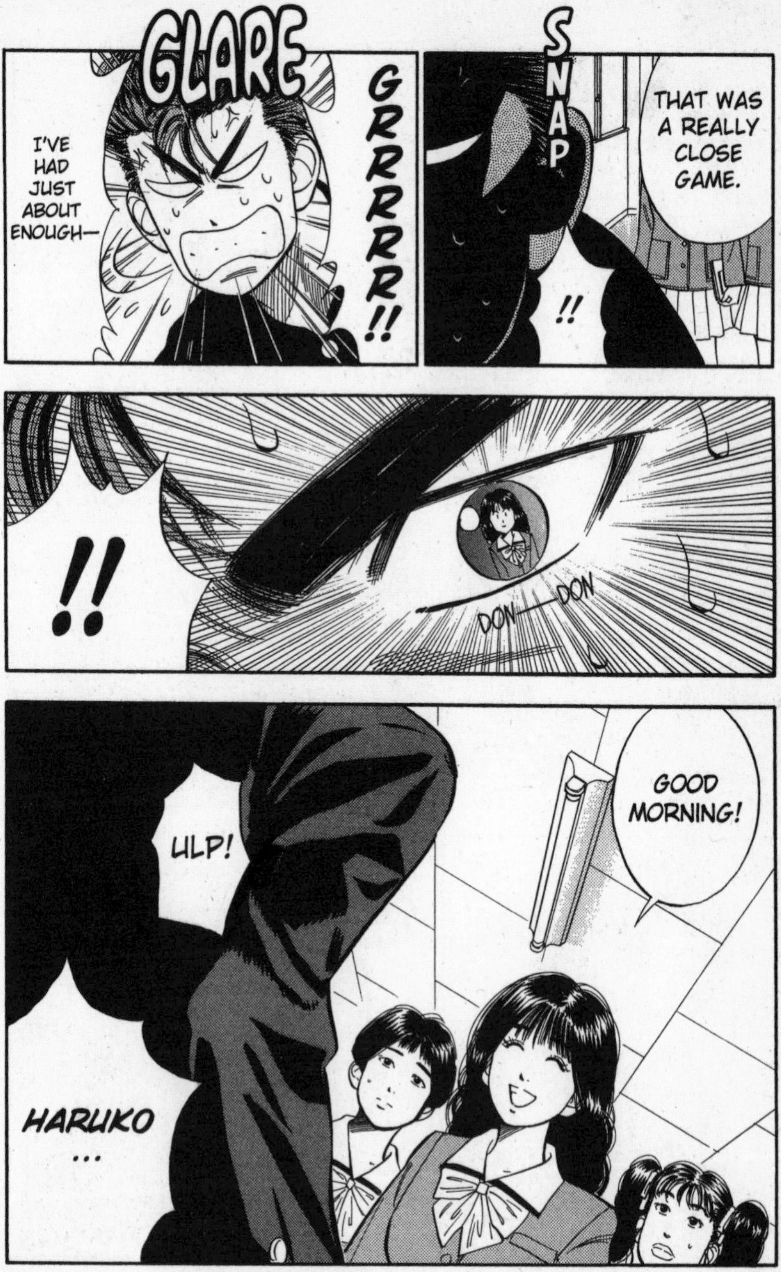
SNAP
THAT WAS A REALLY CLOSE GAME.
!!
GLARE
GRRRRRR!!
I'VE HAD JUST ABOUT ENOUGH—
!!
DON DON
GOOD MORNING!
ULP!
HARUKO ...

READ THIS WAY

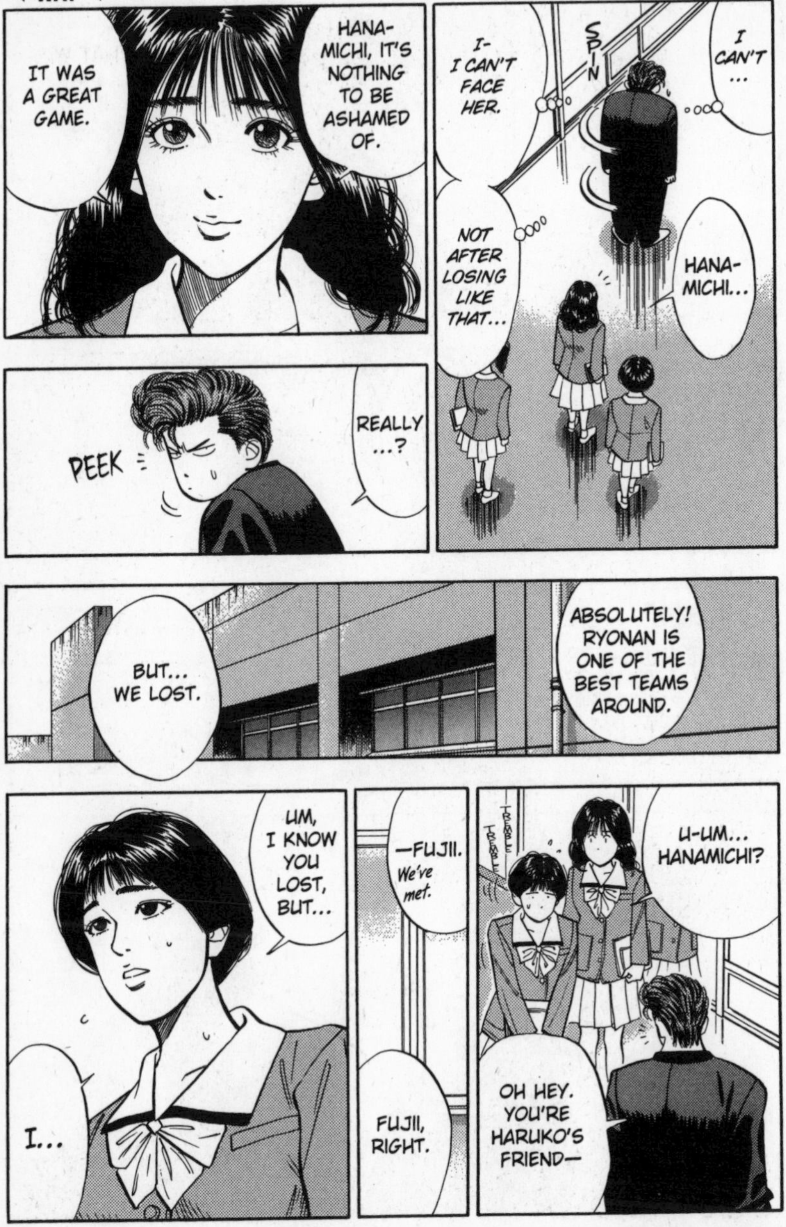
I CAN'T ...
SPIN
I- I CAN'T FACE HER.
HANA-MICHI...
NOT AFTER LOSING LIKE THAT...
HANA-MICHI, IT'S NOTHING TO BE ASHAMED OF.
IT WAS A GREAT GAME.
REALLY ...?
PEEK
ABSOLUTELY! RYONAN IS ONE OF THE BEST TEAMS AROUND.
BUT... WE LOST.
U-UM... HANAMICHI?
TREMBLE TREMBLE
OH HEY. YOU'RE HARUKO'S FRIEND—
—FUJII. We've met.
FUJII, RIGHT.
UM, I KNOW YOU LOST, BUT...
I...

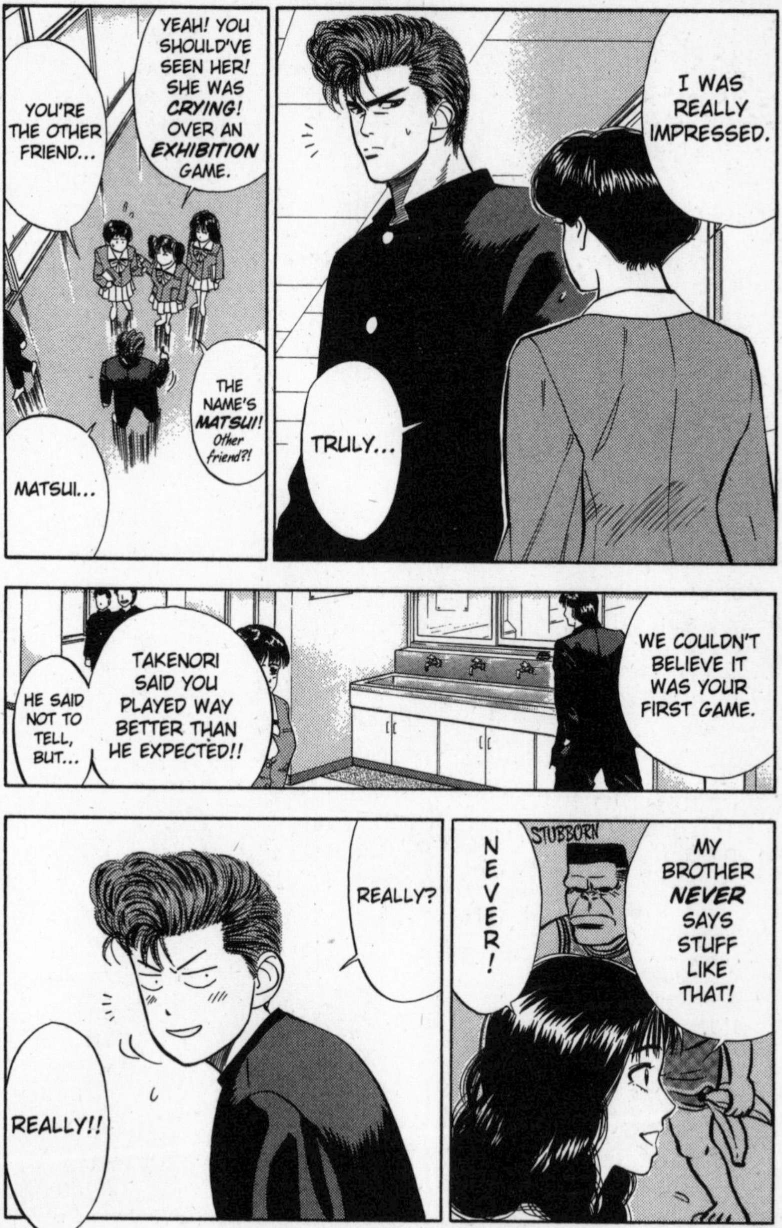

I WAS REALLY IMPRESSED.
TRULY...
YEAH! YOU SHOULD'VE SEEN HER! SHE WAS CRYING! OVER AN EXHIBITION GAME.
YOU'RE THE OTHER FRIEND...
THE NAME'S MATSUI! Other friend?!
MATSUI...
WE COULDN'T BELIEVE IT WAS YOUR FIRST GAME.
TAKENORI SAID YOU PLAYED WAY BETTER THAN HE EXPECTED!!
HE SAID NOT TO TELL, BUT...
MY BROTHER NEVER SAYS STUFF LIKE THAT!
NEVER!
STUBBORN
REALLY?
REALLY!!

READ THIS WAY

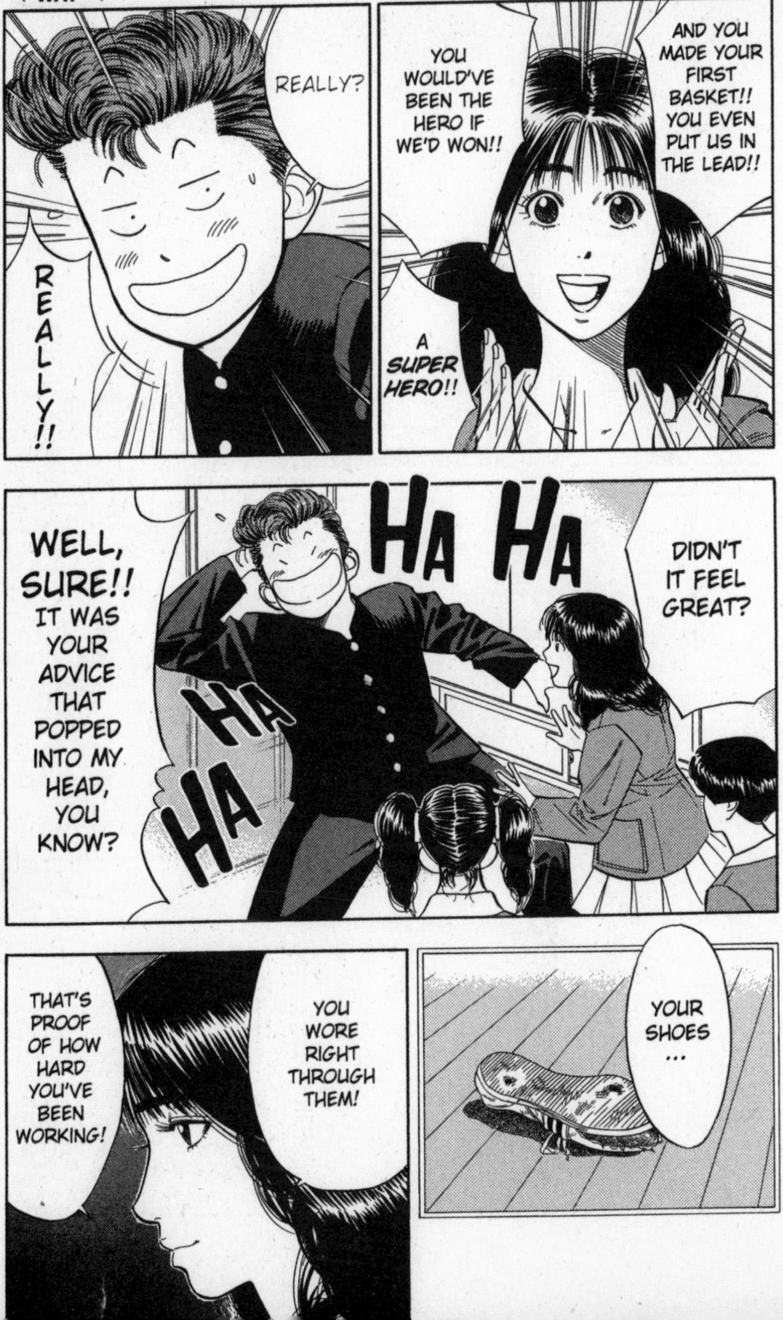
AND YOU MADE YOUR FIRST BASKET!! YOU EVEN PUT US IN THE LEAD!!
YOU WOULD'VE BEEN THE HERO IF WE'D WON!!
A SUPER HERO!!
REALLY?
REALLY!!
DIDN'T IT FEEL GREAT?
HA HA
WELL, SURE!! IT WAS YOUR ADVICE THAT POPPED INTO MY HEAD, YOU KNOW?
HA HA
YOUR SHOES ...
YOU WORE RIGHT THROUGH THEM!
THAT'S PROOF OF HOW HARD YOU'VE BEEN WORKING!

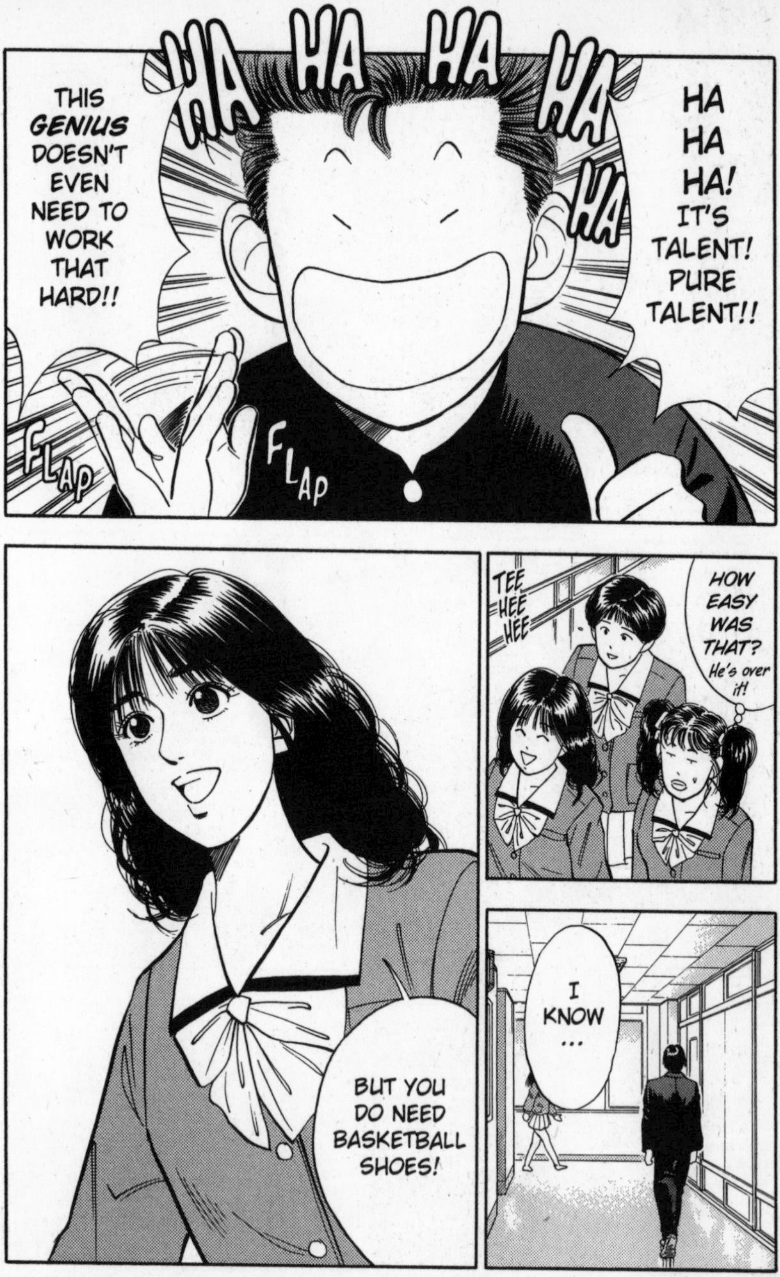
HA HA HA HA HA
HA HA HA! IT'S TALENT! PURE TALENT!!
THIS GENIUS DOESN'T EVEN NEED TO WORK THAT HARD!!
FLAP
FLAP
HOW EASY WAS THAT?
He's over it!
TEE HEE HEE
I KNOW ...
BUT YOU DO NEED BASKETBALL SHOES!

READ THIS WAY

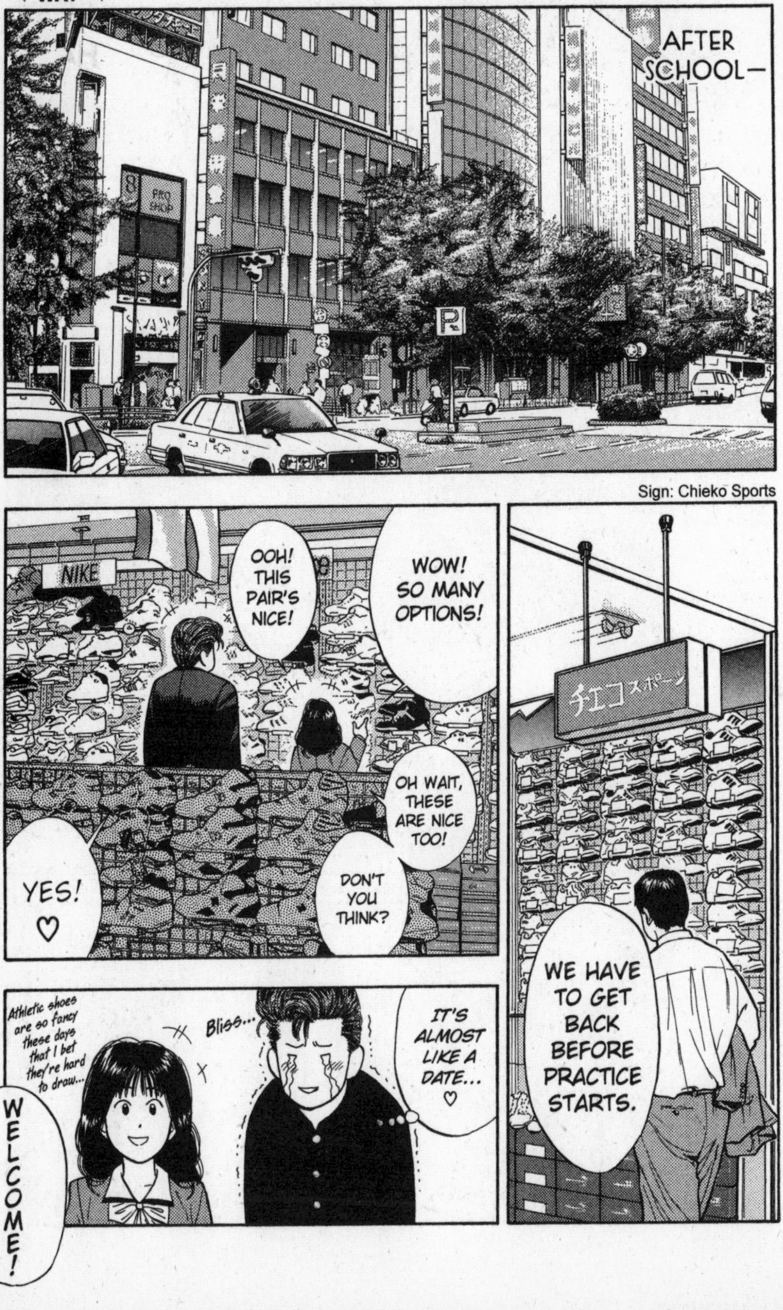

AFTER SCHOOL—
Sign: Chieko Sports
WE HAVE TO GET BACK BEFORE PRACTICE STARTS.
WOW! SO MANY OPTIONS!
OOH! THIS PAIR'S NICE!
OH WAIT, THESE ARE NICE TOO!
DON'T YOU THINK?
YES! ♡
IT'S ALMOST LIKE A DATE... ♡
Bliss...
Athletic shoes are so fancy these days that I bet they're hard to draw...
WELCOME!

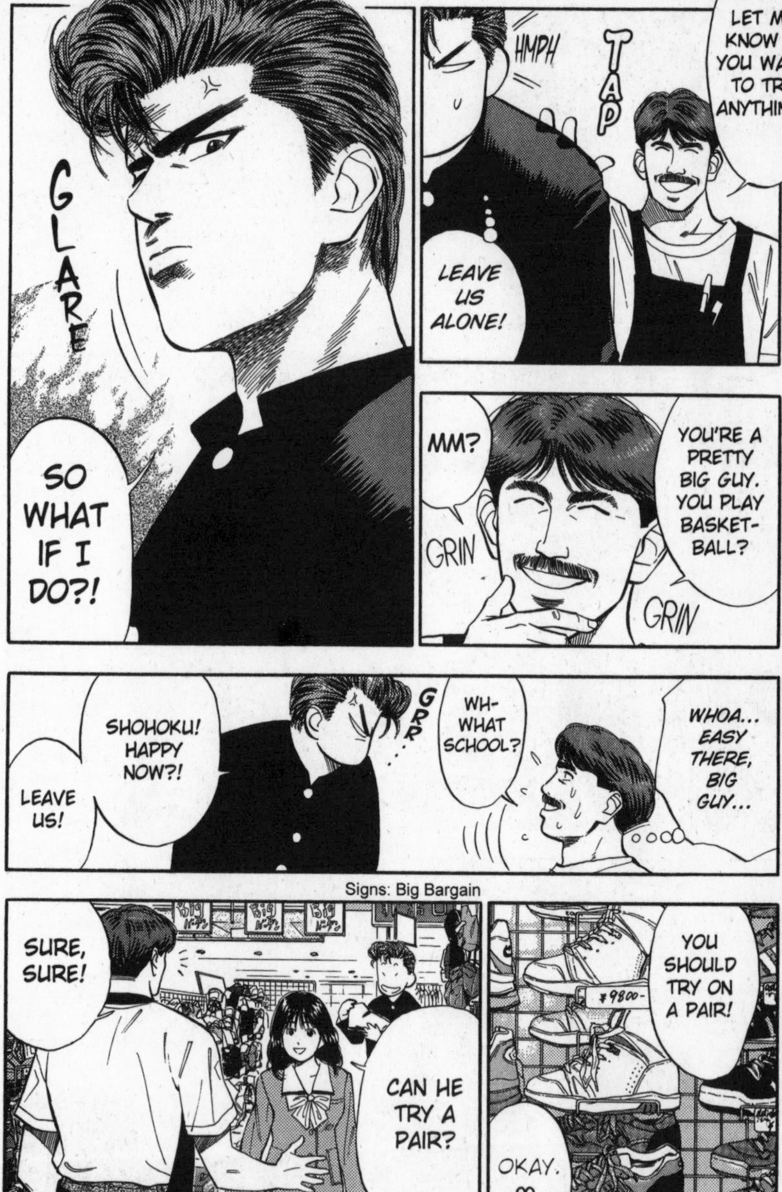
LET ME KNOW IF YOU WANT TO TRY ANYTHING.
TAP
HMPH
LEAVE US ALONE!
YOU'RE A PRETTY BIG GUY. YOU PLAY BASKET-BALL?
GRIN
MM?
GRIN
GLARE
SO WHAT IF I DO?!
WHOA... EASY THERE, BIG GUY...
WH-WHAT SCHOOL?
GRR
SHOHOKU! HAPPY NOW?!
LEAVE US!
YOU SHOULD TRY ON A PAIR!
¥9800-
OKAY. ♥
Signs: Big Bargain
CAN HE TRY A PAIR?
SURE, SURE!

READ THIS WAY

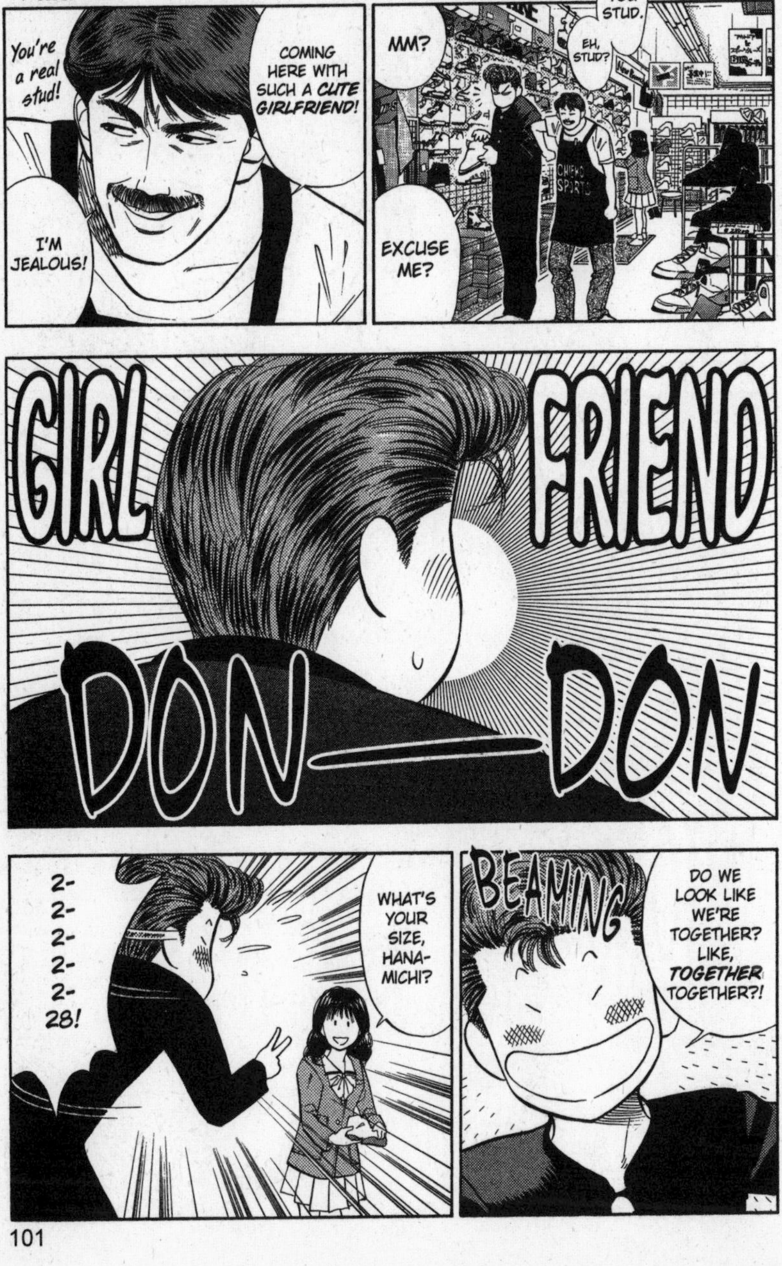

YOU STUD.
EH, STUD?
MM?
EXCUSE ME?
COMING HERE WITH SUCH A CUTE GIRLFRIEND!
You're a real stud!
I'M JEALOUS!
GIRL FRIEND
DON—DON
BEAMING
DO WE LOOK LIKE WE'RE TOGETHER? LIKE, TOGETHER TOGETHER?!
WHAT'S YOUR SIZE, HANA-MICHI?
2-2-2-2-2-28!

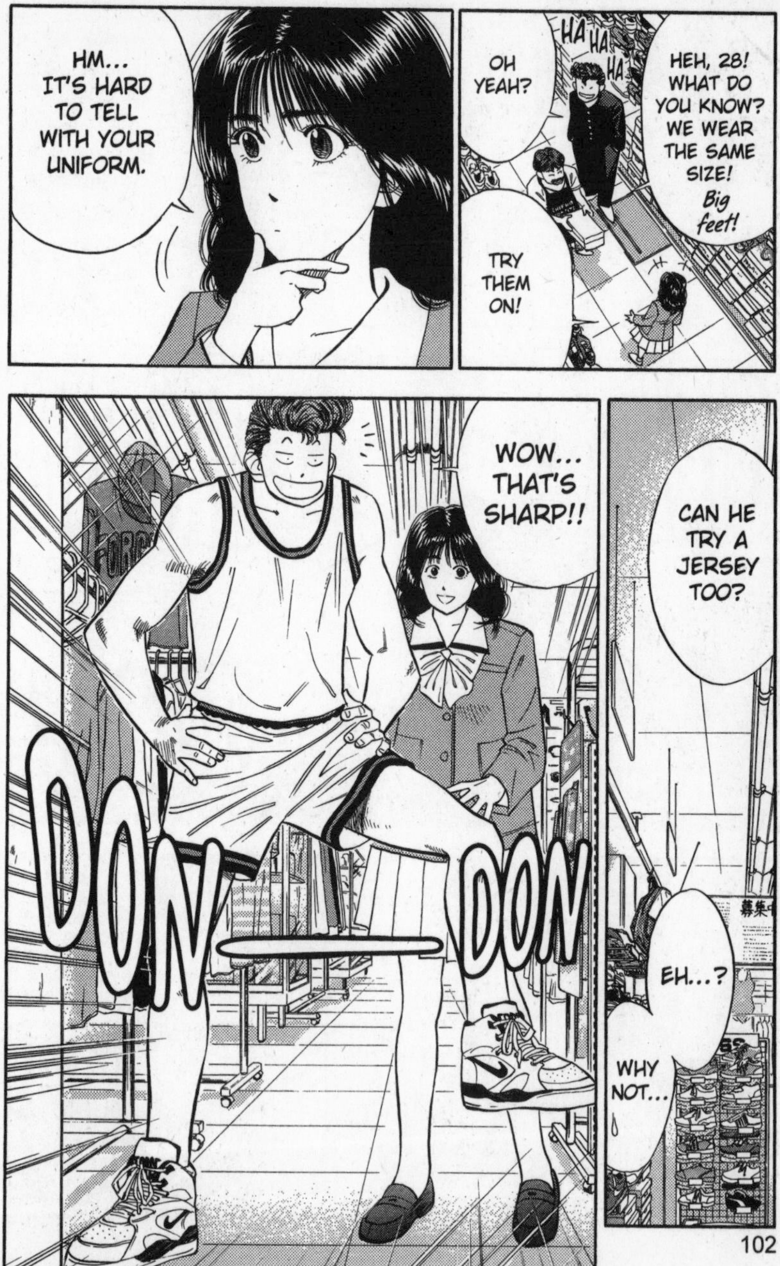
HA HA HA
HEH, 28! WHAT DO YOU KNOW? WE WEAR THE SAME SIZE! Big feet!
OH YEAH?
TRY THEM ON!
HM... IT'S HARD TO TELL WITH YOUR UNIFORM.
CAN HE TRY A JERSEY TOO?
EH...?
WHY NOT...
WOW... THAT'S SHARP!!
DON
DON

READ THIS WAY

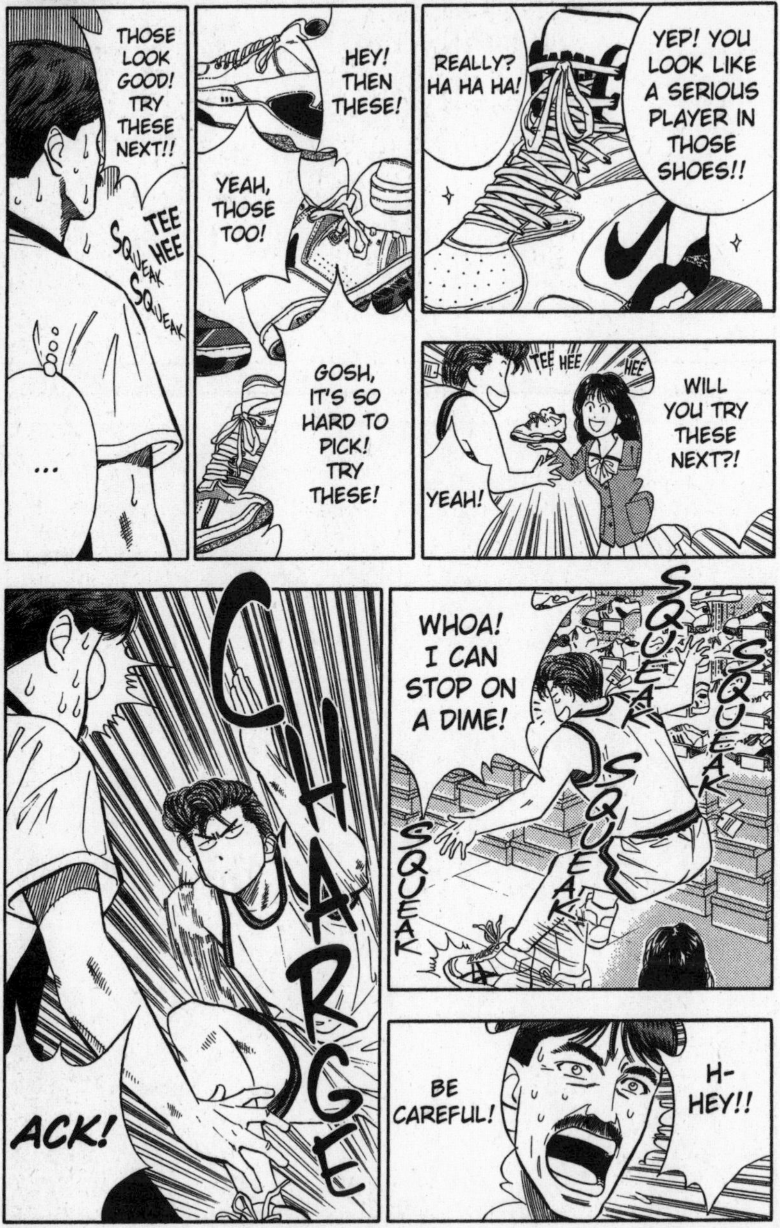
YEP! YOU LOOK LIKE A SERIOUS PLAYER IN THOSE SHOES!!
REALLY? HA HA HA!
WILL YOU TRY THESE NEXT?!
TEE HEE HEE
YEAH!
HEY! THEN THESE!
YEAH, THOSE TOO!
GOSH, IT'S SO HARD TO PICK! TRY THESE!
THOSE LOOK GOOD! TRY THESE NEXT!!
TEE HEE
SQUEAK SQUEAK
...
WHOA! I CAN STOP ON A DIME!
SQUEAK
SQUEAK
SQUEAK
SQUEAK
H-HEY!!
BE CAREFUL!
CHARGE
ACK!

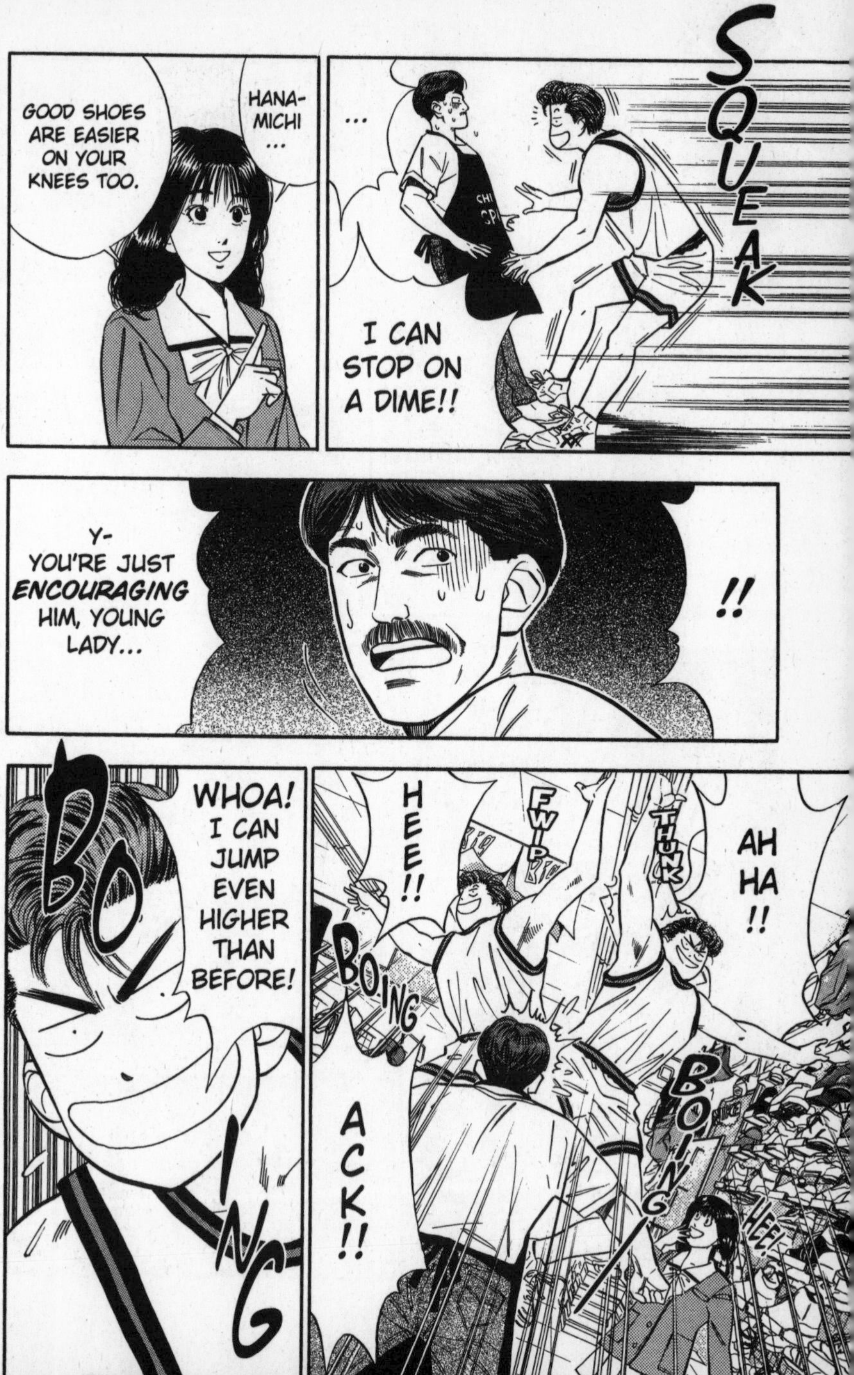
SQUEAK
...
I CAN STOP ON A DIME!!
HANA-MICHI ...
GOOD SHOES ARE EASIER ON YOUR KNEES TOO.
!!
Y- YOU'RE JUST *ENCOURAGING* HIM, YOUNG LADY...
AH HA !!
THUNK
FWIP
HEE!!
BOING
HEE!
BOING
ACK!!
WHOA! I CAN JUMP EVEN HIGHER THAN BEFORE!
BOING

READ THIS WAY

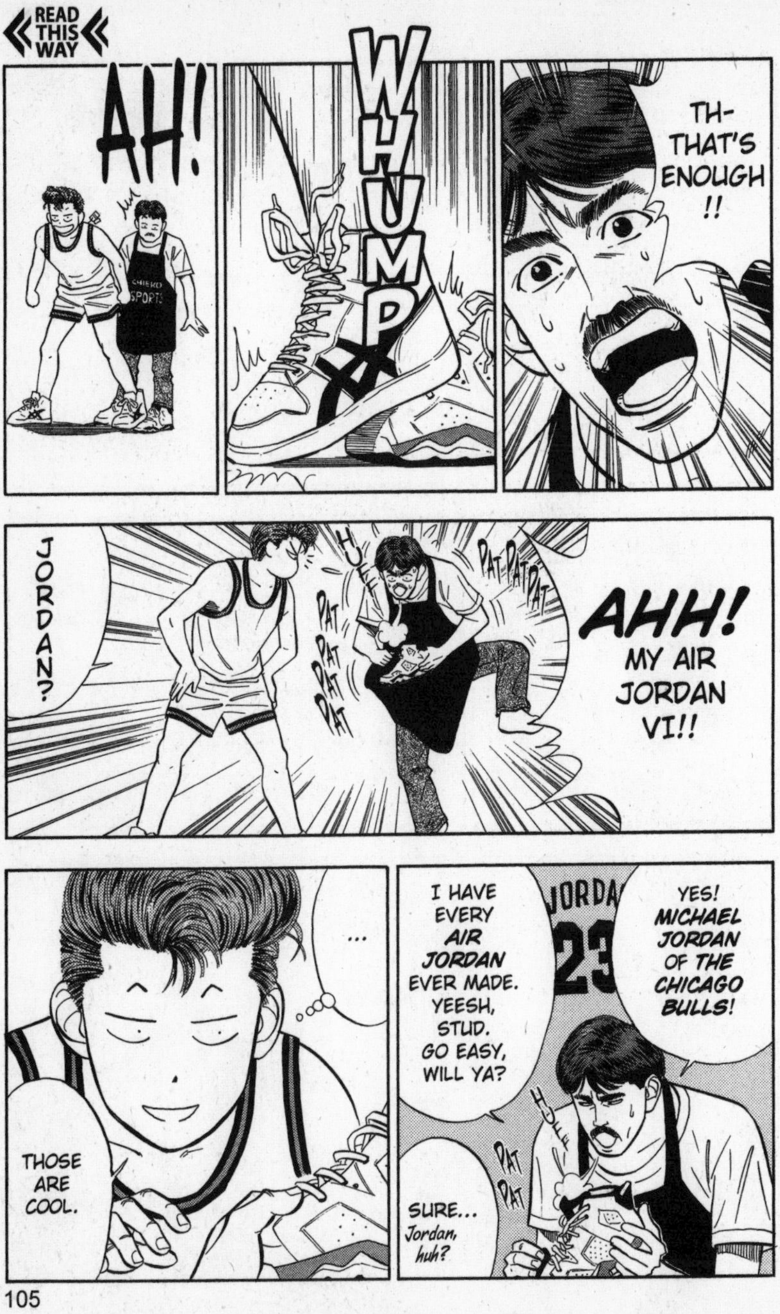
TH- THAT'S ENOUGH !!
WHUMP
AH!
AHH! MY AIR JORDAN VI!!
PAT PAT PAT
HUFF
PAT PAT PAT PAT
JORDAN?
YES! MICHAEL JORDAN OF THE CHICAGO BULLS!
I HAVE EVERY AIR JORDAN EVER MADE. YEESH, STUD. GO EASY, WILL YA?
HUFF
PAT PAT
SURE... Jordan, huh?
...
THOSE ARE COOL.

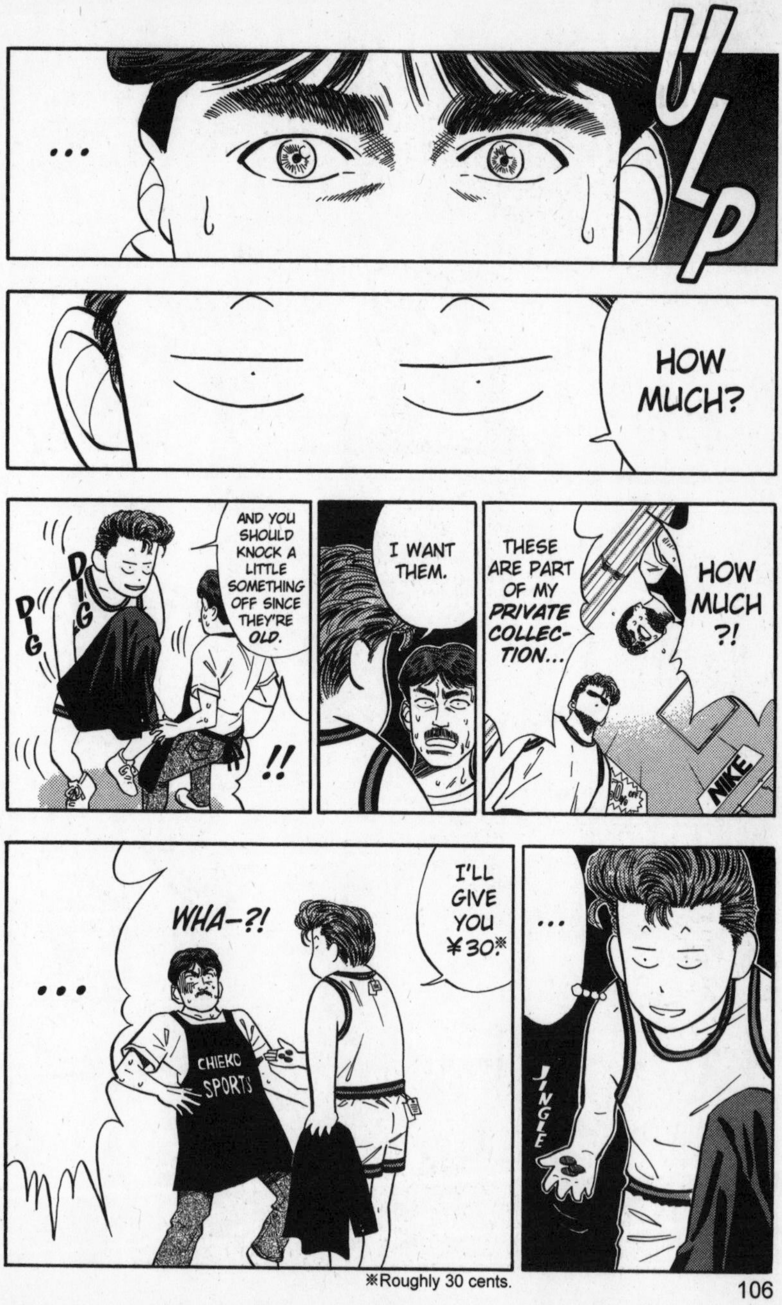
ULP
...
HOW MUCH?
HOW MUCH ?!
THESE ARE PART OF MY PRIVATE COLLECTION...
I WANT THEM.
AND YOU SHOULD KNOCK A LITTLE SOMETHING OFF SINCE THEY'RE OLD.
DIG
DIG
!!
...
JINGLE
I'LL GIVE YOU ¥30※
WHA-?!
CHIEKO SPORTS
...

※Roughly 30 cents.

READ THIS WAY

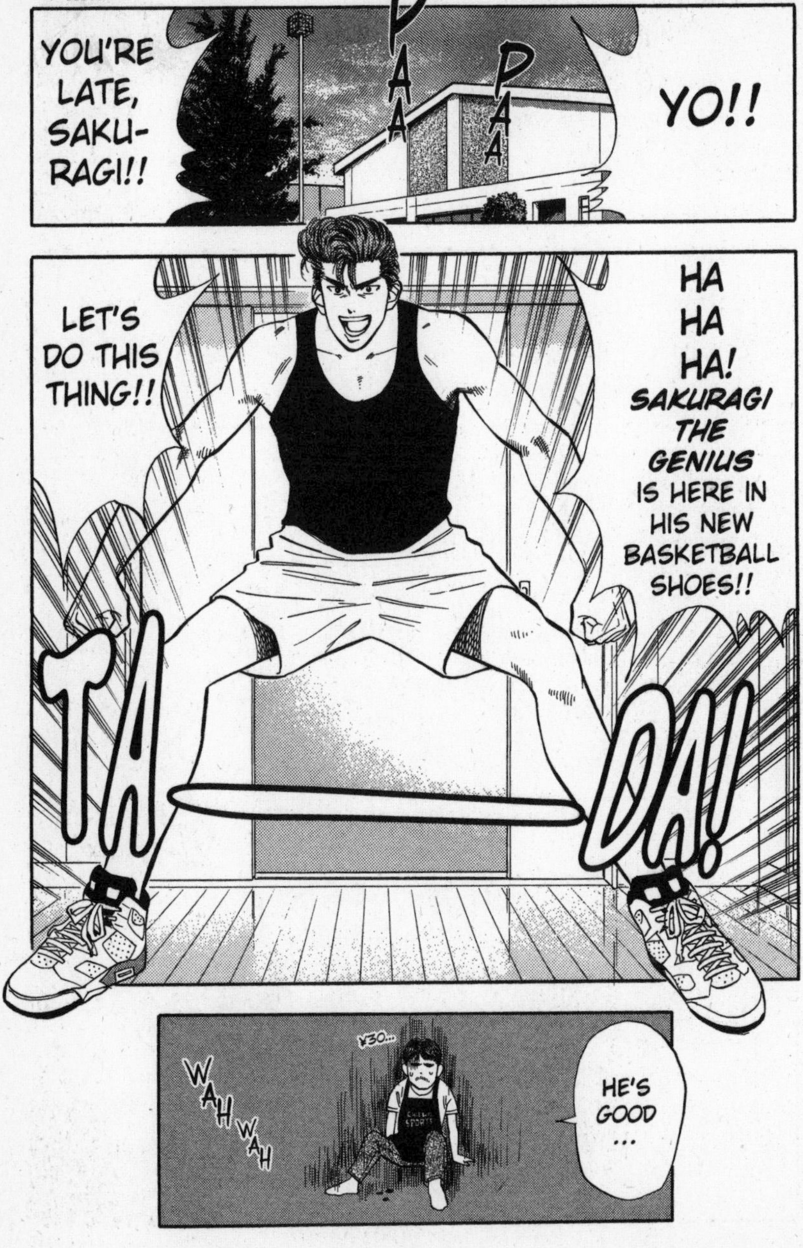
YO!!
PAA
PAA
YOU'RE LATE, SAKURAGI!!
HA HA HA! SAKURAGI THE GENIUS IS HERE IN HIS NEW BASKETBALL SHOES!!
LET'S DO THIS THING!!
DA!
TA
HE'S GOOD ...
¥30...
WAH WAH

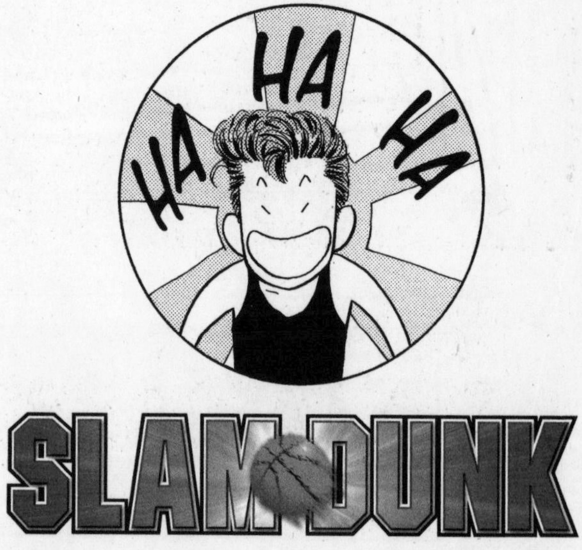
HA HA HA

SLAM DUNK

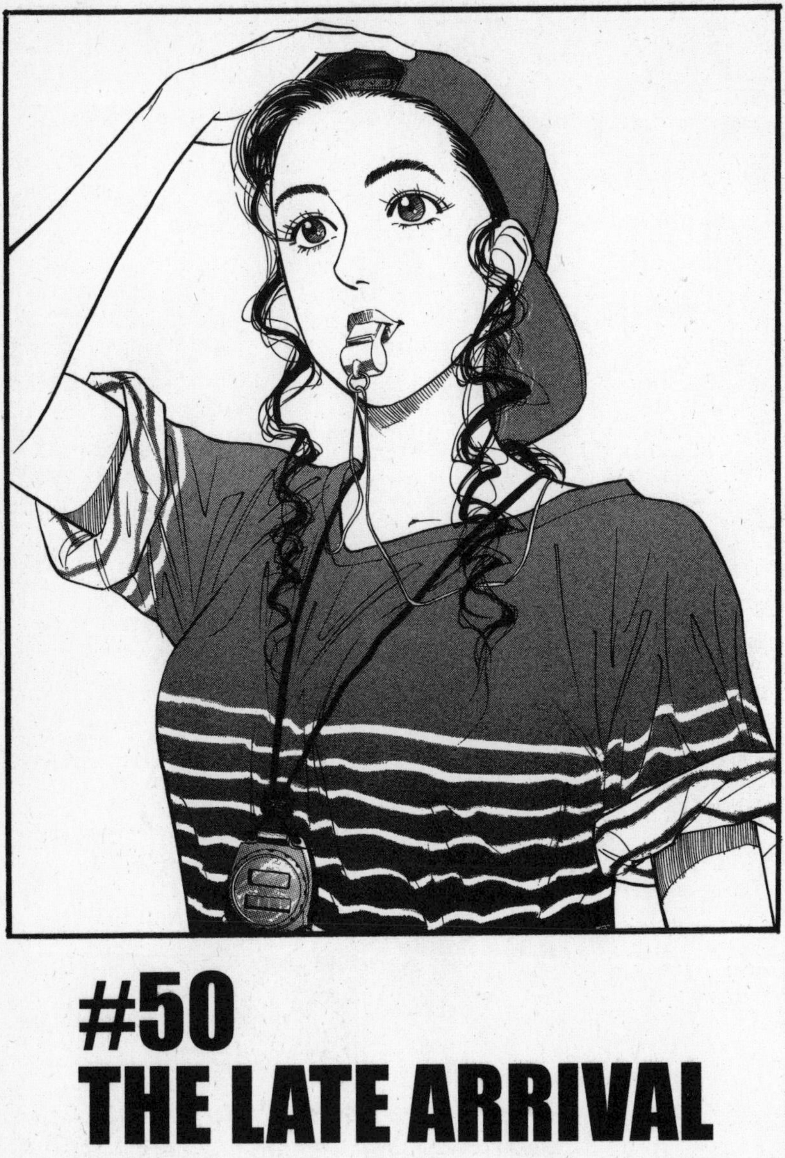

# #50
# THE LATE ARRIVAL

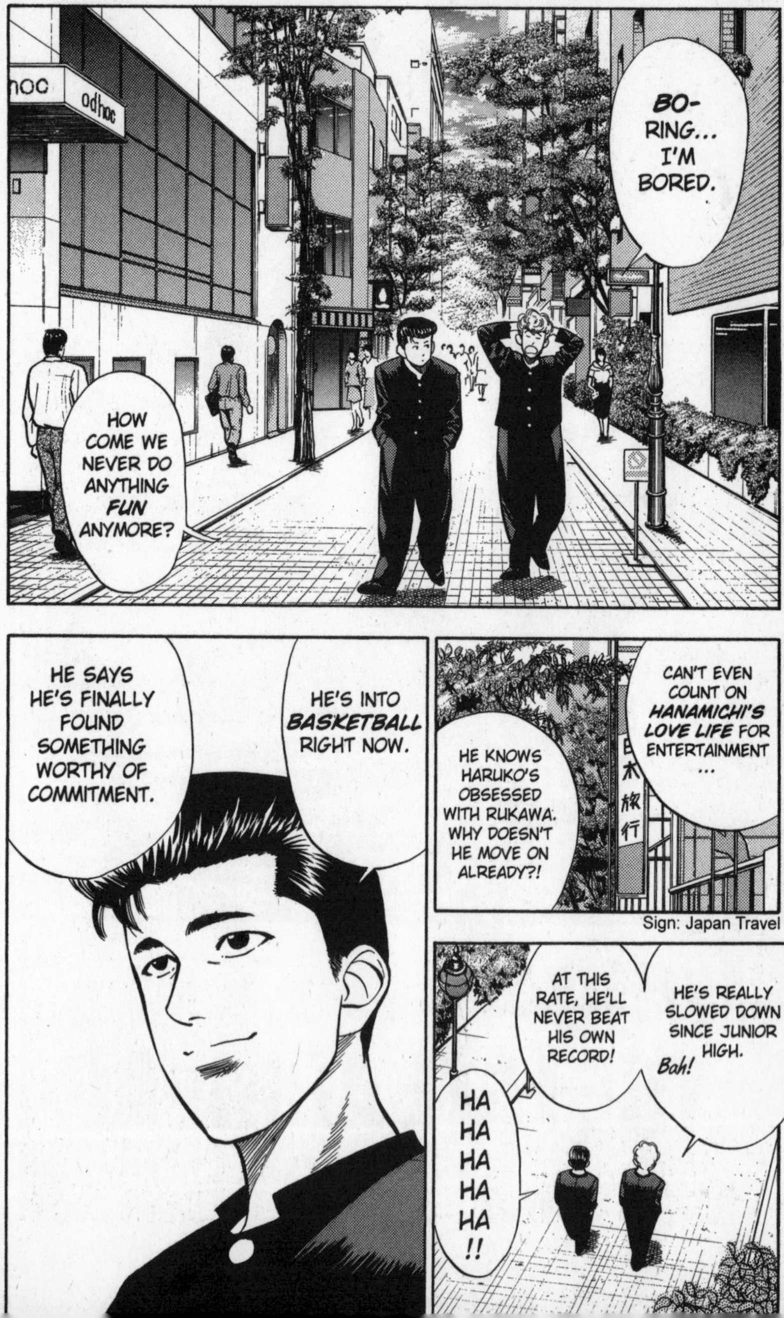
BO-RING... I'M BORED.
HOW COME WE NEVER DO ANYTHING FUN ANYMORE?
CAN'T EVEN COUNT ON HANAMICHI'S LOVE LIFE FOR ENTERTAINMENT ...
HE KNOWS HARUKO'S OBSESSED WITH RUKAWA. WHY DOESN'T HE MOVE ON ALREADY?!
Sign: Japan Travel
HE'S REALLY SLOWED DOWN SINCE JUNIOR HIGH.
Bah!
AT THIS RATE, HE'LL NEVER BEAT HIS OWN RECORD!
HA HA HA HA HA!!
HE'S INTO BASKETBALL RIGHT NOW.
HE SAYS HE'S FINALLY FOUND SOMETHING WORTHY OF COMMITMENT.

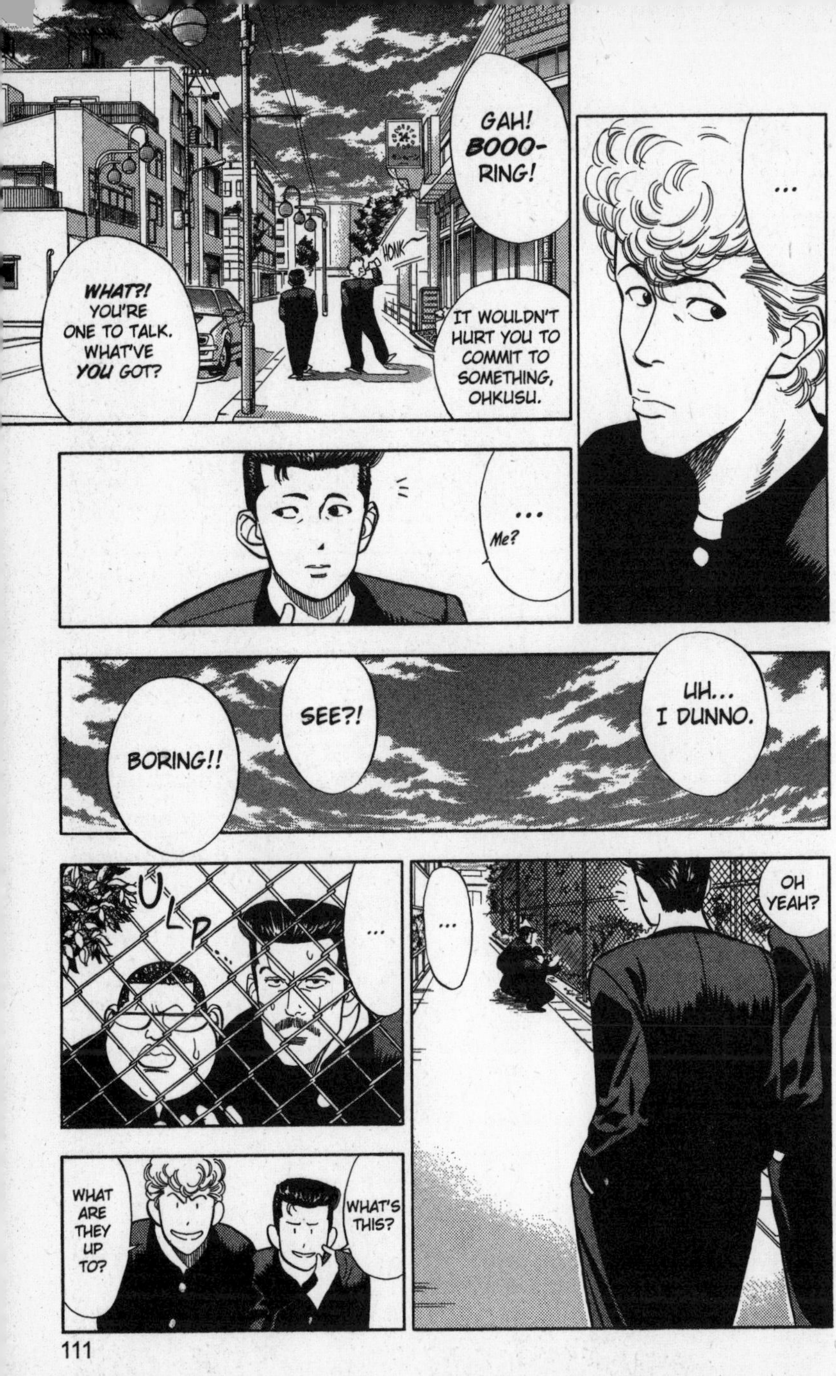
GAH! BOOO-RING!
IT WOULDN'T HURT YOU TO COMMIT TO SOMETHING, OHKUSU.
HONK
WHAT?! YOU'RE ONE TO TALK. WHAT'VE YOU GOT?
...
... Me?
UH... I DUNNO.
SEE?!
BORING!!
OH YEAH?
...
ULP...
...
WHAT'S THIS?
WHAT ARE THEY UP TO?

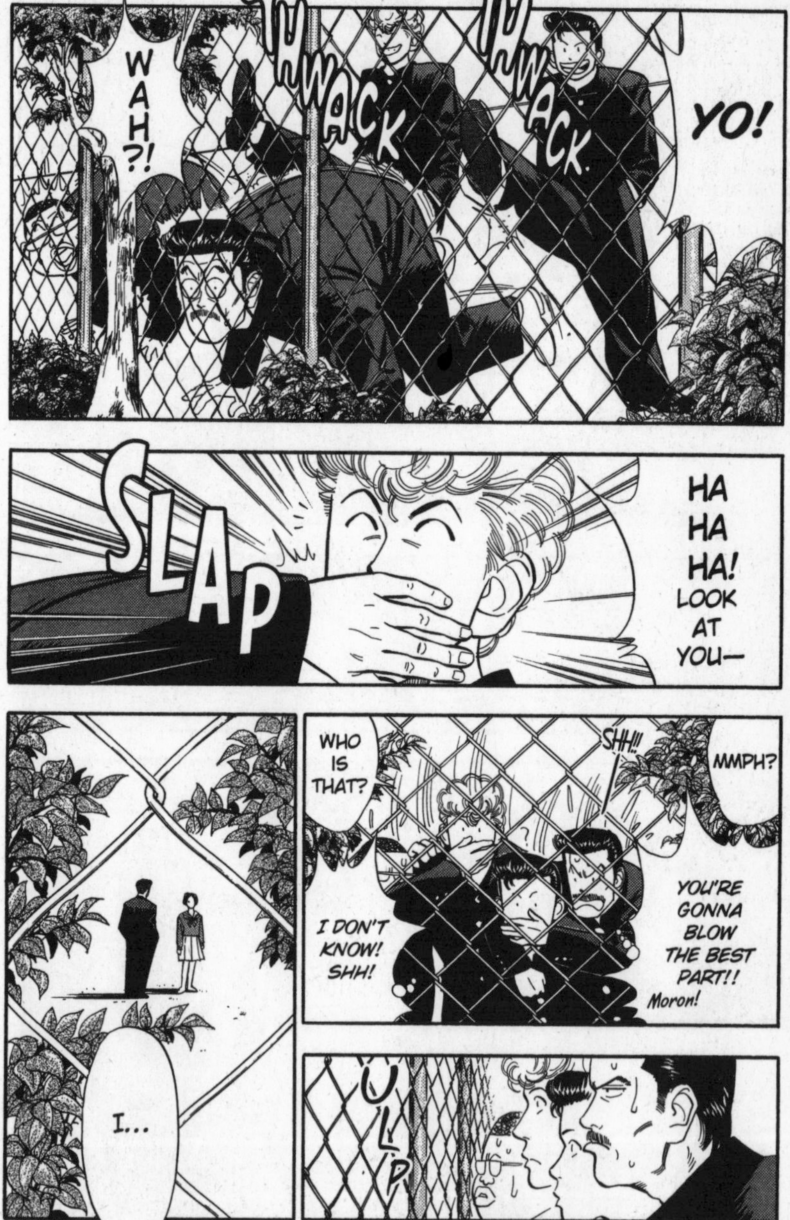
YO!
THWACK
THWACK
WAH?!
HA HA HA! LOOK AT YOU—
SLAP
MMPH?
SHH!!
WHO IS THAT?
YOU'RE GONNA BLOW THE BEST PART!!
Moron!
I DON'T KNOW! SHH!
ULP
I...

READ THIS WAY

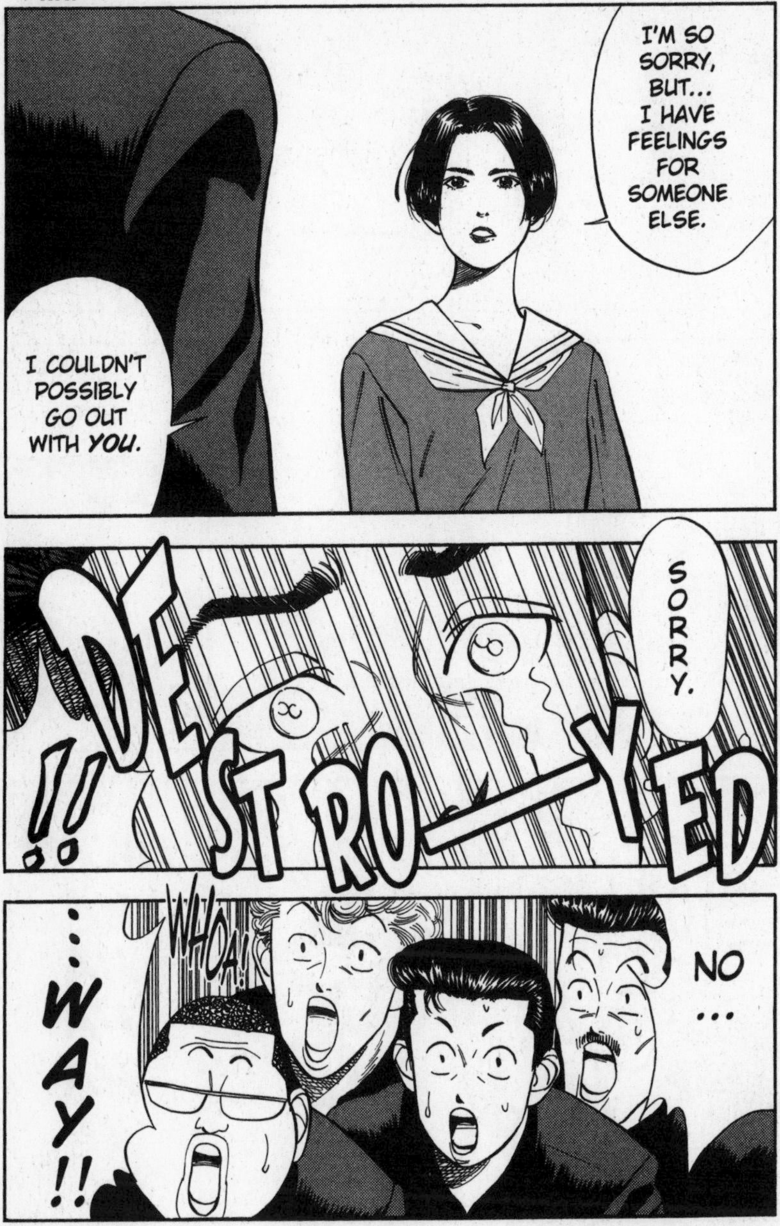
I'M SO SORRY, BUT... I HAVE FEELINGS FOR SOMEONE ELSE.
I COULDN'T POSSIBLY GO OUT WITH *YOU*.
SORRY.
DESTRO—YED !!
NO...
WHOA!
...WAY!!

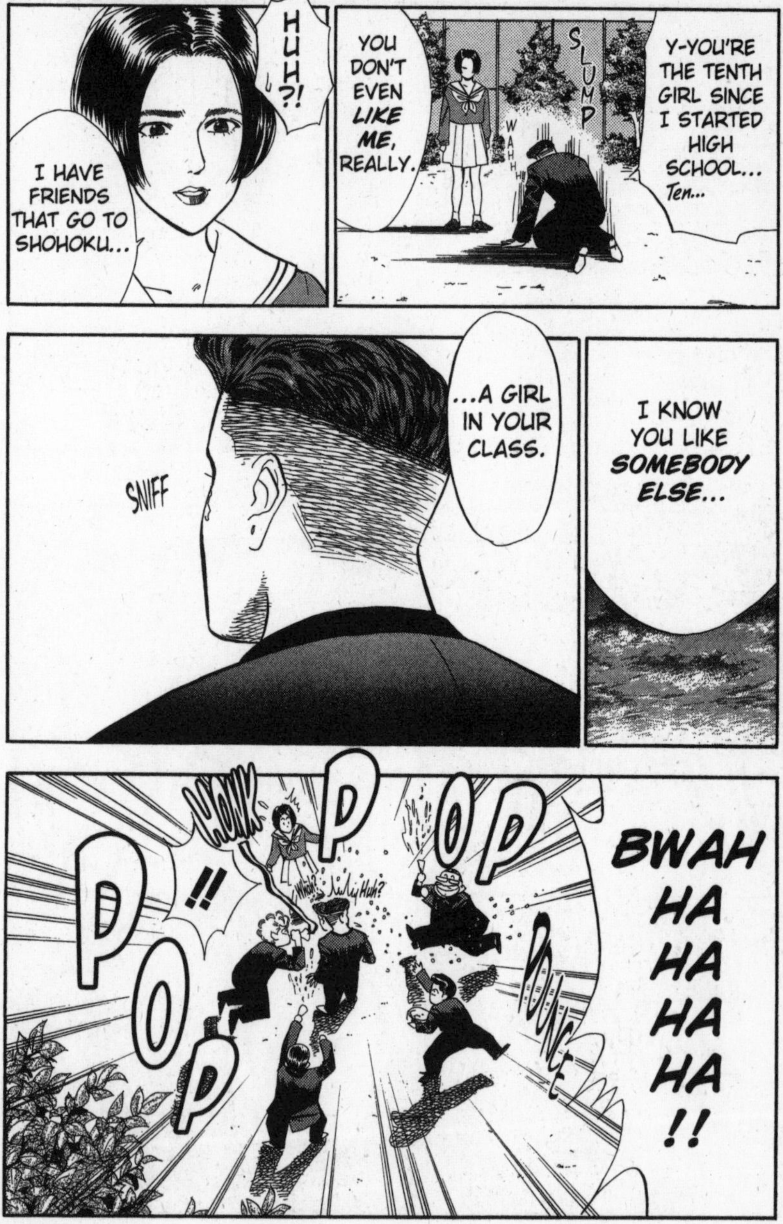
Y-YOU'RE THE TENTH GIRL SINCE I STARTED HIGH SCHOOL... *Ten...*
SLUMP
WAHHH!!
YOU DON'T EVEN *LIKE ME*, REALLY.
HUH?!
I HAVE FRIENDS THAT GO TO SHOHOKU...
I KNOW YOU LIKE *SOMEBODY ELSE*...
...A GIRL IN YOUR CLASS.
SNIFF
BWAH HA HA HA HA HA!!
POP
POP
POP
POP
!!
POUNCE

READ THIS WAY

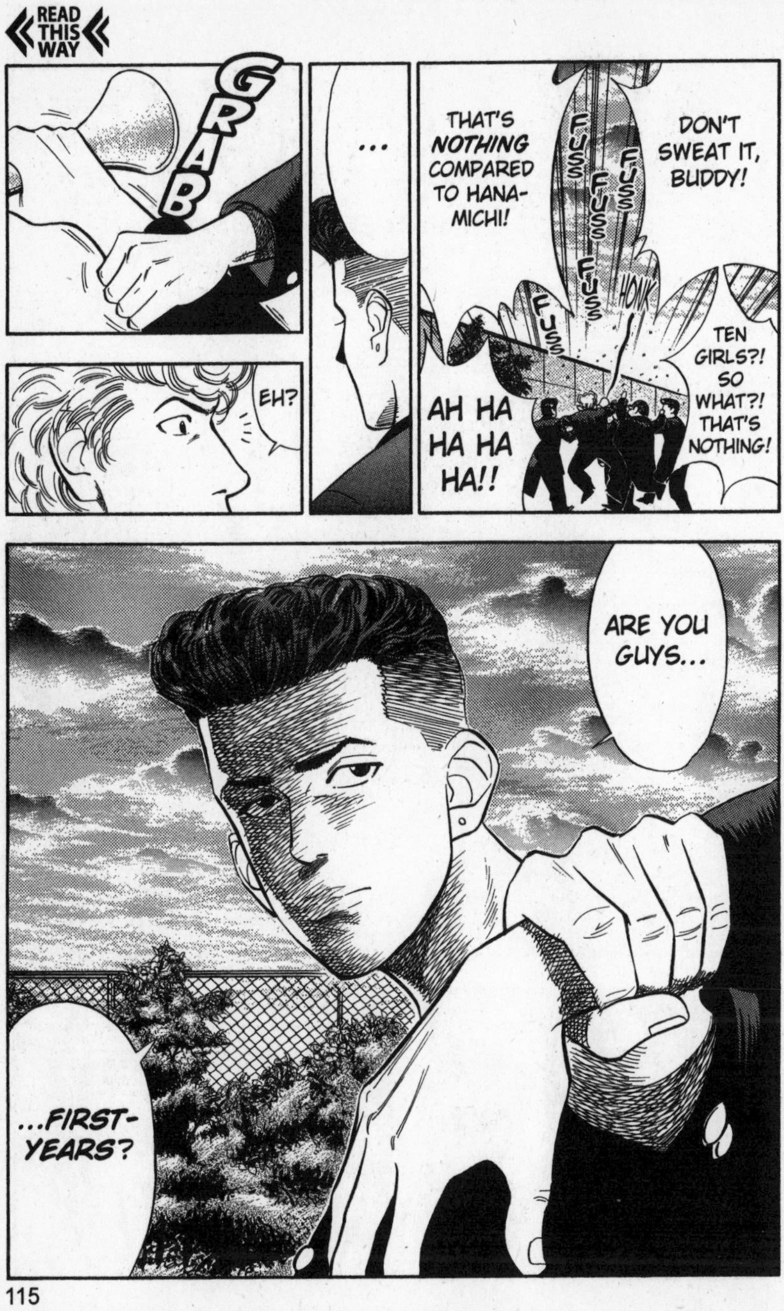
DON'T SWEAT IT, BUDDY!
FUSS FUSS FUSS FUSS FUSS
HONK
THAT'S *NOTHING* COMPARED TO HANA-MICHI!
TEN GIRLS?! SO WHAT?! THAT'S NOTHING!
AH HA HA HA HA!!
...
GRAB
EH?
ARE YOU GUYS...
*...FIRST-YEARS?*

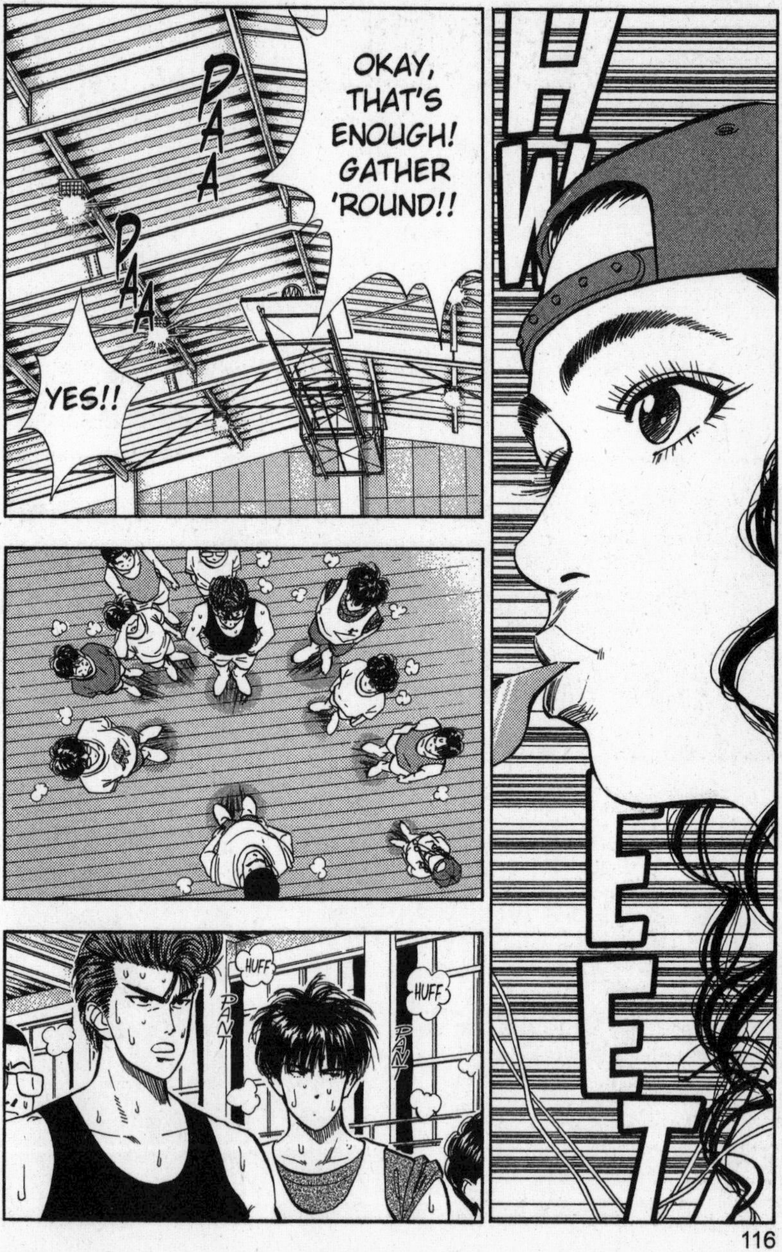
HW
EET
OKAY, THAT'S ENOUGH! GATHER 'ROUND!!
PAA
PAA
YES!!
HUFF
PANT
HUFF
PANT

READ THIS WAY

WHEW...
OKAY, OF ALL THE FIRST-YEARS, WE'RE DOWN TO YOU FIVE!
YEAH...
Pfft! Wusses...
A couple guys dropped out during the game...
Heh...
WHATEVER. IT HAPPENS *EVERY YEAR.*
HEH HEH
IT ACTUALLY WASN'T AS BAD THIS YEAR.
DISTRICT PRELIMS ARE COMING UP!! PREFECTURE GAMES, TOO!
WE'VE GOT TO FINALIZE OUR LINEUP.

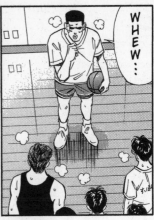

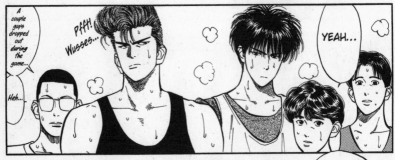

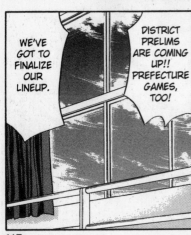

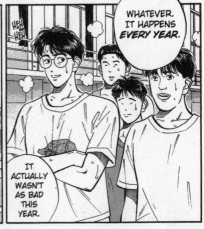

THERE ARE OVER 200 TEAMS IN OUR PREFECTURE.

ONE OF THEM IS KAINAN-DAI FUZOKU HIGH SCHOOL!! THEY'RE A POWERHOUSE. THEY WERE LAST YEAR'S CHAMPS AND THEY'VE MADE NATIONALS TEN YEARS IN A ROW!!

AND, OF COURSE...

THERE'S ALSO SHOYO. THEY'VE BEEN CLOSING IN ON KAINAN AND LAST YEAR THEY TOOK SECOND PLACE.

...RYONAN! AS YOU WELL KNOW, THEY'VE GOT A GENIUS IN SENDOH AND A MONSTER IN UOZUMI!!

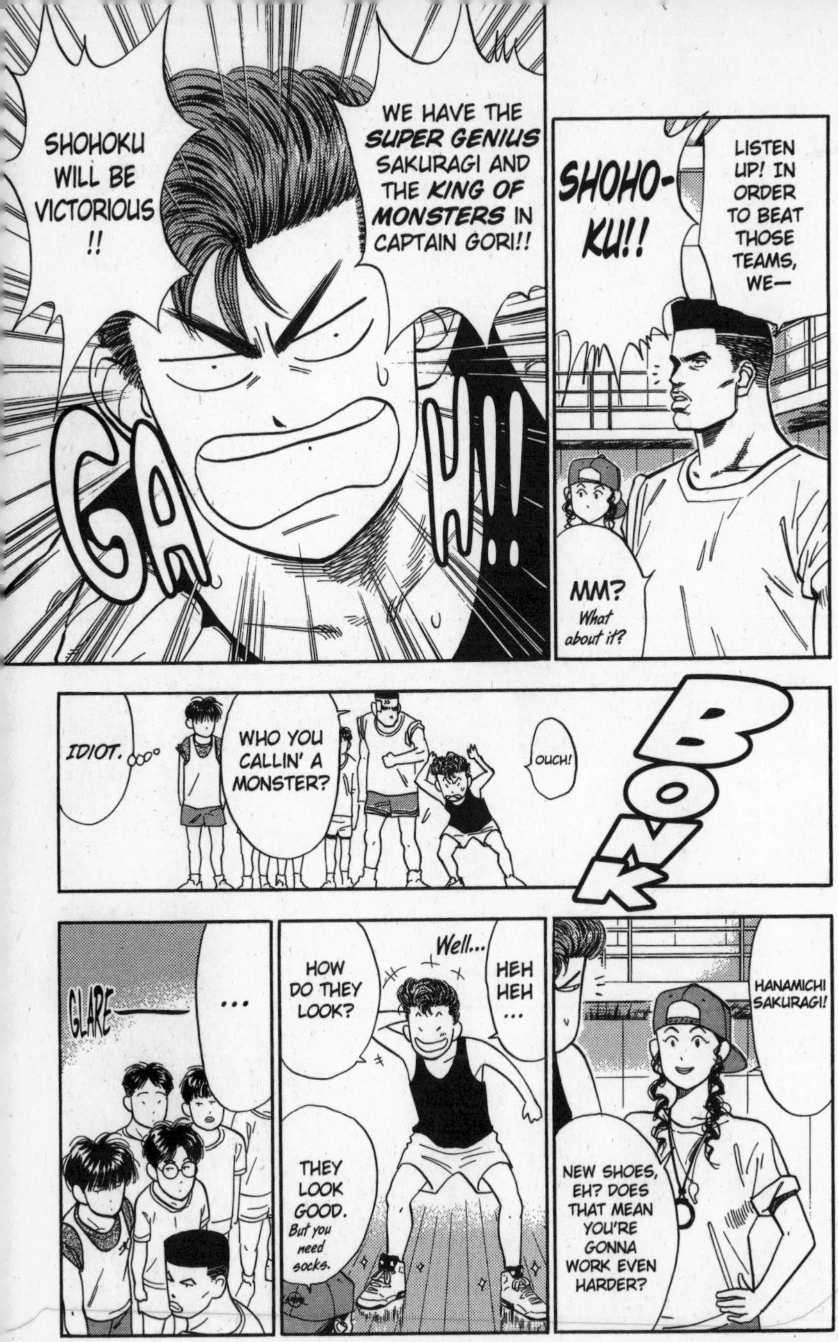
LISTEN UP! IN ORDER TO BEAT THOSE TEAMS, WE—
SHOHO-KU!!
MM? What about it?
WE HAVE THE SUPER GENIUS SAKURAGI AND THE KING OF MONSTERS IN CAPTAIN GORI!!
SHOHOKU WILL BE VICTORIOUS !!
GAH!!
BONK
OUCH!
WHO YOU CALLIN' A MONSTER?
IDIOT.
HANAMICHI SAKURAGI!
NEW SHOES, EH? DOES THAT MEAN YOU'RE GONNA WORK EVEN HARDER?
Well...
HEH HEH ...
HOW DO THEY LOOK?
THEY LOOK GOOD. But you need socks.
...
GLARE——

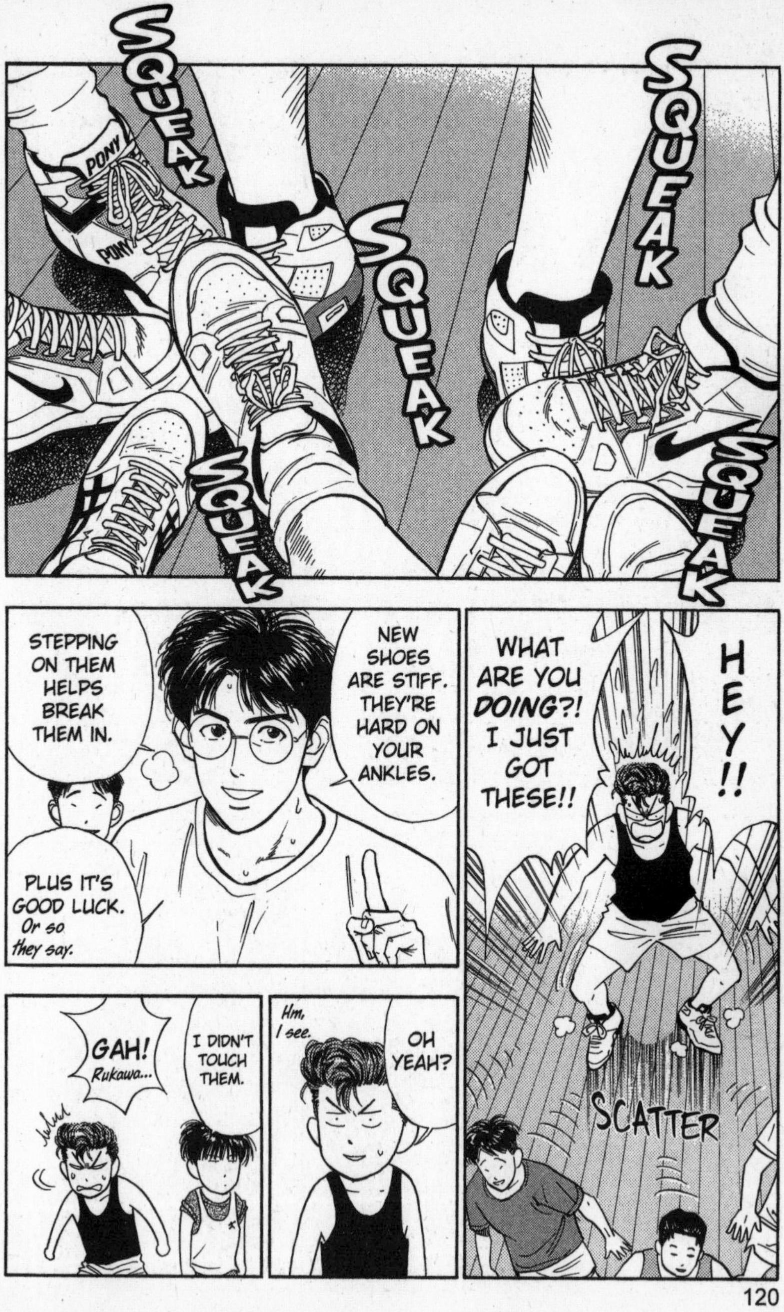

SQUEAK
SQUEAK
SQUEAK
PONY
PONY
SQUEAK
SQUEAK
HEY!!
WHAT ARE YOU *DOING*?! I JUST GOT THESE!!
SCATTER
NEW SHOES ARE STIFF. THEY'RE HARD ON YOUR ANKLES.
STEPPING ON THEM HELPS BREAK THEM IN.
PLUS IT'S GOOD LUCK.
*Or so they say.*
OH YEAH?
*Hm, I see.*
I DIDN'T TOUCH THEM.
GAH!
*Rukawa...*

READ THIS WAY

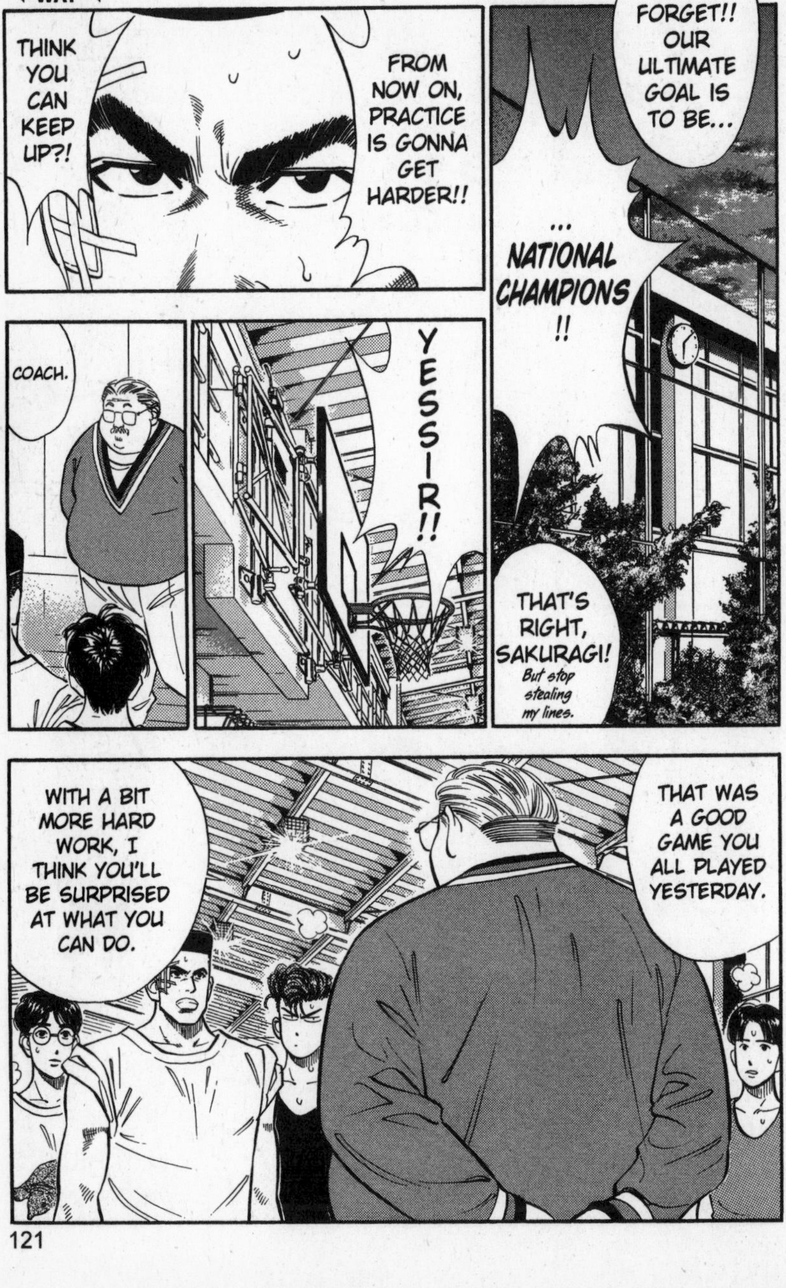

DON'T FORGET!! OUR ULTIMATE GOAL IS TO BE...
...NATIONAL CHAMPIONS!!
THAT'S RIGHT, SAKURAGI!
But stop stealing my lines.
FROM NOW ON, PRACTICE IS GONNA GET HARDER!!
THINK YOU CAN KEEP UP?!
YESSIR!!
COACH.
THAT WAS A GOOD GAME YOU ALL PLAYED YESTERDAY.
WITH A BIT MORE HARD WORK, I THINK YOU'LL BE SURPRISED AT WHAT YOU CAN DO.

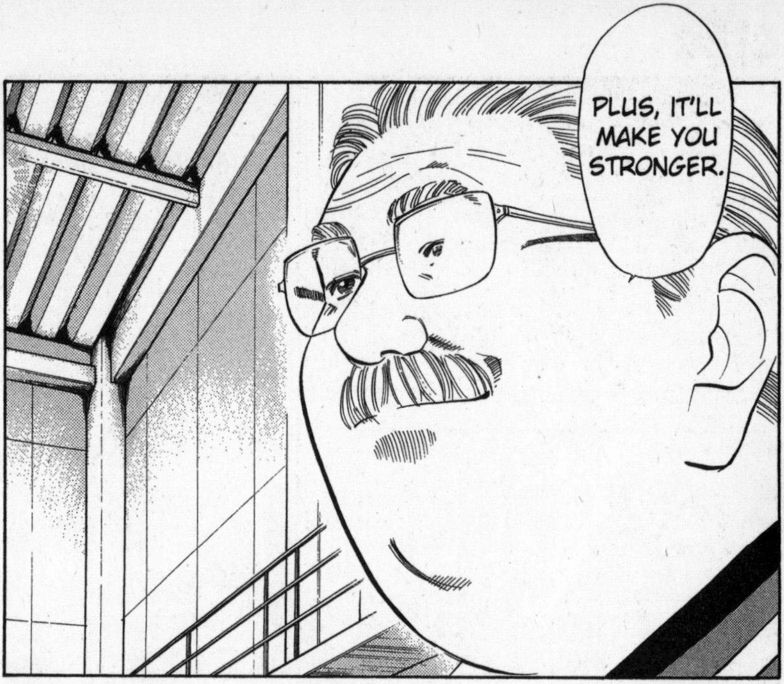
PLUS, IT'LL MAKE YOU STRONGER.
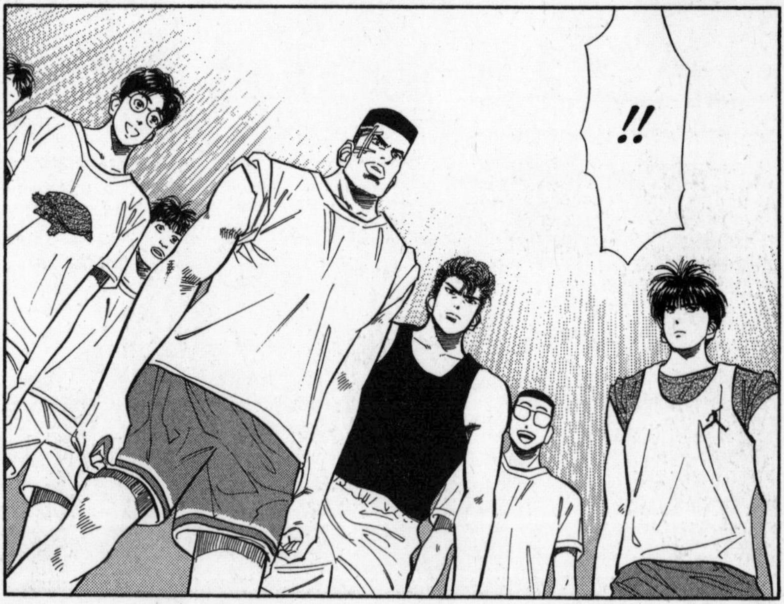
!!

READ THIS WAY

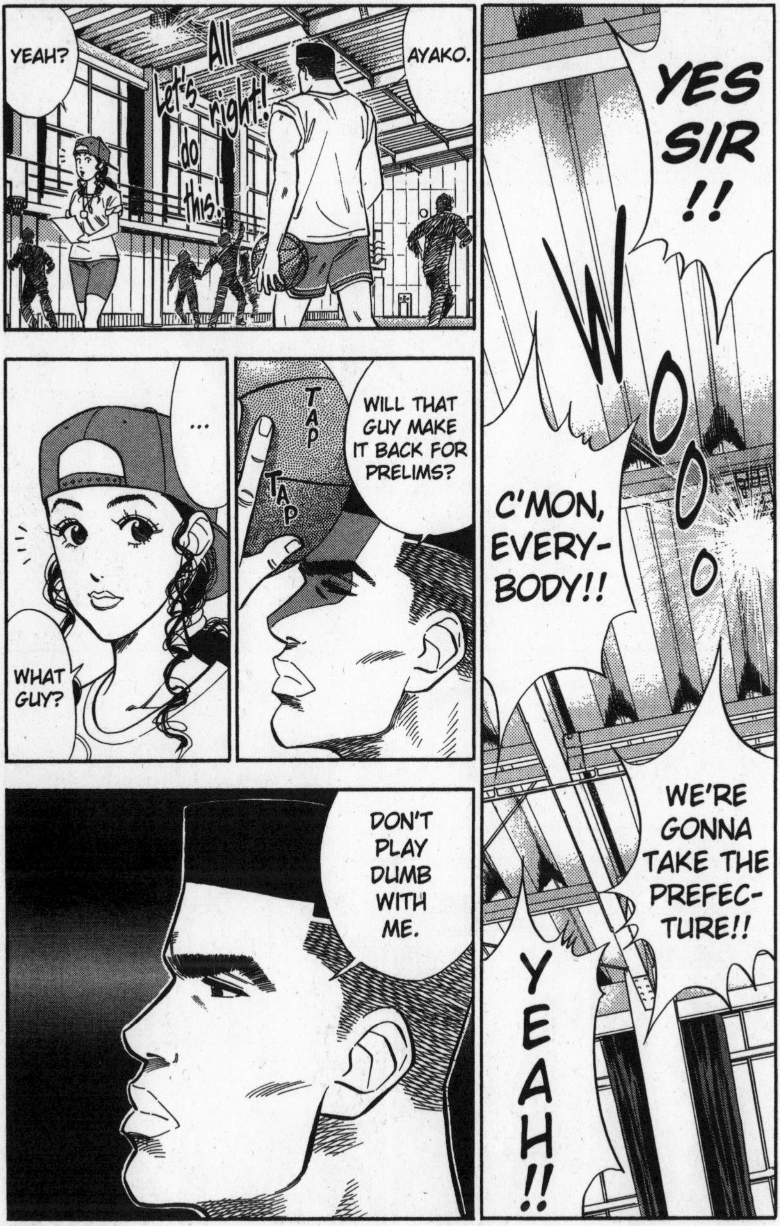

YES SIR!!
WOOOO
C'MON, EVERY-BODY!!
WE'RE GONNA TAKE THE PREFEC-TURE!!
YEAH!!
AYAKO.
All right! Let's do this!
YEAH?
WILL THAT GUY MAKE IT BACK FOR PRELIMS?
TAP
TAP
...
WHAT GUY?
DON'T PLAY DUMB WITH ME.

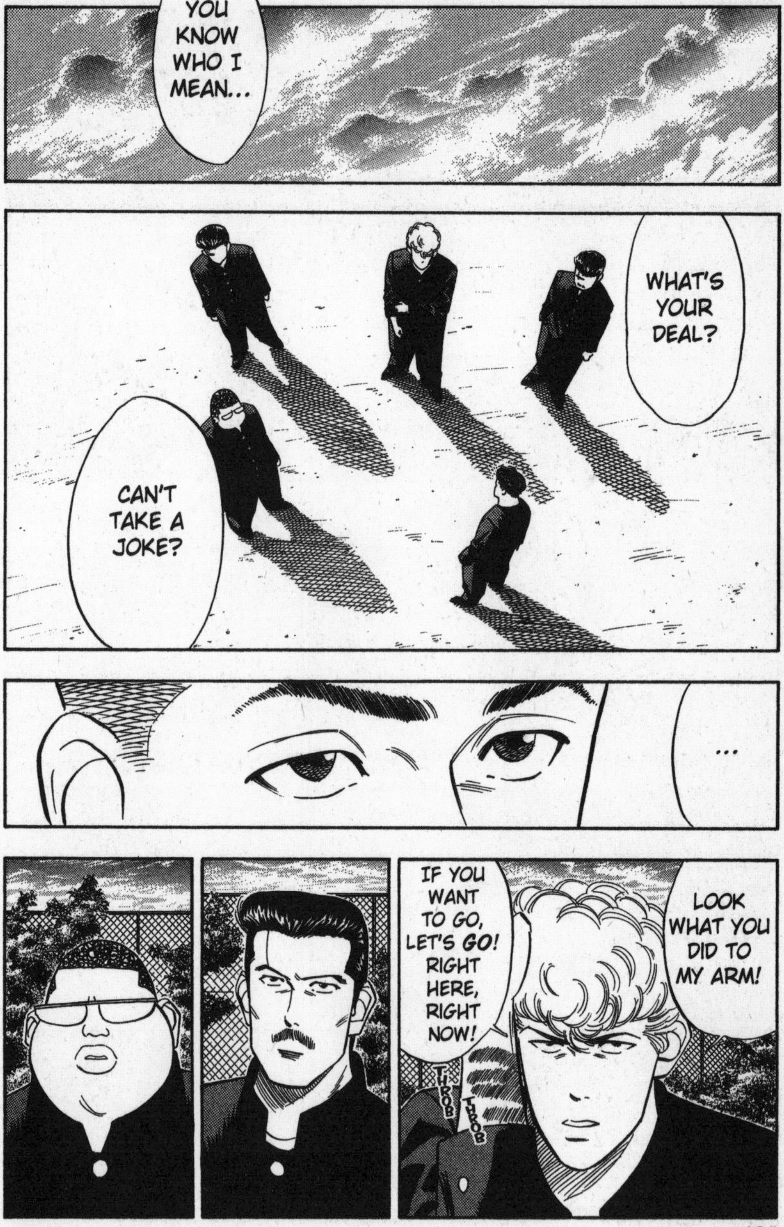
YOU KNOW WHO I MEAN...
WHAT'S YOUR DEAL?
CAN'T TAKE A JOKE?
...
LOOK WHAT YOU DID TO MY ARM!
IF YOU WANT TO GO, LET'S GO! RIGHT HERE, RIGHT NOW!
THROB
THROB

READ THIS WAY

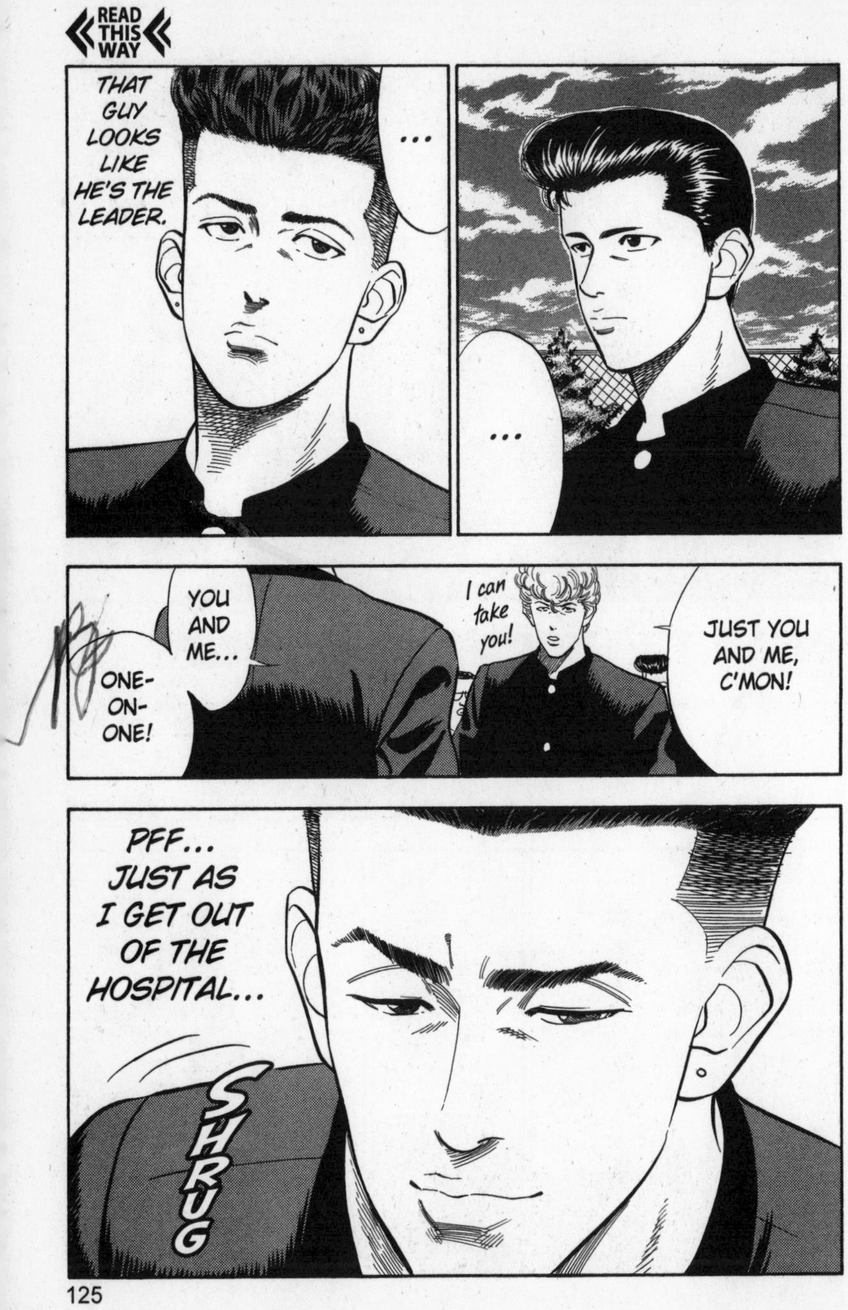
...
...
THAT GUY LOOKS LIKE HE'S THE LEADER.
JUST YOU AND ME, C'MON!
I can take you!
YOU AND ME...
ONE-ON-ONE!
PFF... JUST AS I GET OUT OF THE HOSPITAL...
SHRUG

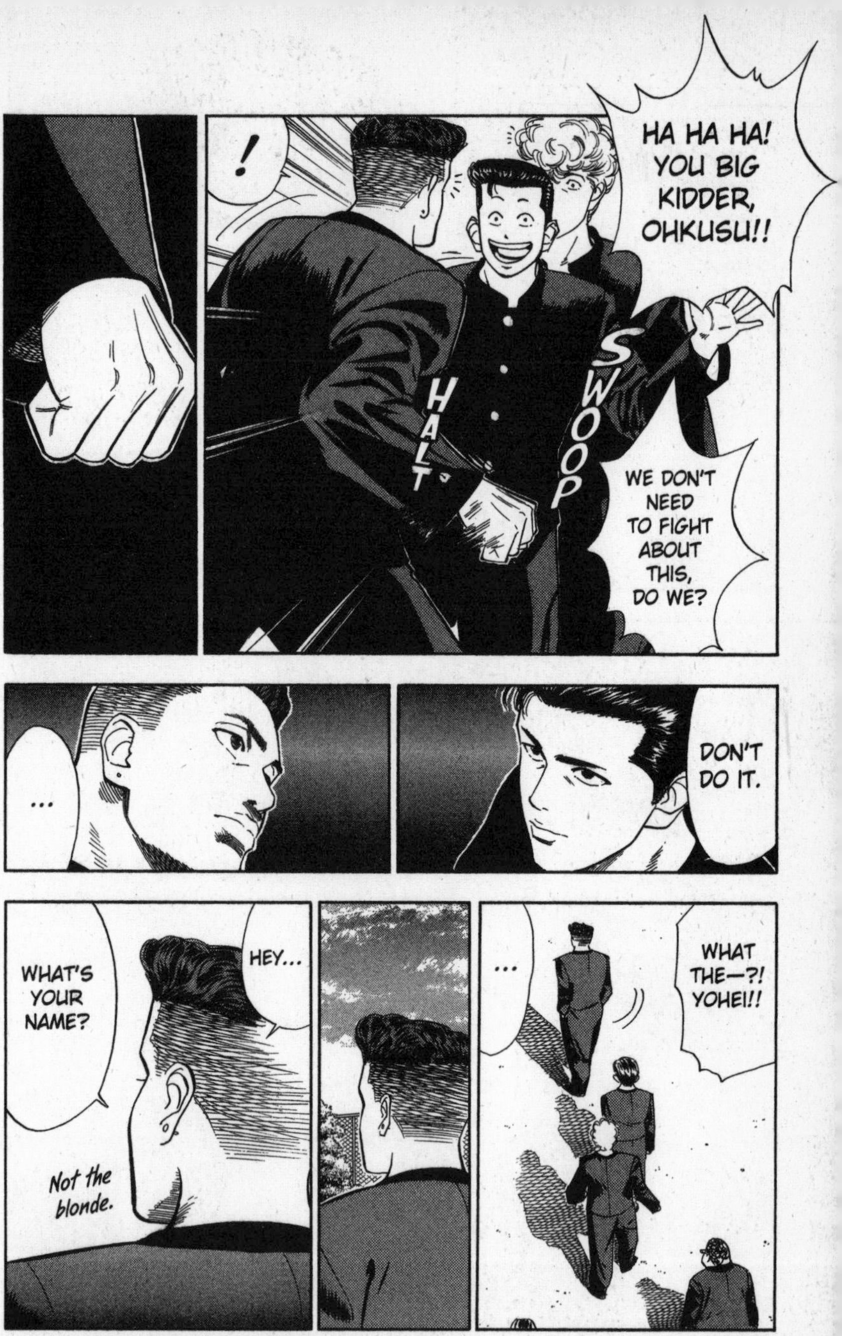
HA HA HA! YOU BIG KIDDER, OHKUSU!!
!
SWOOP
HALT
WE DON'T NEED TO FIGHT ABOUT THIS, DO WE?
DON'T DO IT.
...
WHAT THE—?! YOHEI!!
...
HEY...
WHAT'S YOUR NAME?
Not the blonde.

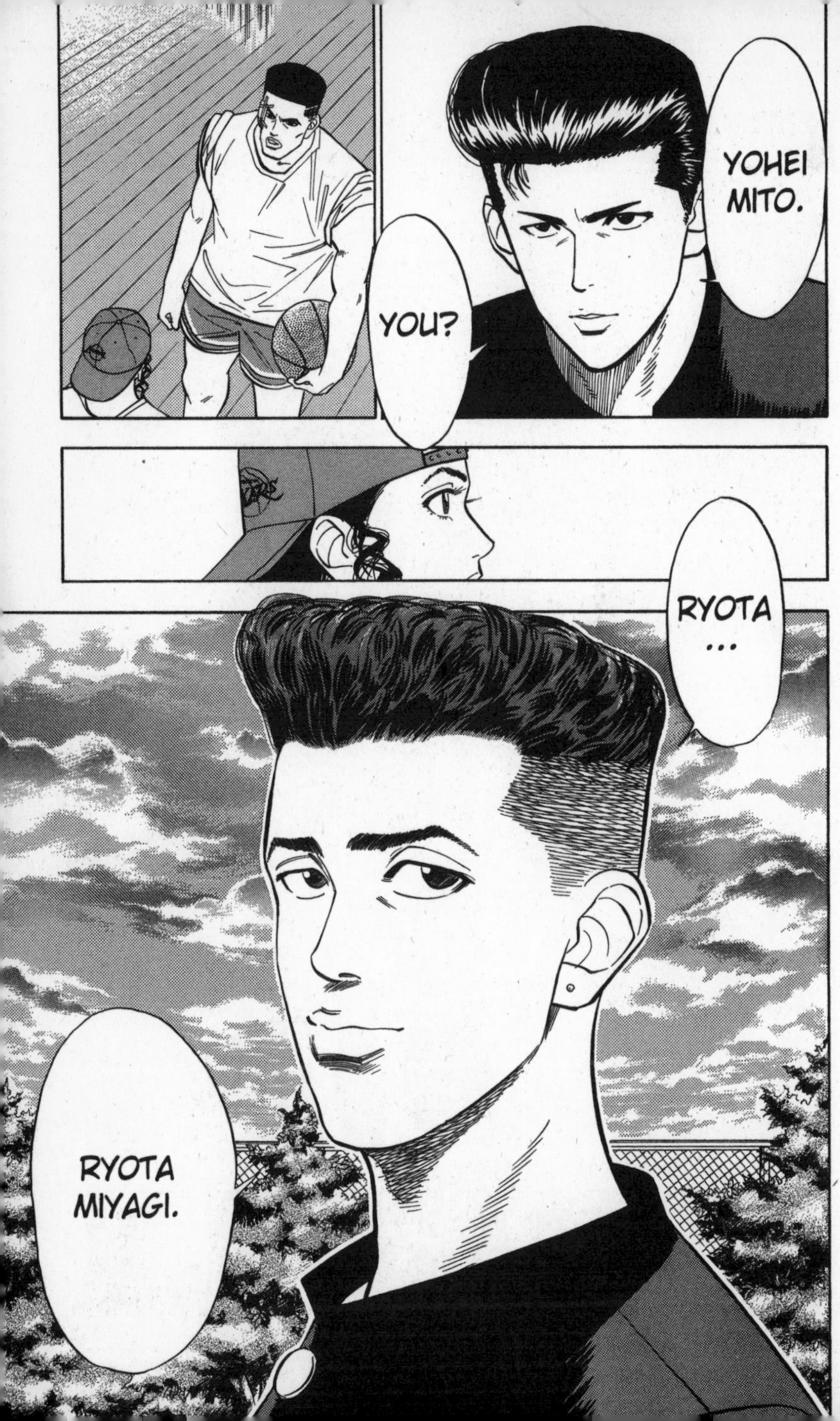
YOHEI MITO.
YOU?
RYOTA ...
RYOTA MIYAGI.

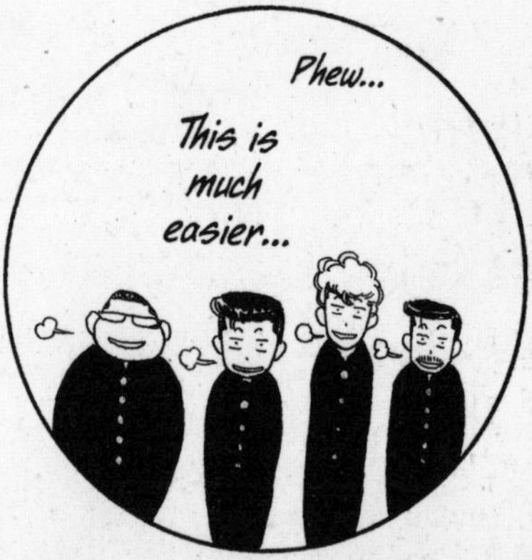
Phew...
This is much easier...

SLAM DUNK

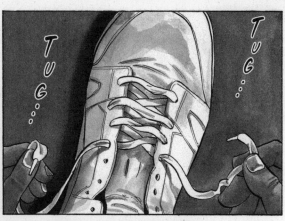

*TUG...*

*TUG...*

*TUG...*

# #51 SUPER PROBLEM CHILD

HM?

MIYAGI!!

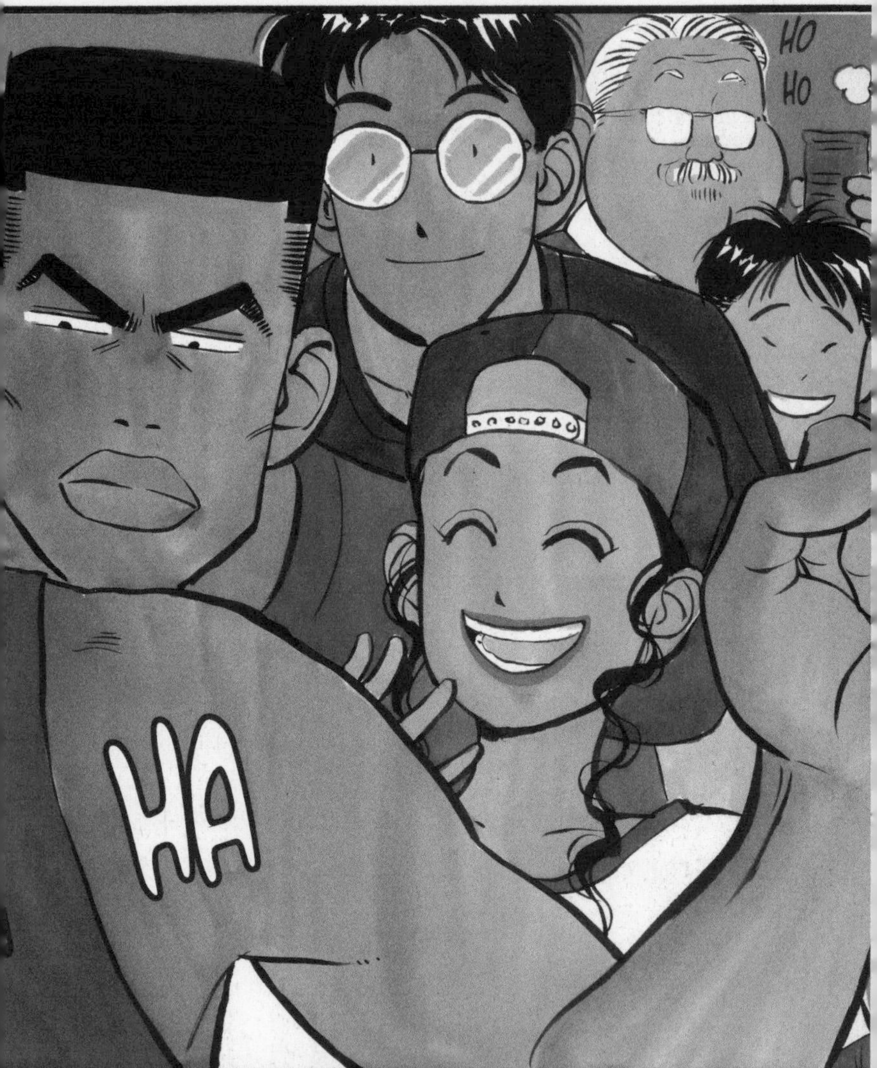
HO
HO
HA

# SUPER PROBLEM CHILD

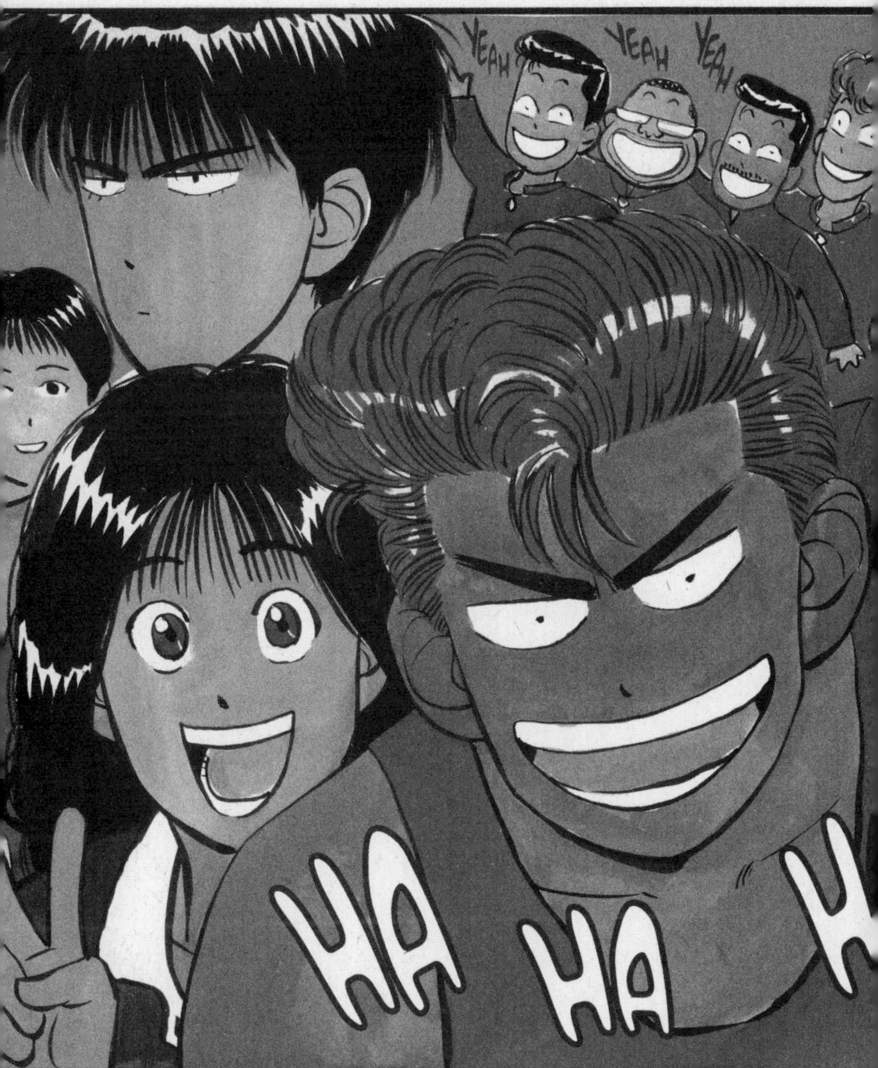
YEAH
YEAH
YEAH
HA HA H

# #51

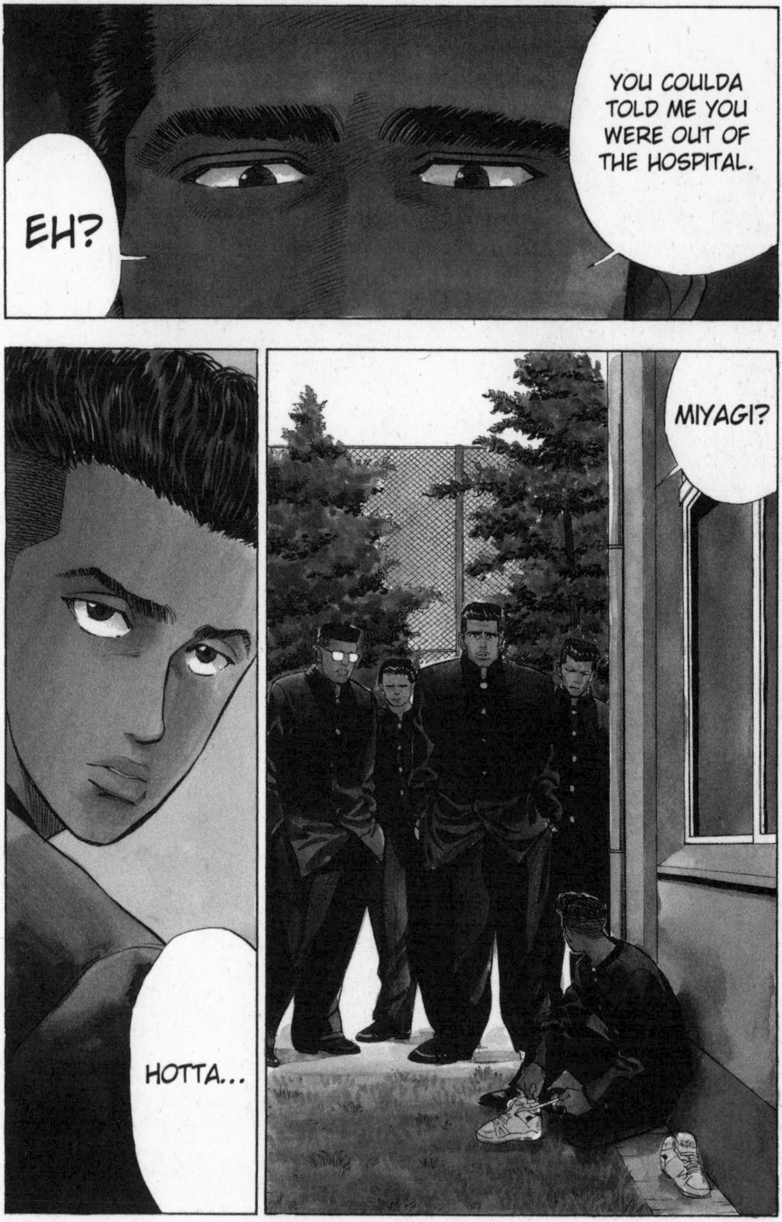
YOU COULDA TOLD ME YOU WERE OUT OF THE HOSPITAL.
EH?
MIYAGI?
HOTTA...

READ THIS WAY

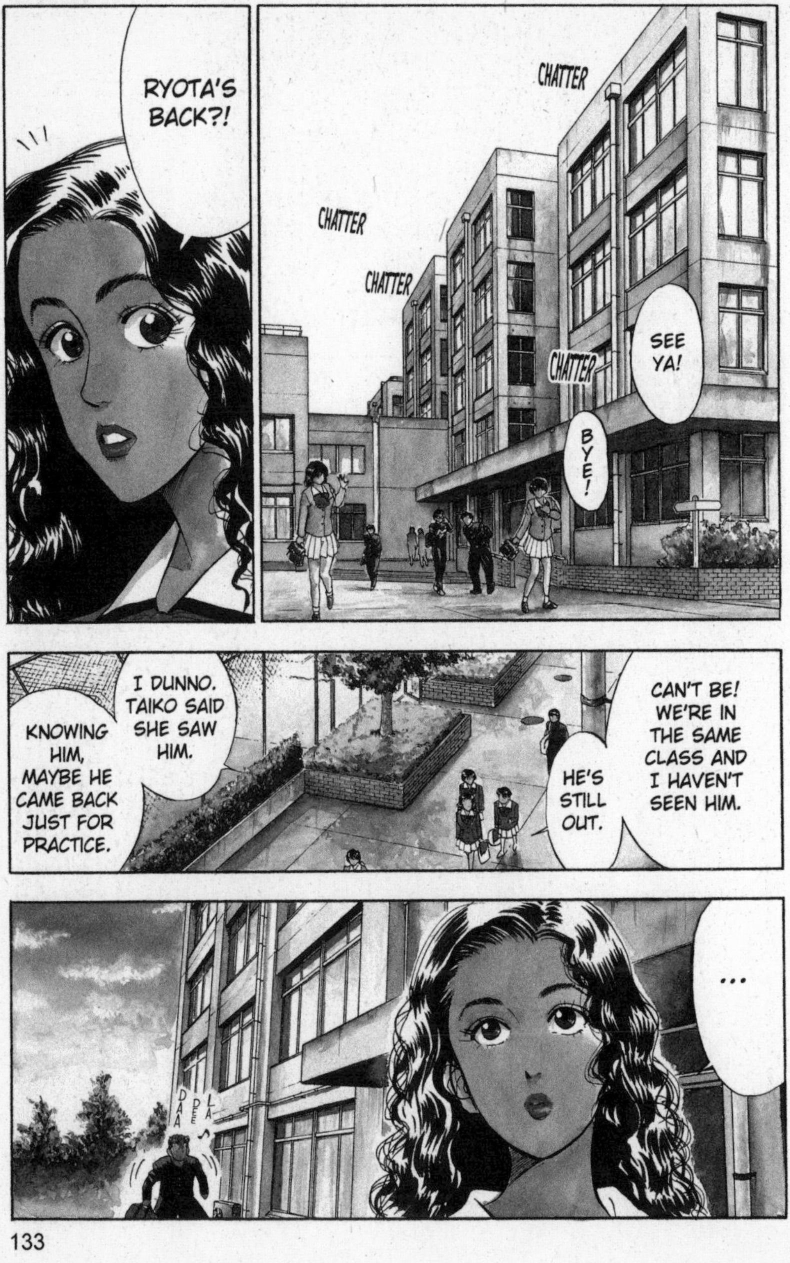
CHATTER
SEE YA!
BYE!
CHATTER
CHATTER
CHATTER
RYOTA'S BACK?!
CAN'T BE! WE'RE IN THE SAME CLASS AND I HAVEN'T SEEN HIM.
HE'S STILL OUT.
I DUNNO. TAIKO SAID SHE SAW HIM.
KNOWING HIM, MAYBE HE CAME BACK JUST FOR PRACTICE.
...
DA DE LA

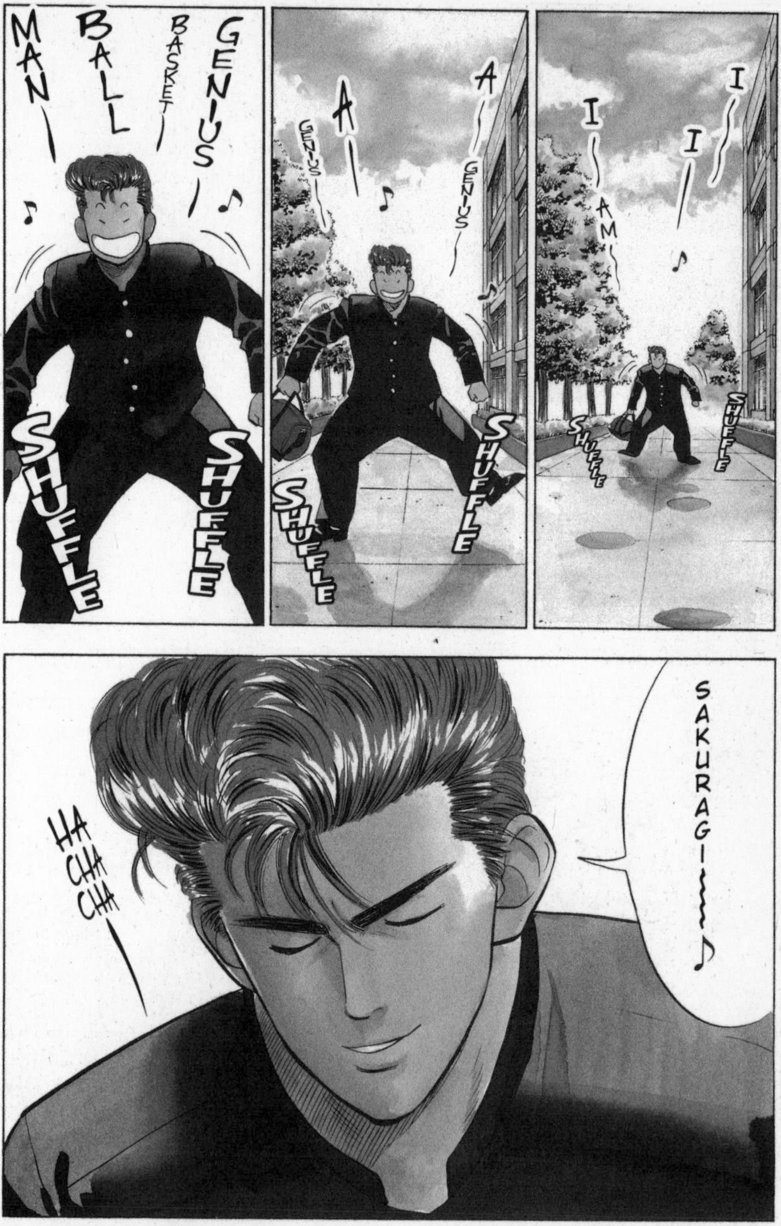
I~
I~
I~ AM~
SHUFFLE
SHUFFLE
A—
GENIUS—
A—
GENIUS—
SHUFFLE
SHUFFLE
GENIUS—
BASKET—
BALL
MAN—
SHUFFLE
SHUFFLE
SAKURAGI~♪
HA CHA CHA—

READ THIS WAY

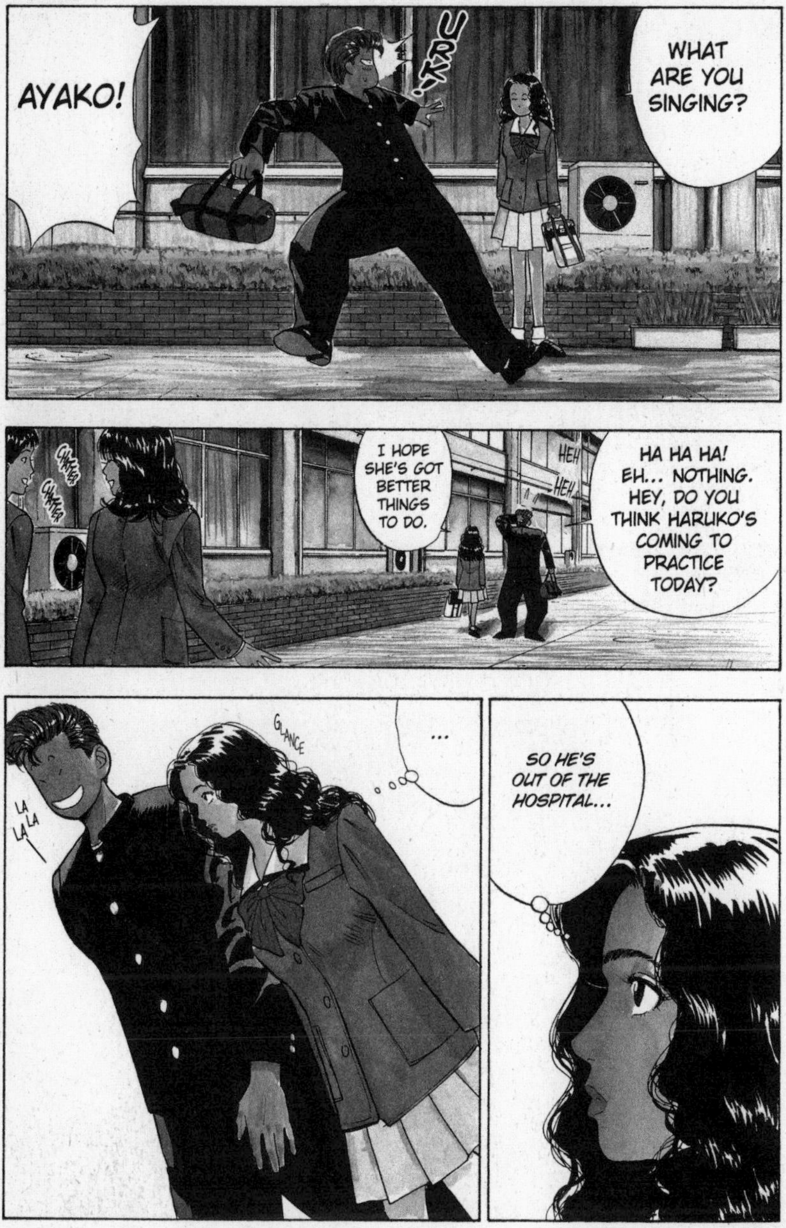
WHAT ARE YOU SINGING?
URK!
AYAKO!
HA HA HA! EH... NOTHING. HEY, DO YOU THINK HARUKO'S COMING TO PRACTICE TODAY?
HEH HEH
I HOPE SHE'S GOT BETTER THINGS TO DO.
CHATTER CHATTER
SO HE'S OUT OF THE HOSPITAL...
...
GLANCE
LA LA LA

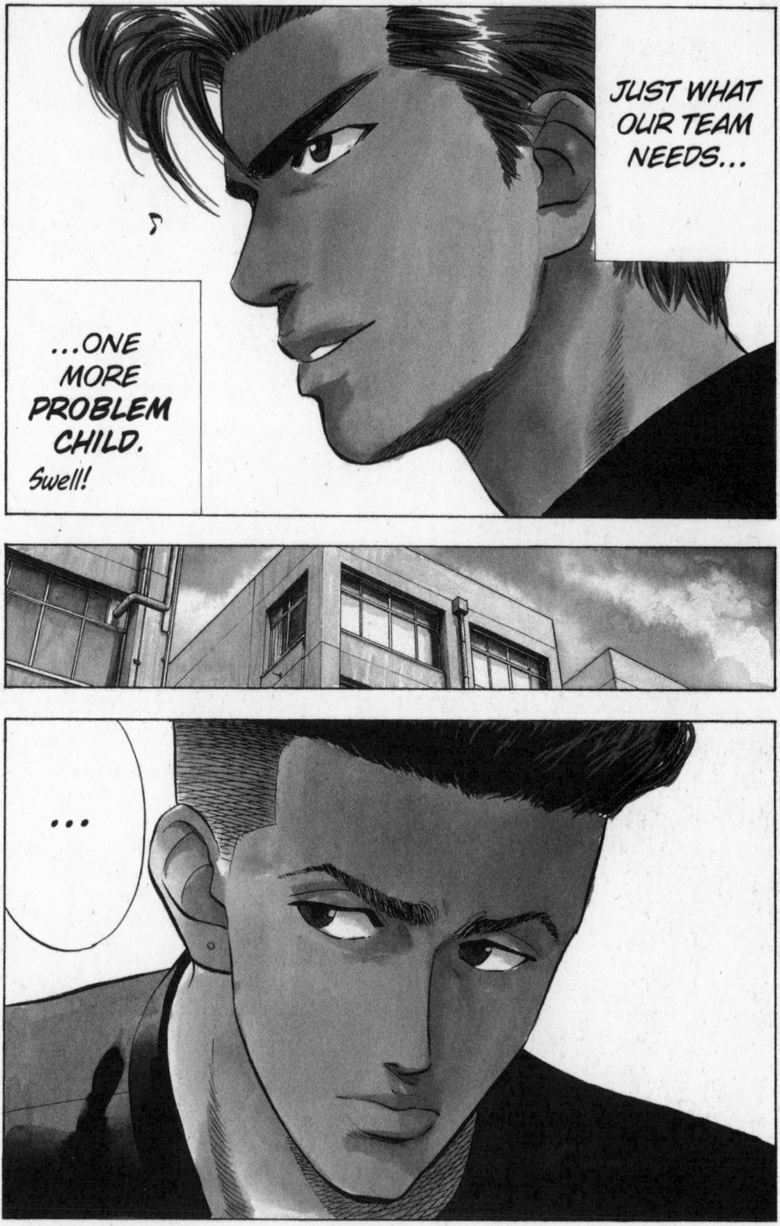
JUST WHAT OUR TEAM NEEDS...
...ONE MORE PROBLEM CHILD.
Swell!
...

READ THIS WAY

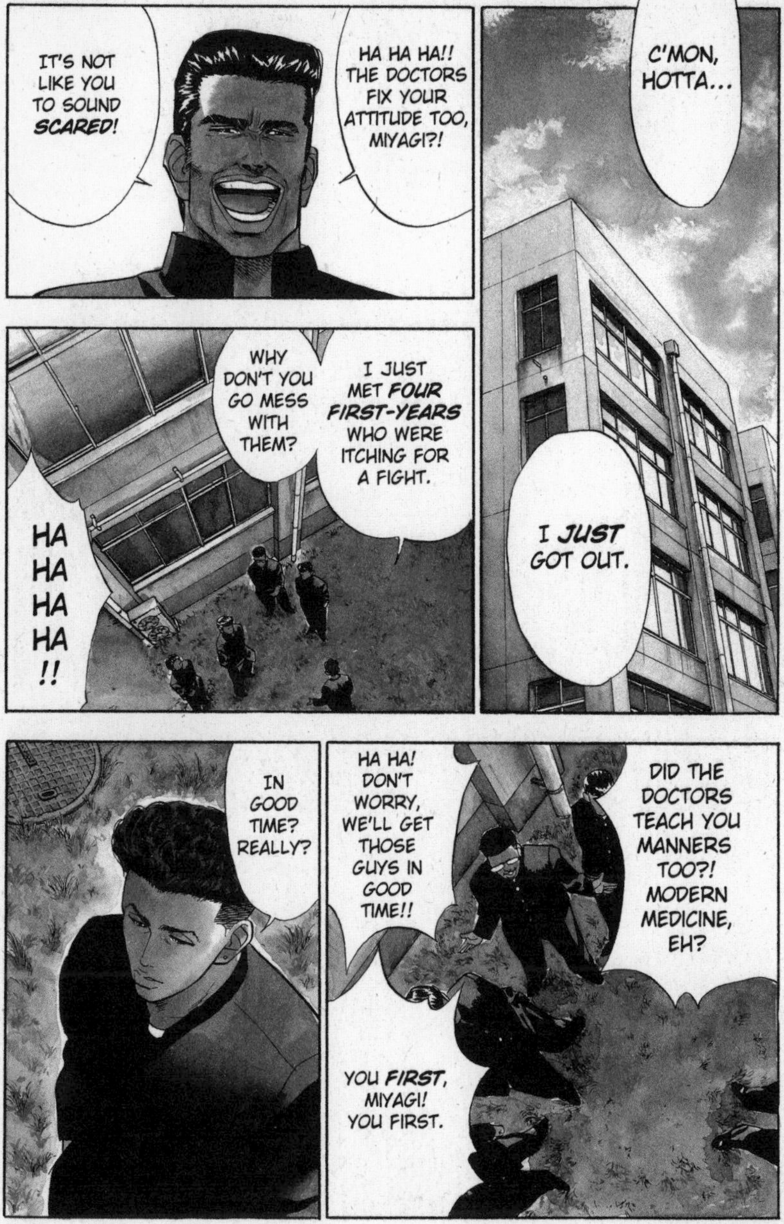

C'MON, HOTTA...
I JUST GOT OUT.
HA HA HA!! THE DOCTORS FIX YOUR ATTITUDE TOO, MIYAGI?!
IT'S NOT LIKE YOU TO SOUND SCARED!
I JUST MET FOUR FIRST-YEARS WHO WERE ITCHING FOR A FIGHT.
WHY DON'T YOU GO MESS WITH THEM?
HA HA HA HA!!
DID THE DOCTORS TEACH YOU MANNERS TOO?! MODERN MEDICINE, EH?
HA HA! DON'T WORRY, WE'LL GET THOSE GUYS IN GOOD TIME!!
YOU FIRST, MIYAGI! YOU FIRST.
IN GOOD TIME? REALLY?

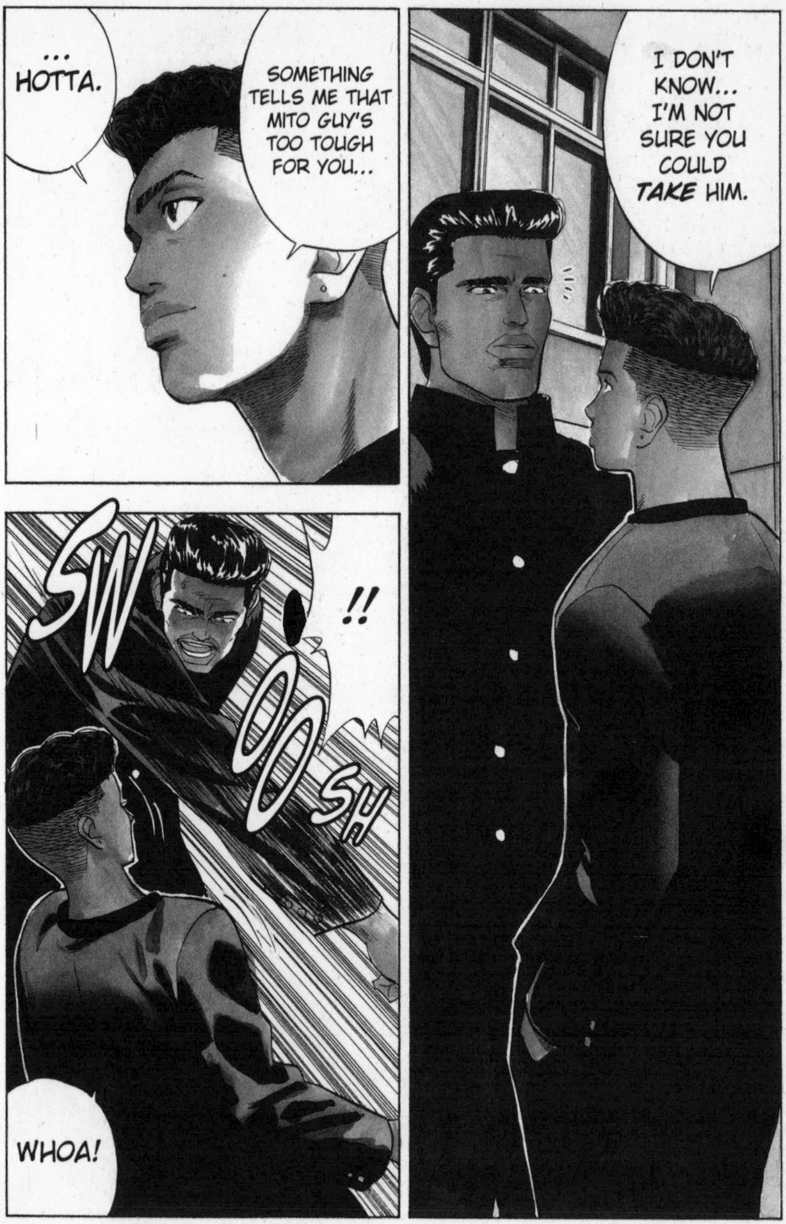
I DON'T KNOW... I'M NOT SURE YOU COULD *TAKE* HIM.
SOMETHING TELLS ME THAT MITO GUY'S TOO TOUGH FOR YOU...
... HOTTA.
!!
SWOOOSH
WHOA!

MITSUI
...

STEP

TAP

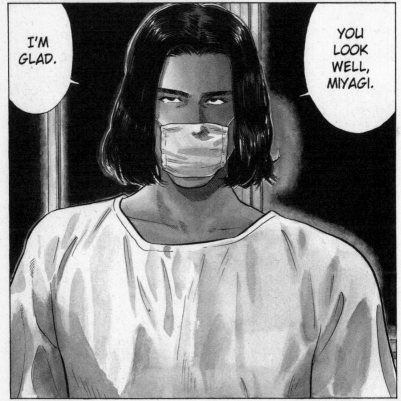

I'M GLAD.

YOU LOOK WELL, MIYAGI.

139

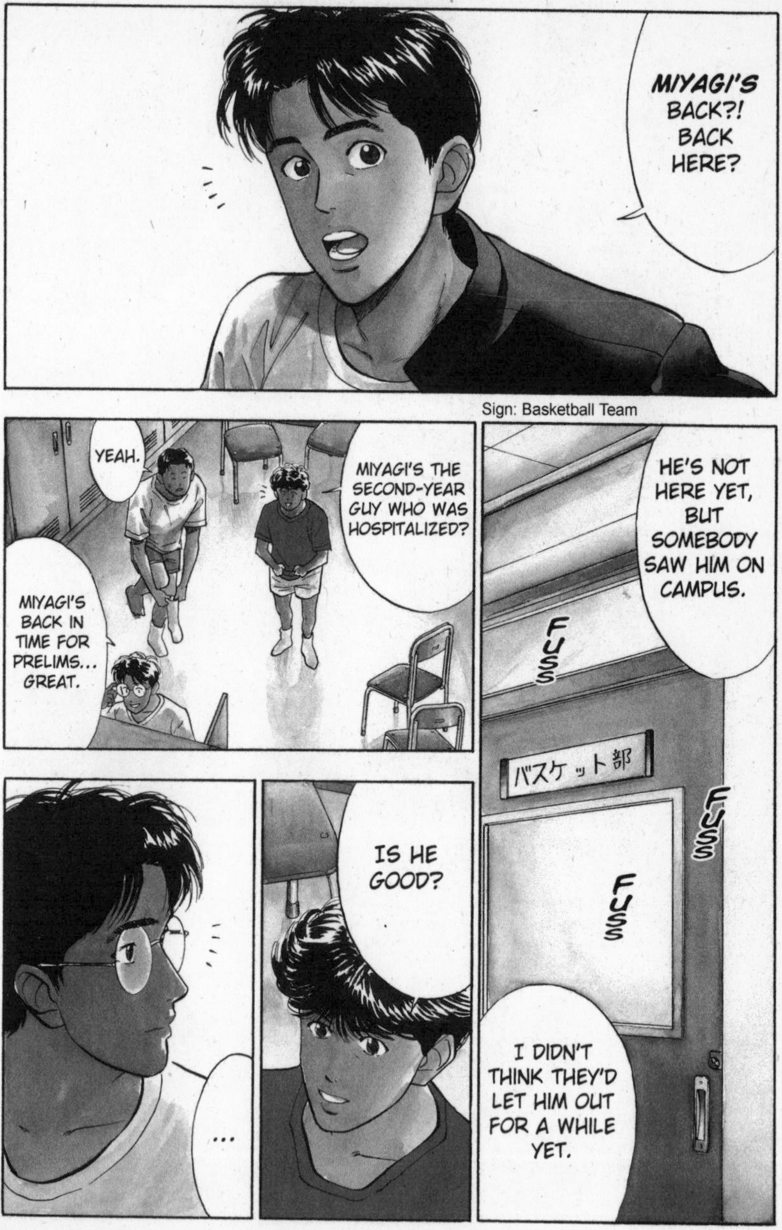
MIYAGI'S BACK?! BACK HERE?
HE'S NOT HERE YET, BUT SOMEBODY SAW HIM ON CAMPUS.
FUSS
バスケット部
FUSS
FUSS
I DIDN'T THINK THEY'D LET HIM OUT FOR A WHILE YET.
MIYAGI'S THE SECOND-YEAR GUY WHO WAS HOSPITALIZED?
YEAH.
MIYAGI'S BACK IN TIME FOR PRELIMS... GREAT.
IS HE GOOD?
...
Sign: Basketball Team

READ THIS WAY

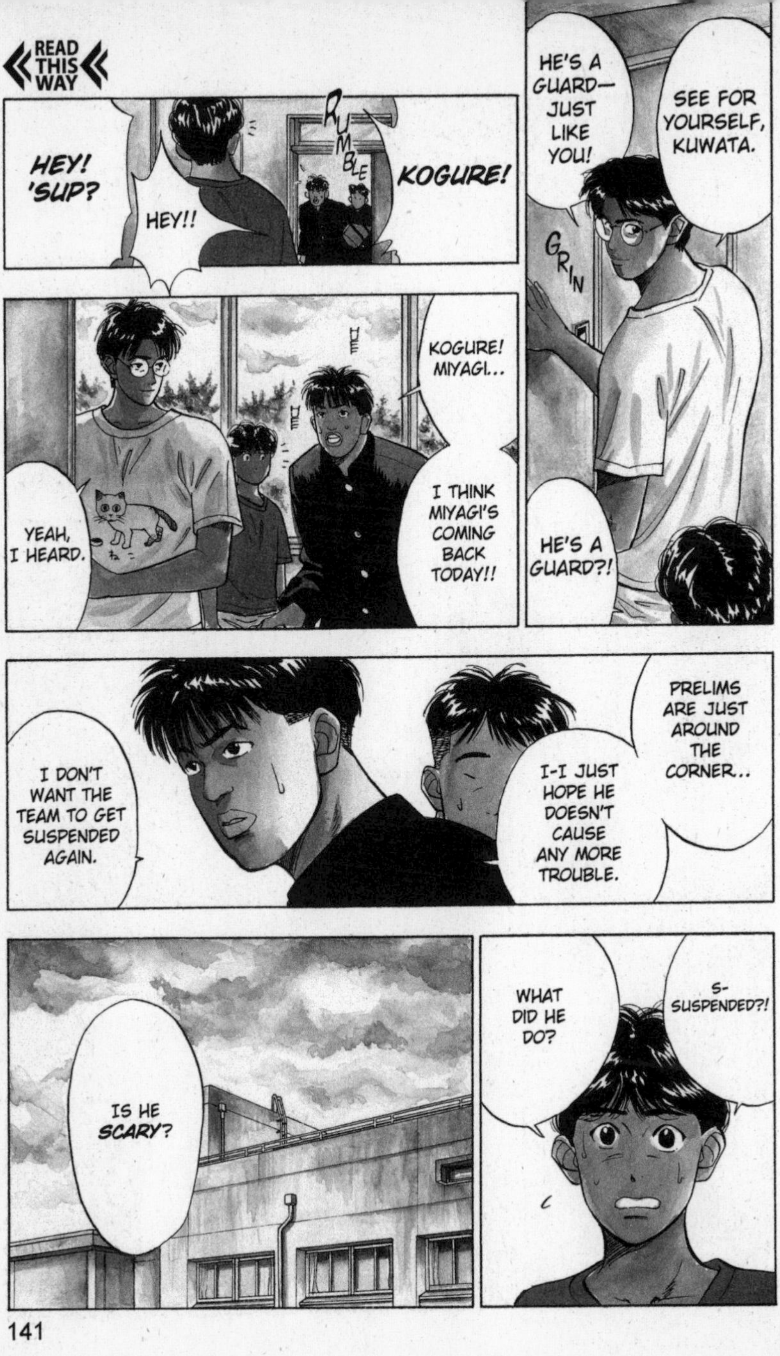
SEE FOR YOURSELF, KUWATA.
HE'S A GUARD— JUST LIKE YOU!
GRIN
HE'S A GUARD?!
RUMBLE
KOGURE!
HEY!!
HEY! 'SUP?
KOGURE! MIYAGI...
HE HE
I THINK MIYAGI'S COMING BACK TODAY!!
YEAH, I HEARD.
PRELIMS ARE JUST AROUND THE CORNER..
I-I JUST HOPE HE DOESN'T CAUSE ANY MORE TROUBLE.
I DON'T WANT THE TEAM TO GET SUSPENDED AGAIN.
S-SUSPENDED?!
WHAT DID HE DO?
IS HE *SCARY*?

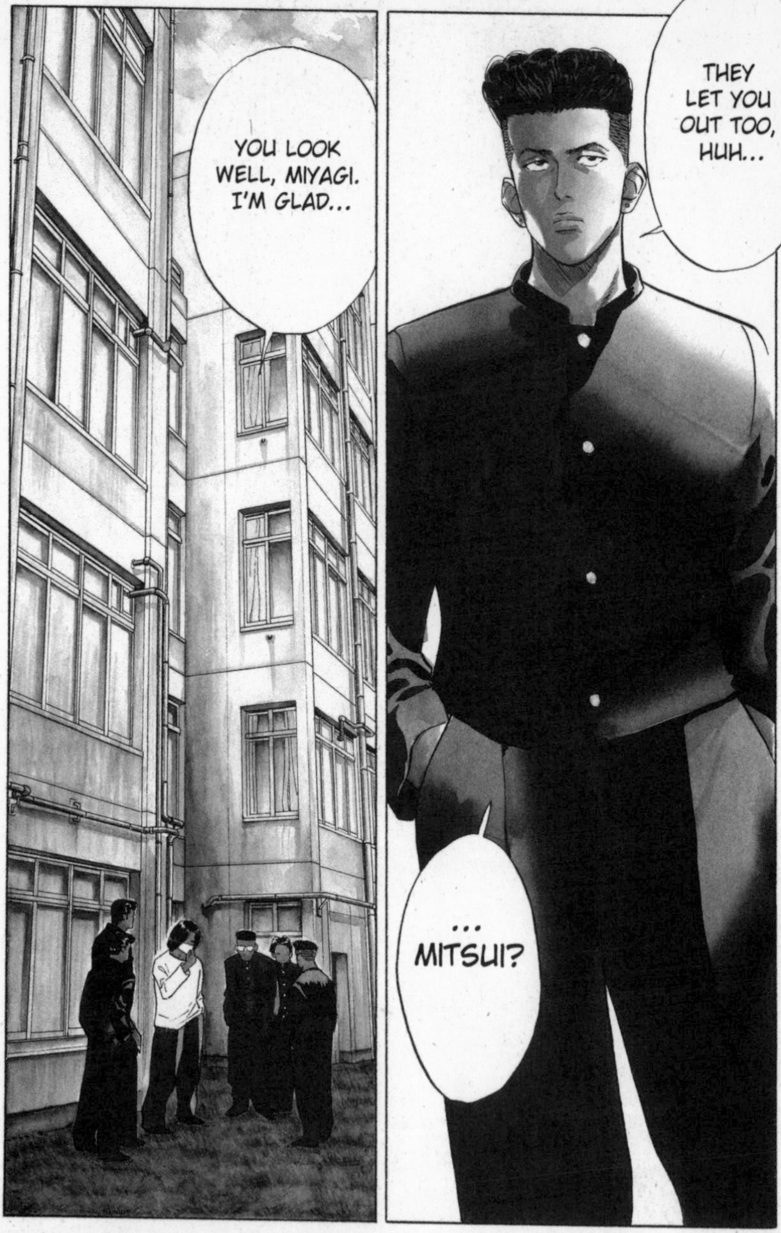
THEY LET YOU OUT TOO, HUH...
... MITSUI?
YOU LOOK WELL, MIYAGI. I'M GLAD...

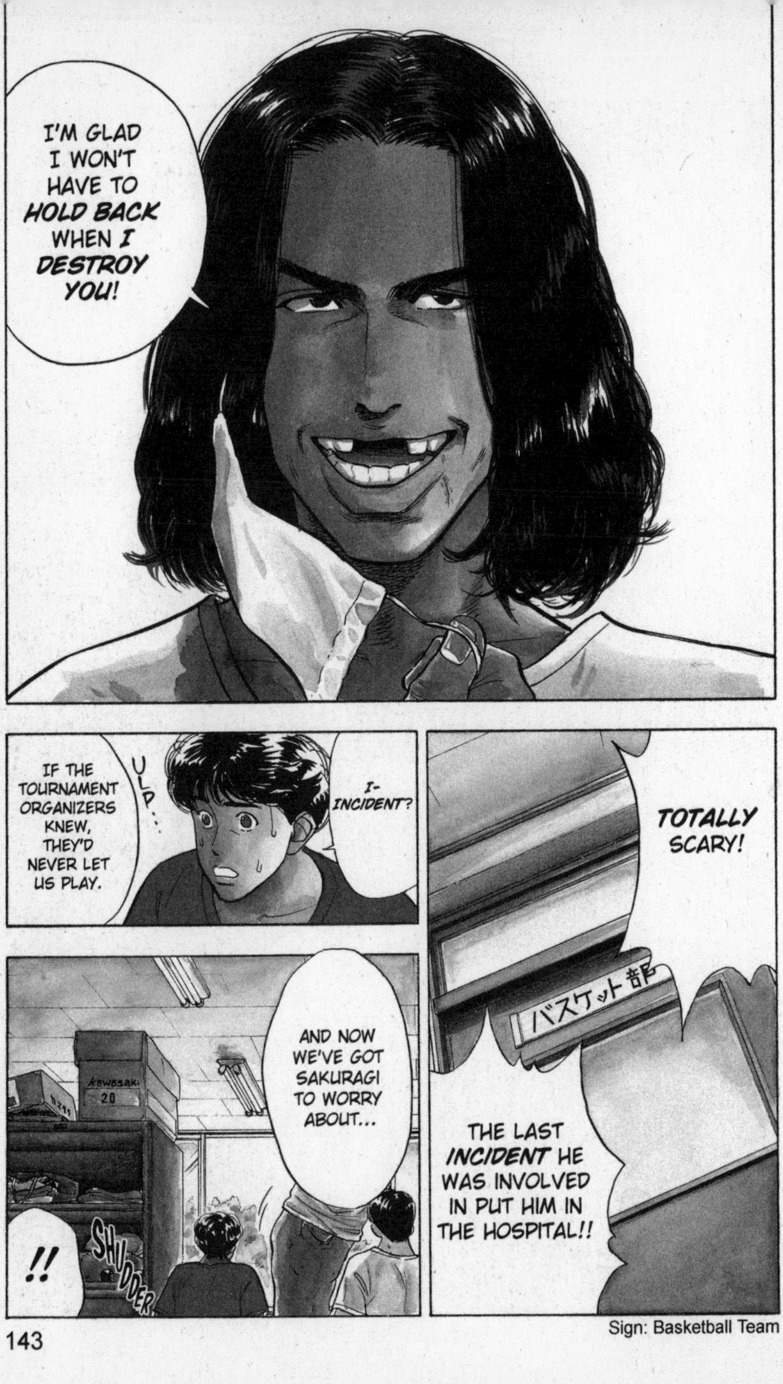
I'M GLAD I WON'T HAVE TO HOLD BACK WHEN I DESTROY YOU!
TOTALLY SCARY!
バスケット部
THE LAST INCIDENT HE WAS INVOLVED IN PUT HIM IN THE HOSPITAL!!
I- INCIDENT?
ULP...
IF THE TOURNAMENT ORGANIZERS KNEW, THEY'D NEVER LET US PLAY.
AND NOW WE'VE GOT SAKURAGI TO WORRY ABOUT...
SHUDDER
!!
Sign: Basketball Team

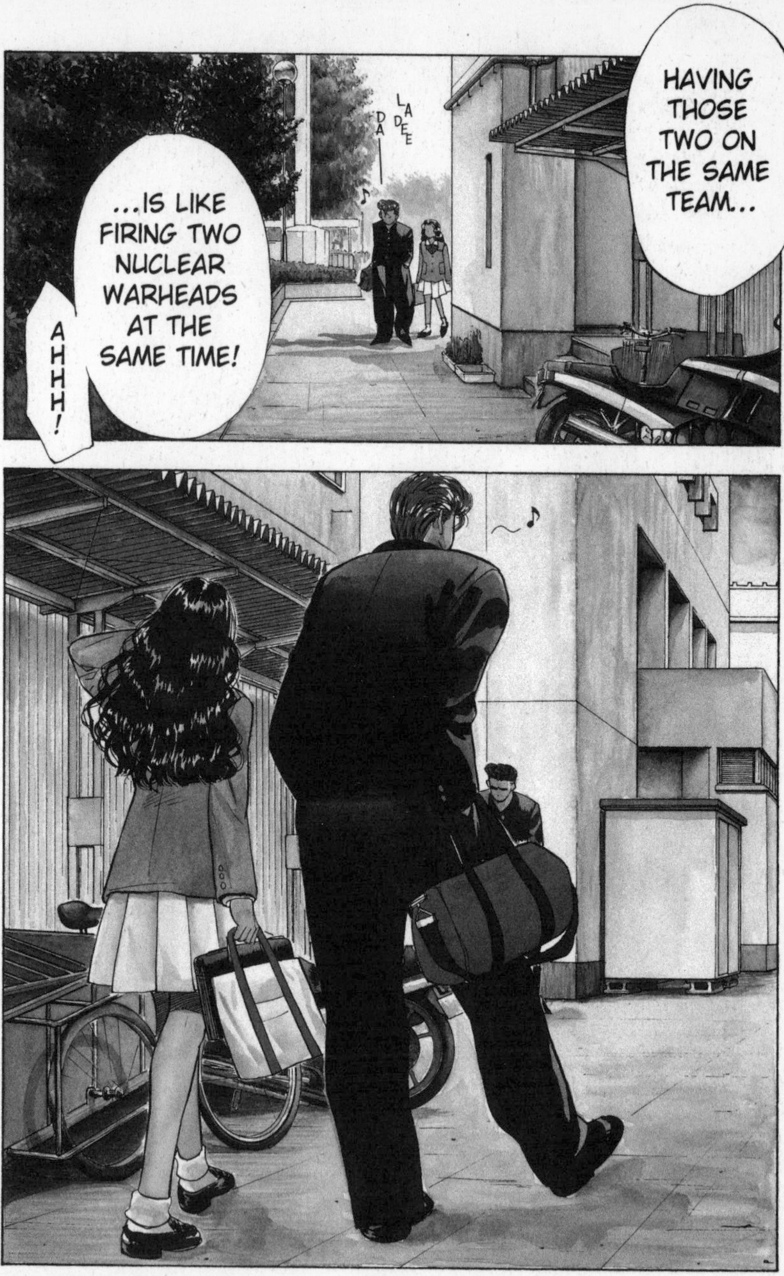
HAVING THOSE TWO ON THE SAME TEAM...
LA DEE DA
...IS LIKE FIRING TWO NUCLEAR WARHEADS AT THE SAME TIME!
AHHH!

READ THIS WAY

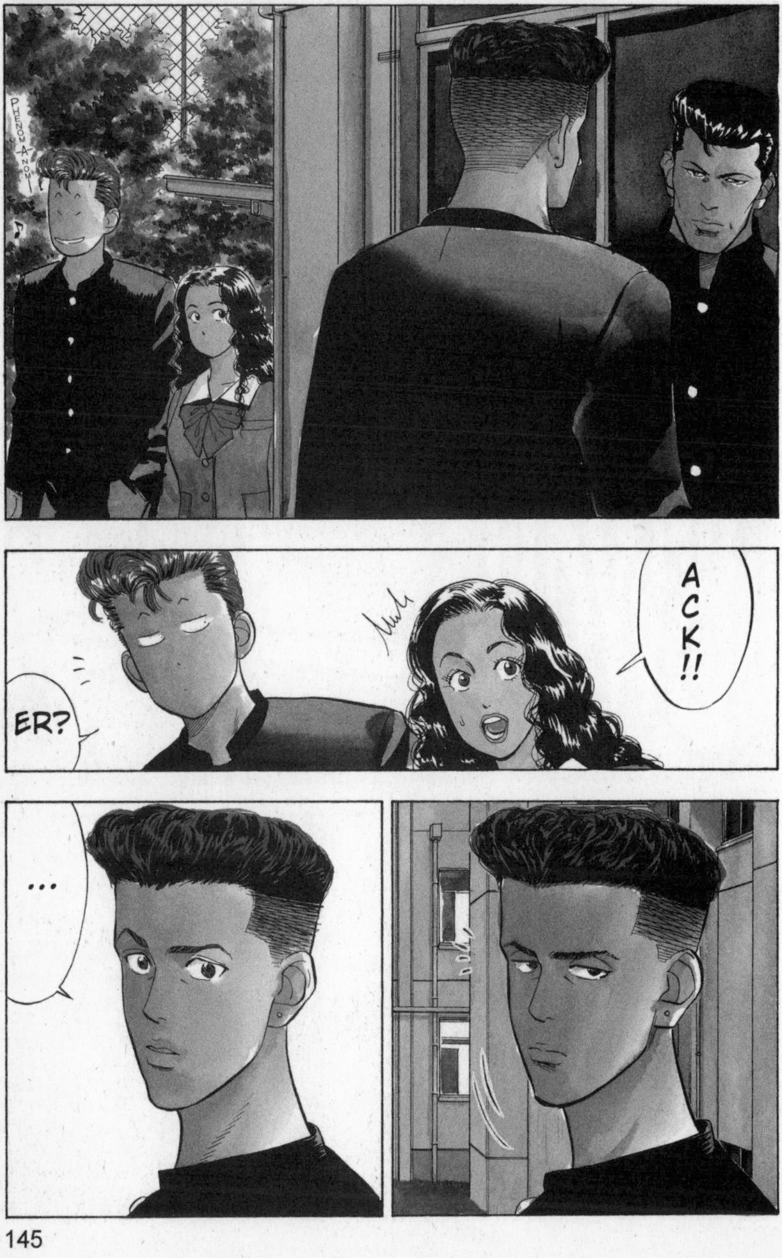
PHENOM-A-NOM
♪
ACK!!
ER?
...

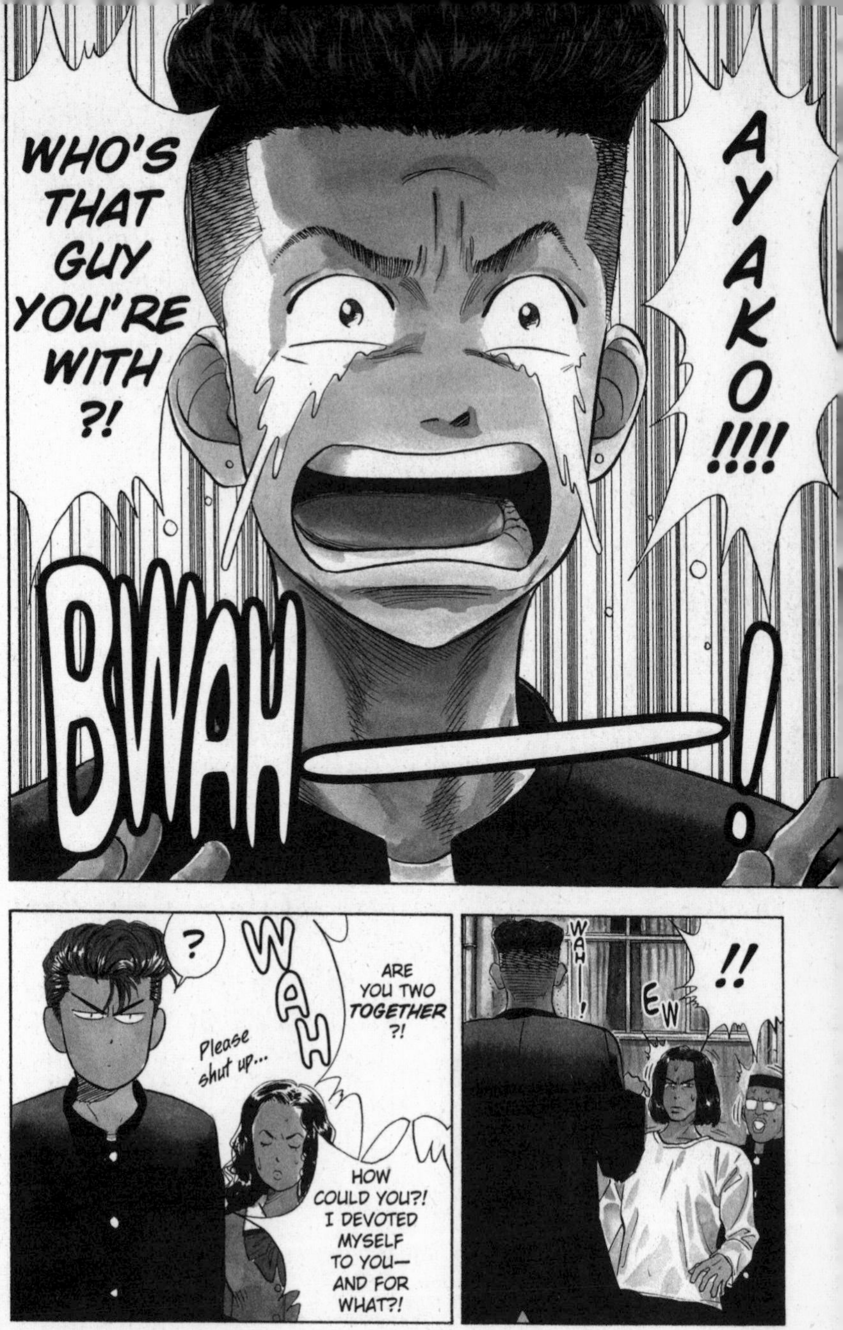
AYAKO!!!!
WHO'S THAT GUY YOU'RE WITH?!
BWAH!
WAH!
EW!!
ARE YOU TWO TOGETHER?!
WAH
?
Please shut up...
HOW COULD YOU?! I DEVOTED MYSELF TO YOU— AND FOR WHAT?!

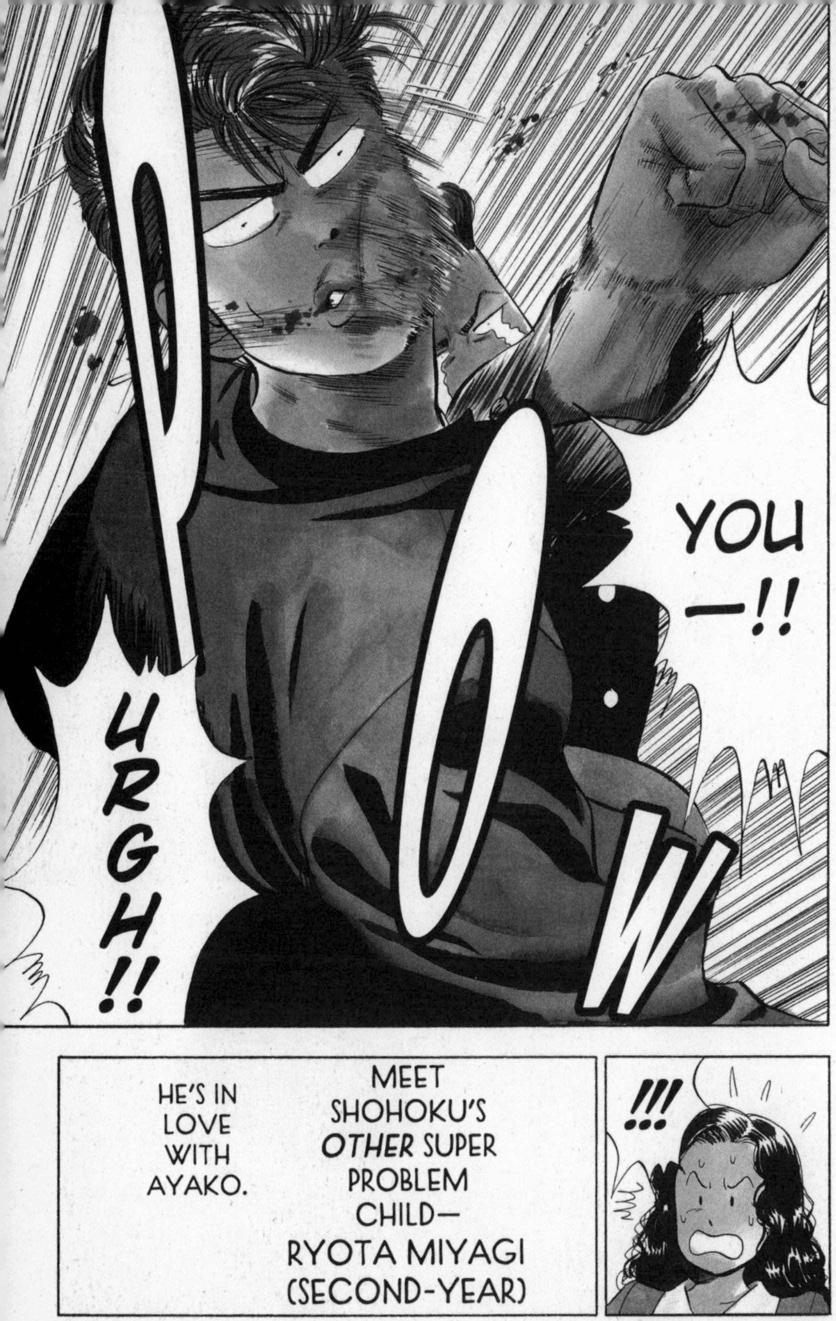
YOU—!!
POW
URGH!!
!!!
MEET SHOHOKU'S *OTHER* SUPER PROBLEM CHILD— RYOTA MIYAGI (SECOND-YEAR)
HE'S IN LOVE WITH AYAKO.

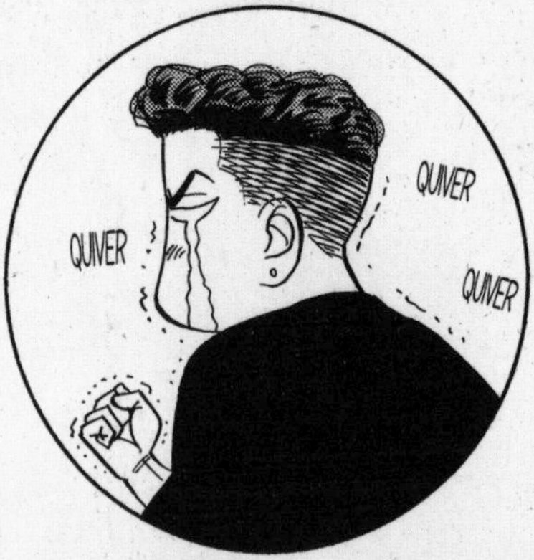
QUIVER
QUIVER
QUIVER

SLAM DUNK

# #52 AN INCIDENT

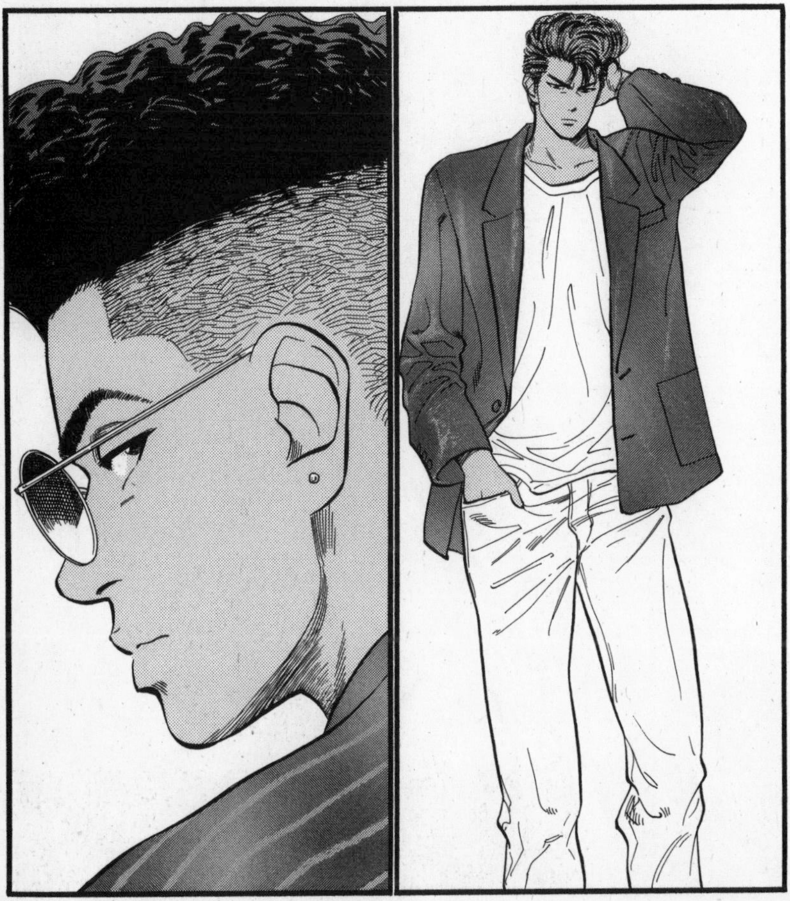

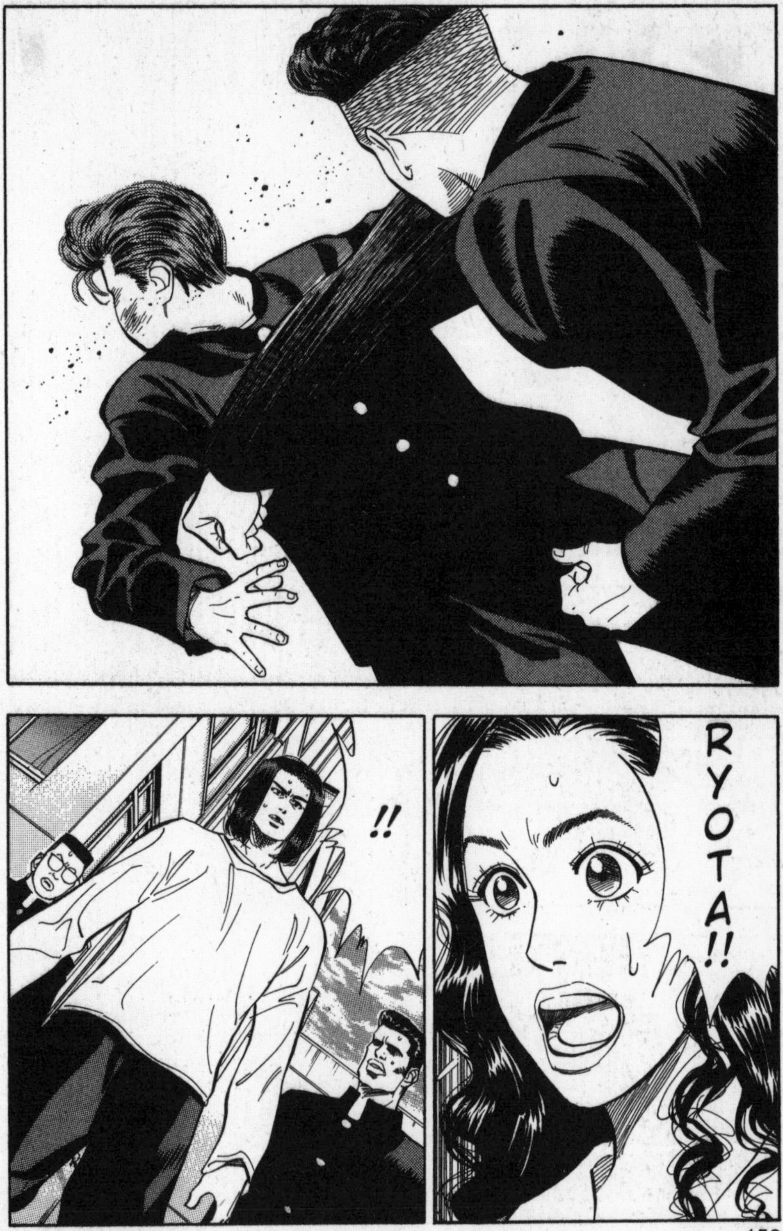

RYOTA!!
!!

READ THIS WAY

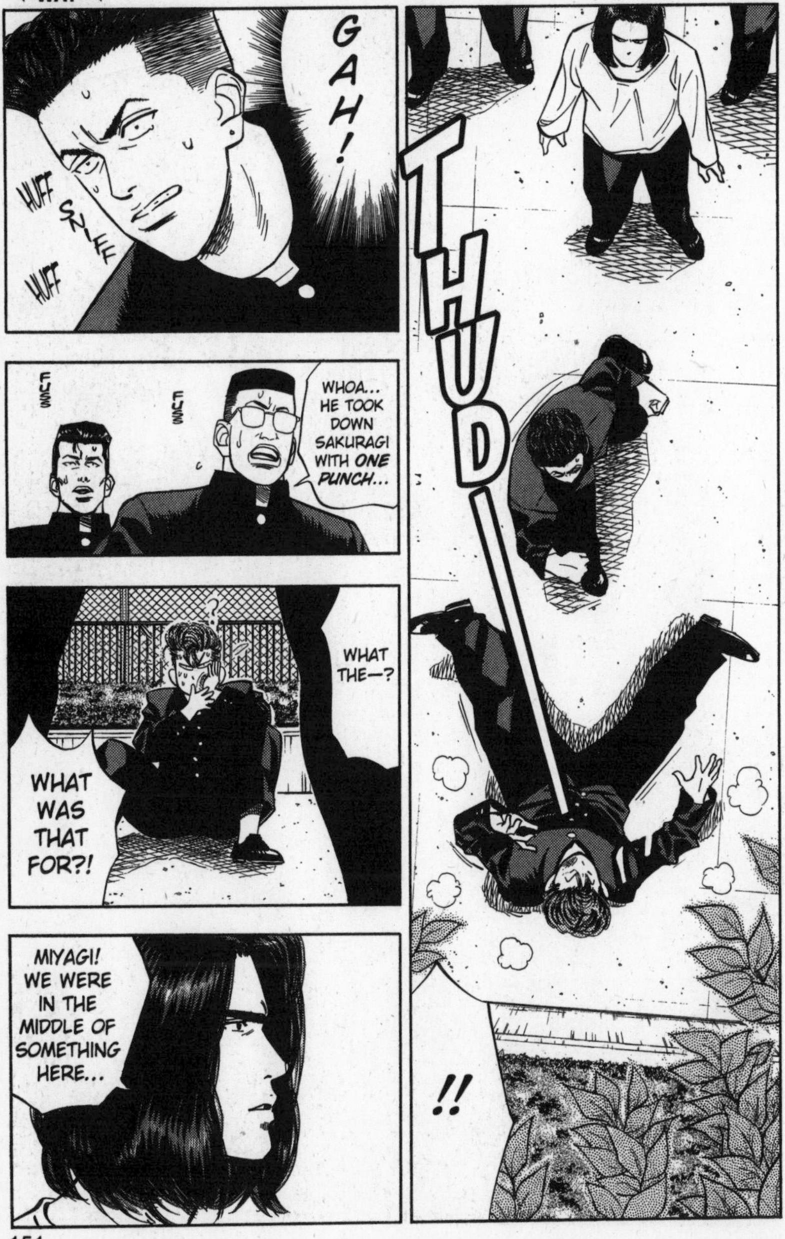
THUD!
!!
GAH!
HUFF
SNIFF
HUFF
FUSS
FUSS
WHOA... HE TOOK DOWN SAKURAGI WITH *ONE PUNCH*...
WHAT THE—?
WHAT WAS THAT FOR?!
MIYAGI! WE WERE IN THE MIDDLE OF SOMETHING HERE...

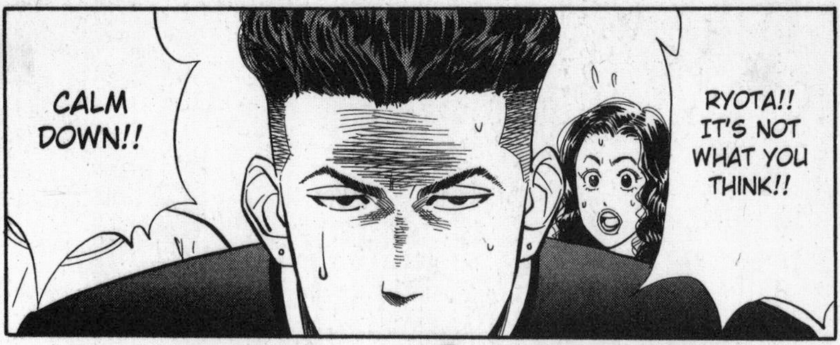
RYOTA!! IT'S NOT WHAT YOU THINK!!
CALM DOWN!!
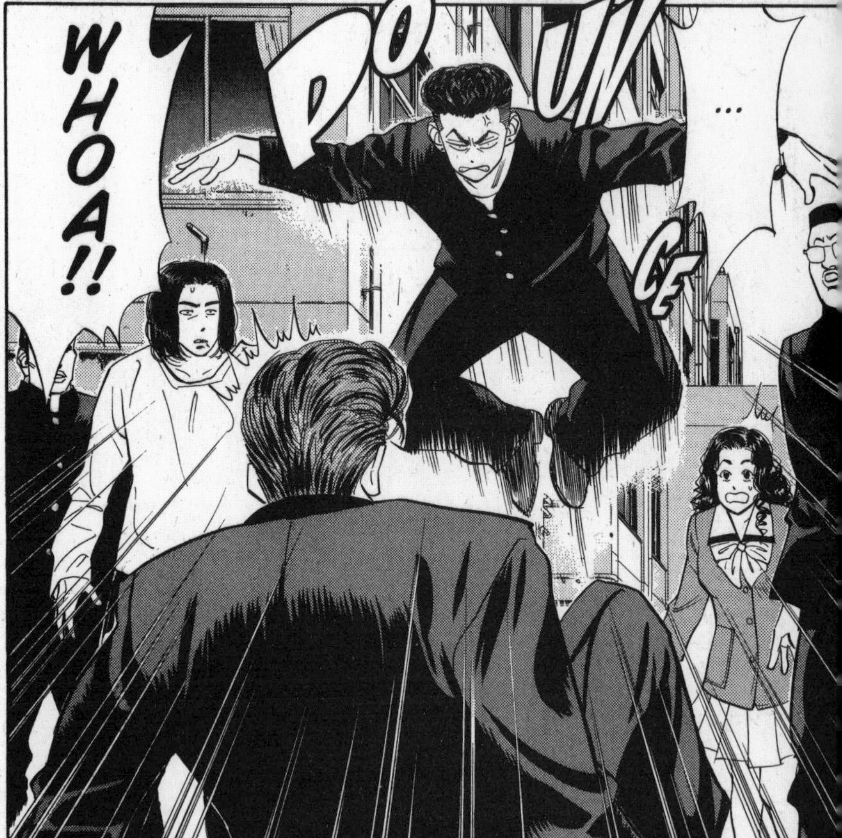
...
DOUNCE
WHOA!!

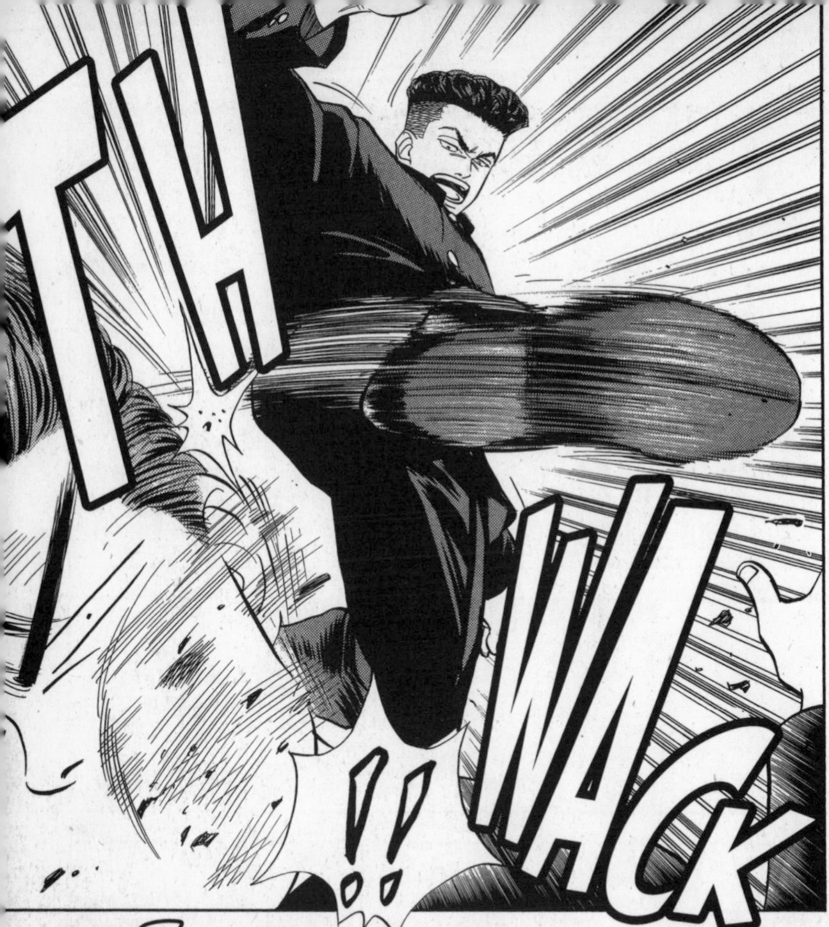
TH
WACK
!!
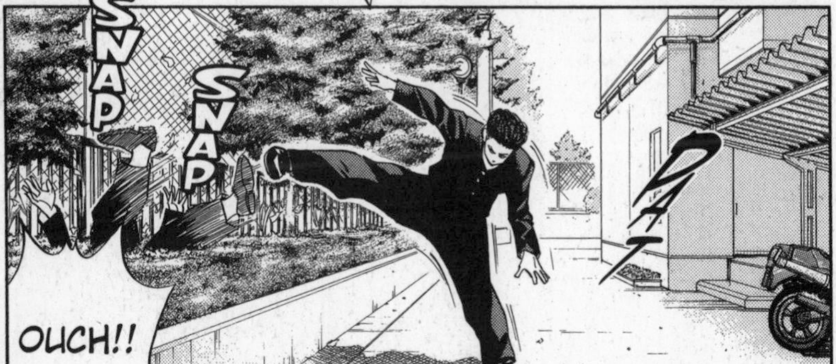
SNAP
SNAP
OUCH!!

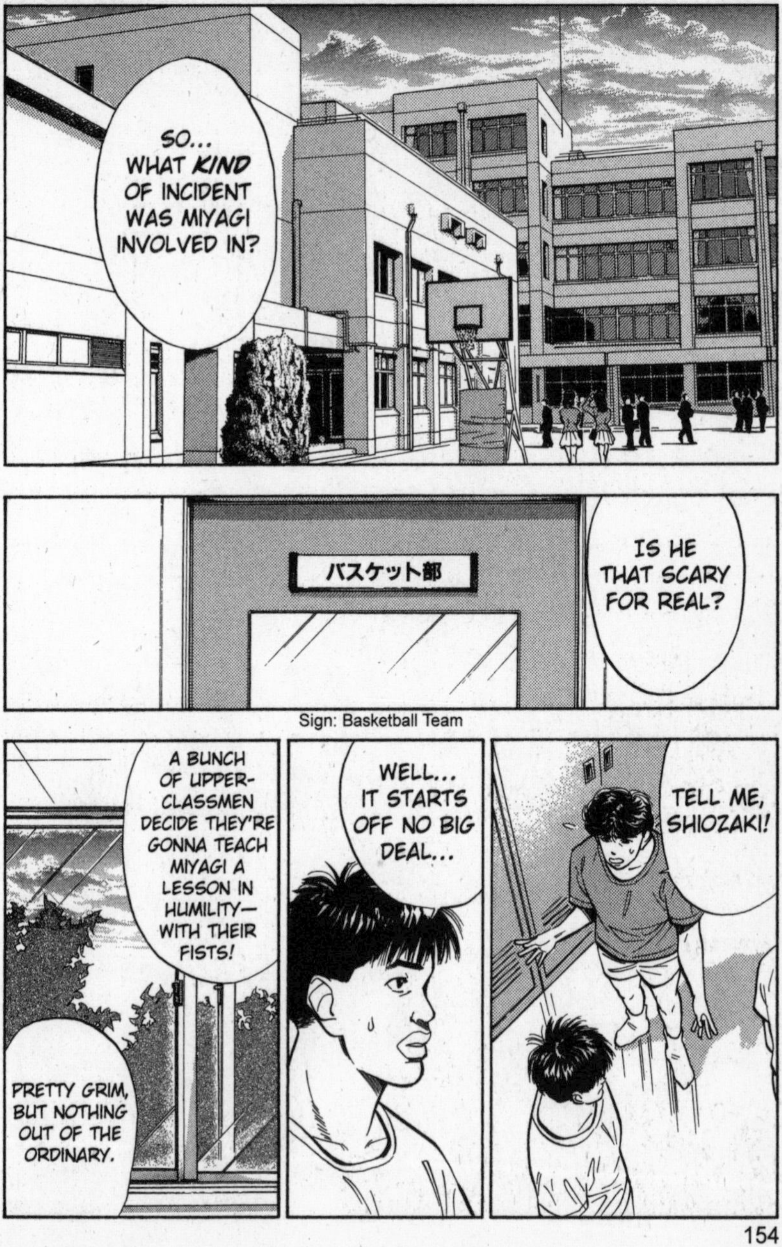
SO... WHAT KIND OF INCIDENT WAS MIYAGI INVOLVED IN?
IS HE THAT SCARY FOR REAL?
バスケット部
TELL ME, SHIOZAKI!
WELL... IT STARTS OFF NO BIG DEAL...
A BUNCH OF UPPER-CLASSMEN DECIDE THEY'RE GONNA TEACH MIYAGI A LESSON IN HUMILITY—WITH THEIR FISTS!
PRETTY GRIM, BUT NOTHING OUT OF THE ORDINARY.

Sign: Basketball Team

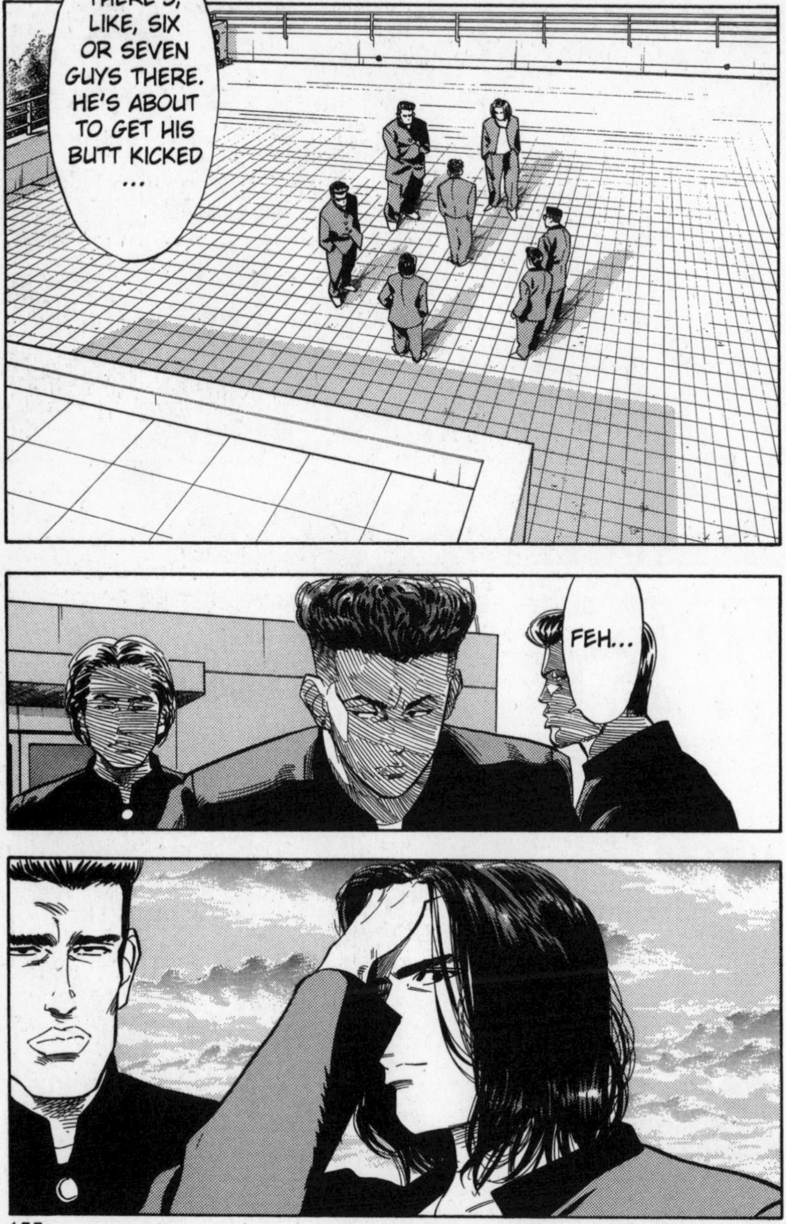
THERE'S, LIKE, SIX OR SEVEN GUYS THERE. HE'S ABOUT TO GET HIS BUTT KICKED ...
FEH...

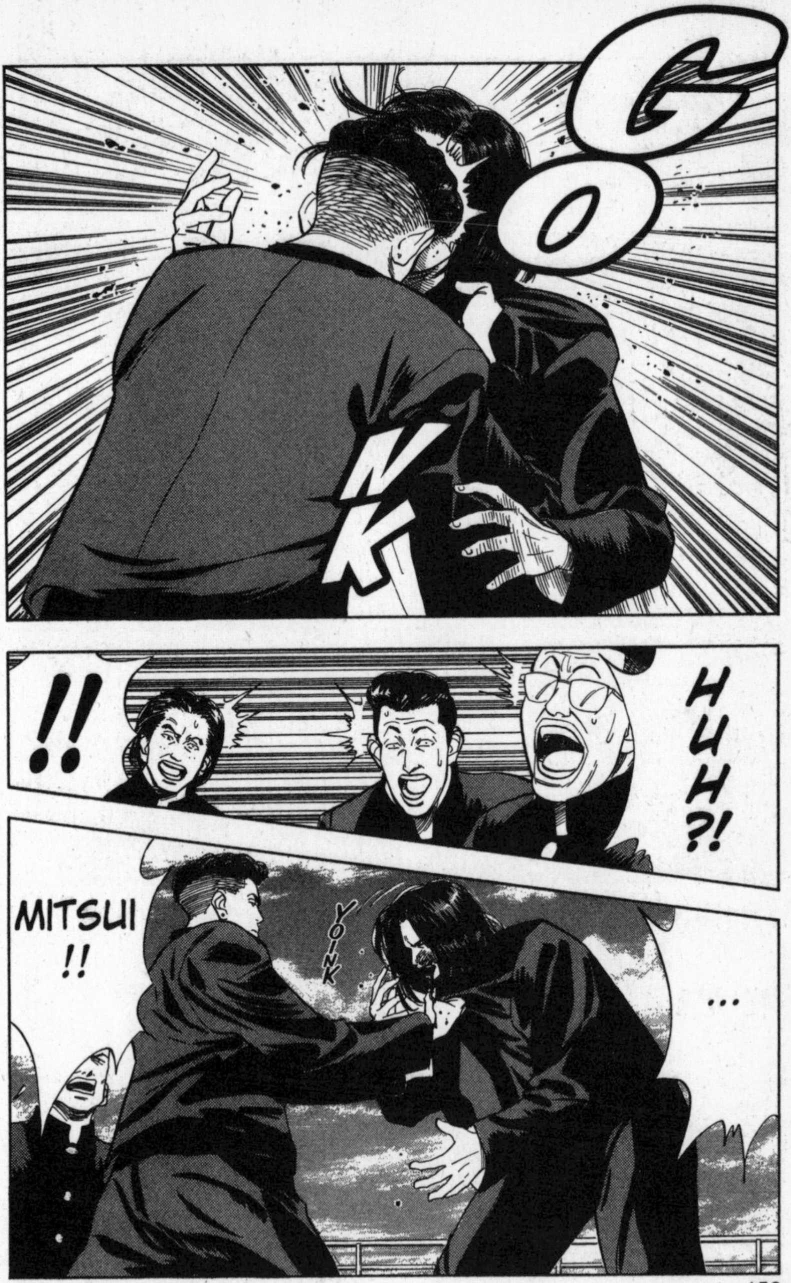

GO
NK
HUH?!
!!
...
YOINK
MITSUI!!

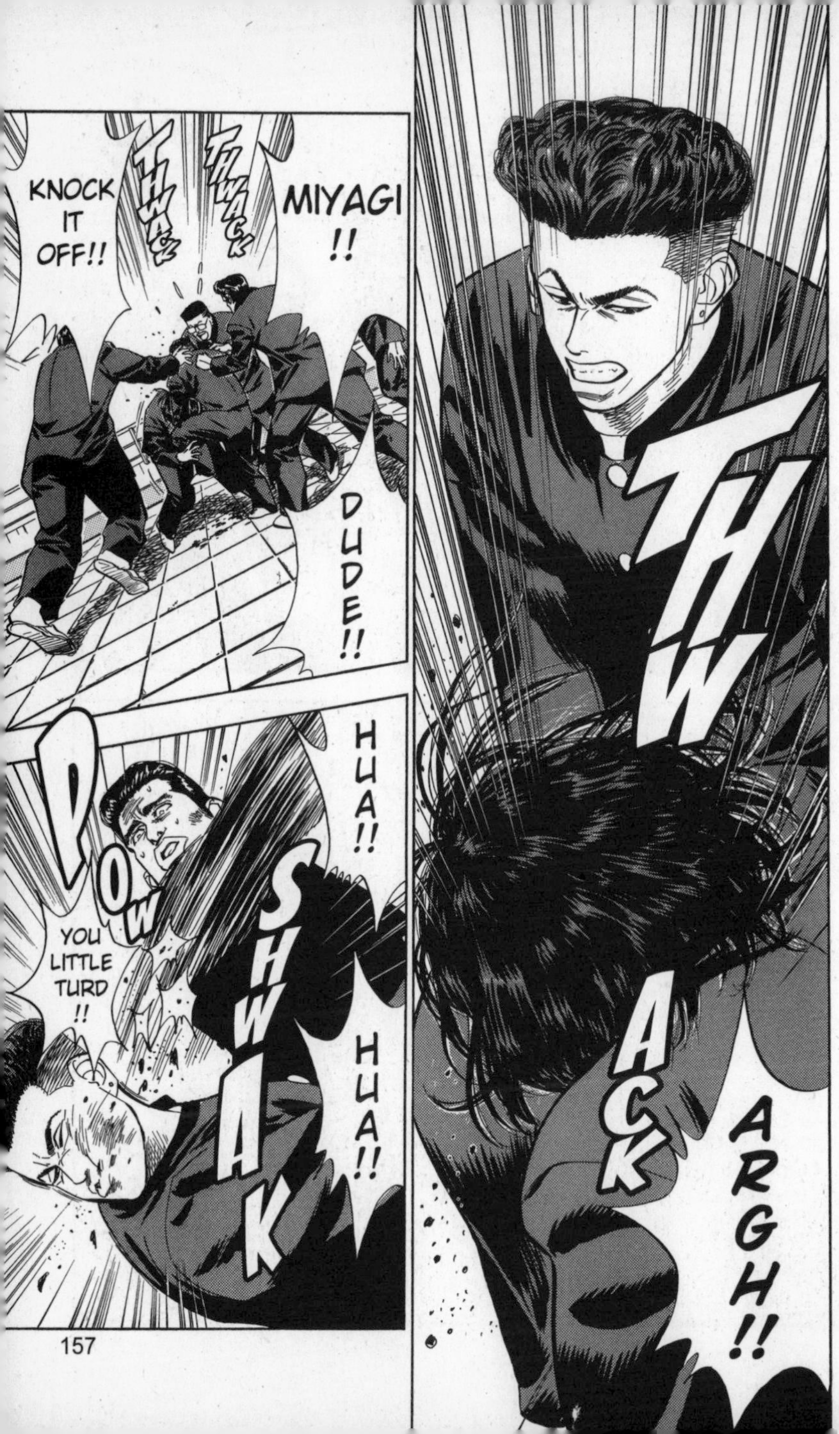
THWACK
ARGH!!
MIYAGI!!
THWACK
THWACK
KNOCK IT OFF!!
DUDE!!
HUA!!
POW
SHWAK
HUA!!
YOU LITTLE TURD!!

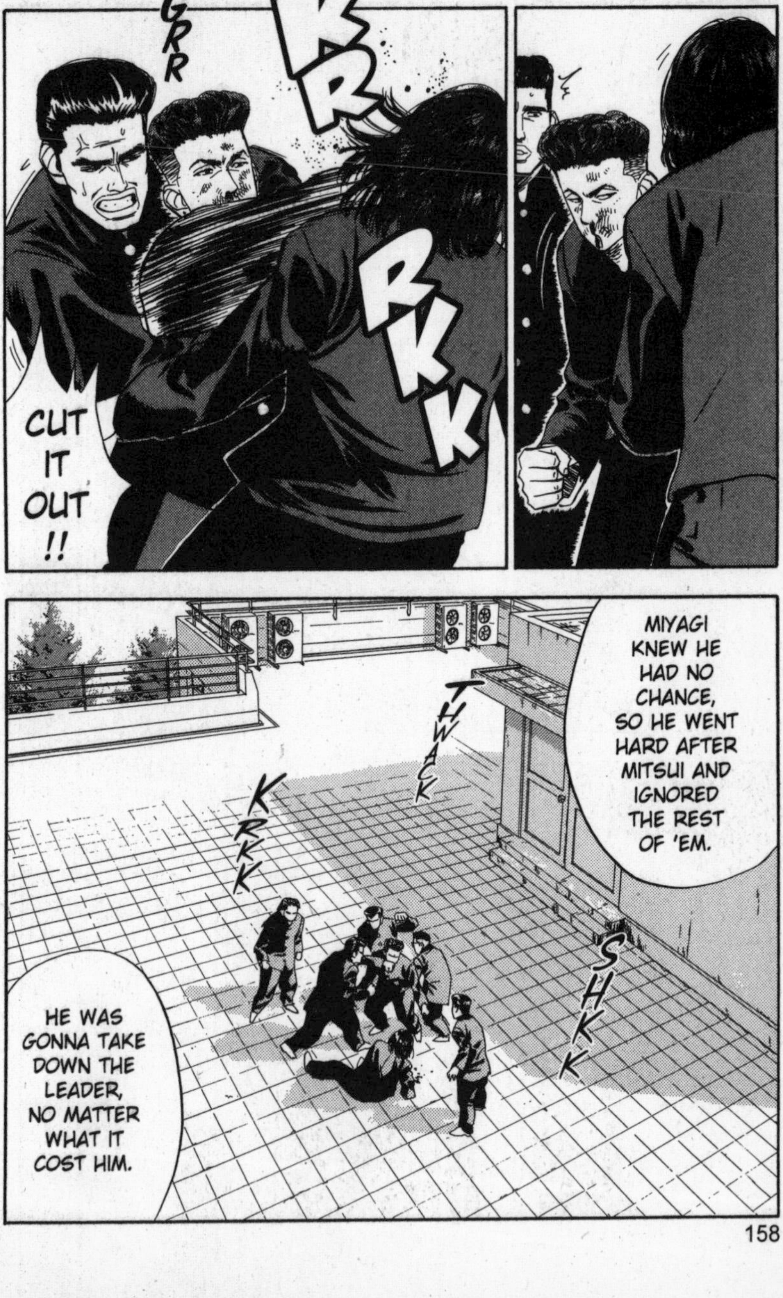
GRR
KRR
RKKK
CUT IT OUT !!
MIYAGI KNEW HE HAD NO CHANCE, SO HE WENT HARD AFTER MITSUI AND IGNORED THE REST OF 'EM.
THWACK
KRKK
SHKK
HE WAS GONNA TAKE DOWN THE LEADER, NO MATTER WHAT IT COST HIM.

READ THIS WAY

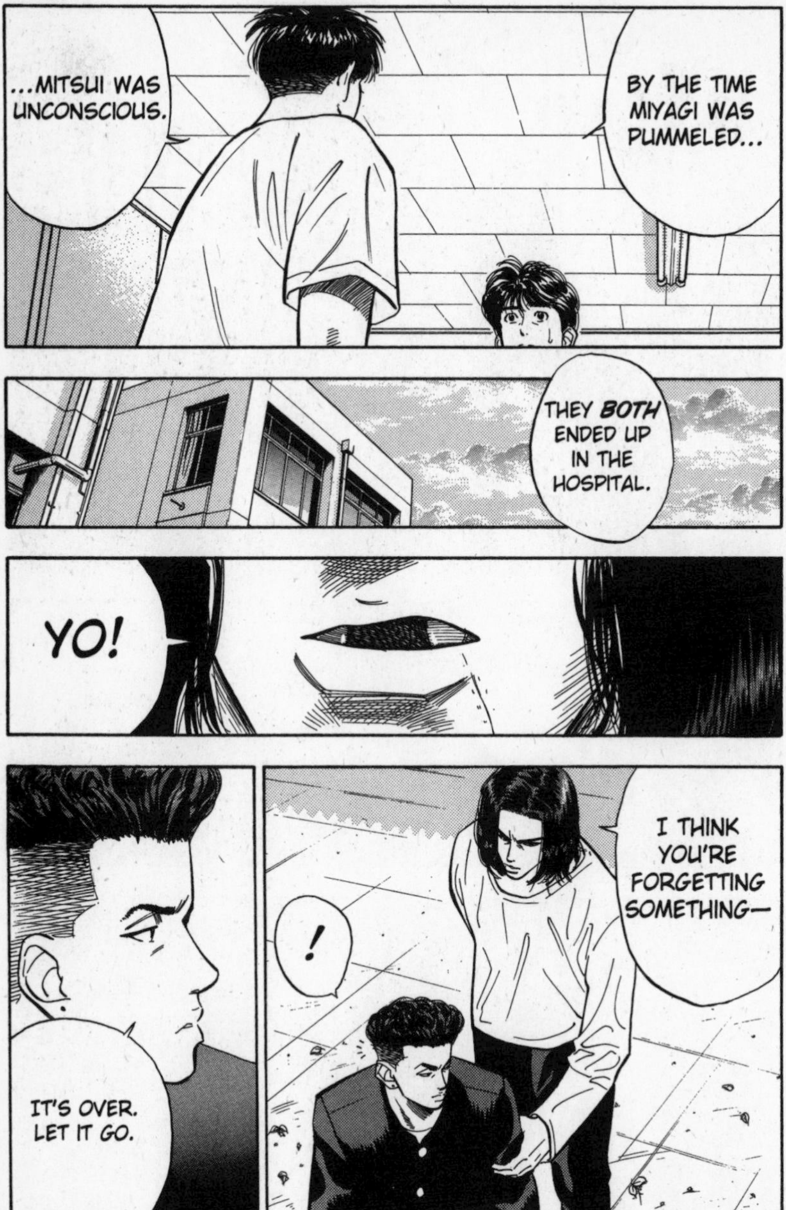
BY THE TIME MIYAGI WAS PUMMELED...
...MITSUI WAS UNCONSCIOUS.
THEY *BOTH* ENDED UP IN THE HOSPITAL.
YO!
I THINK YOU'RE FORGETTING SOMETHING—
!
IT'S OVER. LET IT GO.

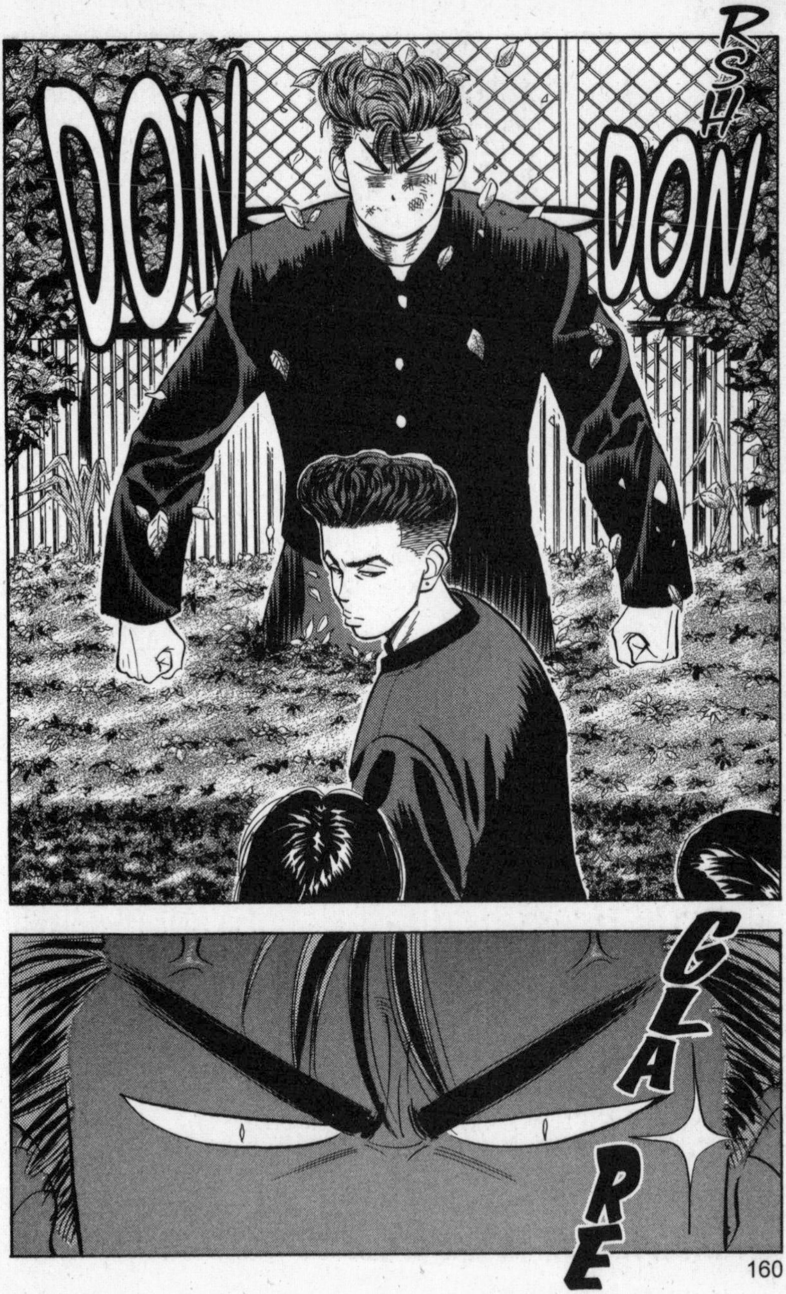
RSH
DON
DON
GLARE

READ THIS WAY

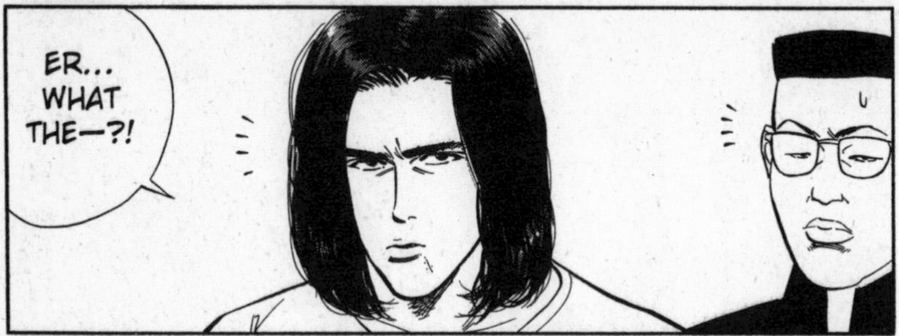
ER... WHAT THE—?!

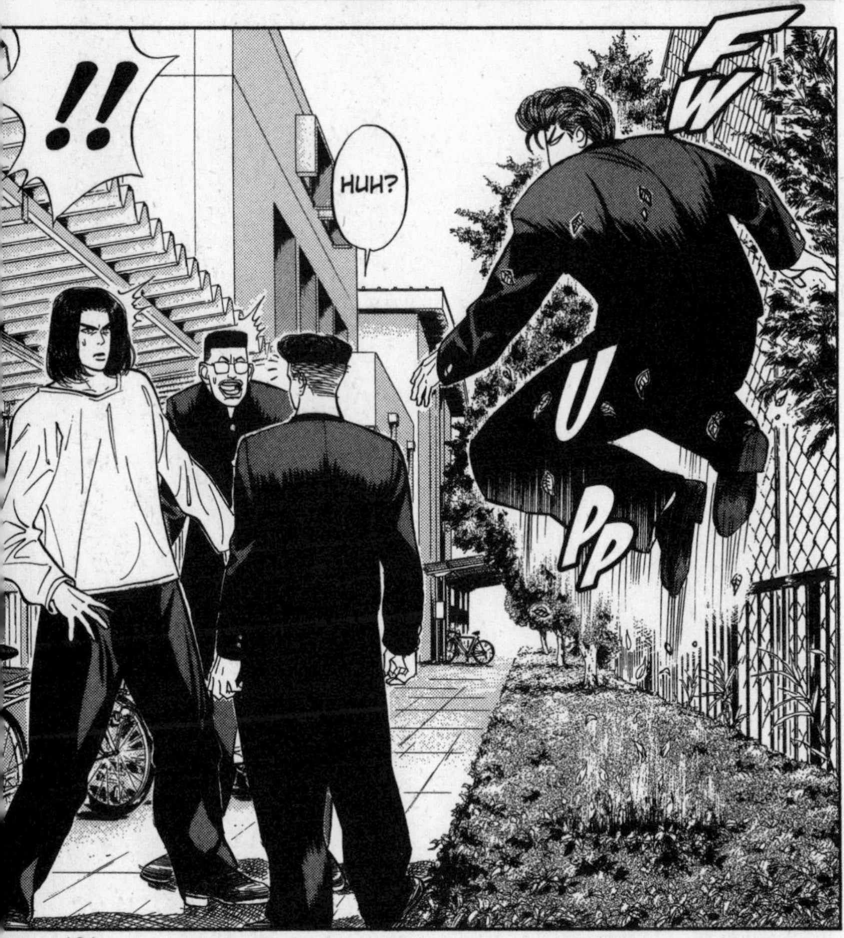
FWUPP
HUH?
!!

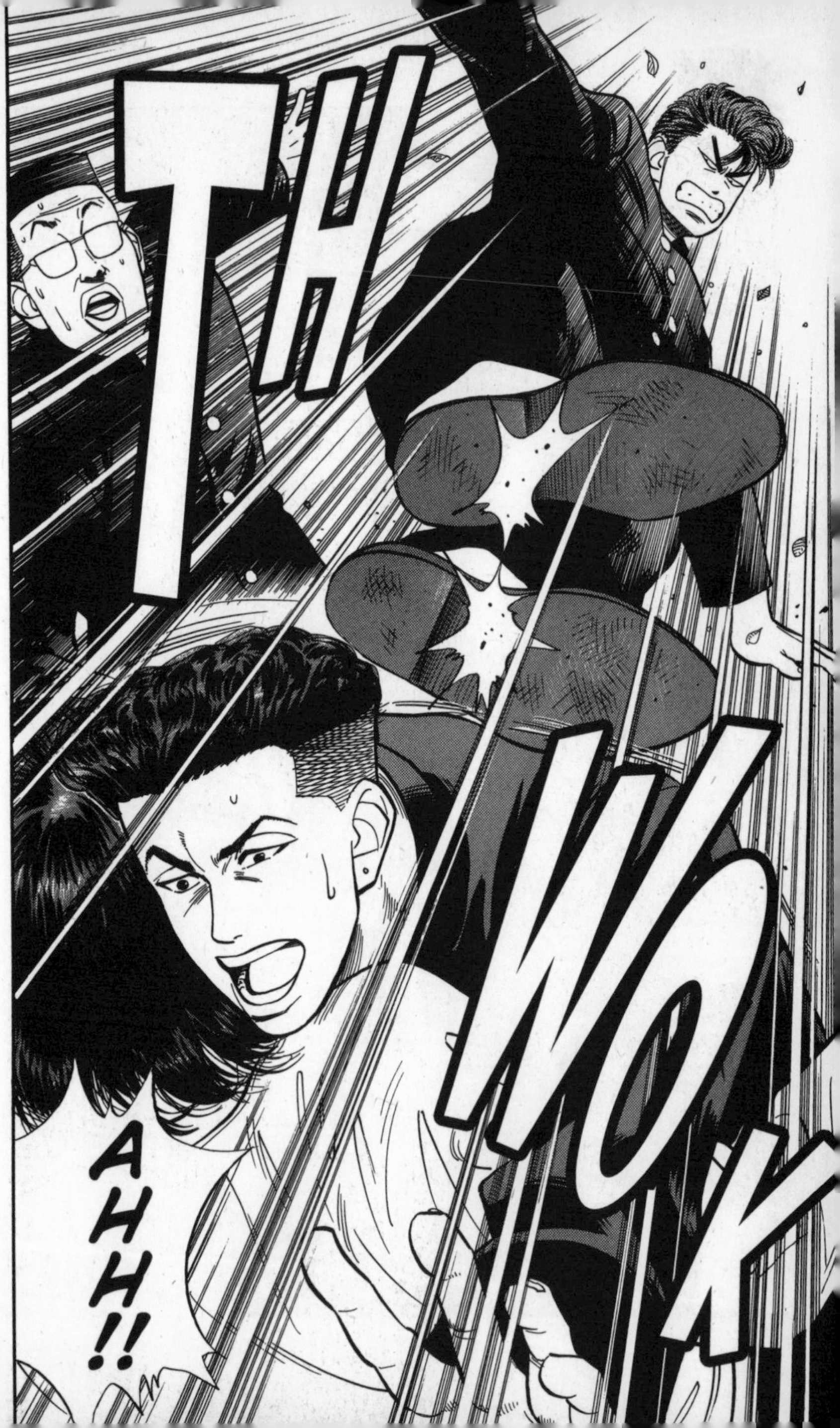
THWOK
AHH!!

READ THIS WAY

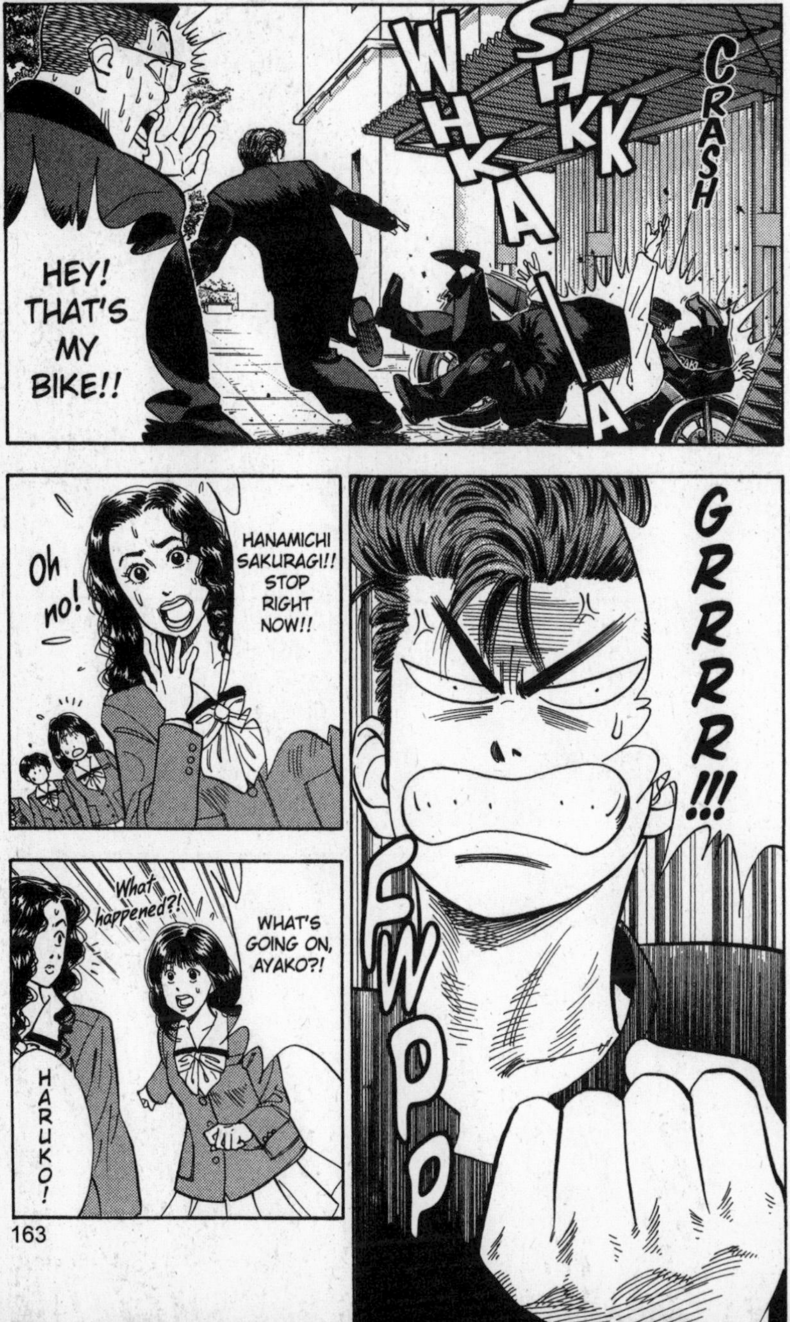
CRASH
SHKK
WHKA—A
HEY! THAT'S MY BIKE!!
GRRRR!!!
FWPP
HANAMICHI SAKURAGI!! STOP RIGHT NOW!!
Oh no!
WHAT'S GOING ON, AYAKO?!
What happened?!
HARUKO!

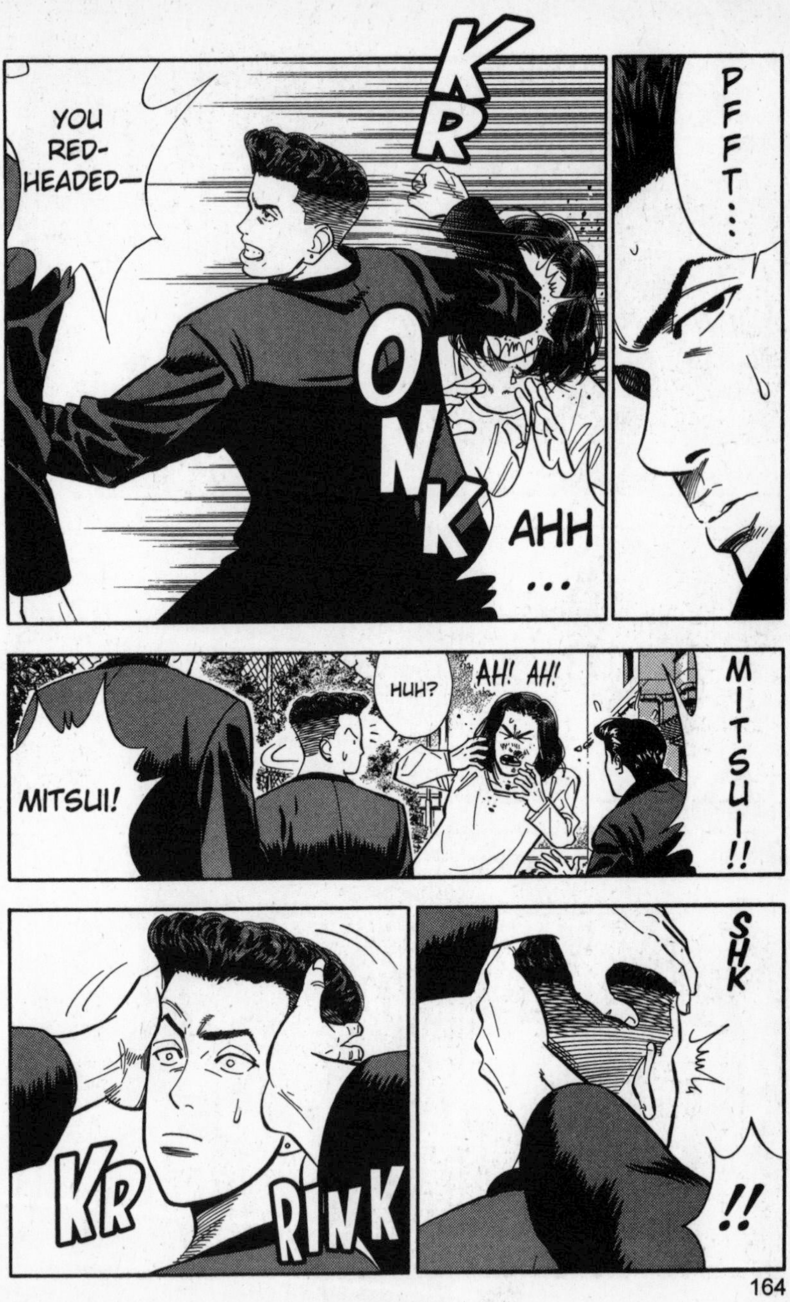
PFFT...
KRONK
YOU RED-HEADED—
AHH ...
MITSUI!!
AH! AH!
HUH?
MITSUI!
SHK
!!
KRRINK

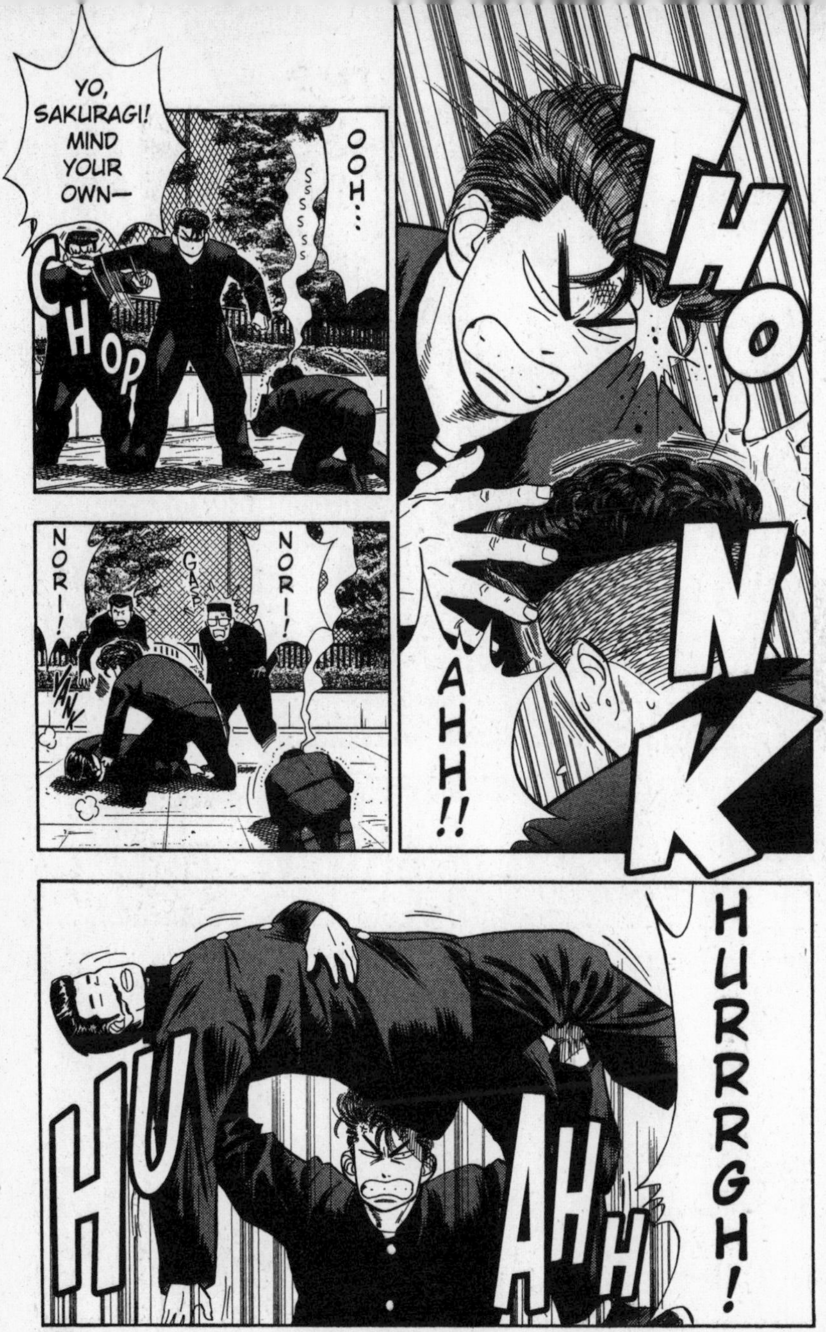
THONK
AHH!!
YO, SAKURAGI! MIND YOUR OWN—
OOH...
SSSSS
CHOP
NORI!
GASP
NORI!
YANK
HURRRGH!
HUAHHH

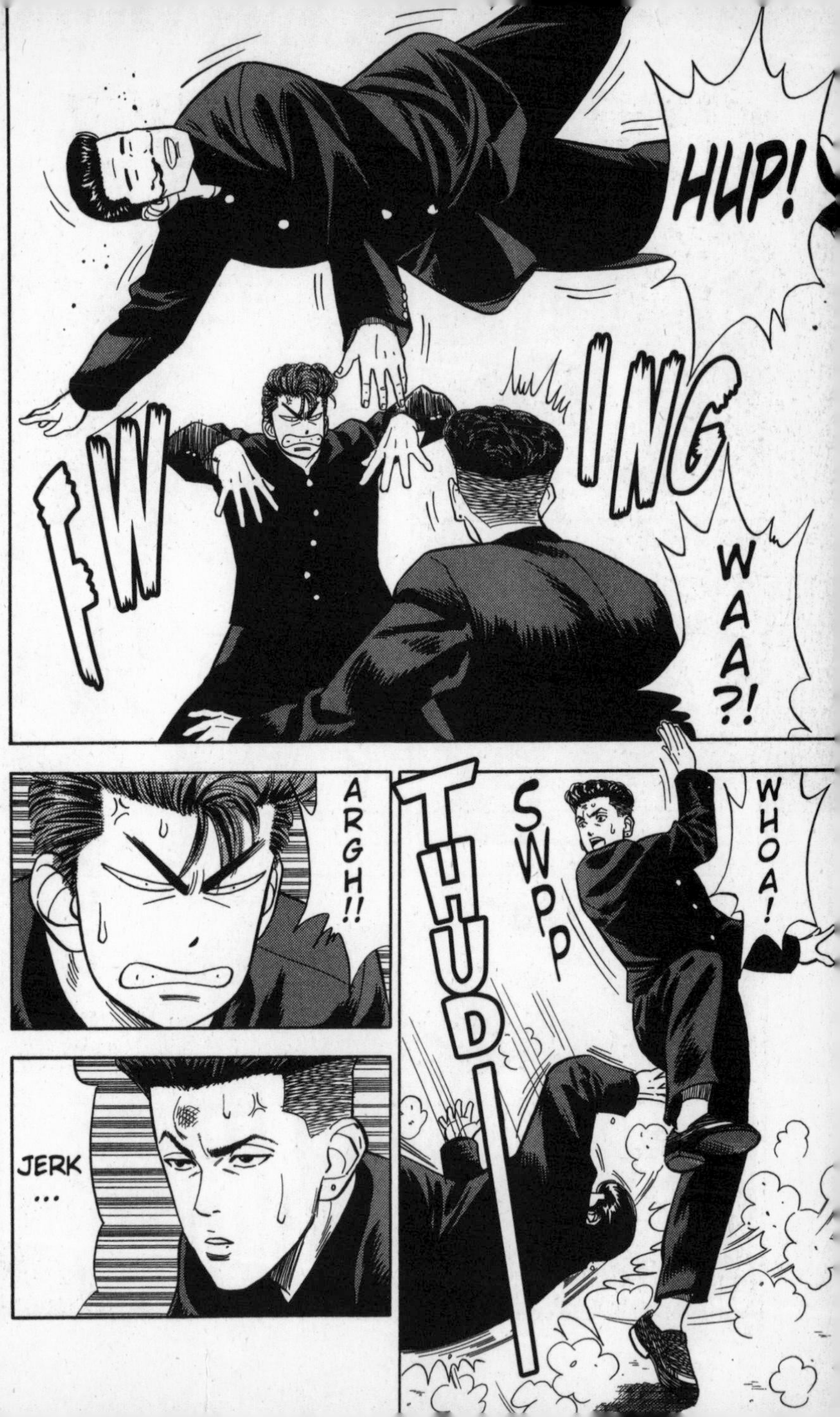
HUP!
WAA?!
SWING
WHOA!
SWPP
THUD!
ARGH!!
JERK...

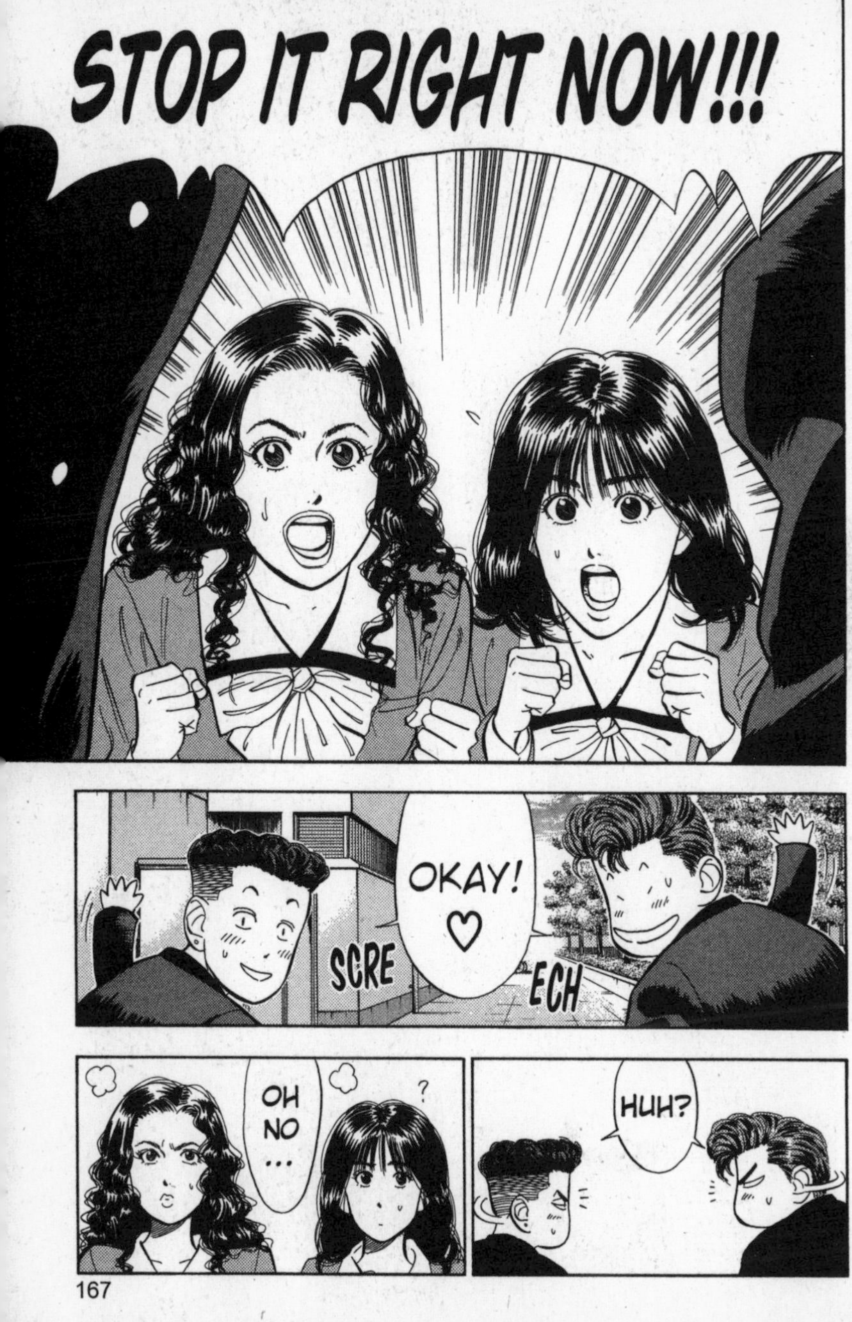
STOP IT RIGHT NOW!!!
OKAY! ♡
SCRE ECH
HUH?
OH NO ...

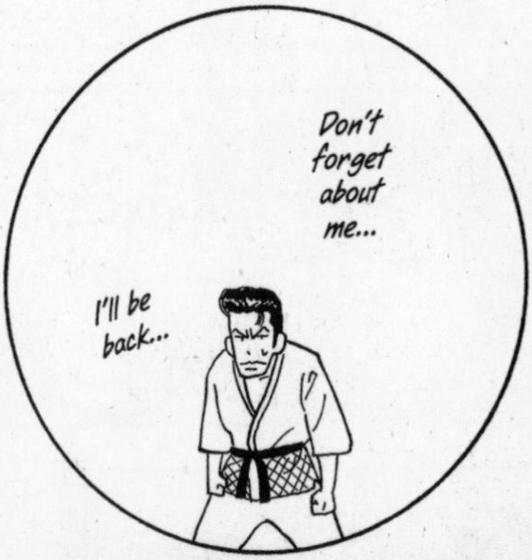
Don't forget about me...
I'll be back...

SLAM DUNK

READ THIS WAY

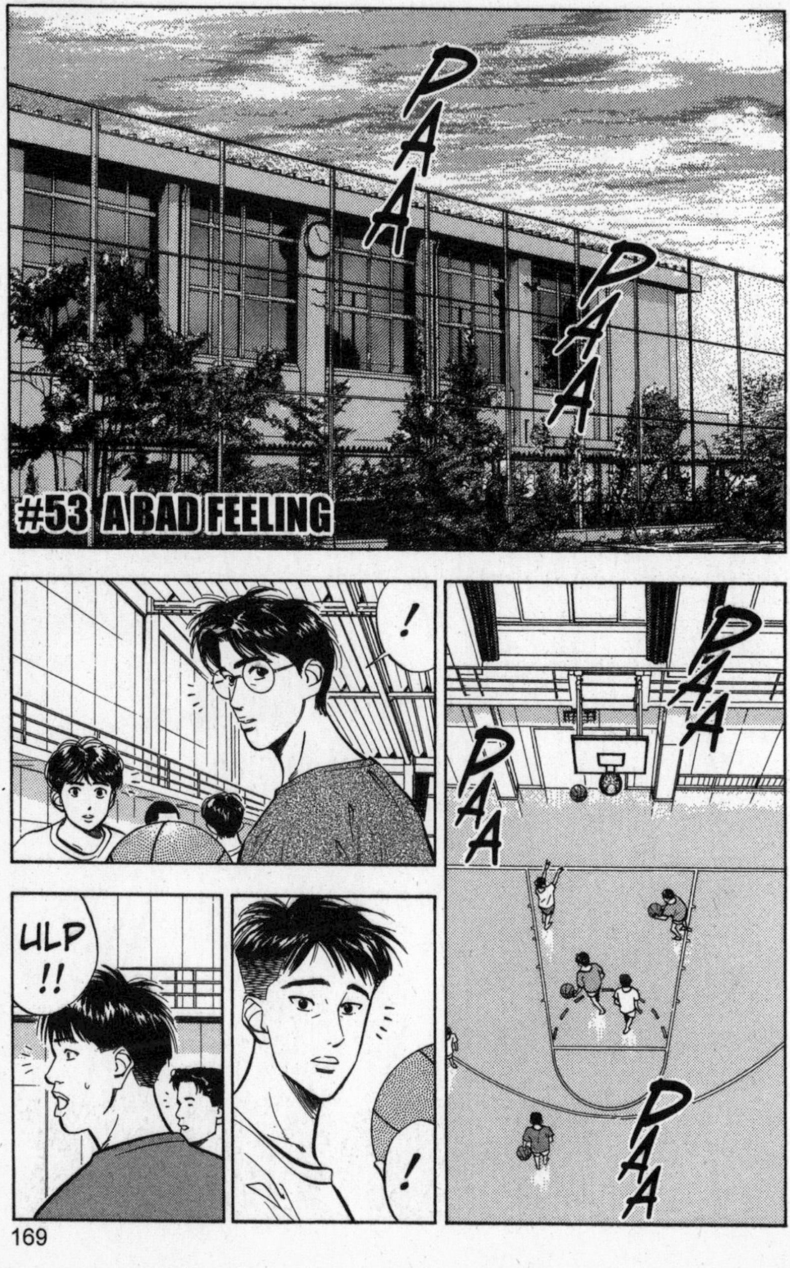

#53 A BAD FEELING
PAAA
PAAA
PAA
PAA
PAA
!
!
ULP !!

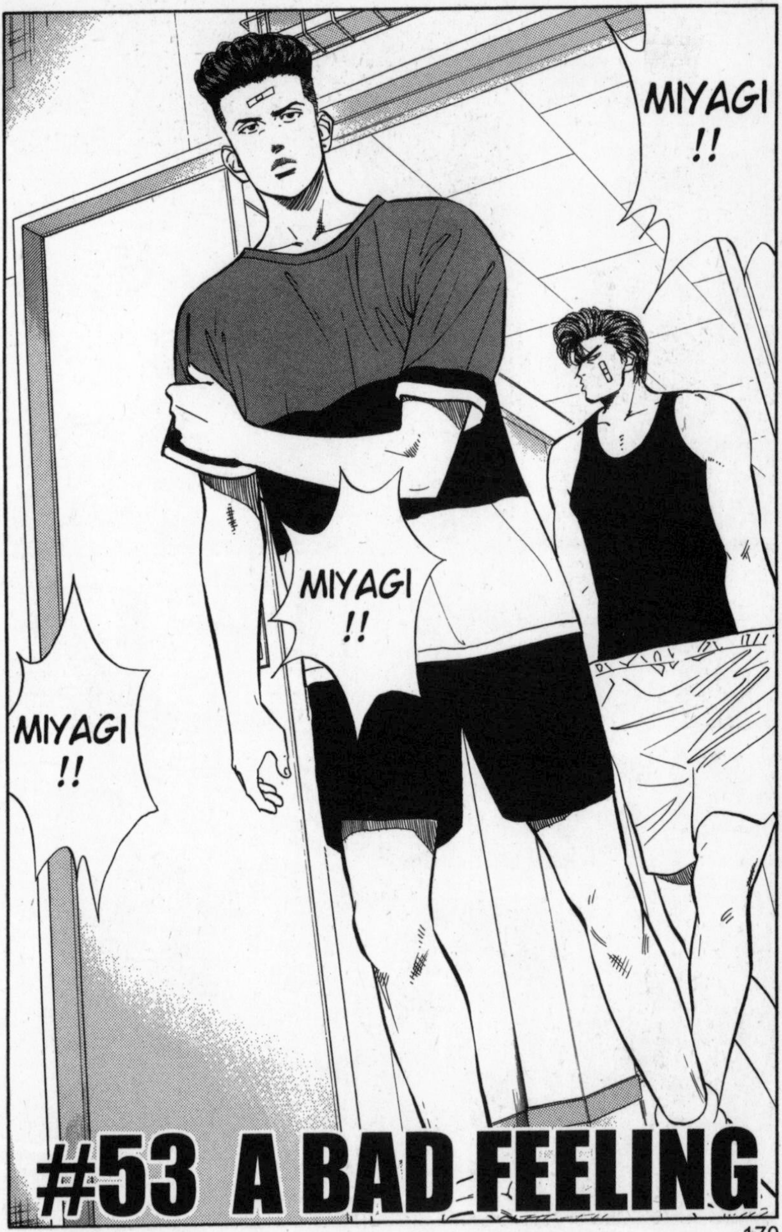
MIYAGI !!
MIYAGI !!
MIYAGI !!

# #53 A BAD FEELING

READ THIS WAY

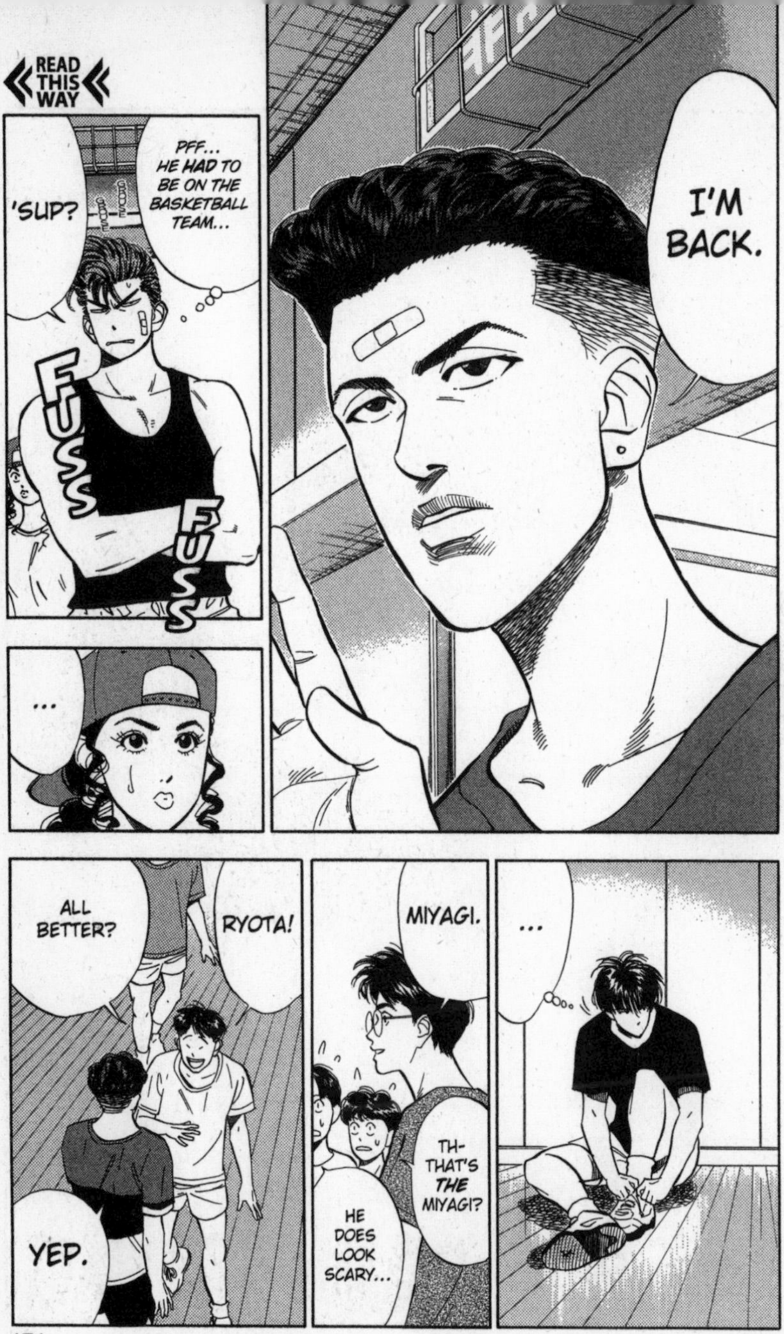
I'M BACK.
PFF... HE *HAD* TO BE ON THE BASKETBALL TEAM...
'SUP?
FUSS
FUSS
...
...
MIYAGI.
TH- THAT'S *THE* MIYAGI?
HE DOES LOOK SCARY...
RYOTA!
ALL BETTER?
YEP.

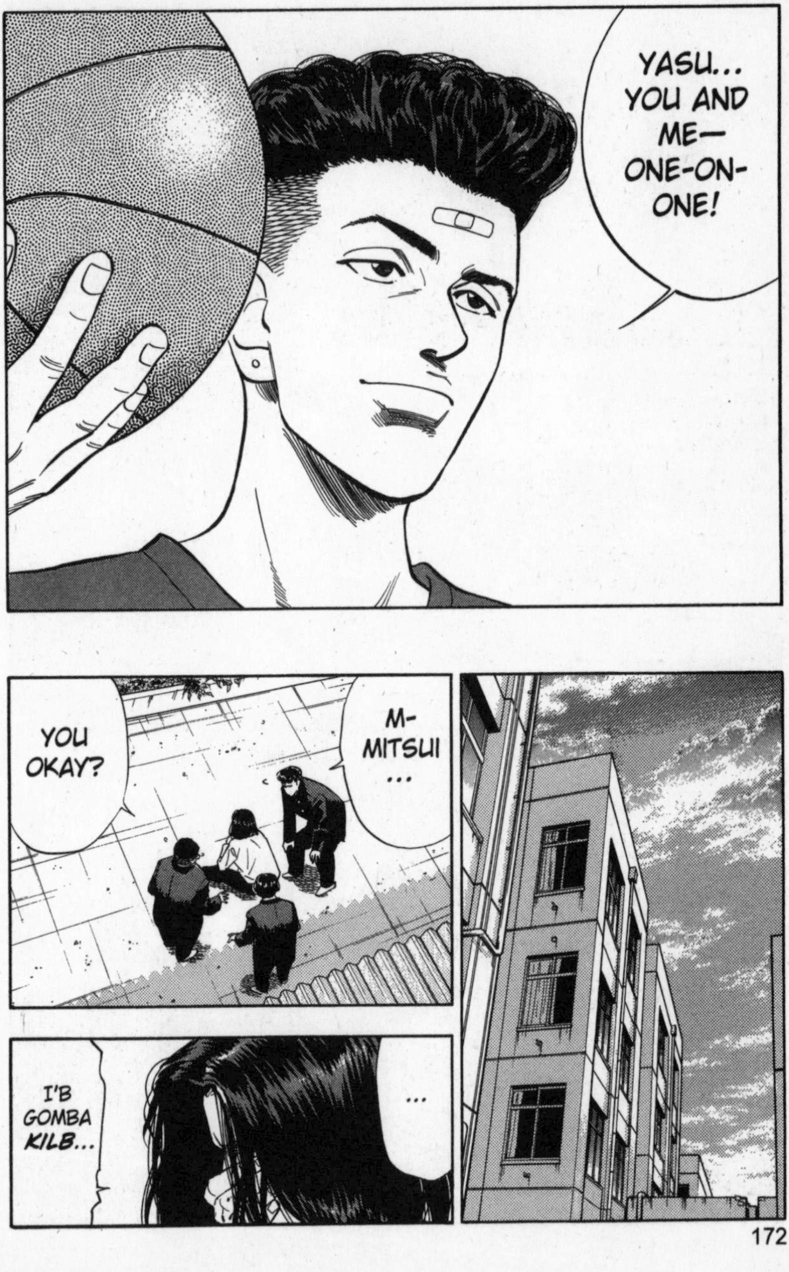
YASU... YOU AND ME— ONE-ON-ONE!
M-MITSUI...
YOU OKAY?
...
I'B GOMBA *KILB*...

READ THIS WAY

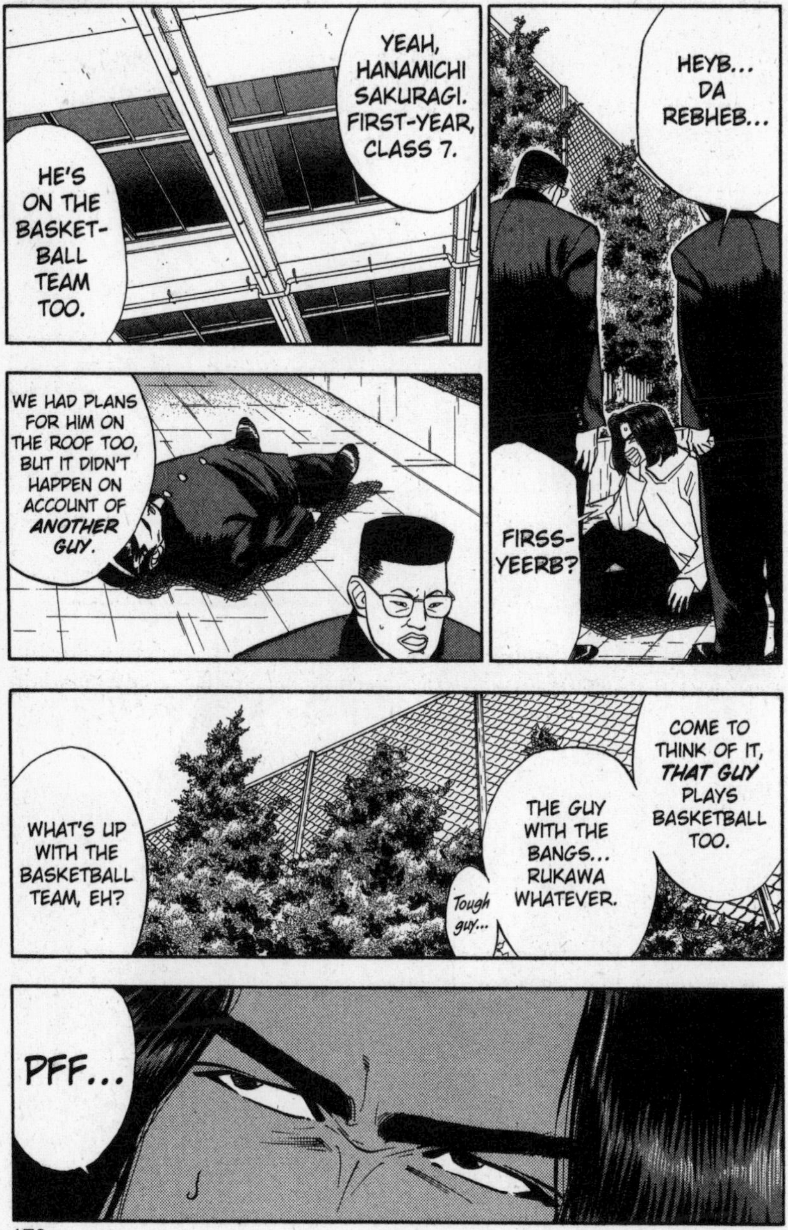
HEYB... DA REBHEB...
FIRSS-YEERB?
YEAH, HANAMICHI SAKURAGI. FIRST-YEAR, CLASS 7.
HE'S ON THE BASKET-BALL TEAM TOO.
WE HAD PLANS FOR HIM ON THE ROOF TOO, BUT IT DIDN'T HAPPEN ON ACCOUNT OF ***ANOTHER GUY***.
COME TO THINK OF IT, ***THAT GUY*** PLAYS BASKETBALL TOO.
THE GUY WITH THE BANGS... RUKAWA WHATEVER.
Tough guy...
WHAT'S UP WITH THE BASKETBALL TEAM, EH?
PFF...

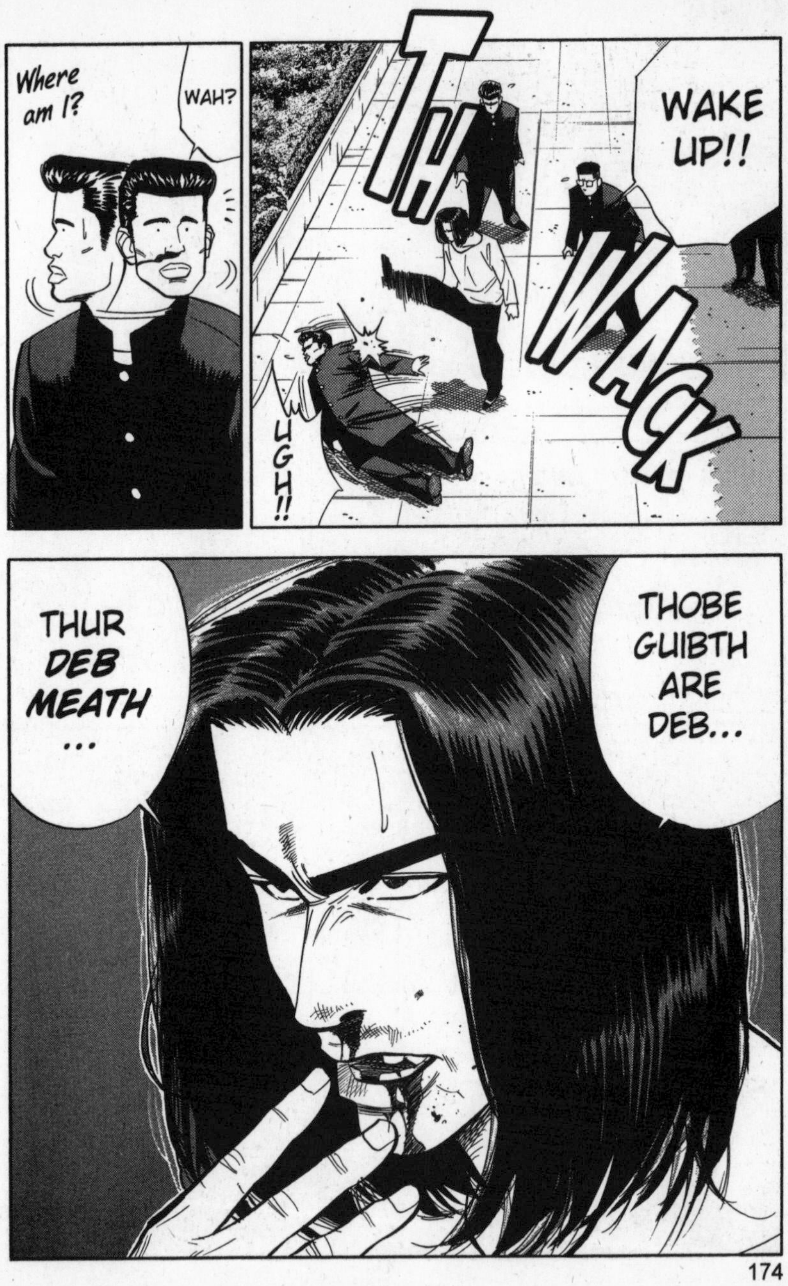
WAKE UP!!
TH
WACK
UGH!!
WAH?
Where am I?
THOBE GUIBTH ARE DEB...
THUR DEB MEATH ...

READ THIS WAY

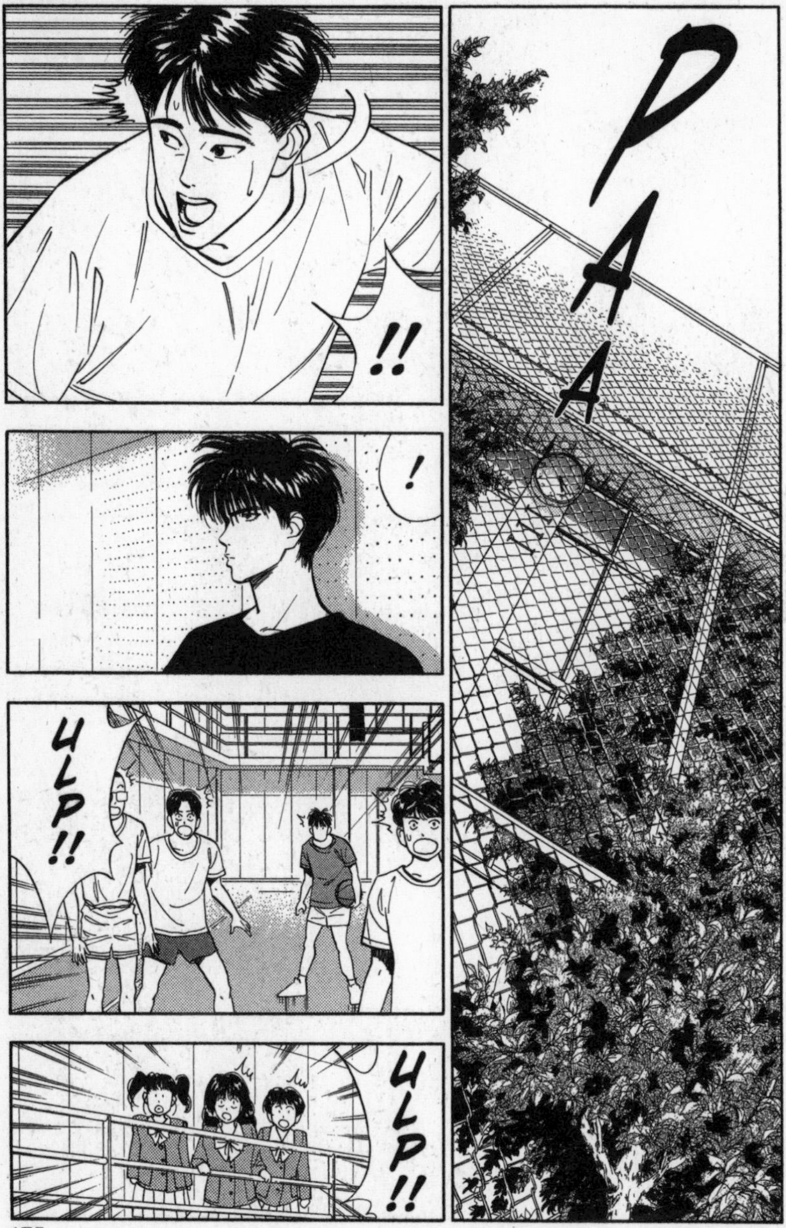
PAAA
!!
!
ULP!!
ULP!!

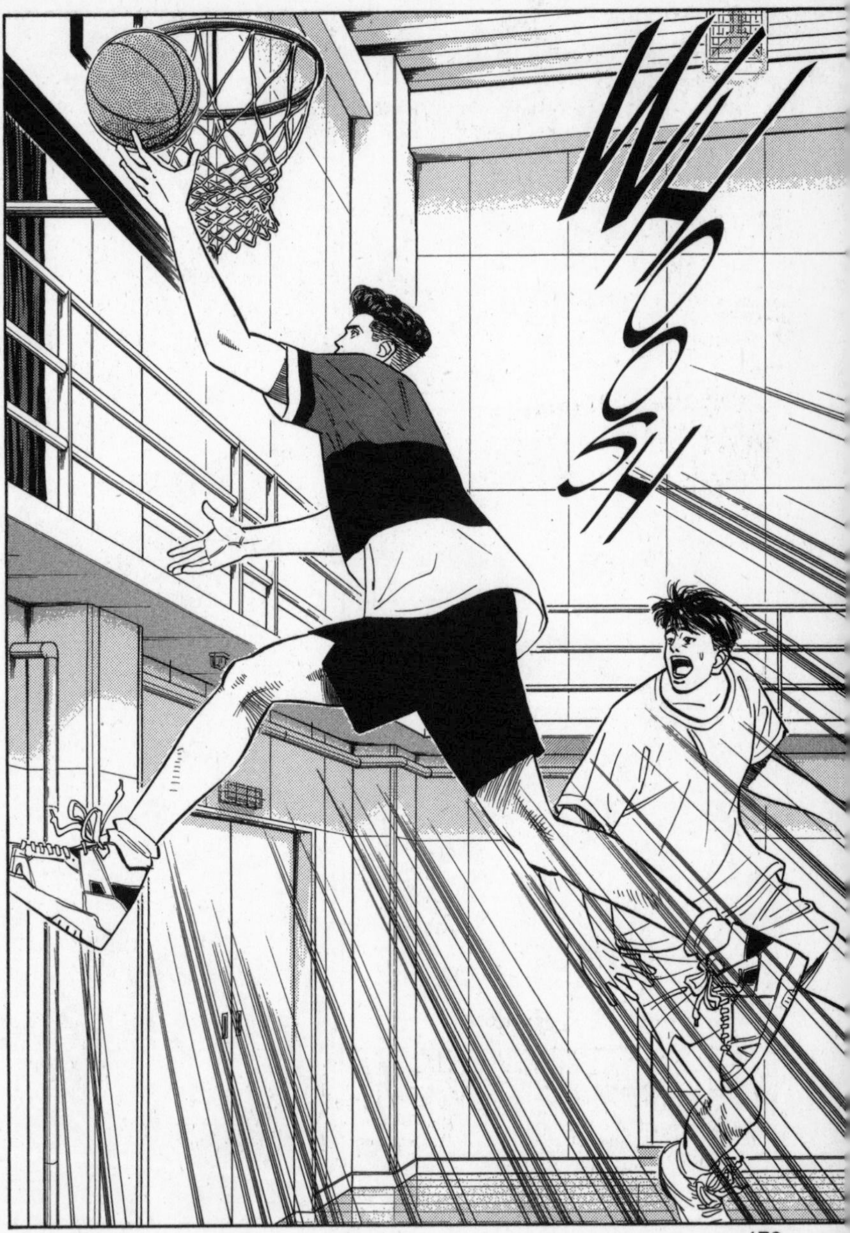
WHOOSH

READ THIS WAY

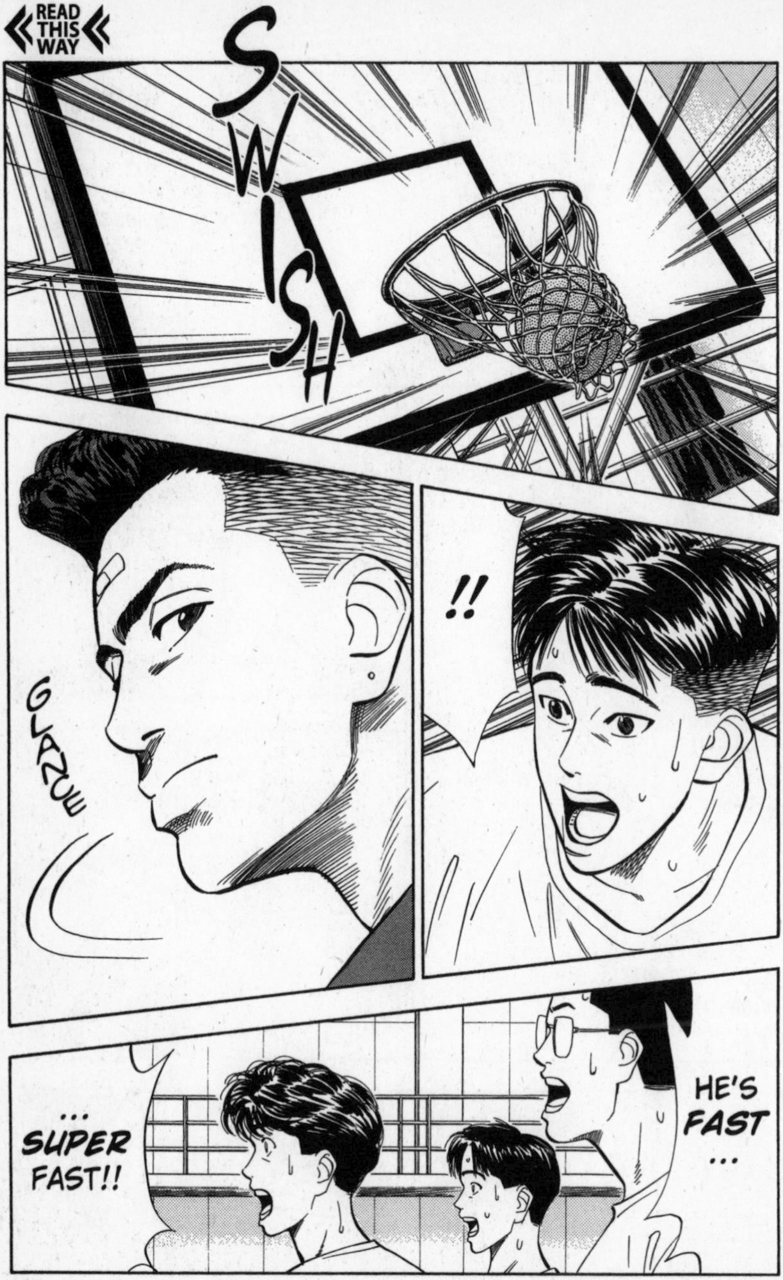
SWISH
!!
GLANCE
HE'S FAST ...
... SUPER FAST!!

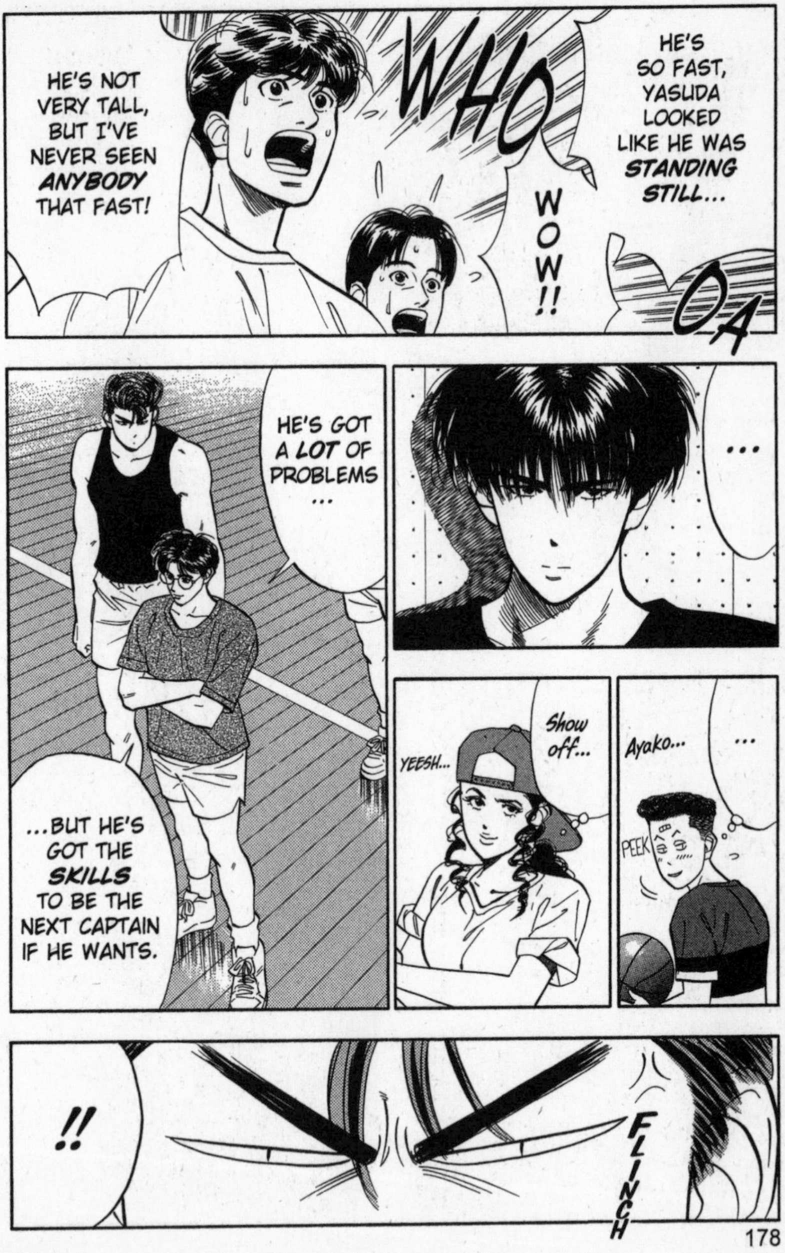
HE'S SO FAST, YASUDA LOOKED LIKE HE WAS STANDING STILL...
WHO
OA
WOW!!
HE'S NOT VERY TALL, BUT I'VE NEVER SEEN ANYBODY THAT FAST!
...
...
Ayako...
PEEK
Show off...
YEESH...
HE'S GOT A LOT OF PROBLEMS ...
...BUT HE'S GOT THE SKILLS TO BE THE NEXT CAPTAIN IF HE WANTS.
FLINCH
!!

READ THIS WAY

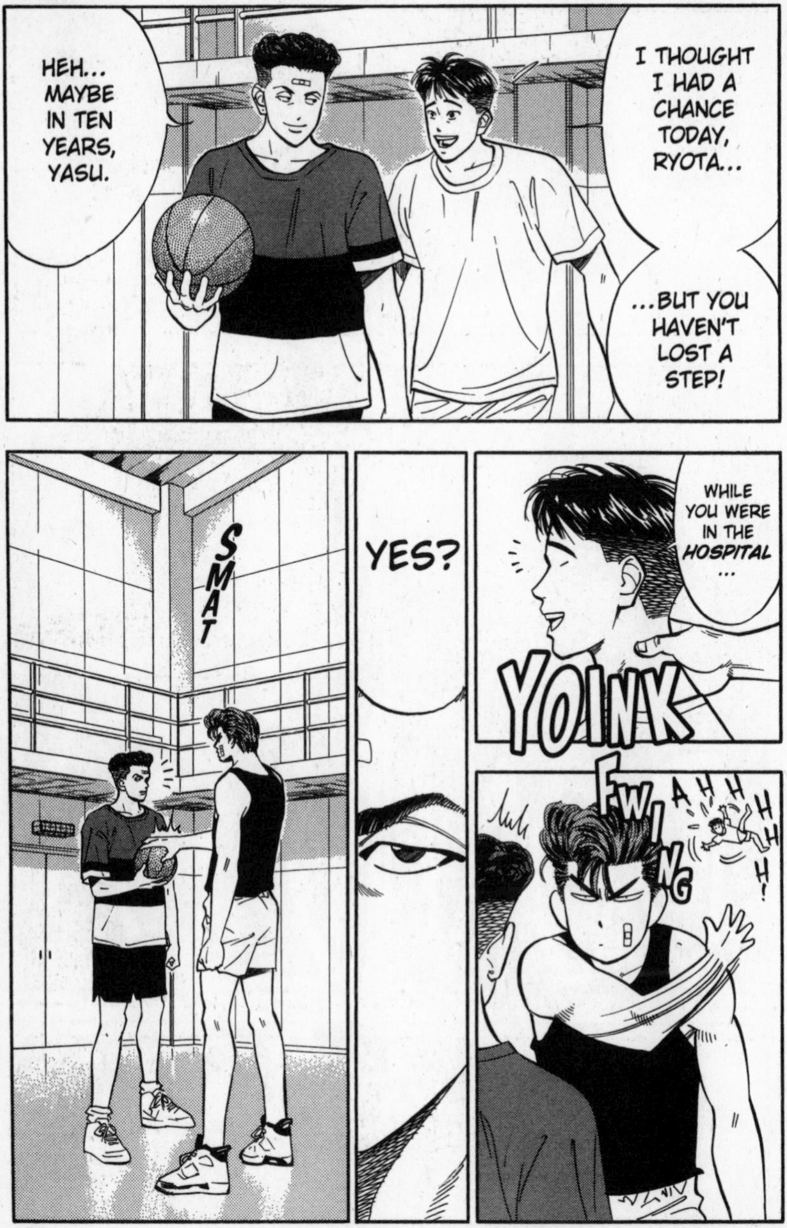
I THOUGHT I HAD A CHANCE TODAY, RYOTA...
...BUT YOU HAVEN'T LOST A STEP!
HEH... MAYBE IN TEN YEARS, YASU.
WHILE YOU WERE IN THE HOSPITAL...
YOINK
FWING
AHHHHHH!
YES?
SMAT

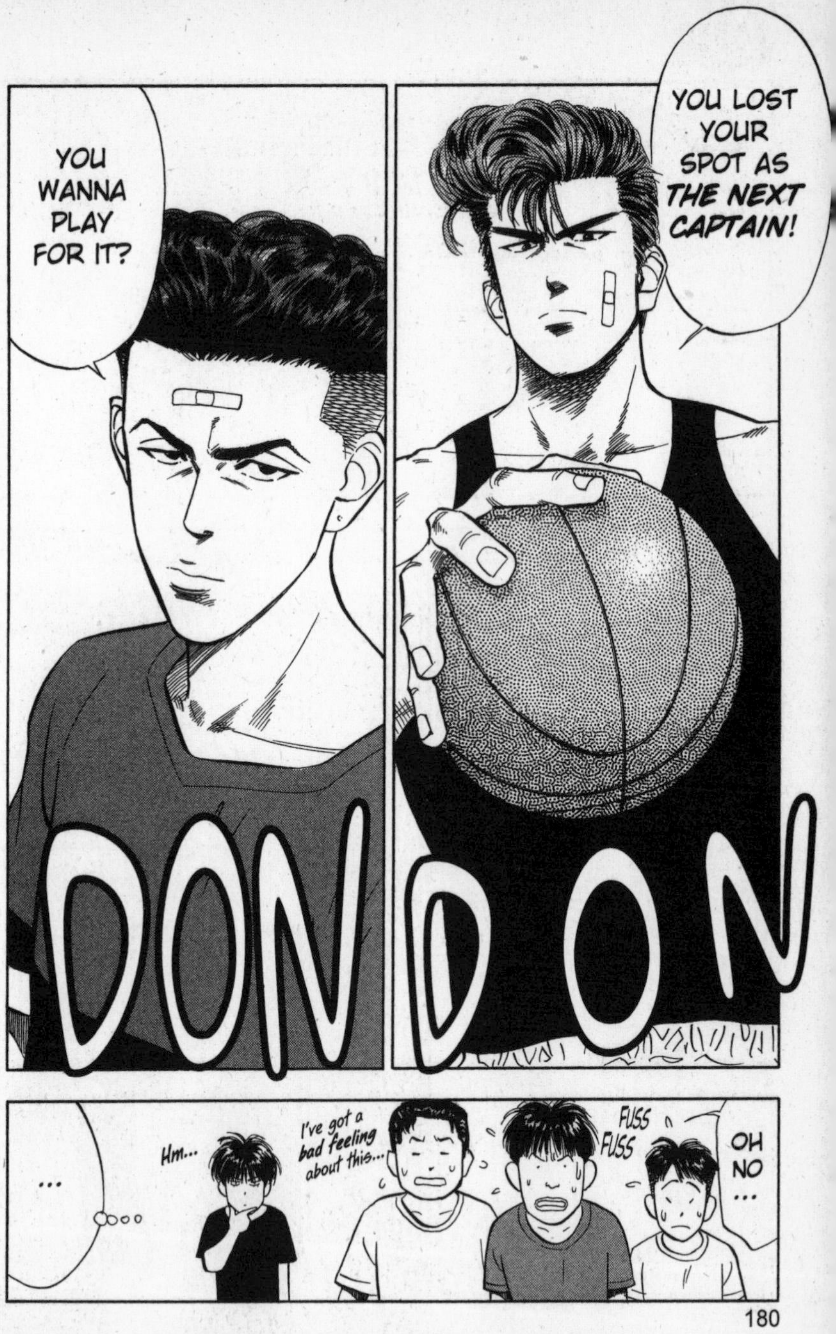
YOU LOST YOUR SPOT AS THE NEXT CAPTAIN!
YOU WANNA PLAY FOR IT?
DON DON
OH NO ...
FUSS FUSS
I've got a bad feeling about this...
Hm...
...

READ THIS WAY

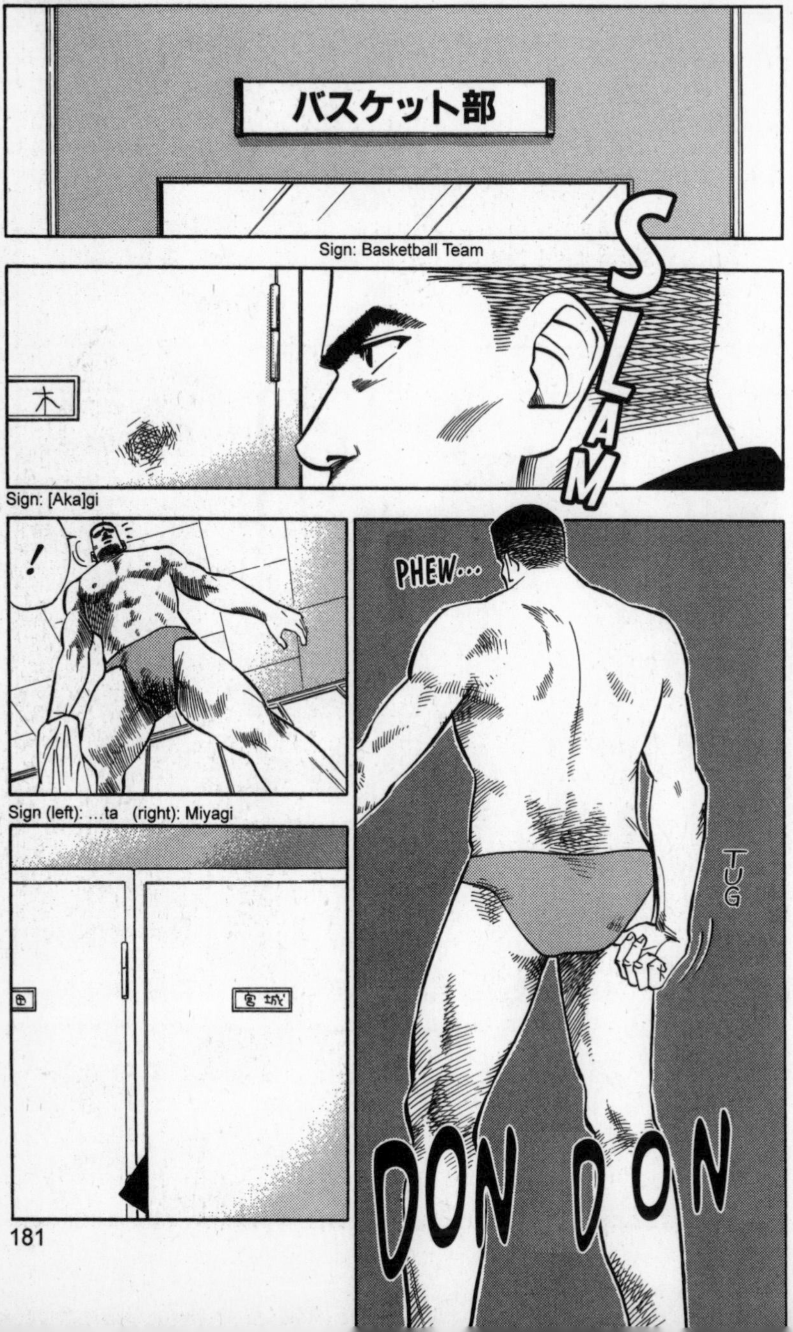
バスケット部
Sign: Basketball Team
SLAM
Sign: [Aka]gi
PHEW...
TUG
DON DON
!
Sign (left): …ta (right): Miyagi

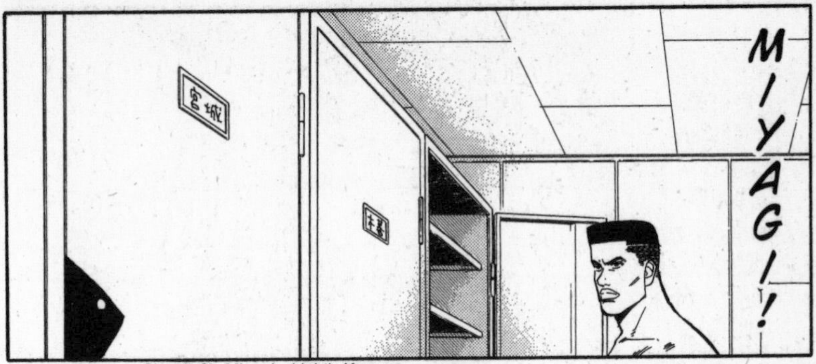
MIYAGI!!
Sign (left): Miyagi (right): Kogure

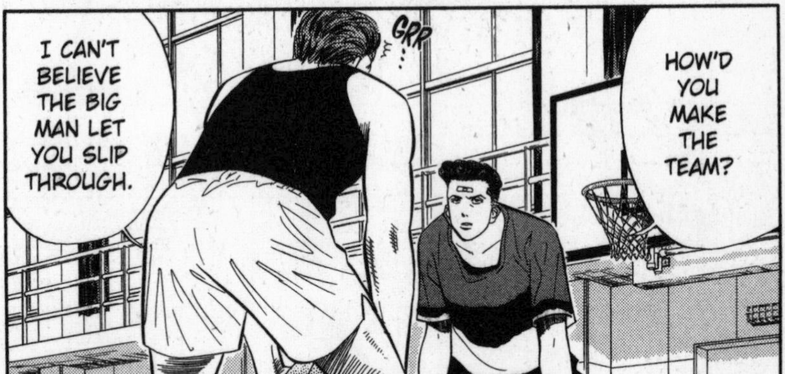
HOW'D YOU MAKE THE TEAM?
GRR...
I CAN'T BELIEVE THE BIG MAN LET YOU SLIP THROUGH.

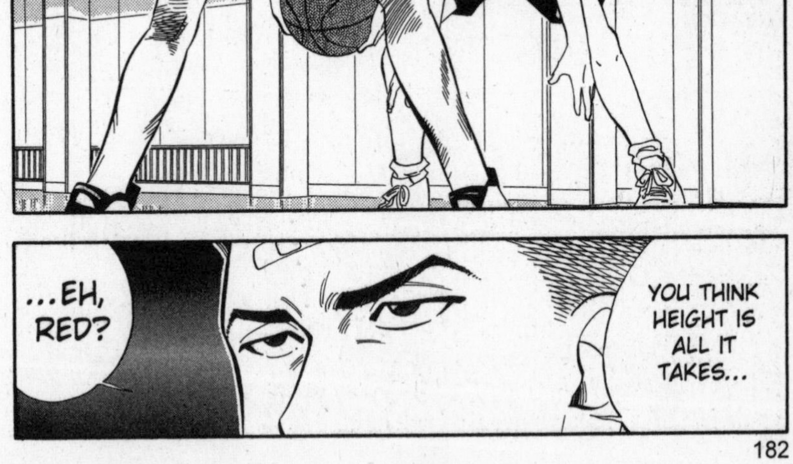
YOU THINK HEIGHT IS ALL IT TAKES...
...EH, RED?

READ THIS WAY

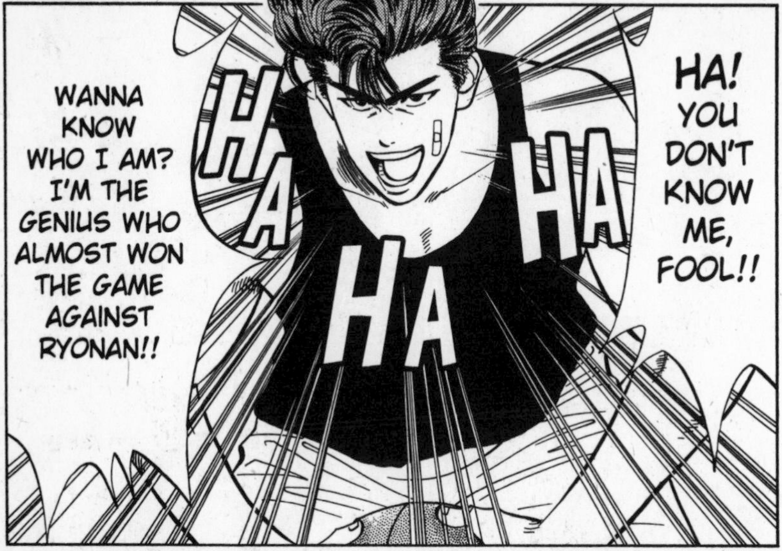
HA! YOU DON'T KNOW ME, FOOL!!
HA
HA
HA
WANNA KNOW WHO I AM? I'M THE GENIUS WHO ALMOST WON THE GAME AGAINST RYONAN!!

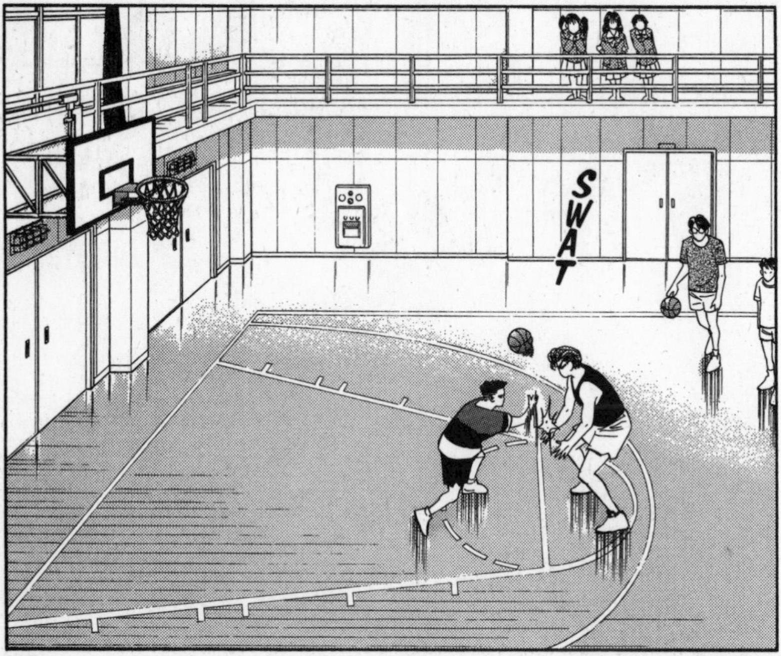
SWAT

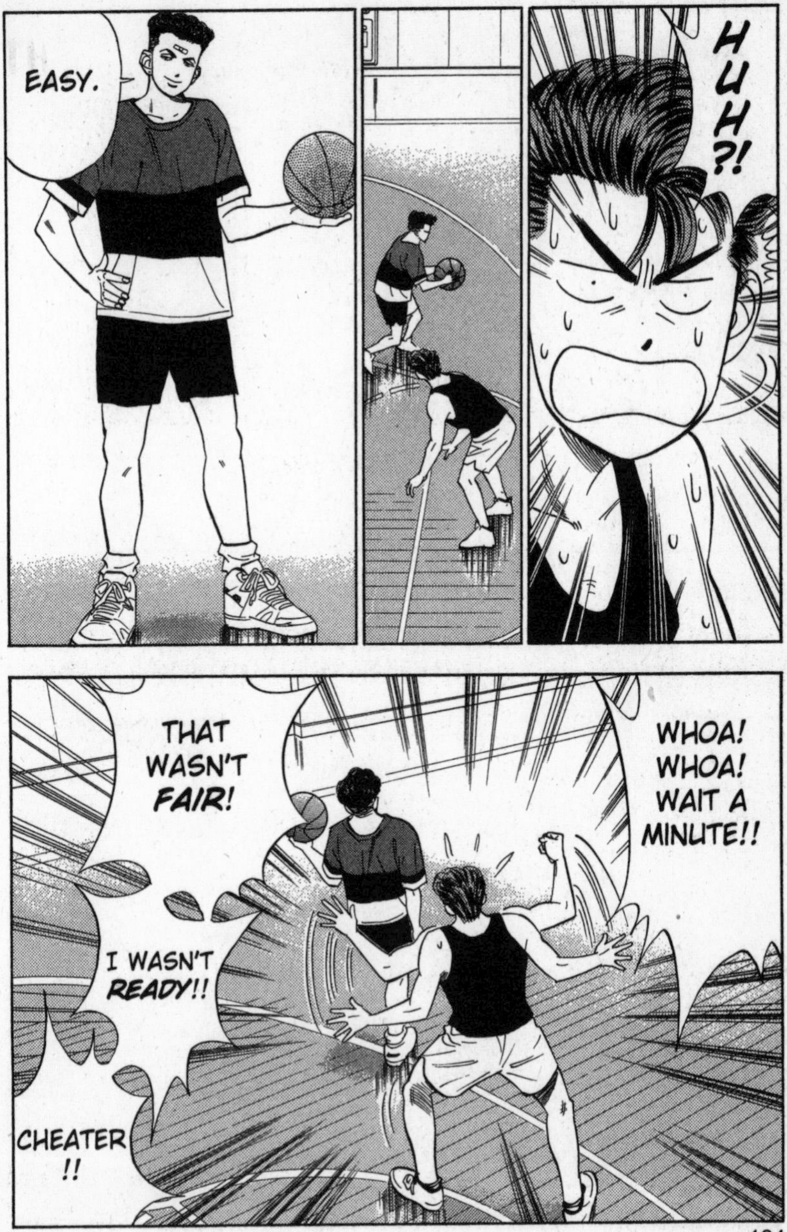
HUH?!
EASY.
WHOA! WHOA! WAIT A MINUTE!!
THAT WASN'T FAIR!
I WASN'T READY!!
CHEATER!!

READ THIS WAY

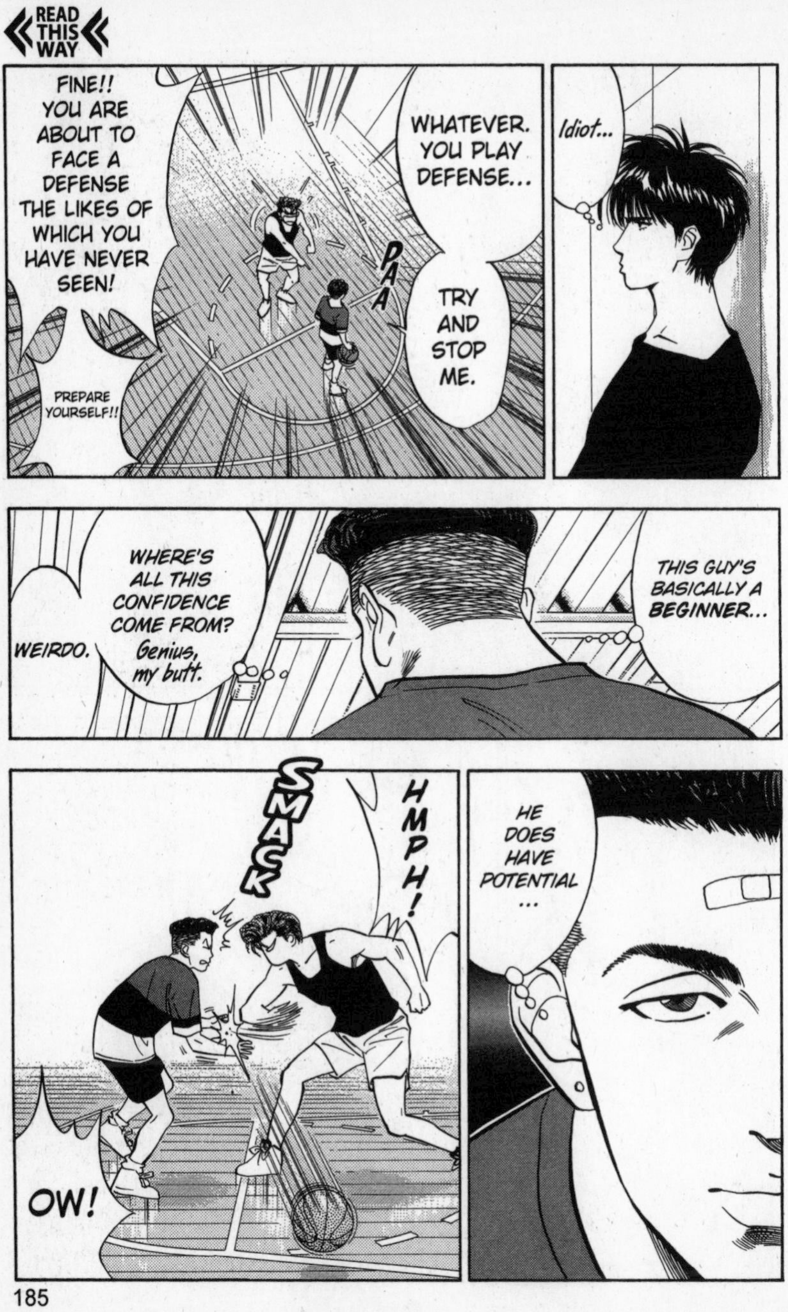
Idiot...
WHATEVER. YOU PLAY DEFENSE...
TRY AND STOP ME.
PAA
FINE!! YOU ARE ABOUT TO FACE A DEFENSE THE LIKES OF WHICH YOU HAVE NEVER SEEN!
PREPARE YOURSELF!!
THIS GUY'S BASICALLY A BEGINNER...
WHERE'S ALL THIS CONFIDENCE COME FROM? Genius, my butt.
WEIRDO.
HE DOES HAVE POTENTIAL ...
HMPH!
SMACK
OW!

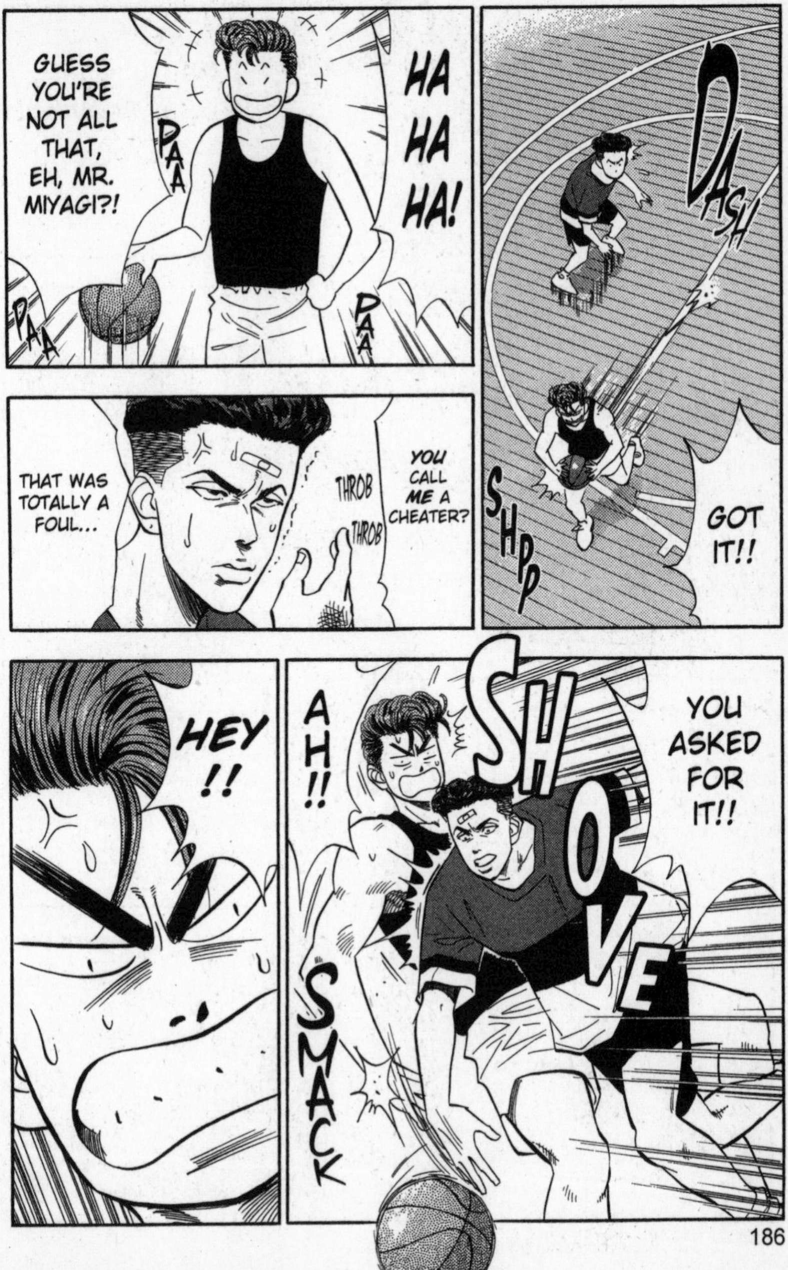

DASH
GOT IT!!
SHPP
HA HA HA!
GUESS YOU'RE NOT ALL THAT, EH, MR. MIYAGI?!
PAA
PAA
PAA
YOU CALL ME A CHEATER?
THROB
THROB
THAT WAS TOTALLY A FOUL...
YOU ASKED FOR IT!!
SHOVE
AH!!
SMACK
HEY!!

READ THIS WAY

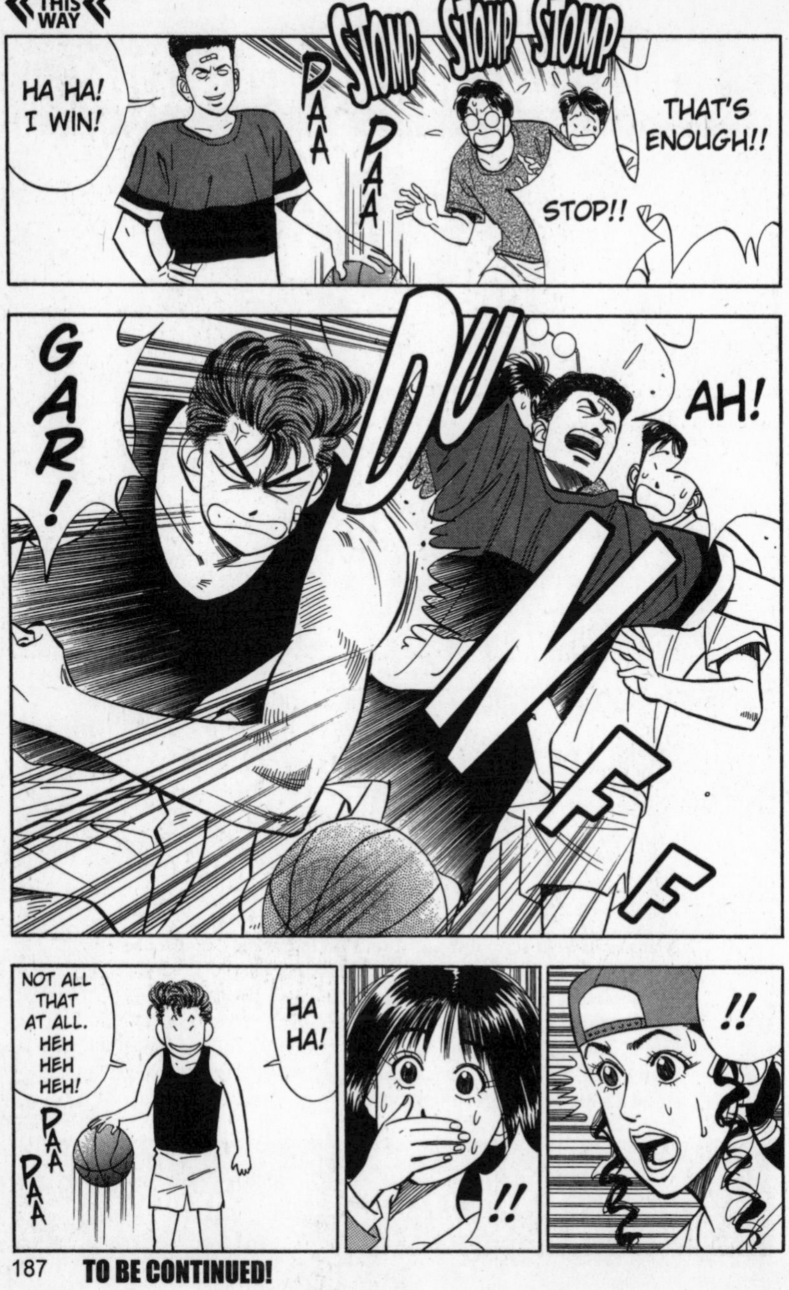
THAT'S ENOUGH!!
STOP!!
STOMP STOMP STOMP
PAA PAA
HA HA! I WIN!
AH!
DUNFF
GAR!
!!
!!
HA HA!
NOT ALL THAT AT ALL. HEH HEH HEH!
PAA PAA



TO BE CONTINUED!

# Coming Next Volume

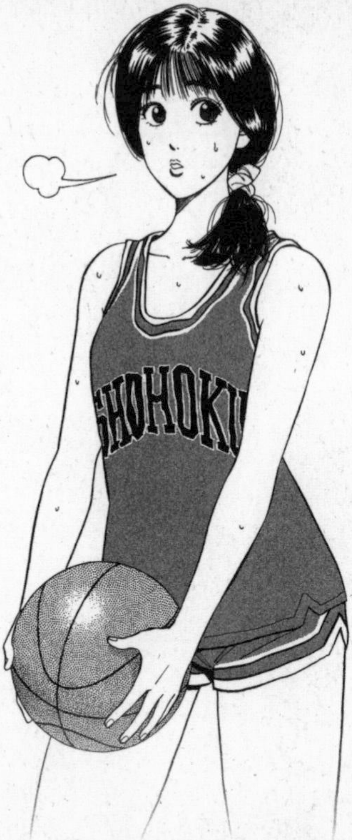

SHOHOKU


A group of high school thugs intent on stomping some sense into the talented (yet arrogant in a Hanamichi sort of way) Ryota Miyagi crash a Shohoku practice session, and the fists (and brooms!) start to fly. Never one to back down from a fight, Hanamichi also gets in on the action as a full-on street brawl breaks out on the basketball court. Will Captain Akagi stand for this reckless roughhousing?

ON SALE DECEMBER 2009

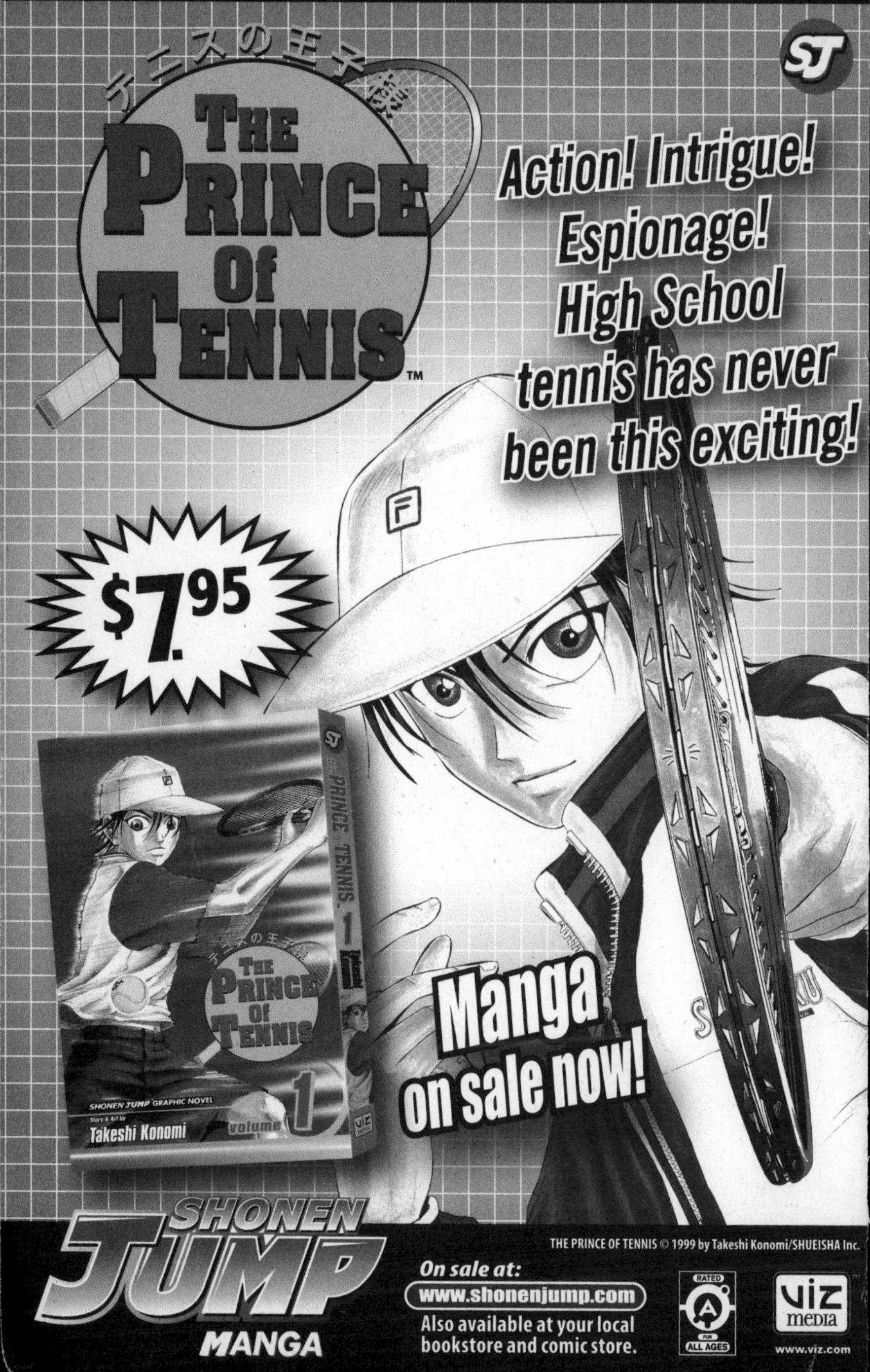
SJ
テニスの王子様
THE PRINCE OF TENNIS™
Action! Intrigue! Espionage! High School tennis has never been this exciting!
$7.95
SHONEN JUMP GRAPHIC NOVEL
Story & Art by
Takeshi Konomi
volume 1
Manga on sale now!
SHONEN JUMP MANGA
THE PRINCE OF TENNIS © 1999 by Takeshi Konomi/SHUEISHA Inc.
On sale at:
www.shonenjump.com
Also available at your local bookstore and comic store.
RATED A FOR ALL AGES
VIZ media
www.viz.com

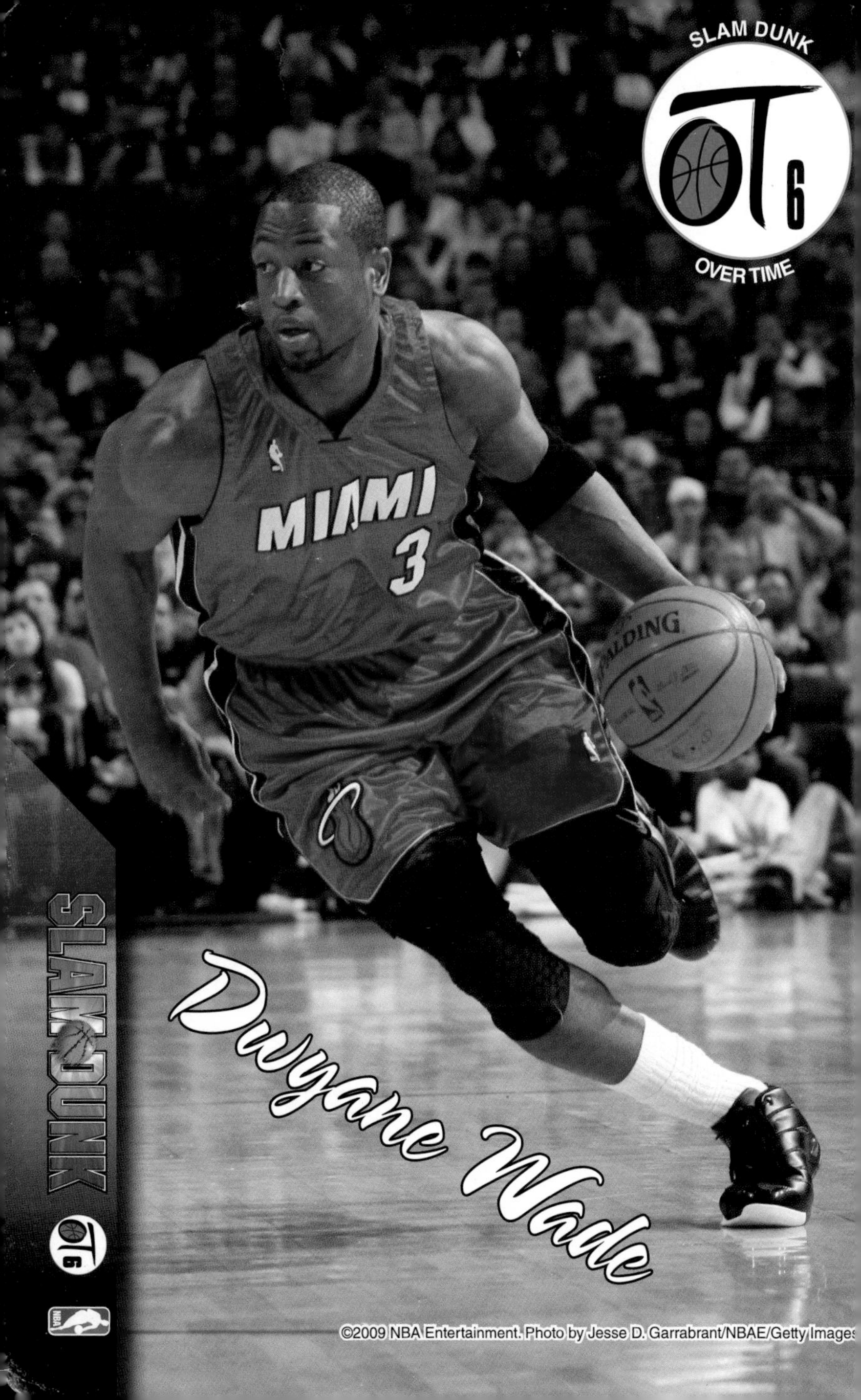
SLAM DUNK
OT 6
OVER TIME
MIAMI
3
SPALDING
SLAM DUNK
Dwyane Wade

***Welcome back to the Omake-Dome, basketball fans! This time out, SDOT returns to the backcourt to profile high-flying Miami Heat guard Dwyane Wade. Next up, Coach will be running S-Dunkers the length of the floor as he breaks down the anatomy of the fast break. Yes, version six is shaping up to be another classic, folks. Think Wilt's 100-point game, Larry vs. Magic, or courtside with Spike and Woody at the Garden—that's the fevered pitch we're aiming for. So break out the face paint and put on those game faces—only true gamers get face time with D-Wade and Coach O!***

## "Flash" Memory

Ditch The Di


Dwyane "Flash" Wade is a bit of an *SDOT* anomaly. He's the superstar that nobody saw coming. Playing his prep ball at Harold L. Richards High School in Oak Lawn, Ill., Dwyane started out as an understudy. His stepbrother, Demetris McDaniel, was the Bulldog's top dog early on. It wasn't until Dwyane's junior year that he began to show "flashes" of brilliance. Before the season started, he grew a fortuitous four inches and went on to average 27 points and 11 rebounds. Despite his breakout season, Dwyane wasn't heavily recruited and wound up at Marquette University. Wade was more than marquee at Marquette but didn't rise to national prominence until the NCAA Midwest Regional Final in 2003. In the game of his life against the storied, top-seeded Kentucky Wildcats, Wade didn't trip up—he scored a triple-double! With his draft stock soaring, Dwyane seemed poised for prime time—he would skip his senior year at Marquette and enter the 2003 NBA draft.

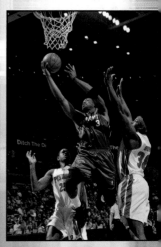

## The Quiet Superstar

If past is prelude, there was certain to be some folks casting shadows over Dwyane's NBA coming-out party. And sure enough, included in the '03 crop of draft picks were two players you might have heard of: Carmelo Anthony and LeBron James. D-Wade was picked fifth by the Miami Heat and would finish third in rookie-of-the-year voting. But if you want to talk titles, it's Wade who's outclassed his recruiting class. Landing Shaquille O'Neal in the Heat-Lakers 2004 mega-trade, Miami had all the pieces in place to compete with Detroit for East Coast dominance. In 2006, Wade would bring Miami two pieces of shiny, gold hardware: the Larry O'Brien NBA Finals Trophy and the NBA Finals MVP Trophy. Besting the Dallas Mavericks, Wade averaged 34.7 points a game—third best in Finals history.

## A Gifted and Talented Education

So what is it that makes this young shooting guard so special? Well, for one, he's versatile. Wade can play the 2 (shooting guard) and the 1 (point guard). He's a fleet-footed, hard-charging slasher and a one-man fast break. D-Wade possesses a breathtaking, improvisational style; changing direction and pirouetting around accomplished shot-blockers and inexplicably converting low-percentage shots. He also plays bigger than his size—posting up, rebounding and blocking shots as if he were a power forward. He's the ultimate little big man. Now if the Heat were to sign a true big man to play alongside him, the Eastern Conference Finals could once again run through Miami. Only time will tell!

**CAREER SEASON AVERAGES**

| Year | Team | G | GS | MPG | FG% | 3P% | FT% | OFF | DEF | RPG | APG | SPG | BPG | TO | PF |
|---|---|---|---|---|---|---|---|---|---|---|---|---|---|---|---|
| 03-04 | MIA | 61 | 56 | 34.9 | 0.465 | 0.302 | 0.747 | 1.4 | 2.7 | 4.0 | 4.5 | 1.4 | 0.6 | 3.21 | 2.30 |
| 04-05 | MIA | 77 | 77 | 38.6 | 0.478 | 0.289 | 0.762 | 1.4 | 3.7 | 5.2 | 6.8 | 1.6 | 1.1 | 4.17 | 3.00 |
| 05-06 | MIA | 75 | 75 | 38.6 | 0.495 | 0.171 | 0.783 | 1.4 | 4.3 | 5.7 | 6.7 | 2.0 | 0.8 | 3.57 | 2.90 |
| 06-07 | MIA | 51 | 50 | 37.9 | 0.491 | 0.266 | 0.807 | 1.0 | 3.7 | 4.7 | 7.5 | 2.1 | 1.2 | 4.24 | 2.30 |
| 07-08 | MIA | 51 | 49 | 38.3 | 0.469 | 0.286 | 0.758 | 0.9 | 3.3 | 4.2 | 6.9 | 1.7 | 0.7 | 4.39 | 2.70 |
| 08-09 | MIA | 73 | 73 | 38.5 | 0.489 | 0.300 | 0.765 | 1.2 | 3.9 | 5.0 | 7.5 | 2.3 | 1.4 | 3.42 | 2.20 |
| **Career** | -- | 388 | 380 | 37.9 | 0.483 | 0.276 | 0.772 | 1.2 | 3.6 | 4.9 | 6.7 | 1.8 | 0.9 | 3.80 | 2.60 |
| **All-Star** | -- | 5 | 4 | 25.2 | 0.541 | 0.250 | 0.615 | 1.6 | 1.0 | 2.6 | 3.0 | 2.6 | 0.6 | 2.20 | 1.60 |

## Too Fast, Too Furious

All right, people—that's enough of the fawning little bio, there. Are we fanboys or are we men? Let's get up off your keisters and move those frumpy otaku frames for once in your lives! Coach O's going to teach you how to run a fast break like the showtime Lakers—so suit 'em up and stretch out those hammies… It's time to play fast and play hard!

## What Is a Fast Break?

A fast break is an offensive strategy designed to push the ball quickly up the floor in advance of the defense. The hope is that, at best, the offensive unit will have a "numbers" advantage. It's like when you hear the play-by-play announcer say, "Look out, they've got numbers!" The opposition has been caught sleeping and the offense has two players for the defense's one (or 3-on-2 or 4-on-3, etc.). At worst, the defense will be caught flat-footed and out of position. Either way, the offense has the upper hand.

### Drill Baby, Drill!

Okay, folks. Let's hit the hardwood and drill this baby just like I drew it up:

### Positioning

1. The point guard (the 1) fills the middle lane and dribbles the ball up the court as fast as possible.
2. The 2 and the 3 (shooting guard and small forward) run with the point guard and fill the far outside wings. They are typically the better shooters on the floor and the second and third quickest (after the point guard). As such, they are the first and second options on the break. It's important that these players situate themselves within one foot of the sideline to spread the floor as widely as possible. Proper spacing creates lanes and holes in the defense.
3. The 4 (power forward) and the 5 (center) run the inside lanes on either side of the point guard. The 4 plays cleanup and follows missed shots. The lumbering 5 is usually last down the floor (the "trailer"). Should there be a turnover, he serves as the last line of defense—or the "safety."

## Execution

1. Good defense usually creates fast break opportunities. Be ready to run the break after a blocked shot or a steal. Long, defensive rebounds can also be pushed ahead and converted into easy layups. In any of these situations, get the ball into the hands of your point guard and get into position!
2. Fill your lanes, stay wide and run the floor.
3. Court awareness: see the entire floor!
4. Take what the defense gives you—find the open man and pass it ahead.
5. Keep passing (but don't overpass) and keep the defense off-balance! A quick touch-pass back to the point guard can be very effective.
6. Play the percentages: once you've found the best shot, take it!

That's a wrap for today's clinic, kids. Be sure to practice your passing for volume 7!

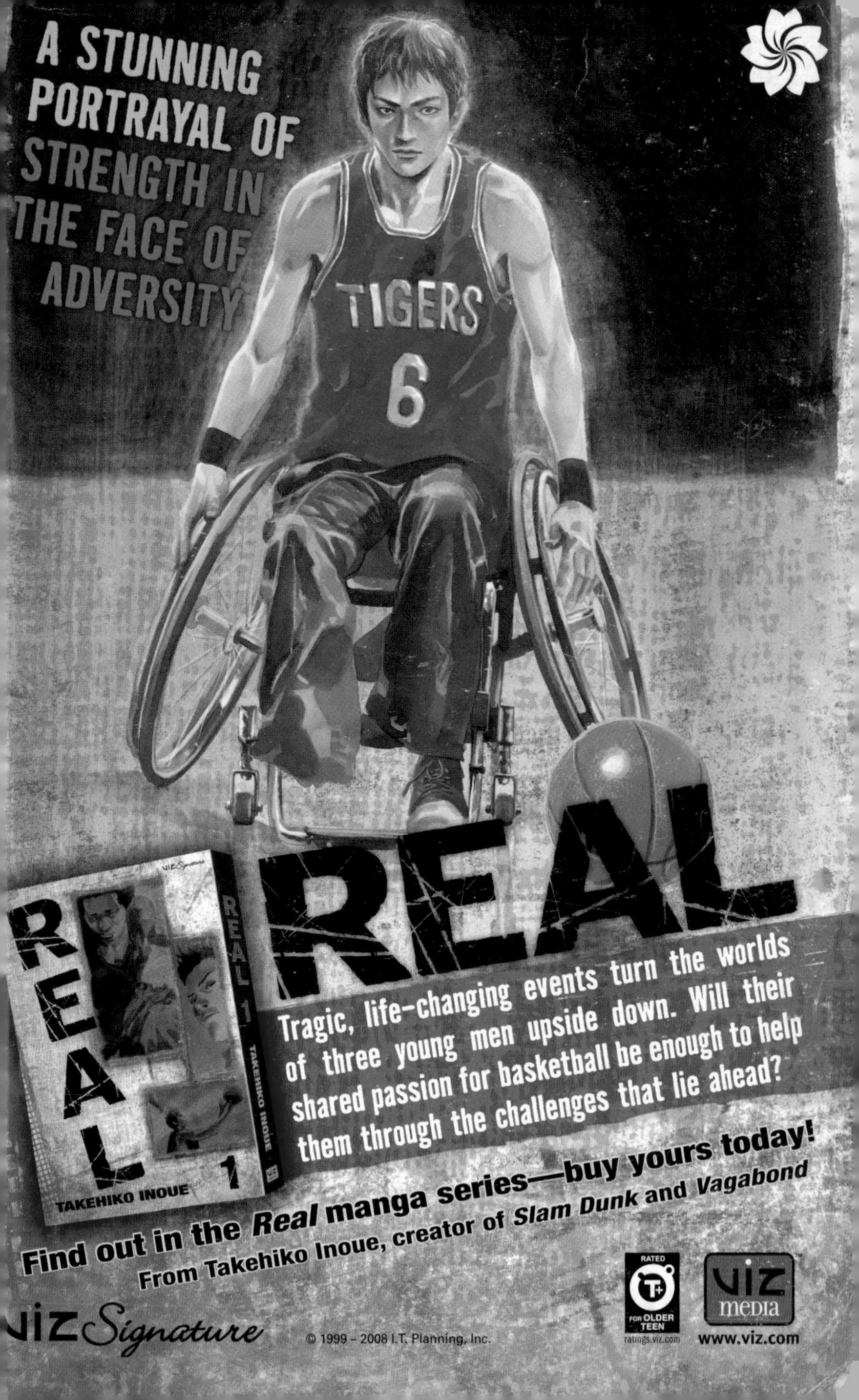
A STUNNING PORTRAYAL OF STRENGTH IN THE FACE OF ADVERSITY
TIGERS
6
REAL
REAL 1
TAKEHIKO INOUE
Tragic, life-changing events turn the worlds of three young men upside down. Will their shared passion for basketball be enough to help them through the challenges that lie ahead?
Find out in the Real manga series—buy yours today!
From Takehiko Inoue, creator of Slam Dunk and Vagabond
VIZ Signature
© 1999 – 2008 I.T. Planning, Inc.
RATED T+ FOR OLDER TEEN
ratings.viz.com
VIZ media
www.viz.com